Free the Land

Justice, Power, and Politics

The Justice, Power, and Politics series publishes new works in history that explore the myriad struggles for justice, battles for power, and shifts in politics that have shaped the United States over time. Through the lenses of justice, power, and politics, the series seeks to broaden scholarly debates about America's past as well as to inform public discussions about its future.

More information on the series, including a complete list of books published, is available at http://justicepowerandpolitics.com/.

Free the Land

The Republic of New Afrika and the
Pursuit of a Black Nation-State

∙∙∙

EDWARD ONACI

The University of North Carolina Press Chapel Hill

This book was published with the assistance of the Fred W. Morrison Fund of the University of North Carolina Press.

The University of North Carolina Press has been a member of the Green Press Initiative since 2003.

Library of Congress Cataloging-in-Publication Data
Names: Onaci, Edward, author.
Title: Free the land : the Republic of New Afrika and the pursuit
   of a black nation-state / Edward Onaci.
Other titles: Justice, power, and politics.
Description: Chapel Hill : The University of North Carolina Press, 2020. |
   Series: Justice, power, and politics | Includes bibliographical references
   and index.
Identifiers: LCCN 2019046674 | ISBN 9781469656137 (cloth) |
   ISBN 9781469656144 (paperback) | ISBN 9781469656151 (ebook)
Subjects: LCSH: Republic of New Africa (Organization)—History. |
   New Afrikan Independence Movement—History. | Black nationalism—
   United States—History—20th century.
Classification: LCC E185.615 .O58 2020 | DDC 320.54089/96073—dc23
   LC record available at https://lccn.loc.gov/2019046674

Cover art by Matt Avery, https://monograph.studio.

To my ancestors

Reverend Walter and Eunice Brown

Cleo and Esser Mills

Felix and Pernilla Sanford

Bessie and Willie Smittick

Eugene Mills

Joery E. Smittick

And all of those whose names I do not know.

Asé!

Contents

Acknowledgments, xi

Abbreviations in the Text, xv

Introduction, 1

1 Birth of the New Afrikan Independence Movement, 15
   A Historical Overview

2 The Fruition of Black Power, 43
   Paper-Citizenship and the Intellectual Foundations
   of Lifestyle Politics

3 Revolutionary Name Choices, 79
   Self-Definition and Self-Determination

4 New Afrikan Lifestyle Politics, 113
   Personal Histories of Political Struggle

5 Cointel's Got Blacks in Hell, 158
   State Repression and Black Liberation

6 For New Afrikan People's War, 184
   Lessons and Legacies of the New Afrikan Independence Movement

   Epilogue, 205
   On Terrorism, Lingering Silences, and the Inextinguishable
   Determination to Free the Land

Notes, 209

Bibliography, 243

Index, 271

Illustrations

"Let No Man Question Us!" *The New Afrikan Journal* 6, December 25, 1976, 3

Robert F. Williams painting by Khalid Abdur-Rasheed, 2016, 28

New Afrikan territory behind bars, *The New Afrikan Journal* 3, no. 2, ca. 1982, 109

The New Afrikan couple, *Suggested Guidelines for the Land Development Cooperatives*, n.d., 144

"Educate to Liberate," *The New Afrikan Journal*, ca. 1980, 149

Acknowledgments

This book benefited from generous support of longtime participants in the New Afrikan Independence Movement. Many of them joined the ancestors as I was working on this project. Because speaking with people was essential for my research and because those with whom I spoke willingly made themselves vulnerable to me—a complete stranger—to tell me about their lives and experiences in the New Afrikan Independence Movement, I want to begin by honoring and thanking them for what they gave me. They include Hamid Abdul-Aziz, Baba Hannibal Tirus Afrik, Herman Ferguson, Dr. Njeri Jackson, Mama Marilyn Killingham, Chokwe Lumumba, Dr. Imari Obadele, Sekou Owusu, and Fulani Sunni-Ali. Asé.

I am equally grateful to their comrades who, as elders in the movement for black liberation, continue to guide their communities. Some of them took time to speak with me so that I could develop a history of the New Afrikan Independence Movement. Included here are Dr. Muhammad Ahmad, Elder Balogun Anderson, Mama Iyaluua Ferguson, Nana Kwesi Jumoke Ifetayo Frimpong, Hekima and Tamu Kanyama, Aneb Kgositsile, Ukali Mwendo, Saladin Muhammad, Brother-D.B. Aammaa Nubyahn, Shushanna Shakur, Bilal Sunni-Ali, Hondo T'Chikwa, Bokeba Trice, Ohenewaa White, Malik Yakini, and others. Baba Khalid Abdur-Rasheed has been especially generous with his time, his art, and mentorship. The same is true of Sister Nkechi Taifa (the world needs your book!) and General Rashid, who were always available to answer questions, granted me access to their collections, and more. They are featured in the pages that follow, and no words of thanks will ever be adequate. I am also grateful to those whose stories did not make it into this project. I hope that they recognize the spirit of their dedication to improving humanity in this text.

Because this book is a work of history, I also depended on the archivists at Michigan State University's Special Collections, the Mississippi Department of Archives and History, the Moorland-Spingarn Research Center at Howard University, the Special Collections Research Center at the University of Michigan, the Special Collections Research Center at Temple University, the Archives & Special Collections at Tougaloo College, and the Wayne

State University Archives. Gaining access to the personal papers of Nkechi Taifa and General Rashid also proved extremely valuable.

I covered a lot of ground to visit the people and collections that provided the information for this project. Several people opened their homes, lending me space to rest without asking for anything in return. The small acts of friendship and kindness that Tayo Banjo, Evan and Stephanie Jones, Paul Karolczyk and Doris Garcia, Manju Rajendran, Gee Yawson-Sharpe, and Elizabeth (Liz) Whittaker-Walker, among others, gave continue to resonate with and impress me. Liz also enthusiastically supported the project from the beginning and helped me establish contacts with people in the movement. Her intervention was critical to my ability to meet and build relationships with the people who shared their time, resources, and personal experiences. Thank you.

Several other friends and comrades in scholarship contributed to my ability to make it through the research for and writing of this book. Included are Tahir Abdullah, Folayemi Agbede, Richard D Benson II, Dan Berger, Tage Biswalo, the Chenault family, Genevieve Clutario, Comrade Brad Duncan, Kwame Essien and family, Nicholas Gaffney, Rondee Gaines, Maurice Hobson, Kwame Holmes, the Ashley Howard and Chris Sang family, Nicole Ivy, Joseph Jordan, Julilly Kohler-Hausmann, Brandon Mills, Asantewa Sunni-Ali, Willie Wright, and Brian and Erica Hill Yates. Much love to my friends from the McNair Scholars Program, including Angel Miles, Mckenna Philpot-Bowden, and Tayo Banjo. Special thanks go to Keisha Blain, Ashley Farmer, Ibram Kendi, and Quito Swan, who, through word and deed, encouraged me on numerous occasions to finish this book.

My DJ buddies, fellow foodies, and just good people kept me grounded. They include the People's DJs Collective, Makalani Adisa and Martine Caverl, the Barrett family, Juan and Karina Bustamante, Gabriel Bryant, Gabe Carryon, Bryan Flowers, Amanda Klonsky, the David Marques and Tiffany Hinton family, Jermont Montgomery, DuiJi and Kara Mshinda and family, Femi and Sulaiha Olatunji, Samyra Rogers (whose support, generosity, and love have been unyielding), Greg Scruggs, and Sheena Sood. Even before I really knew them, members of the Malcolm X Grassroots Movement were helping me stay enthusiastic about this project. The Philadelphia chapter has been especially supportive of me and my work.

This book also benefited from some very generous readers, including Folayemi Agbede, Sarah Frohardt-Lane, Toussaint Losier, Kerry Pimblott, and Patti Schroeder. They pushed me to develop greater clarity and critical analysis, as did the peer reviewers for this project. I hope that they see their influence in the pages that follow.

A number of scholarly and life mentors offered guidance and support as I worked on this book. They include Derrick Alridge, Jim Barrett, Cornelius Bynum, Mia Henry, Alphine Jefferson, Mariame Kaba, Clarence Lang, Trayce Matthews, Erik McDuffie, and Robyn Spencer (who has been an inspiration since I was an undergrad at Virginia State University). Sundiata Cha-Jua and Akinyele Umoja were especially helpful. Their insights and critical feedback pushed me to dig deeper into this topic than I thought was possible.

My editor, Brandon Proia, and the entire UNC Press staff have been amazing. The process of publishing a book has given me a greater appreciation of the effort and resources needed to prepare a manuscript for publication and distribution. I knew very little about this process, but everyone has been patient and generous with their time and expertise. Thank you.

I treasure my colleagues at Ursinus College. The folks on Olin 3 have been invaluable—and they really know how to party! The Faculty and Staff of Color group has been a life vest in this sea called academia, as have our allies. Special thanks go to Hugh Clark; Ross Doughty (Rest in Power); C. Dallett Hemphill (Rest in Power); Nzadi Keita and her husband, Maghan; Richard King (Rest in Power); Reverend Charles Rice (Rest in Power), Tonya Rice and their sons; and Susanna Throop. The Office of Academic Affairs and library staff were also extremely helpful. The former awarded small research grants that helped me complete this project, in addition to helping me adjust to the demands of being a professional scholar. The library staff never seemed to tire of my steady stream of interlibrary loan requests, purchasing suggestions, and chattiness when looking for an excuse to avoid heading back to my office.

I had the honor of working with two undergraduate research assistants as I pursued this project. Rachael Carter and Shy'Quan Davis helped me catalog and digitize several fragile documents. I am grateful to them for their contributions to the completion of this project.

I cannot thank my Love, Dr. Patricia Ann Lott, enough for her support, expert editing, critical feedback, encouragement, and friendship. Together, we journeyed through the completion of our respective PhD programs, had memorable (mis)adventures moving back and forth between Chicago and various points along the East Coast, and remained dedicated to our joint mission to discover healthy and delicious food. Our families have also provided the love and encouragement that I needed. I am especially thankful to my grandmothers, Carrie Mills and Chesterine Smittick; my parents, Edward and Jorine Mills; my siblings, Jasmine and Jordan; my nephews, aunts, uncles, and cousins; and the entire Lott family, who have accepted me and showed me nothing but love. Respect and Eternal Love to you all.

Abbreviations in the Text

AD NIP   African Descendants Nationalist Independence Partition Party

AME   African Methodist Episcopal

APP   Afrikan People's Party

BLA   Black Liberation Army

BPP   Black Panther Party

CAP   Congress of Afrikan Peoples

FBI   Federal Bureau of Investigation

FNP   Freedom Now Party

GOAL   Group on Advanced Leadership

HOU   House of Umoja

MXGM   Malcolm X Grassroots Movement

NAACP   National Association for the Advancement of Colored People

NAIM   New Afrikan Independence Movement

NAPO   New Afrikan People's Organization

NAPS   New Afrikan Political Science

NBEDC   National Black Economic Development Conference

NBHRC   National Black Human Rights Coalition

NOI   Nation of Islam

PG-RNA   Provisional Government–Republic of New Afrika

RAM   Revolutionary Action Movement

RATF   Revolutionary Armed Task Force

RNA   Republic of New Afrika

SNCC   Student Nonviolent Coordinating Committee

UNIA   Universal Negro Improvement Association

Introduction

· ·

During the final weekend in March 1968, five hundred activists and Pan-African nationalists came together at the Black Government Convention to determine the destiny of the "captive black nation" in America. Participants included Lawrence Guyot of the Student Nonviolent Coordinating Committee and director of the Mississippi Freedom Democratic Party, Betty Shabazz, Maulana Karenga, Amiri Baraka, and highly revered reparations activist "Queen Mother" Audley Moore. The convention's main organizers, Gaidi (Milton Henry) and Imari Obadele (Richard Henry), brought them together so they could discuss their historic political conditions and the legal remedies available under international human rights law. After deliberating about religion, culture, sexism, and government repression, on Sunday, March 31, several dozen attendees in convention agreed to sign a document declaring to the world that they would struggle for the complete independence and statehood of the black nation, which they named the Republic of New Afrika (RNA). By advocating for a UN-monitored plebiscite, they would ensure that their people, whom they began referring to as "New Afrikans," could once and for all determine where to place their consent of citizenship.[1]

As the document was revealed before the crowd, one attendee, a young soldier from an Ohio paramilitary organization, felt a pang of fear. He understood the implications of signing his name to the Declaration of Independence, especially considering his and other people's knowledge that those who attended the convention were subject to government monitoring and police harassment. Among other potential outcomes, he worried that his position at General Motors would be terminated by the following morning when he was supposed to return to work. But then he observed the elderly Queen Mother Moore's response to the document. According to a witness, upon hearing the text read aloud, she rose from where she was sitting, extended her arms, and exclaimed, "Hallelujah, Hallelujah[,] I've lived to see the day!" At that moment, she volunteered to be the first person to place her name in ink on the document. That sight, the genuine excitement of the moment, and no doubt his sense of masculine self-worth eventually carried him through the line, though not with confidence. "I mean, i'll never forget [how] i could hardly hold my pen when i got up there," he stated. "But i was still going by my slave name, Ulysses X." And that was the name the ninety-ninth signer placed on the RNA Declaration of Independence.[2]

Ulysses X and the other attendees represented various organizations and local and regional efforts that had come together to develop a strategy for securing a UN-monitored plebiscite whereby their nation, then captive to the United States, could exercise self-determination. By calling themselves "captive," New Afrikans were indicating that they were members of an internal colony that, like colonized nations elsewhere, had the right to self-determination.[3] Their timing was significant: they committed to their New Afrikan Independence Movement (NAIM) in 1968, *after* black people had struggled for and won full legal recognition as citizens and federally guaranteed protection of their rights. The people who signed the Declaration of Independence believed they could create an independent black nation-state from Louisiana, Mississippi, Alabama, Georgia, and South Carolina and that a significant portion of the African-descended population from the United States of America would join them. This decision to "free the land" following landmark civil and voting rights legislation indicted the United States as unredeemable and uninhabitable for the descendants of the country's enslaved.[4]

This declaration of the right to independence had a lasting impact on many dedicated activists' lives. The young man who went by Ulysses X recognized that officially declaring himself a self-styled soldier in the Pan-African nationalist movement meant that he would face heightened surveillance and potential threats to his employment and personal safety. Yet there were many more potential effects of his decision. How would his family and friends outside of the movement respond to his decision? Would participation in the movement have any noticeable impact on his spirituality, his romantic relationships, and any children under his care? Could he be confident that government monitoring would be just that, monitoring? Or did Ulysses X have to prepare himself mentally and physically for other encounters with the American government? Ulysses X and everyone else who became a signed supporter of the NAIM would have to deal with such questions.

Considering the Republic of New Afrika "the *name* of [their] nation," advocates framed the NAIM in terms of achieving political independence and statehood. Their ranks consisted of a "Provisional Government" (PG-RNA)

'Let No Man Question Us!'

"WE apply to ourselves - and believe it also logical, humane, and legally correct for the world to apply to us - the same standards that permit the Cubans, who are descendants of Indians, Africans, and Spaniards, to claim the land they claim; Jamaicans to claim the land they claim, and Haitians, Trinidadians, Guyanese, and Mexicans to claim the land they each claim. All of us and each of us are migrant peoples who came into possession of the land as the majority and traditional populations in the wake of a campaign of Genocide waged by Europeans - English, French, Dutch, and Spanish - against the original and rightful possessors: the Amerindians.

"We, the New Africans, gladly acknowledge the fundamental rights of the Indian in the land.

"But, if no one questions the claims of the Cubans or the Jamaicans or the Mexicans, let no man question ours."

— Brother Imari
Jackson, Mississippi,
KUSH DISTRICT,
Republic of New Africa
21 May 1975

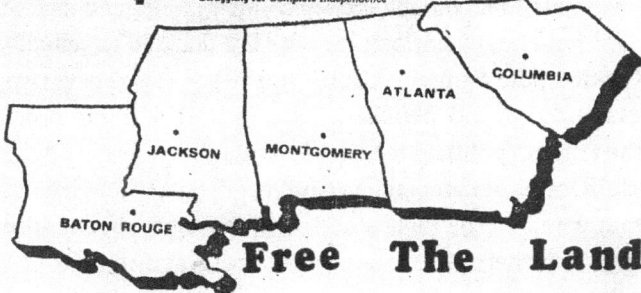

Brother Imari Abubakari Obadele, I
President

The Provisional Government of

THE REPUBLIC OF NEW AFRIKA

An African Nation in the Western Hemisphere
Struggling for Complete Independence

COLUMBIA

ATLANTA

JACKSON   MONTGOMERY

BATON ROUGE

Free The Land!

FREE THE RNA-11 AND ALL "PRISONERS OF WAR"

"Let No Man Question Us!" *The New Afrikan Journal* 6, December 25, 1976.
Courtesy of Nkechi Taifa.

and "citizens," many who were also members of various organizations that achieved more visibility during the Black Power era and are referenced frequently in historical literature of the period.[5] New Afrikans claimed that their own territorial liberation would strike a debilitating blow to global oppression, making the overthrow of white supremacy and capitalist domination more achievable. Equally important, they advocated for a reparations settlement as restitution for the United States' role in the international trafficking of African peoples, their enslavement in the United States, and the persistent violence, degradation, socioeconomic inequality, and consistent efforts to suppress black self-determination.[6] New Afrikans consciously fashioned a culture and a lifestyle that accommodated their political actions and revolutionary goals. Although there was no single way to embody New Afrikan citizenship, multiple attempts to do so helped form the contours of the ongoing and protracted struggle.

To the twenty-first-century observer, the basic goals of the NAIM may sound familiar, even if unsettling, during a moment of international tensions revolving around the interrelated issues of sovereignty, border security, and human rights responsibilities of various nations and peoples. In 2011, following brutal warfare and a widely spread human rights campaign, South Sudan gained its independence using an independence referendum. In 2014, Scotland held a nationwide vote but decided to remain within the United Kingdom, the country's historic oppressor. In the next two years, Catalonia revitalized its independence movement, leading to protests and arrests of the region's political leaders, as well as changes in Spanish law that made certain forms of independence protest illegal. Though citizens of Quebec had not voted on the issue since 1995, Quebec's sovereignty advocates have maintained their right to govern themselves and their physical territory.[7] At the same time, the far right in Europe and the United States has gained power using rhetoric reminiscent of fascism from the 1930s and 1940s. Climate change and war have exacerbated decades of fiscal and military instability, pushing migrants from Africa, the Arabian Peninsula, South and Central America, and elsewhere to economically dominant countries, including Australia and Canada. However, these relocations have been accompanied by fear about terrorism (as carried out by nonwhite persons) and violent enforcement of border security. Brexit is just one example, albeit an extreme one, of the latter.[8]

Taken together, issues of sovereignty, self-determination, national identity, and attempts to maintain the global status quo through legal and extralegal enforcement demonstrate that the basic idea behind New Afrikan independence and self-determination, is more commonplace than some may realize. The difference between the New Afrikan struggle and the others is that New Afrikans frame theirs as a revolutionary war against oppression and that it has been carried out by historic nonpersons and U.S. "paper-citizens" (see chapter 2) who consider themselves captives forced to reside and die on land stolen from indigenous nations. The NAIM is most often associated with the PG-RNA; however, the movement has included people and organizations that pursued independence using different, though complementary, methods. Despite disagreements about approach, these various formations have shared a vision of New Afrikan nationality and the intentional lifestyles that they believed would help deliver independent statehood, secure reparations, and win the global war against white supremacy and capitalist domination.[9]

Free the Land tells the history of New Afrikan independence efforts, primarily as they have been carried out by the PG-RNA. While placing a spotlight on those who sought to exchange residence in the United States with self-determined citizenship, it examines the effects of this struggle on the lives and lifestyles of participants. Activism influenced interpersonal exchanges, routine practices, and varying individual rationales that compelled New Afrikans to commit themselves to their very ambitious goals. As each individual evolved within the protracted struggle, each individual reinterpreted the overarching ideology and shifted his or her practices according to these new frames of reference. Therefore, a dialectical and reciprocal relationship bound New Afrikan activists, their movement and its concomitant ideas, and the impact of their revolutionary work. These "lifestyle politics" may offer some insight into why their movement continues, even though the overwhelming majority of their Black Power contemporaries demobilized.[10]

"Lifestyle politics," as it has been used by political scientist W. Lance Bennett, describes everyday practices that may have political intent outside of the purposeful mass organizing and civic culture activists utilized more regularly prior to the 1980s. His version of lifestyle politics outlines the various ways individuals "organize social and political meaning around their lifestyle values and the personal narratives that express them." Bennett bases his definition on U.S. activists' major retreat from mass political organizing in the 1970s and 1980s due to state repression, globalization, and technological innovations such as the Internet.[11] Distinct from Bennett, I define lifestyle politics as the everyday lived enactment of political ideology and argue that New Afrikans consciously and actively made lifestyle politics central to their framework for understanding revolution and essential in their strategy for liberation. Lifestyle politics are the constant interpretation, contestation, negotiation, and reproduction of activists' shared ideas within both civic arenas and domains deemed "personal" and/or "private." This helps explicate New Afrikan social and legal positioning, collective political identity, and the group-centered nature of individual choices and actions. Through the practice of lifestyle politics, New Afrikans lived their evolving interpretations of the ideas that drove their movement from the Black Power era and beyond. Those formative ideas, or "New Afrikan Political Science" (NAPS), manifest as RNA activists' pursuit of self-determination in every facet of their lives, including name choices, educational endeavors, occupations, family, and spirituality. Lifestyle politics also account for the personal ramifications experienced as a consequence of the political repression of black leftists.

This in-depth engagement with the axiom "the personal is political" also provides insight into how New Afrikan activists constructed their unique, proudly African, and revolutionary, collective political identity. However, as a Black Power project, these efforts were neither solely about settling on nor affirming who they, as a people, were. For New Afrikans, Black Power was based on the concept of self-determination, or the ability of a nation to govern itself within its own territory. The greatest achievement of Black Power would therefore be the creation of an independent nation-state. Identity, or self-definition, mattered inasmuch as it helped New Afrikans overcome centuries of white supremacist oppression and helped them achieve their ultimate goals. For New Afrikans, dedication to the daily practice of being a revolutionary and fighting to achieve structural and political goals were key to carrying on the Black Power tradition.

Free the Land presents the full history of the NAIM and explains how NAPS guided the movement's adherents. It accepts the challenge leveled by New Afrikans to interrogate the limits and potential of citizenship, to question the political meanings of black identity during the Black Power era and following, and to reconsider the goals of black political activism. Doing so permits us to draw connections between New Afrikans, their predecessors, and contemporaries, demonstrating the intellectual fertility found in the nexus of distinct activist groupings. For example, the Black Panther Party at some point demanded reparations and a U.N.-monitored plebiscite through which the descendants of enslaved Africans in America could determine their collective destiny. Some of their members pledged allegiance to the RNA. Yet this group's position on black self-determination and reparations has not undergone significant scholarly scrutiny. This history of New Afrikan independence foregrounds these ideas, showing that some activists kept them alive within broader political discourses until these ideas became embedded in some of the major current-day conversations about reparations. Telling this history highlights the importance of the NAIM to preserving and expanding upon the legacy of Black Power.

Narrating such a history requires a multifaceted inspection of the more day-to-day aspects of movement building and participation. Such a project intentionally brings forth the perspectives and experiences of the people whose voices were muffled under the booming soundtrack of charismatic, highly visible, and often male representatives of the Black Power era. These people were also silenced and rendered invisible by the tear gas, tanks, and media representations that facilitated government-sponsored repression. In order to amplify their voices above the raucousness of war, this book consciously and humbly participates in a multidisciplinary conversation that includes history, sociology, cultural studies, geography, political theory, and onomastics (the study and history of naming conventions). More than offering just a nod to these scholarly disciplines, *Free the Land* attempts to speak to and through them in productive ways. Because this social movement history includes diverse people with a variety of outlooks, the study of it should be as holistic as the people whose lives and experiences are interpreted in the following pages.

Carving out Intellectual Space for the New Afrikan Independence Movement

Although mentioned in several studies of Black Power–era political activism, the NAIM has not received sustained scholarly analysis. To date, only political scientist Christian Davenport has devoted a book-length study to the movement. He uses RNA activists in Detroit, Michigan, and Jackson, Mississippi, from the 1960s until the early 1970s to analyze the factors that cause social movement organizations to demobilize. Akinyele Omowale Umoja devotes a chapter to RNA efforts in *We Will Shoot Back*, as does Robert L. Tsai in *America's Forgotten Constitutions*. Similarly, the anthologies *Black Power in the Belly of the Beast* and *The Hidden 1970s* each include one chapter on some aspect of New Afrikan organizing efforts. Otherwise, New Afrikans receive varying levels of analysis in the existing scholarship on the Black Power era, African American political thought, (anti)prison activism, and reparations.[12]

Although the NAIM has not received extensive scholarly coverage, the issues at the heart of this study have. This book's interrogation of lifestyle politics builds on social movement theory with a particular focus on the biographical consequences of social movements. Sociologists Doug McAdam, Nella Van Dyke, and Brenda Wilhelm, among others, have argued that participation in the social movements of the 1960s caused activists to question and critique the ways that societal norms governed their personal lives. They explained that for activists, more than nonactivists, the social upheaval of that era had an indelible influence on their life-course patterns.[13] According to Darren E. Sherkat and T. Jean Blocker, social movement activism "inevitably forges opinions, orients activities, and affects the lifestyles of participants" for several reasons. Among them, one's "participation in social movements constitutes a link to a variety of resources," which "will help sustain distinctive schemata, and will be sustained by the schematic orientations that constitute the social structure of social movements." Further, they state, "individuals' commitments to particular schemata may become codified, providing cognitive resources for other decisions and understandings—thereby generating cognitive structures." In other words, activists begin their social movement activism with a certain perception of the world which, through their sustained contact with the people, ideas, and experiences that accompany social movement activism, change and, ultimately, reshape such individuals' worldviews. What they learn becomes codified and then forms the basis of their understanding outside of that particular set of experiences with activism. Finally, "the transposability of schematic orientations across structural domains implies that shifting preferences will lead to different choices among diverse resource options— such as choice of job, political affiliations, religious ties, and family structure."[14] This claim captures what the New Afrikans shared for this study. Their childhood and early adult experiences guided their decisions to become involved with social movement activism. Activism then reshaped their worldviews and became a reference point for decisions New Afrikans eventually made about their careers, families, and other aspects of their daily lives.

This sociological literature provides a useful beginning point for exploring the manifold ways that activists changed and evolved because of their participation with social movements, but their analysis is limited because of scholars' focus on vaguely conceptualized and narrowly depicted versions of civil rights, women's rights, and a mostly white New Left. With few exceptions, these scholars utilize information from random national surveys in order to develop their research, making it difficult to identify who exactly were social movement activists and what their participation entailed.[15] These studies also pose imprecise questions about participation in electoral politics, Christianity, nonmarital cohabitation, and childbearing as their main devices to measure each respondent's level of activism. Those aspects of people's lives are excellent ways to determine one's political orientation, but as employed by the extant literature, they provide incomplete assessments of the impact of social movement activity on participants. Mainly, they determine that heteronormative, nonmarital cohabitation, delayed marriage and childbearing, reluctance to join Christian churches, and voting for Democratic Party candidates all constitute the politics of former social movement activists. Further, even though concerned with activists' life courses, scholars typically present social movements and the ideas that they produce as static by ignoring the evolution of the movements and organizations in which their subjects participated. They do the same with the people involved, mainly beginning analysis with the moments when individuals decided to participate in a cause.

Because such studies avoid Pan-African nationalists and black radicals, those studies miss a wide range of potential outcomes. For example, they do not interrogate the ways in which many social movement participants utilized marriage and childbearing as the basis from which to organize newly conceptualized communities, which could potentially strengthen activists' ability to undermine oppressive political structures. Such studies overlook the many revolutionaries who ended up in prison or in exile abroad because of their activities and associations, which dramatically affected their life courses. Finally, they do not discuss how activists' lived experiences and interactions with various cognitive resources produced an internal evolution within movements, changed the political orientation of social movement organizations, and helped (re)define the parameters of their agendas. Attention to a person's life from childhood through activism provides the breadth required to adequately understand the biographical consequences of social movements on one's life.[16]

Some historians have begun exploring the ways that social movement participation impacts activist lifestyles, and conversely how activists push social movement organizations to change and adapt to evolving contexts. Specifically, Tracye Matthews and Robyn C. Spencer each explain how Black Panther Party (BPP) cadres reoriented their entire lifestyles in order to live in alignment with their political ideology and the directives of the BPP's Central Committee. In the process of negotiating their new lifestyles with previous worldviews and social understandings, these Panthers prompted the expansion of their organization's ideology in ways that caused it to be more theoretically viable for participants. Both Matthews and Spencer contend that Panthers, women especially, fought diligently to minimize sexism by creating nonsexist lifestyle practices.[17] They participated equally with men as cadre leaders and theorists; they sold newspapers, fed children, and risked ostracism from their families just as their male counterparts did. Also, these scholars appropriately consider how the offensive waged against black revolutionaries by the federal government impacted Black Panthers' lifestyles. However, neither Matthews nor Spencer discusses the long-term outcomes of this process of living one's political ideology.[18]

This book, then, utilizes the most promising aspects of the sociological and historical scholarship on the biographical impact of social movements in order to determine the various effects of New Afrikans' dialectical relationships with their movement. It builds on the existing scholarly work to develop an understanding of New Afrikans' lifestyle politics and to push the boundaries of life course studies. The NAIM encouraged activists to pursue self-determination and independence culturally and politically from the United States and Western societies more generally. The theory and practice of NAPS created space for rethinking names and for reconceiving and reframing concepts of family, spirituality, and one's relationship with the mode of production.

In focusing on RNA members' practice of lifestyle politics, this book demonstrates the significance of the relationships between New Afrikans and their political ideologies. I contend that highlighting such commonplace interactions illuminates the strengths and shortcomings of the people involved in social movement activism. These interplays allow us to observe and critically analyze how New Afrikans' varying beliefs about citizenship, self-determination, reparations, and other matters were shaped by and filtered through preexisting, evolving, and sometimes dubious formulations of "nation," "revolution," "colonization," and other concepts. The multitude of ways that individual New Afrikans interpreted their own subject positions in relation to the surrounding world posed both advantages and limitations to their abilities to contribute to the group's goals. Leaders struggled to maintain equal power between men and women at all levels of the PG-RNA's organizational structure. However, their vision of gender equality was limited in scope, especially when examined retrospectively with the critical interventions made by the 1970s and subsequent black feminist and womanist critiques of U.S. society, social movements, and Pan-African nationalism. As a point of intentional struggle, New Afrikans in the PG-RNA and formations such as the Malcolm X Grassroots Movement took steps over time to minimize that contradiction.

Each chapter of this book attempts to provide a nuanced analysis of such issues to clarify how New Afrikans challenged and, in some instances, failed to address contradictions in their movement. Chapter 1, "Birth of the New Afrikan Independence Movement," introduces the NAIM, providing a historical overview from its inception to the early 1980s. It explains how two brothers from South Philadelphia became the motivating persons behind the Black Government Convention in 1968. Tracing the birth and early development of the movement will help readers consider the ways that political geography, historical context, and personal circumstance helped shape activism. After relocating to the Detroit metropolitan area in the 1950s, the Henry brothers became community activists and political leaders. Working through the Group on Advanced Leadership and the Freedom Now Party, political struggle taught them the limits of seeking full entry into a nation that circumscribed their political power. At the same time, the Henry brothers witnessed decolonization in Africa, especially Ghana, which challenged them to reconsider the meaning of black liberation. Under the tutelage of people like Malcolm X and Queen Mother Moore, they shifted their politics from reform and inclusion to revolution and self-determination. They eventually called for the 1968 convention, during which they helped declare black people's right to independence from the United States of America.

The moments following the founding convention are also important, because they provide the full context in which New Afrikan citizens attempted to comport their lives and lifestyles to NAPS. In that time, the PG-RNA experienced two internal disputes and a number of violent engagements with the state and its law enforcement officials. These nearly destroyed the Provisional Government, eating away at important financial resources, straining relationships between key personnel, and undermining the confidence of would-be supporters. Yet the self-proclaimed governing body and a number of associated organizations survived. By detailing some of the important developments during the first fifteen years or so of NAIM history, chapter 1 introduces readers to the basic ideas, important people, and events that have come to define the movement.

After describing the NAIM's founding and the aftermath of the call for independence, chapter 2, "The Fruition of Black Power," explains and analyzes the movement's intellectual and theoretical foundations. It utilizes the theoretical power of the New Afrikan concept "paper-citizen" to explain the various founding documents, including the RNA Declaration of Independence, the New Afrikan Oath, and more. Highlighting the major ideas from these documents reveals several important concepts through which New Afrikans critiqued U.S. paper-citizenship and developed their concept of New Afrikan citizenship. Besides the question of citizenship, New Afrikan political identity, Third World solidarity, and the governmental—not organizational—apparatus anchored a significant portion of known New Afrikan activism. Specific actions, such as supporting the independence of Puerto Rico, seeking out political relationships with U.S. indigenous nations, and running for political office, exemplify NAPS as a lived experience of ideology. An assessment of those outcomes and ideas behind them prepares readers for a deeper exploration of how and when NAPS and everyday life intersected within individual persons. The term "lifestyle politics" captures this phenomenon.

The discussion of lifestyle politics continues in chapter 3, "Revolutionary Name Choices," focusing primarily on name choices, which I argue are the most fundamental form of self-determination developed by New Afrikans (and Black Power activists more generally). Chapter 3 historicizes black naming practices in the United States and explains why choosing one's name was important for New Afrikans, especially during the 1960s and 1970s. Specifically, it examines the ways that individual and group names, cartography, and orthography became effective tools for the mechanics of liberation struggle. Because activists' name choices have been taken for granted by both the name studies scholarship and histories of the Black Power movement, my consideration of naming encourages scholars and activists to think more deeply and critically about the value of politically conscious naming practices.

Using interviews with RNA citizens and participant observation, chapter 4, "New Afrikan Lifestyle Politics," seeks to understand other aspects of New Afrikan life and political struggle.[19] Personal stories about the real and imagined RNA family and educational and career choices as paper-citizens in an oppressive nation add more depth to the historical and sociological discussions about social movement activism. Because much of the NAIM has been organized around a provisional government and multiple New Afrikan grassroots organizations and political parties, and because of citizens' decades-long pursuit of revolutionary goals, studying the people who have carried the movement into the twenty-first century provides unique opportunities to question and review the life course consequences of social movement activism. The stories presented for analysis demonstrate and begin to correct the shortcomings of the extant literature on these topics. Such literature tends to overemphasize survey data while presenting narrowly constructed categories of political leanings, participation, and outcomes. The use of an enduring territorial nationalist movement with revolutionary goals troubles the methods and conclusions of the extant scholarship.

New Afrikans, like their counterparts from the Black Power era to the present, remind us that the lived experience of one's ideas and activism was never wholly an internal process faced in isolation and independent of outside forces. Instead, state agencies such as the Federal Bureau of Investigation and local policing agencies, along with U.S. print and broadcast media, helped shape activists' goals, sociopolitical positioning, collective New Afrikan identity, and the outcomes of their participation. Therefore, chapter 5, "Cointel's Got Blacks in Hell," considers the dangerous and dispiriting aspects of social movement participation. Even so, it is important to avoid too quickly confirming the various declension narratives that populate such discussions. Nor will the chapter easily fit various "long Civil Rights Movement" models that historians of African American activism have proffered.[20] Instead, chapter 5 underscores the importance of external forces in shaping the development of social movements, as well as lifestyle politics. Although the outcome of repression is often negative, in the sense that it causes harm to activists and their loved ones, government hostility also helps shape the goals of movements, causes activists to rethink their beliefs and ideology, and has the potential to be a generative force in their collective political agenda. Chapter 5, therefore, will clarify how New Afrikans thought about and acted as the result of hostility and violence as they pursued their goals.

Chapter 6, "'For New Afrikan People's War,'" considers the NAIM beyond the PG-RNA. It highlights some of the organizations and parties that struggled for New Afrikan independence alongside the Obadele-led formation. These groups shared varying though similar interpretations of what New Afrikans meant and could bring about. Their ideas and actions demonstrate some of the ways that activists carried the struggle into the twenty-first century. Chapter 6 then traces the history of New Afrikan efforts to build the reparations movement in America, showing how New Afrikans worked with a variety of groups and individuals to give lasting momentum to ideas that many attribute to the efforts of the Student Nonviolent Coordinating Committee's (SNCC) former executive secretary James Forman. Revealing how New Afrikans distinguished their claims from Forman's, it shows that while Forman singled out churches and synagogues for their role in the slave trade, the PG-RNA focused on what the U.S. government owed African people. New Afrikans also connected the reparations claim to questions about the Fourteenth Amendment and how the federal government applied it to people of African descent. Another distinction was the PG-RNA's interpretation of UN language about national self-determination for historically oppressed groups. From its foundations in the RNA Declaration of Independence, the New Afrikan reparations claim eventually made its way into the formation of the National Coalition of Blacks for Reparations in America in 1989. Therefore, chapter 6 shows how New Afrikan politics have informed certain aspects of the broader black political agenda today.

The epilogue offers a short meditation on issues that scholars and activists have yet to fully explore as we continue to study and learn from past and present black political struggles. It asks: How will scholars and activists respond to state-sanctioned political violence? And what can we learn from the history and legacy of movements, such as the movement for New Afrikan independence, which have survived efforts by the state to destroy them? This history of the NAIM offers only one part of the story. It will take various efforts from a variety of disciplines to do justice to the movement to free the land and the people who helped normalize advocacy for reparations and political prisoners in modern black political struggles.

Taken together, these chapters tell the history of the New Afrikan Independence Movement while simultaneously exploring some ways that social movements might continue to live and evolve based on their specific historical contexts. Written in the age of #BlackLivesMatter, #MeToo, "Black Identity Extremists," the rise of the "Alt Right," humanmade climate-related challenges, and other important developments, the portions of this history that are accessible—and much is hidden due to government repression—have the ability to teach readers how certain aspects of the current situation arose and what lessons we might learn from our past. Because we continue to live in a society that sees the challenges of African-descended people as of little significance at best, or as extremist and terrorist at worst, the attention we give the NAIM and other social movement histories may help determine the ways that we respond now and shape our collective future.

1 Birth of the New Afrikan Independence Movement

A Historical Overview

· ·

On March 29, 1969, New Afrikans assembled at New Bethel Baptist Church, Reverend C. L. Franklin's ecumenical home, during a weekend-long celebration of the Republic of New Afrika's first anniversary. Active in grassroots organizing, Reverend Franklin at times worked on civil rights campaigns with two Republic of New Afrika (RNA) cofounders, Milton and Richard Henry, including the 1963 "Freedom March" at which Dr. Martin Luther King Jr. delivered his famous "I Have a Dream" sequence. Even though Reverend Franklin never claimed to support the creation of an independent black nation-state, he sometimes rented his church for black political activities.[1]

As the day's festivities were coming to a close, between forty and fifty police officers burst into the building. According to newspaper reports, they trained their weapons on the two hundred or so attending men, women, and children; and they may have exchanged shots with a rifleman in open view near the altar, as well as someone shooting from a semiconcealed location in the ceiling. The assault came moments after officers Michael Czapski and Richard Worobec observed armed guards from the Black Legion (the RNA military) outside the church building. Newspaper accounts claimed the guards shot the two officers—one fatally—as Czapski and Worobec approached to question the black men. Detroit police suggested the armed Legionnaires then ran into New Bethel, still shooting, as more officers arrived to rescue the dying Czapski and wounded Worobec. The onslaught left four attendees injured and resulted in 143 arrests. To the displeasure of local police and the *Detroit News*, black judge George Crockett released most of the arrestees the following morning.[2]

The "New Bethel Incident" and its immediate aftermath drew national attention and sensationalistic media coverage to the year-old RNA Provisional Government (PG-RNA). Police-community relations were already tense, and the battle at New Bethel strained them severely. It seemed to confirm fears that Black Power was indeed going after Anglo America's "mama," as former member of the Student Nonviolent Coordinating Committee

(SNCC) Julius Lester quipped.[3] For some white Detroiters, the gun battle evidenced another violent clash between "black militants" and the police, and provided one more justification for their flight from the inner city to more guarded homes in the suburbs.[4] For New Afrikans, the events of March 29 served as a reminder that the U.S. government would use its extensive resources to prevent RNA activists from bringing their version of Black Power, the attainment of New Afrikan independence, to fruition. Many New Afrikans also understood it as the first battle in what promised to be a long and drawn-out war for self-determination.

The PG-RNA and the New Afrikan Independence Movement (NAIM) it initiated developed out of Detroit's legacy of black struggle. The PG-RNA emerged specifically from the activism of the 1960s with the goal of independent statehood. Essential in this story were brothers Gaidi and Imari Obadele (also known as Milton and Richard Henry, respectively), leading figures in the Group on Advanced Leadership (GOAL) and the Malcolm X Society. Their activism and ideological evolution led to the call for the National Black Government Conference, later considered a convention, that birthed the PG-RNA. Following the convention, the PG-RNA weathered two major splits, two well-known shootouts, and other forms of overt and covert repression. Nevertheless, the PG-RNA and the movement survived.

The NAIM came into existence during an era that witnessed profound shifts in America's political atmosphere that ended Black Power and ushered in a new, more conservative sociopolitical moment. The growing state oppression and conservatism of the years that followed would effectively end the Black Power movement. New Afrikans' success in making it through this era set the context of the "New Afrikan Political Science" and the ways that participation in the NAIM was more than just a form of political activism—it came to shape activists' whole lives.

Black Struggle in Detroit and the Prehistory of the RNA

Detroit's story is one of migration, racial conflict, and black liberation struggle against a backdrop of industrial growth and decline. From the 1880s through World War II, the opening of new industries in Detroit prompted a migration that dramatically changed the city's population density and demographic makeup. Detroit's renown as the "Motor City" beckoned immigrants from all over the nation and world whose residency, in turn, helped the city become the fourth largest in the United States by 1920. In one period of tremendous growth between 1910 and 1920, black migrants increased the city's African American population by 611.3 percent. This dramatic increase resulted partially from the expansion of the auto industry and the "relaxation" of discriminatory employment practices. Detroit met steady streams of black migrants originating from almost every state in the Deep South and several northern Atlantic states. With World War I and the anti-immigrant legislation that followed, black migrants found unprecedented success in Detroit's labor market. Despite new work opportunities and growth in the African American population, black Detroiters had not overcome the major racial obstacles that characterized their quest for employment and decent housing in the wartime era and its aftermath. Companies hired black job seekers out of desperation and fired them at whim, and tensions between black workers and their white peers often led to violence.[5]

In their search for economic security, some African Americans began joining and organizing within labor unions such as the Congress of Industrial Organizations. Black union participation gained momentum during the 1930s following President Franklin D. Roosevelt's National Labor Relations Act, which gave more flexibility to workers trying to collectively organize for their rights. Although many black workers were initially skeptical of unions, talented organizers in Detroit managed to recruit enough of them to give black laborers some presence and power.[6]

Notwithstanding these opportunities in industrial workspaces, factors such as restrictive covenants, discriminatory loan practices, racialized violence, and "blockbusting" kept black Detroiters packed tightly in the city's East Side. When African Americans like Ossian Sweet moved into white neighborhoods, they were greeted with enmity and violence. Sweet was a gynecologist who moved into a segregated neighborhood in September 1925. Anticipating a hostile welcome into his new home, Sweet and his family arrived with several guns, ammunition, and food. As he expected, a group of white Detroiters gathered outside his home and at one point surrounded and threatened Sweet's brother and a friend. During this tense moment, someone fired a weapon from Sweet's house, killing a white man who was standing on a porch across the street. Sweet and ten others were arrested and charged with murder. An all-white jury ruled in Sweet's and his ten codefendants' favor. The historic victory encouraged some African Americans to continue pushing to live where they pleased and to remain resolute in their right to enjoy all aspects of life uninhibited. Still, the antagonism toward black Detroiters' ambitions continued, and tensions erupted into anti-black violence during the race riot of 1943, the worst disturbance the United States had seen to date.[7]

Black Detroiters' campaigns included strong showings of African American women activists and met with government repression of the early Cold War. As they did in other cities throughout the 1940s, African American women fought thoroughly for economic security, demanded equal access to public accommodations, hosted voter registration drives, and contested police brutality, among other activities. For example, the Detroit Association of Women's Clubs sponsored "voters' institutes" to educate its members about the voting process, pressing social issues, and political candidates. These women involved the National Association for the Advancement of Colored People (NAACP), the United Auto Workers (UAW), the Detroit Commission on Community Relations (DCCR), and other national and local organizations in their often successful enterprises.[8] However, black women and men's activism was complicated by coordinated repression against communism and anything mainstream politicians could label as "subversive." As a defense attorney for the Communist Party and lead attorney with the U.S. Department of Labor, George Crockett experienced high levels of repression, including a four-month sentence in federal prison for contempt after defending future Detroit mayor Coleman Young and other targets of the House Un-American Activities Committee. Crockett's work made him ineligible for public elected office until 1966, after nationwide black civil rights activism pushed enough reforms for him to operate freely.[9]

White people, too, gave varying levels of support to black equality. Henry Ford began implementing a seemingly more egalitarian business strategy, and the UAW and other unions became more open to promoting civil rights. Together, such shifts, when combined with the efforts of black activists, helped bring welcome changes. Although these efforts did not end racism in Detroit, by the 1950s, the city's African Americans achieved more economic and political power than ever before. Together, the various factors prompted some to revere Detroit as a "Model City" and "one of the major centers of black progress." As scholars August Meier and Elliot Rudwick point out, "this [progress] came at the very time that the multiplying NAACP legal victories and the dramatic rise of Martin Luther King to public prominence signified a revolution of expectations that was spawning a new militancy among black Americans." New modes of struggle that favored direct confrontation instituted a new era in black activism.[10]

Shifts in direction and strategy caught the attention of the forty-first, forty-second, and forty-third governors of Michigan, G. Mennen Williams, John B. Swainson, and George Romney, respectively, who each utilized the power of the position to aid civil rights causes. From 1948 through 1969, they gave state-funded efforts unprecedented power to investigate and address violations of their constituents' civil rights, thus making the state one of the most racially progressive in the nation. In Detroit, this racial progressivism manifested through the Civil Rights Commission's involvement with housing and employment discrimination and police brutality. Though the Michigan governors, particularly Romney, deserve some credit for their willingness to use their executive powers toward the advancement of black civic equality, it was the national civil rights movement that determined Detroit activists' successes.[11] Where the governors and civil rights activists failed, discrimination and racial violence persisted. Those oppressive tendencies influenced how black political organizations in Detroit evolved into the 1960s.

One organization that attempted to create a more equitable Detroit was the Trade Union Leadership Council (TULC), created in 1957 with the help of Horace Sheffield, an international representative for the UAW, to improve the conditions of black workers in their workplaces and unions. In a field of labor veterans who were still recovering from recent anticommunist assaults that spread to and weakened a range of left and liberal activists and organizations, Sheffield and the TULC's role in the black community resulted from political assaults on the National Negro Labor Council's Detroit body and the Local 600. Carrying on the work of those radical organizations, the TULC made visible the rifts in the "liberal-labor coalition, which had grown out of the black-union alliance during and after World War II." This coalition included the NAACP, Detroit Urban League, UAW, Jewish Community Council, various black churches, the Civil Rights Commission, and the American Civil Liberties Union (ACLU), among others. The TULC fought racism within labor unions and staged frontal attacks on racist restaurants, skating rinks, bars, and many other accommodations and recreational facilities, all while providing financial support to the southern movement. The council also supported the election of racial liberal Jerome Cavanaugh as mayor in 1962. In some ways, the undertakings of the TULC proved to be a liberal dress rehearsal for the activism staged by black leftist groups, including those that would involve Milton and Richard Henry.[12]

One such group was the Freedom Now Party (FNP), an all-black political party founded by journalist William Worthy and others just before the 1963 March on Washington for Jobs and Freedom. Party organizers sought to make the FNP national but gained momentum primarily in Michigan.[13] Grace Lee and James Boggs, Reverend Albert B. Cleage, and several other activists helped create the Detroit FNP directly following the 1963 Grassroots

Leadership Conference at which Malcolm X delivered his speech "Message to the Grassroots." They sought to make the FNP a recognizable force in Detroit city and Michigan state politics. With the hopes to transform U.S. party politics, several fairly well-known black Detroiters ran for local and state offices, including Milton Henry for Congress, radical lawyer Christopher Alston for senate, and Reverend Cleage for governor. With the interracial support of the Socialist Workers Party, the membership of GOAL, and Uhuru, a militant black student group whose leaders would later play instrumental roles in the creation of the Revolutionary Union Movements (RUMs), it seemed the FNP would achieve its desired results. However, disappointment reigned as the primary victor when all FNP candidates lost their respective elections. The party quickly declined thereafter but was succeeded by the RUMs, the League of Revolutionary Black Workers (the League), the Revolutionary Action Movement (RAM), the Black Panther Party (BPP), the Malcolm X Society, and the PG-RNA.[14]

The League was a coalition of RUMs that formed at various auto manufacturing plants (e.g., Dodge or DRUM and Ford or FRUM) and sought to organize black workers as the revolutionary vanguard of the United States. The League's ideology fused activists' understanding of the capitalist exploitation of workers with theories concerning the racial exploitation of the black colony in the United States. League members argued that if black workers could take control over the means of production, these laborers would provide leadership to oppressed groups and eventually create a society free of racial, economic, and gender oppression. The League also anticipated that revolutionaries in the United States would aid similar movements against imperialism abroad. Moreover, leaders from the League were central participants in the National Black Economic Development Conference (NBEDC). Resolutions from the conference allowed the League to secure funds for the creation of the Black Star line of press, publications, film productions, and a bookstore. They also made a film, *Finally Got the News*, which documented the League's struggles and ideals. Although the League and the PG-RNA disagreed on the issue of reparations, they had a generally amicable relationship and even worked together on activities related to Robert F. Williams.[15]

RAM was another important organization in Detroit. It was a revolutionary organization created by Donald Freeman and Maxwell Stanford Jr., student activists from Cleveland and Philadelphia, respectively. It had a national and largely underground membership, and it boasted the support of Malcolm X and Robert F. Williams. Stanford (later known as Akbar

Muhammad Ahmad) established a RAM group in Detroit in 1963 and maintained close relationships with many prominent Detroiters, including the Henry brothers. Though details of RAM's history in Detroit are still largely a mystery, Ahmad (Stanford) has made it clear that the organization held a consistent presence in Detroit between 1963 until it dissolved in 1968 with the intention of becoming the PG-RNA's left wing.[16]

Members of the League attempted to organize a local chapter of the BPP in hopes of attracting young activists and pushing the national BPP away from an ideology that envisioned the lumpen proletariat as the vanguard of black revolutionary struggle. However, it was instead the branch of the Detroit BPP founded by Ron Scott and Eric Bell about one year after RAM's demise that ultimately earned recognition by the national party's central committee. Among the Detroit branch's contributions to Detroit's political landscape was its work with the National Committee to Combat Fascism, a BPP front group that, in Detroit, invited white radical groups to participate. More important, the Panthers established an underground membership in Detroit that established a close relationship with the RNA's army, the Black Legion.[17]

A long-standing pillar of the black political scene was the Nation of Islam (NOI), born in Detroit on July 4, 1930. Besides promoting black nationalism and spreading its brand of Islam among African Americans, the Nation was responsible for one of African Americans' most celebrated icons, Malcolm X. The NOI provided Malcolm Little with the basic spiritual and cultural tools he needed to transform himself from a street hustler to Minister Malcolm X, and later El-Hajj Malik El-Shabazz. He underwent his initial training in Detroit, where he made several memorable appearances. The NOI, through Minister Malcolm, had a tremendous influence on the two brothers from Philadelphia who helped shape the goals and strategies of black revolutionary activism in Detroit, most notably through founding the PG-RNA.[18]

The elder brother, Milton Henry, moved from Philadelphia to the Model City in 1950 because it was one of the few cities in the United States where he could utilize his legal practice explicitly for the benefit of African Americans. In 1952, his younger brother Richard joined him, and they worked together in several civil rights organizations. In November 1961, the Henrys, Reverend Cleage, and other militant civil rights activists created GOAL, a civil rights group that sought to introduce what Richard Henry called "a new dimension in the fight against bias." Then GOAL chairperson, Richard added that the NAACP and other organizations "can at times benefit from outside help in accomplishing their goals faster." Although GOAL began with a stated purpose of assisting groups like the NAACP achieve their objectives, the organization quickly distinguished itself when some of its members began "Re-Thinking Integration," considering it "almost as dangerous as it is desirable." With a stated membership roster of 750 names, GOAL championed a "catalytic" method of activism that included using boycotts and legal battles to achieve the goals of getting African people's contributions to history added to public school textbooks and halting urban renewal projects, or "Negro Removal," according to some GOAL members. Members even helped sponsor and win a campaign to demand that white merchants carry a black-owned company's barbecue sauce.[19] Many of these reform-oriented activities built on the momentum of GOAL's liberal predecessors such as the TULC.

Over the years, GOAL developed bonds with radical leftist organizations and participated in militant activities. It was involved in study groups and actions against police brutality with the members of Uhuru and RAM, as well as the Boggses.[20] On occasion, Milton Henry gave talks at the Friday Night Socialist Forum hosted by the Socialist Workers Party, and he held a leadership position within RAM. Together, RAM and GOAL members co-founded and participated in self-defense groups, the Medgar Evers Rifle Club and the Fox and Wolf Hunt Club. The first honored the slain NAACP activist. Activists likely named the other in recognition of Malcolm X's December 4, 1963, characterization of white liberals as foxes and conservatives as wolves. Learning from the example set by the Deacons for Defense and Justice, Richard Henry explained that they formed the clubs to deter potential violent attacks on African American activists in their city. It is conceivable that they were also training for potential guerilla warfare. With these associations and the lessons they learned from years of struggle, the Henrys began to advocate for a separate nation as a viable solution to African Americans' problems.[21]

Taking their cue from Brother Imari, scholars William Van Deburg and Raymond L. Hall credit Malcolm X/Malik Shabazz with pushing the Henry brothers to accept territorial black nationalism as the most practical option for liberation. Milton met and developed a relationship with the minister, and the Henry brothers used GOAL to sponsor three lectures for him when he visited the Model City. In addition to his "Message to the Grassroots," Malcolm X delivered "The Ballot or the Bullet" and his "Last Message" in Detroit. After Shabazz's death, Milton and Richard changed their names to Gaidi and Imari Abubakari Obadele, respectively, and created the Malcolm

X Society, which they charged with working toward Shabazz's unmet goals for territory and revolution. The Obadeles believed the minister's primary concern was to create a sovereign black nation that would help Third World revolutionaries destroy global oppression.[22]

Even though Malcolm X was essential to the Henrys' political development, the brothers' life experiences in Philadelphia and over a decade spent in Detroit wielded as much of an impact on their political perspectives as did the NOI minister. Milton was a World War II veteran and a pilot whose refusal to accept racial discrimination led to his dishonorable discharge from the military and contributed to his inability to practice law in Pennsylvania. As a youth, Richard, who viewed his older brother as a hero, was an activist with the NAACP and a journalist who used his media talents to challenge racism. Also worthy of recognition are the siblings' organizing experiences in Detroit with groups and individuals who, as early as December 1961, had begun "Re-Thinking Integration." The Obadeles' associations with Reverend Cleage, the Boggses, RAM, Uhuru, and others who formed DRUM and the League should not be minimized. Indeed, the brothers' decision to work with these groups and individuals, as opposed to the NAACP or the TULC—organizations they deemed to be peopled with "Uncle Toms"—reflects the lessons they learned from their experiences struggling for freedom from under U.S. sovereignty.

By the time they met Minister Malcolm, the Obadeles' experiences already prepared them for his 1963 "Message." For Milton in particular, traveling in Ghana confirmed the importance of attaining political and physical independence as a basis of power. He was inspired by seeing Kwame Nkrumah and other African "guys [he]'d gone to school with at Lincoln . . . in their offices making decisions" that affected their country. In contrast, as the only black member of the Pontiac City Commission, Milton became discouraged because he was not able to make decisions that he believed would benefit African Americans. This inability confirmed his conviction that African Americans would never gain the power necessary to change the United States according to their needs. With these influences in mind, rather than single out Malcolm X as the primary reason the Henrys marched leftward to "Revolution and Nation-building," we should situate the martyred minister's influence within the broader context of their personal experiences working to improve conditions for black Detroiters.[23]

By 1964, the Obadeles had evolved into territorial nationalists with revolutionary goals. When they created the Malcolm X Society in 1967, they initially saw it as an apparatus to "work within [the] governmental framework and state structure of the United States, winning black people, first in Mississippi, to the cause of independent land and power, follow[ed] . . . with election victories (the sheriffs' offices, particularly) within the U.S. federal system, and, finally, tak[ing] the black state out of the U.S. federal union at the moment when white power could no longer be successfully resisted or neutralized in its efforts to prevent the creation of a new society in the black state."[24] The Malcolm X Society's aspirations became evident through its calls for black people to secure control over their own communities in the aftermath of the 1967 rebellion.[25]

Considered by many as the worst urban rebellion of the decade, the 1967 Detroit uprising deserves brief mention here because it helps explain the trajectory of the Obadeles as they approached the creation of the PG-RNA.[26] The Malcolmites, like most other political organizations, attempted to use the insurgency and the widespread fear of violence it spawned to leverage their demands as they organized shortly thereafter. They claimed to represent "the political side of the black Revolution" and insisted they could manage street revolutionaries if the city and state governments met their demands for community control. Apparently, the FBI and local police took such assertions seriously enough to increase their surveillance of the Obadeles immediately following the insurgency.[27] The rebellion, the Malcolmites' demands, and the local police and U.S. government's increasing surveillance of black activists all came to form the specific context in which the Obadeles organized the National Black Government Convention. The events of 1967 also signify the definite bookend of the political organizing strategies the brothers and their allies favored during much of the 1960s. Leading up to the establishment of the PG-RNA, the Malcolmites changed their strategy to include gaining African Americans' consent to create a separate nation through diplomatic and, if necessary, military means.[28]

The 1967 rebellion marked a turning point for black Detroiters. For their part, the Obadele brothers recognized the moment's revolutionary potential and used the lessons they had drawn from it to hasten their call for the creation of an independent black nation-state. But their appeal for land and power was not due solely to the violence of, or in response to, the uprising. Instead, decades of lived experience in the Motor City crystallized when the seeming opportunity to dismantle the status quo appeared within reach. For the Malcolm X Society, the events of July 1967 created space for their political project. Less than one year later, they would meet in hopes of bringing their ideas to fruition.

The National Black Government Convention
and the Creation of the PG-RNA

New Afrikans argue that the NAIM is the broad-based struggle seeking an independent black nation-state in the Black Belt region of the United States. Although they trace the movement's birth to the 1968 Detroit convention, former PG-RNA official Chokwe Lumumba indicates that its roots go back to the mid-seventeenth century when European settlers began racializing enslaved Africans with legislation that passed the mother's status to her children, naturalizing matrilineal enslavement. He indicates that the enslaved often liberated themselves and attempted to create their own maroon communities—at times with indigenous nations—outside of the European slave system.[29] According to Lumumba, the foundation of this long-standing movement grew stronger when black emigrationists in the United States such as Paul Cuffe, Henry Highland Garnett, and Martin Delaney sought land in Africa and elsewhere. It continued in the twentieth century with Marcus Garvey and the Universal Negro Improvement Association, whose estimated two million members took up the call "Africa for the Africans." That same era marked the inauguration of the African Blood Brotherhood (ABB), which supported the institution of an independent black state in the southern portion of the United States. Although it is estimated to have included between five thousand and eight thousand adherents at its height, the small organization influenced the Communist Party (CP) to accept and promote the idea of black sovereignty, a maneuver that increased black support of the CP tremendously. The CP adopted the "Black Belt Thesis," which identified portions of several southern states in which black people were entitled to self-determination. Lumumba claims that although the CP eventually dropped the idea and lost much of its black backing, several former black Communists and Garveyites, including "Queen Mother" Audley Moore, continued promoting territorial autonomy independently and through the NOI. In fact, Lumumba and Muhammad Ahmad both credit Queen Mother Moore for influencing Malcolm X and Elijah Muhammad to take up the struggle for independent land.[30]

Malcolm X and Queen Mother Moore were largely responsible for making the notion of an independent black nation palatable to the activists who founded the PG-RNA. Taking up and revising the Black Belt nation argument, the Malcolmites sought to liberate five southern states—Louisiana, Mississippi, Alabama, Georgia, and South Carolina. They recognized that the South was the region where the majority of enslaved Africans and their descendants resided. Further, as enslaved laborers and then sharecroppers, Africans built on and tilled the earth in those states, thus helping Anglo Americans prosper. Therefore, according to the Malcolmites, the five aforementioned states represented African Americans' historical "homeland" in the United States. The Malcolmites presented these and other ideas at the National Black Government Convention held in Detroit on March 30–31, 1968.[31]

The Obadeles and the Malcolm X Society were not alone in these efforts. A variety of middle- and working-class individuals, paramilitary organizations, socialists, former SNCC and Organization of Afro-American Unity activists, Black Panthers, Pan-Africanists, and non-affiliated Black Power advocates who participated in the national Black Power Conference in 1967 attended the 1968 Detroit convention. Lumumba states, "The fact that most prominent cultural and revolutionary nationalists of the period at least lent their name to the effort was indicative of the high regard which existed for the founding of the New Afrikan Independence Movement throughout the New Afrikan nation and within grass roots New Afrikan communities." Among these well-known supporters were Queen Mother Moore, the Us Organization's Maulana Karenga, Malcolm's widow Betty Shabazz, famous playwright and poet Amiri Baraka, John Bracey of RAM, and several other black nationalists, including some who held high rank within the original provisional governmental structure of the RNA.[32]

Convention participants dedicated both days of their meetings to discussing and resolving issues concerning citizenship, national sovereignty, taxes and governmental functioning, opening diplomatic relations with other nations and the United Nations, and "achieving status for black guerillas under the Geneva Convention," in addition to ratifying a declaration of independence. Brother Gaidi invited "three categories of persons" to the convention: "(1) Participants, who are Black nationalists ready now for separation, (2) Observers, black people who are genuinely interested in separation as a possible solution to our problems in America, and (3) Technical Advisors."[33] The last group of invitees included "black people, whether nationalists or not, who have something to offer the new government and its founding efforts: such as lawyers, scientists, economists and industrialists." The conversations held during the convention demonstrated such people's importance. Talks centered on international human rights law, reparations, women's equal participation, and military strategy—or some combination or derivative of them. An example is participants' agreement that New

Afrikan citizens who might be captured by the U.S. police or other law enforcement and/or armed agencies when carrying out the military work of the Provisional Government should receive prisoner of war (POW) status. Attendees concluded that POW status should not be dependent on an actual "declaration of war against the U.S. (and [they] recommend[ed] no declaration of war)" so that "members of [black revolutionary] military forces would have rights under the Geneva Convention."[34]

During the second day of the convention, participants spent considerable time discussing and signing the Declaration of Independence of the black nation. Questioning the legitimacy of U.S. citizenship and demanding restitution for African enslavement and its legacies of discrimination, racial violence, economic oppression, and more, the document connected the struggle of African-descended people in the United States with a global effort "to destroy this oppression wherever it assaults mankind in the world." The declaration promoted a "New Society" and a "New State Government" that would assure individual and collective human rights and that renounced discrimination or persecution for one's religious beliefs, race, color, and sex. Pledging to pursue these ideals "without reservation," Queen Mother Moore signed first, marking the founding of the Provisional Government and the NAIM. At a rally later that day, convention participant Raymond Willis announced that the new nation would be called the "Republic of New Africa," as opposed to the originally proposed name, the "Songhay Republic."[35]

As a "provisional government," the PG-RNA designated itself as the temporary leadership of the captive black nation in the United States. The original structure consisted of executive, judicial, and legislative branches. The executive branch included a president, first and second vice presidents, several regional vice presidents, a treasurer, and ministers of diverse functions. At the RNA's founding, participants elected exiled former Monroe, North Carolina, NAACP president and RAM chairman Robert F. Williams as president; Brother Gaidi as first vice president; Sister Betty Shabazz as second vice president; and Brother Imari, a leading theorist, as minister of information. And so things remained for one year. Gaidi restructured the leadership following the New Bethel shootout of March 29, 1969. The move resulted in replacing the first and second vice presidents with four regional vice presidents whose primary task was to help the president carry out his or her duties of defending the captive black nation and securing reparations and sovereign territory.[36]

Following the convention, the PG-RNA's first step in achieving its goals was to open negotiations with the U.S. government. Brother Imari attempted

Robert F. Williams painting by Khalid Abdur-Rasheed, 2016. Courtesy of the artist.

to initiate this process in late May 1968 when he delivered a message requesting a diplomatic conversation with then Secretary of State Dean Rusk. Vice President Gaidi Obadele signed the request as "Milton Henry" in lieu of the exiled Robert Williams. The Obadeles hoped that requesting diplomatic negotiations with the United States immediately after the RNA's founding would demonstrate to conscious New Afrikans and potential "citizens of record" that the Provisional Government (PG) was serious about achieving physical separation and political independence. This appeal to conduct negotiations brought the RNA into compliance with the various steps necessary to take its struggle for independence to the United Nations. Furthermore, the PG-RNA understood that the U.S. government would not willingly open discussions to hand over 10 percent of the nation's land resources. Thus, the anticipated response to the letter would serve as more proof to African Americans that they could not rely on the U.S. government for liberation. Liberation was something for black people to take on their own terms. This necessary confiscation justified the creation of "a strong, disciplined Black Legion in America—a black army to fight for black rights."[37]

Brother Imari provided an overview of the PG's total agenda to achieve political independence, territorial sovereignty, and reparations in a speech called "The Eight Strategic Elements Necessary for Success of the Black Nation in America." He characterized the first three elements as "the nation's wealth": natural resources, a labor force, and "the genius that our people possess," each of which would allow the burgeoning nation to develop the skills necessary to make the nation strong. The fourth aspect was "a limited objective": the acquisition of five states. Brother Imari expected a relatively smooth turnover of the five states because they encompassed the poorest and contained the largest concentrations of African Americans. Therefore, he justified, the U.S. government would not find the domain desirable and would not try too hard to keep it once "giving up something [became] inevitable" for the United States.[38] However, he was not as naïve as the statement may seem to indicate. Instead, he expected that it would take serious effort on the part of New Afrikans to convince America to give up that land. It would require solidarity from other Africans in the United States, as well as support from international allies.

The fifth factor, "internal domestic support," helps explain why the PG-RNA sought to establish consulates in several major cities across the United States. Officers of the PG-RNA reasoned that maintaining a presence in cities where African Americans held "positions as Congressmen, judges, and other officials" would enable them to develop relationships with black people who could "be used to stay the hand of the United States in its efforts at repression of New Africa's campaign for liberation." Further, black communities could use their collective resources to achieve control over local schools and other institutions that brought African Americans into close contact with one another and the bureaucratic state apparatus. Representing a departure from other Black Power–era liberation efforts, "community control" was not an end in itself for the RNA, but part of a larger procedure to gain land and power. RNA leadership anticipated that influential allies throughout northern cities would lend useful bargaining tools in negotiations with the U.S. government for New Afrika's independence. RNA officers expected to trade on the social and political capital wielded by black-controlled northern cities and people for land in the South and presumed that RNA-controlled southern land would serve as the foundation of their black nation.[39]

The sixth necessary strategic element emphasized gaining international allies. The PG-RNA apparently began meeting with representatives from several potential ally nations and groups including the USSR, Tanzania, and Sudan. Although there is no clear indication of how extensive such conversations were, attempts at developing these relationships confirm that New Afrikan leadership hoped to be taken seriously by established nations. The New Afrikan leaders also hoped to gain the support of the United Nations as they demanded reparations for the human rights violations committed by the United States against enslaved Africans and their progeny up to the contemporary moment. Brother Imari later claimed he initiated deals with China, and these negotiations seemed to be going well until the PG-RNA ran into complications in its relationship with Robert Williams. The titular president began losing faith in China, Cuba, and "all third world liberation-type organizations" whom he accused of being prejudiced against African Americans.[40]

With such ambitious goals, RNA leaders did not disregard potential repression; in fact, they expected violence from the U.S. government and racist vigilante organizations such as the Ku Klux Klan. Therefore, Brother Imari's final two essential elements addressed the RNA's military strategy, which he divided into three levels of participation: the above-ground army, the Black Legion (later named the New Afrikan Security Forces); Third World military support; and the so-called second-strike capability of underground urban guerillas. Brother Imari argued that the combination of these varying levels of military strength would be threatening enough to prevent possible violent confrontation and/or preserve the fledgling nation in potential battle.[41]

Never simply violent militants, Detroit New Afrikans planned to implement several programs aimed at spreading their ideas and attracting new cadres. First and most important was their political education, "nation-building" classes. Held at their office on Puritan Street, New Afrikans met regularly with new recruits to prepare them for RNA citizenship. They also wanted to create all-black schools modeled after Ocean Hill–Brownsville in Brooklyn, New York, an institution whose struggles for community control Brother Imari participated in and tried to get to support the independence movement. The Detroit consulate ran the Frederick Douglas [sic] Shooting Club, which seemingly served as a recruiting tool for the Black

Legion. The club encouraged interested persons to frequent its daily meetings, which included nation-building classes taught by Brother Imari. The RNA also conducted conversations about running free food and clothing programs to address some of the immediate material needs of black Detroiters, but there is no evidence to determine whether these ideas ever materialized. Finally, New Afrikans initiated a "Freedom Petition" in April 1969 that sought to "place police, central banking and industrial development under a black City Council and create [an] all-powerful black school board and a black court system in the black community." The League of Revolutionary Black Workers and Eastside Voice of Independent Detroit helped circulate the petition, yet it is unlikely that the petition gained widespread endorsement. Further, it is difficult to ascertain which programs the RNA actually carried to fruition and what efforts survived in Detroit, especially considering the many internal and external challenges New Afrikans faced.[42]

Obstacles: Robert F. Williams and the RNA's First Constitutional Crisis

The early years of the PG-RNA were plagued with overlapping obstacles that culminated in a split and led to Imari Obadele moving the RNA headquarters to the South. The first obstacle that they had to overcome was the absence of their elected president, Robert F. Williams. New Afrikans devoted considerable attention to meeting with Robert Williams and devising a way to bring home their president-in-exile. In early June 1968, the Obadele brothers took a seven-day trip to Tanzania, where Williams and his family were spending some time. Many of the meeting's specific details remain unclear, but Williams did "signal some agreement" with being elected RNA president. Williams likely came to this decision due to Brother Gaidi's promise that the PG-RNA would help him return to the United States and "keep him on the streets for at least two years." The Obadeles believed that if Williams "were on the streets for two years [New Afrikans] could build a movement so strong that nobody could touch him and the movement would be a power." With Williams confident in this promise, Brother Gaidi became one of Williams's key legal representatives as the exiled activist negotiated the conditions of his return home with the U.S. government. Meanwhile, the Obadeles expected Williams to secure diplomatic relations between the RNA, China, and newly independent African nations. In fact, he was reported to have a close friendship with Abdul Rahman Mohamed Babu, one of Tanzania's governmental officials. The PG-RNA delegation revealed that the trip also brought them into contact with Tsepo Tiisetso Letlaka, an exiled South African and member of the Pan African Congress, one of the major political parties fighting apartheid.[43]

Despite these highlights, the Obadeles' trip revealed the first of many points of tension between Williams and the RNA, as well as within the PG-RNA. Brother Imari reported that Williams expressed reluctance to accept the presidency of the RNA, and instead exhibited a preoccupation with receiving money to build a hospital in Tanzania and returning safely to the United States to face the kidnapping charges that resulted in his family's exile. Informants for the Detroit police and federal government claimed the Obadeles shared this and other discouraging news at a meeting with RNA leadership. These disclosures suggested that Williams's intentions did not correspond with New Afrikans' desires. Also, in this situation, a test of trust and loyalty was becoming apparent. The leadership decided not to reveal those complications to the general citizenship for fear that such news would jeopardize their movement.[44] Eventually, however, issues surrounding Williams rose to the surface and contributed to the internal conflict that led to the first constitutional crisis.

In the meantime, at Williams's suggestion, Brother Imari began a petition drive to notify the U.S. government and the United Nations that New Afrikans gave the PG-RNA their consent to enter negotiations for reparations and the independence of their nation. Obadele soon reported to Williams that several PG-RNA representatives attended a medical conference in Boston "and won a resolution of support from [some] doctors indicating their willingness to provide medicines and certain equipment to Tanzania." Brother Imari also mentioned to Williams growing support for the RNA from advocates who in 1968 attended the Third Annual Black Power Conference in Philadelphia as well as nationalist-minded students from various colleges and universities across the United States. The 1968 Black Power conference and a student conference at Howard University both passed resolutions recognizing the Provisional Government and pledging to establish consulates at black colleges as well as white colleges with black student caucuses. These students' purpose was to "organize to advance the fight for land and power." Finally, Brother Imari notified Williams that a conscious citizen in Atlanta donated over one hundred acres of land to the RNA, a potential site for the republic's capital. RNA leaders planned to use another plot of land they were purchasing in Mississippi to establish a library, infirmary, and community house. According to Brother Imari, Williams never acknowledged having received word of these updates. In fact, once back in the United States, Brother Imari maintained that the president did not want any information regarding the RNA's plans and insisted his unawareness would help him "say truthfully that he didn't know anything" during his looming Senate testimony.[45]

It was in the midst of these troubles with Williams that the infamous 1969 New Bethel shooting occurred. New Afrikans were meeting at New Bethel Baptist Church in Detroit on the final weekend of March to celebrate their movement and to plan its future course. After several discussions and festivities, Brother Gaidi gave the closing address and then departed the church building with several Legionnaires who escorted him to his car. Just seconds after he drove off, the powder charge that fueled the shootout between Legionnaires and police became volatile. Characterized by the late historian Ahmad Rahman as a tension-filled display of manhood that was bound to explode, the Legion's first shootout with Detroit police exacted innumerable short- and long-term repercussions for the RNA's nation-building process. Arrested attendees complained that the police stole over "$800 in cash and bus and airline tickets" and tortured several Legionnaires, including Brother Imari's teenage son and namesake. The RNA also lost some of its priceless, original documents. Among the arrestees were Clarence "Chaka" Fuller and Rafael Viera, both whom the city of Detroit eventually tried for second-degree murder and assault with intent to kill. Both were acquitted, but Brother Chaka soon thereafter met his death in a stabbing incident that his sister and the RNA's Detroit consulate claimed was police retaliation for the killing of Officer Michael Czapski.[46]

Given the violently repressive atmosphere in which black activists from all political persuasions operated, it is somewhat difficult to imagine the full impact of the New Bethel shootout on potential RNA supporters and the Detroit consulate. For many people who learned about the shootout, it may have been just another battle between the police and black "radicals." On the other hand, the news of a slain police officer may have attracted some African American adventurists who were tired of police brutality and wanted to participate in such gun battles for retaliation. It is also reasonable to assume that the shootout (or "shoot-in," as some have called it) repelled people otherwise drawn to the idea of a black nation-state. In fact, one New Afrikan stated that the shootout frightened people who were otherwise willing to sell land to the Provisional Government.[47] By March 1969, Black Power activists had lost many of their few white supporters. With rare exceptions, black nationalists depended solely on African American support and black activists experienced severe fragmentation among their ranks, despite their utilization of Black Power conferences to unify with one another. What is more, in an era when the most visible ideological thrust advocated working within the U.S. political system for black liberation, the New Bethel Incident may have done more to justify that approach than to encourage African Americans to struggle for political and physical independence. However, like the BPP, the RNA gained some allies who believed the police provoked violent exchanges in order to justify their repression of black nationalists and revolutionaries. Within the PG-RNA, the shootout proved to Brother Gaidi and his supporters that a calculated educational organizing process in the North was the safest way to bring about their desired results. Because he considered the RNA to be at war, Brother Imari believed the RNA's best move was to head south and begin building their nation in their desired land. Disagreement over this relocation soon caused the Provisional Government to implode.[48]

In September 1969, RNA President Robert F. Williams made his triumphant return to the United States after eight years of exile. Brother Gaidi arranged for his arrival in Detroit, where New Afrikans built enough legal, military, and political support to ensure his safety. Still, Williams's arrival provoked a lot of confusion. First, authorities in London, England, briefly detained and incarcerated Williams and refused to permit him aboard any aircraft for fear that he would hijack it. Because they considered him "dangerous cargo," the British Home Office instead offered him passage by ship. As several British Black Power advocates demonstrated outside of Pentonville Prison, the facility where Williams was detained for a couple of days, Brother Gaidi negotiated with British officials. After much bargaining, it finally seemed the PG-RNA president-elect was making his way home. Meanwhile in Detroit, Legionnaires and police made their way to the metropolitan airport to meet the exiled activist upon noticing that a man with the surname Williams would soon land in the city. However, the RNA president-elect was not on the expected flight. In his stead, and quite by accident, a "neatly dressed English businessman" named Edward Williams met the confused police and Legionnaires. When the correct Williams finally arrived in the Detroit area on September 12, 1969, members of the Black Legion, FBI agents, and local police welcomed him. High tensions between U.S. armed forces and the Legion notwithstanding, no violence erupted. After yet another brief detention, Williams walked the Detroit streets on bail.[49]

Many New Afrikans expected Williams's highly anticipated homecoming to reenergize and organize the New Afrikan Independence Movement. It instead presented yet another hindrance for the PG-RNA. Williams's return brought to the surface internal conflicts that had been brewing for over a year. In that time, Brother Imari gained a reputation as a suicidal militant and an impulsive authoritarian whose ideas clashed with those of the other leadership. He threatened the British government with international demonstrations when it apprehended Williams, and he was accused of planting a bomb at the Detroit Metropolitan Airport. Further, it was rumored that several people did not trust some RNA leadership and cadres, including Chokwe Lumumba, because he and others were suspected to be FBI informants.[50] Police provocateurs and actual informants played no small role in creating and exacerbating that distrust. They doctored counterfeit letters from "Concerned Brothers" and drafted fake correspondences from Brother Imari to members of the Detroit BPP with whom local New Afrikans enjoyed cordial relationships. By November 1969, informants contended that the Detroit Consulate was "falling apart." Brother Imari and other leaders constantly requested money from New Afrikans and Black United Front members with whom they had formed an alliance to protect Williams. This money was to go to Williams's defense fund and to assist less fortunate New Afrikans and members of the local community. To make matters worse, funds allocated to purchase land in Mississippi disappeared, thus causing further disharmony within the RNA.[51]

The collective damage done by these and other factors proved irreparable by November 1969, when Brother Imari resigned from his positions as minister of interior and Midwest regional vice president. During that same month, Brother Rob stepped down from the presidency. Brother Imari charged that Williams and Brother Gaidi violated RNA law by unilaterally making important decisions, including their suspension of Brother Imari for allegedly withholding membership information from Gaidi and threatening to start his own organization. In light of these allegations and his suspension, Brother Imari abdicated his posts in protest. Shortly thereafter, Williams told the *Detroit News* that he was more interested in solving his legal problems and fighting for integration than building an independent black nation-state. He did assert, however, that if white Americans refused to allow African Americans to actualize their self-determination, he would again support the creation of a separate black nation. Muhammad Ahmad, one of the resigned president's associates from RAM, insisted Williams left because he sensed that the ranks of the PG were heavily infiltrated with agents of the state and "romantic leftwing adventurism."[52]

During that same moment, the long-percolating ideological and strategic conflicts between Brothers Gaidi and Imari bubbled to the surface. Although Brother Imari described the dispute as a "family squabble" of little consequence to the RNA, the dispute's roots lay partially in very important strategic disagreements that profoundly affected the Provisional Government and its supporters. On one side, Imari and his supporters favored moving RNA headquarters to Mississippi in order to implement their nation-building process within the "captive" homeland. On the other side, Gaidi and several others argued that RNA headquarters should remain in Detroit and New Afrikan leadership should focus on deliberate organizing and legal strategies. The former faction seemed determined to present a direct challenge to the United States in a manner that would bring about unavoidable violent confrontation more quickly. The latter camp's approach appeared safer; it intended to mitigate any further violence between the RNA's military and local authorities.[53] The *Detroit News* and *Detroit Free Press* publicized this conflict, thus preventing the brothers and their respective supporters from hiding their rifts.

Still, there was more to the conflict than what the Obadele brothers stated in public. The RNA was also undergoing what some refer to as its first "constitutional crisis." Since the 1968 Black Government Convention, the Provisional Government had yet to ratify a constitution. Instead, the RNA's governing body based its decisions and actions on original documents such as the New Afrikan Declaration of Independence and the *Government Administration* handbook. An established constitutional commission was not able to approve a constitution by its deadline of December 1, 1969.[54] Divided by strategy, the Obadeles proposed two different courses of action to rectify the crisis. Brother Gaidi argued for an open election of PG officers during a convention in January, while Brother Imari recommended that regional representatives carry out PG elections, a measure he believed ensured all New Afrikans a voice. The acting judges in this dispute decided that if 40 percent of the general population could attend a meeting to cast their votes, then Brother Gaidi's suggestion would win. Gaidi rejected the ruling.[55]

On January 1, the PG's authority lost its legal basis due to the PG's expired "terms of office." In his stated attempt to carry out already planned business, Brother Imari hosted an RNA constitutional convention in Detroit on January 23–24. About thirty New Afrikans attended as representatives "from seven or eight cities," and they elected interim officers to serve for three months. Brother Gaidi, Queen Mother Moore, and eight other officials in the PG-RNA boycotted the meeting and planned a convention for July. Others, including Chokwe Lumumba, a respected Detroit elder named Anwar Pasha (also known as Henry "Papa" Wells), and several members of the Black Legion, attempted to support both factions as they sought to bring unity back to the RNA leadership. Despite those attempts, by July, Brother Gaidi, Sister Betty Shabazz, and several other leaders resigned from their positions, giving Brother Imari and his newly assembled governing body complete control over the RNA.[56] Brother Gaidi, still "absolutely a political separatist" by his own admission, moved to a Detroit suburb to enjoy a break from the movement. With his newly attained power and a newly approved constitution, "the Code of Umoja," RNA president Imari Obadele moved the organization's headquarters south, first to New Orleans in May 1970. In March 1971, New Afrikans moved the RNA headquarters to Mississippi. During a land dedication ceremony, they declared El Malik, in Bolton, the capital. With between three thousand and five thousand estimated citizens of record, the PG's move south marked a new chapter in RNA and NAIM history.[57]

Intense national organizing, ideological struggle, and difficulty with government infiltration characterized the first two years of the PG-RNA's existence. In that period, New Afrikans made national headlines due to the audacity of their goals and because of their violent interactions with police. Also during that time, they experienced forceful growing pains resulting from their divergent views regarding the issue of independence and territorial sovereignty for African people in the United States. Those growing pains did not ease up with the PG-RNA's strategic move to the South. Instead, New Afrikans encountered a new series of challenges that determined the course of their organizing for over a decade.

Incarceration, Contention, and Persistence

The early 1970s marked an important moment in the political evolution of Black Power ideologies. Urban rebellion subsided as black elected officials became mayors and congresspersons and held many other positions previously unavailable to them due to de jure and de facto racism. Further, activists incorporated the Black Power slogan into everything from hair products to urban development programs, and even Nixon-sanctioned black city development. African Americans from across the political spectrum strove to develop strategies to make the most of this political environment. They devised plans through institutional formations such as the Congressional Black Caucus and meetings such as the Gary Convention of 1972. Political science scholar Cedric Johnson describes these political moves as the shift from progressive grassroots activism to elitist, stagnated, institutional political participation.[58] In contrast to the either/or changeover outlined by Johnson, during the early 1970s, the PG-RNA and others who championed the NAIM focused on grassroots organizing and cadre development, as well as establishing the PG as an electorally based institution.

Having moved their governmental headquarters to Jackson, Mississippi, New Afrikans began to execute their strategy for political independence. In the process, they were involved in another shootout with police and the FBI, which occurred on August 18, 1971. In a predawn raid, the local police and FBI shot tear gas into the RNA residency on Lynch Street. In response, the New Afrikans present shot back, killing one police officer and injuring an FBI agent. The incident also resulted in the arrests of several New Afrikans, including Imari Obadele, which was devastating and diverted attention from their plans. Whereas the PG-RNA previously focused its energy on organizing New Afrikan communities and recruiting and developing new cadres, following the shootout, it allocated a tremendous amount of money and energy into defending the "RNA-11," the alleged participants in the shootout, in their various court cases.[59] The deposed president Imari Obadele and Midwest regional/first vice president Hekima Ana lost their legal authority per the Code of Umoja, the RNA constitution, thereby transferring power to Alajo Adegbalola, Dara Abubakari, and Chokwe Lumumba.

According to Lumumba, Adegbalola trained the aforementioned younger New Afrikan leaders in order to build up cadres and instill discipline across the RNA cadres. It was this group, he stated, "that really began the work to free the land." They planned and implemented a course of action that involved moving people to the South and raising money for "new communities" with the hopes of developing the new nation around those communities. Under those auspices, they also generated enthusiasm for the 1975 general RNA elections aimed at simultaneously educating black people about the New Afrikan Independence Movement and creating a people's government to help lead them to liberation. Although considered a success by some RNA leaders, the 1975 elections revealed the moment during which many of the more experienced organizers began developing critiques of the PG-RNA's direction. They learned several lessons about organizing based on their experiences with the election.[60]

In particular, some in the younger contingent questioned the timeliness of the Provisional Government apparatus. After studying the Palestinian and Vietnamese struggles, the younger activists decided that a provisional government would be most effective *after* the masses of black people acquired education about the need for independence and after a revolutionary organization helped bring coherence to the resistance that would develop out of that need. Lumumba and others' experiences during the 1975 elections also convinced many organizers that having a provisional government was premature because the NAIM had not yet developed any broadly recognizable and committed leadership. When organizers canvassed for the elections, people typically voted for whomever the New Afrikan canvasser presented. In other words, there was a lack of serious engagement with the process on the part of the voters. For that reason, PG activists concluded that voters did not have any strong political connection with the election or the people for whom they voted.[61]

Alongside this lack of connection, elected officials neglected to show up to meetings or assume responsibility for the positions to which voters elected them. Brother Chokwe and others attributed this problem partially to a lack of discipline, which Alajo Adegbalola endeavored to foster among much of the cadre. However, practical obstacles also factored into this seeming dereliction of duty. The RNA organized its leadership nationally and regionally, holding meetings in locations that required extensive travel for some. Not everyone had the financial means or excess time needed to get to all of the meetings. Therefore, attending an important meeting in Philadelphia might be impossible for an RNA official living in California, especially since the PG-RNA lacked funds to provide travel stipends to help its leaders assemble. Regardless of the reasons for their absence, the People's Center Council (PCC), the top decision-making body of the RNA, could not meet during an important meeting in late November 1977. When it could not make a quorum for doing business, the PG-RNA entered its second constitutional crisis in less than ten years.[62]

Such problems caused many within the PG-RNA to question their methods for obtaining New Afrikan liberation. After much careful dialogue, Brother Chokwe proposed changes to the RNA constitution, which gained the consent of the PCC. As a result of their experiences since the 1971 shootout, the available PG-RNA leadership (Brother Imari was imprisoned until 1973 and then returned to prison in 1977) decided unanimously that the concept of the provisional government needed to undergo some significant rethinking. New Afrikans in the PG were not alone in their reasoning; members of the Afrikan People's Party (APP) and the House of Umoja (HOU), two successor groups to RAM, and several other black liberation veterans and neophytes argued that the NAIM needed a strong revolutionary political party or activist formation to organize at the grass roots for New Afrikan independence. Beginning in 1978, some of the PG-RNA leadership began to talk seriously about the possible changes. Led by Chokwe Lumumba, Dara Abubakari, and Ahmed Obafemi, this group of New Afrikans earned the enmity of Brother Imari, who was incarcerated in federal prison on a conviction stemming from the Jackson shootout.[63]

Largely from prison and with the indispensable help of energetic young New Afrikan organizer Nkechi Taifa, Brother Imari assembled a group in Washington, D.C., and Philadelphia under the banner of the Malcolm X Party. The Malcolm X Party accused the Abubakari-Lumumba faction of planning a seditious counterrevolution that needed to be stopped and attempted to remove Brother Chokwe from his office of "Acting President." Next, the Malcolm X Party held a National Black Election in Washington, D.C., by soliciting votes "mainly at black meetings . . . and in several prisons." The Association of Black Psychologists counted and verified the votes, but the PCC disavowed legitimacy of the election. According to Brother Imari, the PCC agreed "to pursue, in 1979, the sterile (based on past experience) goals of (a) building cadres and (b) a human rights campaign. Worse, the August 1978 PCC voted to amend the constitution in such a way as to wipe out the popular basis of the Provisional Government, *and* it voted to conduct an election on these amendments in a manner which [was] clearly unconstitutional." The animosity between the Malcolm X Party and the "Lumumba-Abubakari tendency" exacerbated the tensions within the movement.[64]

The second constitutional crisis, like the first, split New Afrikans and led to what political scientist Gary King considers political "taunting." In other words, both sides of the split posed questions about the validity of the other's stance and actions.[65] Each camp alleged that the other carried on in discordance with the Code of Umoja and acted out of its desires for personal gain to the detriment of the revolutionary principle. After about five years of ideological struggle and negotiation, the Malcolm X Party and the Abubakari-Lumumba group—both asserting their legitimacy as the PG-RNA—met in Washington, D.C., where they agreed to form a temporary "Reconciliation Provisional Government." It allowed officers from both sides to hold equal status in the Provisional Government. The coalition appointed Imari Obadele and Dara Abubakari as temporary copresidents until the election of 1984.[66] Many within the Abubakari-Lumumba group opted not to run for office within the PG-RNA, as they believed their continued presence would prolong disharmony and render the PG ineffective. Instead, they left to help form the New Afrikan People's Organization (NAPO), a revolutionary party that worked toward the goals that New Afrikans from various non-PG organizations had been formulating since the previous decade (if not sooner). These include New Afrikans from HOU and APP who were also essential in the development of NAPO and brought their own ideas and programs, such as the New Afrikan Scouts (a youth organization), into it. Since its inception in 1984, NAPO considered itself the sister organization to the PG-RNA, and it focused on building cadres at the grassroots level.[67]

The ideological battles of the 1970s proved significant to the development of the NAIM. They indicate that in the process of trying to obtain independence, New Afrikan activists cultivated new theories and arguments in order to identify the best methods to proceed based on their experiences with organizing and repression. As they struggled with their ideas, the movement grew beyond the Provisional Government to include grassroots organizing that sought to prepare people for political struggle around the notion of New Afrikan independence. While the PG-RNA seemed to evolve into a constituency-based formation in harmony with the general course of Black Power organizing, NAPO and other NAIM groups continued to engage in forms of grassroots organizing that waned among other black political formations in the closing moments of the 1970s. Some examples include the efforts organized through the National Black Human Rights Coalition, the National Task Force for Cointelpro Litigation and Research, and the Afro-American Anti-Bicentennial Committee. Because various blocs within the NAIM emphasized different aspects of the independence struggle, they created space for the involvement of new activists opposed to practices based on a provisional government.

• • • • • •

The RNA developed amid the great political upheaval of the 1960s, and especially grew from a legacy of black political activism in Detroit. Although the city benefited from relatively progressive white elected officials, there were still limitations that prevented African American activists from achieving black liberation. Through their experiences in Detroit and interactions with other activists, the Henrys/Obadeles came to recognize that they could not achieve their goals within the existing political system. Instead, they adopted a revolutionary agenda. The 1967 Detroit rebellion and its aftermath crystallized those sentiments, presenting an opportunity for them to become most vocal advocates for political independence and statehood. The Black Government Convention proved a significant outcome of their personal experiences struggling for liberation in Detroit.

Also significant were the changes that took place internally due to the lessons activists learned during the early years of independence struggle. As young activists experienced and reflected on their actions, as well as government repression, in the name of the RNA, they developed new ideas and analysis. They began incorporate what they had learned into the corpus of tenets that became New Afrikan Political Science. But old ideas and new developments did not always coincide easily, and many of the changes that younger activists wanted to implement moved them into organizations that ultimately struggled alongside the PG-RNA, even as they maintained critiques of the governmental apparatus. Despite the various internal and external elements that could have brought about the NAIM's demise, the NAIM survives to this day.

Though in many ways the PG-RNA's unique goals resonated with the plethora of objectives animating black nationalist organizing during the 1960s and 1970s, New Afrikan activism reminds us that Black Power had different meanings to a range of people and organizations. As their contemporaries organized around Black Power objectives that sought liberation within the United States, New Afrikans promoted independence and statehood. Their end goal required them to reframe the popular political slogan in terms that departed from their peers, even as they promoted some of the same immediate objectives. New Afrikan Political Science provided a framework through which RNA activists developed alternative understandings of such common political terminology and its iconography.

2 The Fruition of Black Power

Paper-Citizenship and the Intellectual Foundations of Lifestyle Politics

The Republic of New Afrika's flag is green, red, and black. According to an article titled "The Flag of Our Nation," the color black is on the bottom to symbolize the political and economic positions of African people throughout the world. Green takes up the top position of the RNA flag because New Afrikans have recognized obtaining land as the most important aspect of their struggle for liberation. Only by gaining land and independence could they expect to help rearrange the economic conditions that made African people among the poorest in the world. Finally, the thin red stripe in the middle stands in for the blood of people who must secure land through any means necessary, though New Afrikans hoped to lose "as little *Black* blood as possible" in pursuit of their goals.[1] Around the same time the RNA released an article explaining its flag, Edward Vaughn, a black business owner and former Citywide Citizens Action Committee member (alongside Milton Henry), published a small book explaining the history, meaning, and use of the red, black, and green flag. In elaborating the flag's colors and their order, Vaughn argues that they follow the tradition of Garveyism, the political movement that made them popular in African liberation struggle worldwide, and insists that the colors should never be changed or reinterpreted.[2] As colorful markers of ideology and end goals, the variations between the RNA's account and Vaughn's rendition indicate the wider body of arguments that distinguished the Provisional Government–Republic of New Afrika (PG-RNA) from its Black Power–era counterparts.

The PG-RNA gained life during a moment of great social and political upheaval in the United States and across Africa and other formerly colonized locales. New Afrikans viewed theirs as just one of the many nations participating in the global effort to end worldwide white supremacy and win independence for colonized peoples. Global revolutionary fervor provided New Afrikans with an opportunity to educate African Americans about the PG-RNA's role in that collective uprising. The independence movements resonated with the founders of the Provisional Government who, following African, Asian, and North American black revolutionary traditions, produced similar ideas in their foundational texts. One finds the RNA's central tenets articulated in its 1968 Declaration of Independence, the Code of Umoja, the New Afrikan Creed and Oath, and the *New African Ujamaa*, the texts at the foundation of New Afrikan Political Science (NAPS). Largely written and published within the first five years of the Provisional Government's founding, each document provides a glimpse into the ideas that have guided many New Afrikans' daily decisions.

The early articulations and documentation of NAPS reveal the basis upon which New Afrikans developed their lifestyle politics. Anticolonial revolutions generally and, more specifically, African and African-descended people's struggles in North America provided inspiration to PG-RNA founders, and through it all, the concept of citizenship looms large. The project of RNA sovereignty, independence, and reparations rests on the premise that African people in the United States have never been legitimate citizens. Instead, the Fourteenth Amendment made them "paper-citizens," people who were deprived of the chance to decide where to place their political consent. The goal of independence compelled some of the first conscious New Afrikans, or those who were aware of their belonging to the New Afrikan nation, to frame their formation as a "provisional government." Others, such as the Afrikan People's Party (APP), continued to organize through a variety of revolutionary nationalist formations. In addition, their perception of African-descended peoples as paper-citizens in relation to the United States also compelled them to forge alliances with other peoples whom they considered colonized, including Native Americans and Puerto Ricans. Such ideas and goals, even when not fully achieved, have guided New Afrikans through life.

The RNA's Foundational Documents

NAPS is the foundation of principles that guides citizens' thinking.[3] RNA founding documents impart a basic understanding of New Afrikan concepts by defining the republic, indicating who may be considered a New Afrikan, and mapping out the Provisional Government's goals and strategies. NAPS can be distilled into the following principles:

1. Black people in the United States make up a "captive" African nation. Black people had citizenship imposed on them when it

should have been offered with the passage of the Fourteenth Amendment to the U.S. Constitution.

2. According to international law, New Afrikans have the right to determine for themselves whether they want to remain citizens of the United States or take their consent of citizenship elsewhere. No matter what they choose, they are due monetary reparations that will help them make the best of their situation.

3. The RNA cannot become truly independent and fully self-determined if the United States remains intact as a capitalistic and imperialist force.

4. New Afrikans are consciously fighting a war against U.S. imperialism and for their (and all oppressed nations') self-determination.

5. A prerequisite for winning the war for independence and self-determination is the personal transformation of black people into conscious New Afrikans.

The founding documents of the RNA are the cornerstone of NAPS and, therefore, the basis of New Afrikans' lifestyle politics. The documents disclose the extent to which New Afrikan founders were inspired by and built on a tradition of activism that preceded and overlapped the New Afrikan Independence Movement (NAIM).

Declaration of Independence

The RNA's Declaration of Independence embodies the essence of what the Black Government Convention sought to achieve in bringing together various black nation enthusiasts in 1968. The declaration constitutes one of the most important outcomes of that meeting and illustrates the moment in which the NAIM took definitive shape. Also, the declaration represents the fundamental viewpoints that eventually framed other key documents. The document sums up the predicament of African people in the United States and proffers an approach to resolving it. Writers framed the plight as an enduring *Maafa* that effectively "warped the bodies and minds" of African people in the United States. As the great suffering or calamity visited upon Africans in the Western Hemisphere, the *Maafa* dimmed their "raging desire" to live independently of the normalized assaults of oppression. When at least one hundred Black Government Convention attendees signed the RNA's Declaration of Independence, they proclaimed New Afrikan people "forever free and independent of the jurisdiction of the United

States of America and the obligations which that country's unilateral decision to make our ancestors and ourselves paper-citizens placed on us."[4] In announcing the desire for New Afrikan autonomy, the signers simultaneously reaffirmed the long-standing pursuit of self-determination expressed in African American political thought and action, and they forged a path for the NAIM to follow.

The RNA's Declaration of Independence consists of three other parts. One part asserts New Afrikans' right to self-determination and emphasizes that they desire nothing from the United States except the basic human rights that they believed were guaranteed to all people. More specifically, the authors demanded their own freedom to become independent of the United States and that black people in the United States receive reparations for the damage done to them and their ancestors. Addressing the probability that their oppressors would refuse to provide the requested restitution, the authors also positioned New Afrikans as revolutionaries prepared to back their demand with struggle against the injustices done to all oppressed peoples of the world.[5]

The second part of the document specifies particular goals and objectives, or "aims of [the New Afrikan] revolution." The fourteen aims form roughly three overlapping categories: individual rights and responsibilities; procedures for developing the black nation; and statements of commitment to overturn global oppression. Individual responsibilities include being "industrious" and producing scholarship in service to the RNA and the revolution. One goal indicates that such work would be rewarded. Some goals concern both building up the Republic and living cooperatively as a consequence of creating "the New Society" in which New Afrikans would reside for the benefit of their nation. Other aspirations for the New Afrikan nation include attaining religious and spiritual freedom, "assur[ing] equality of rights for the sexes," and calling for the end to racial discrimination. Also, the declaration seeks to place the means of production under the control of the New Afrikan government, thereby assuring that all citizens benefit from industry. The document's authors deem all of the aforementioned elements important for the envisioned New Society because they insist "self-respect and mutual respect among all people in the Society" cannot exist if the said nation's citizens harm each other in the very ways founders hoped to destroy.[6]

The third part closes the declaration by charging New Afrikans with devoting all of their physical, economic, and intellectual resources to bringing about a successful revolution and winning independence. The authors believed that only with independence could they create their New Society.

Building upon the aspirations set by their predecessors in various abolitionist, emigrationist, and communist formations, the authors believed the New Society would be "better than what we now know and as perfect as man can make it."[7] It is probable that the declaration's authors employed vague wording in order to leave room for future New Afrikans to conceive of their own interpretations. That way, activists could be flexible and dynamic as they struggled for New Afrikan independence and Third World liberation. For example, in 1968 a strong black feminist and queer movement had yet to develop. But beginning in the 1970s with the Combahee River Collective and other black feminist and woman of color organizations, a critique of heterosexism gained momentum.[8] Thus, the RNA declaration's lack of any steadfast description of the New Society theoretically made room for New Afrikans to embrace changes necessitated by such analyses. Also, like many other Black Power–era revolutionaries, New Afrikan theorists understood that their ability to gain independence from the United States was both reliant on and instrumental to the success of various Third World revolutionaries.[9]

In many ways, the RNA's Declaration of Independence existed within the trajectory of a black revolutionary tradition that sought to define African people's problems and have them decide on appropriate solutions for themselves. For example, one can see parallels between the RNA founders' intentions and the aims of those who overthrew the French government in order to create the Republic of Haiti. The new country's 1804 Declaration of Independence listed Haitians' grievances and committed those who signed on (both literally and ideologically) with the task of creating a better world. It stated: "It is not enough to have expelled the barbarians who have bloodied our land for two centuries; it is not enough to have restrained those ever-evolving factions that one after another mocked the specter of liberty that France dangled before you. We must, with one last act of national authority, forever assure the empire of liberty in the country of our birth; we must take any hope of re-enslaving us away from the inhuman government that for so long kept us in the most humiliating torpor. In the end we must live independent or die."[10] Because of their successful revolution against enslavement, Haitians became an inspiration to their contemporaries as well as future generations of freedom fighters, including some African Americans active in political organizing during the Black Power era.

The RNA declaration echoes such sentiments as it ends with an agreement that the signers would "pledge without reservation, ourselves, our talents, and all our worldly goods" to bring about a successful revolution.

RNA counterparts such as the League of Revolutionary Black Workers and the Black Panther Party expressed similar ideas. The League, for example, sought to wage "relentless struggle against racism, capitalism, and imperialism." In so doing, it strove to help create a free world for all oppressed peoples.[11] The RNA's pledge also parallels Huey P. Newton's concept of "revolutionary suicide," which he summed up in a poem that reads, "By surrendering my life to the revolution / I found eternal life."[12] Many New Afrikan revolutionaries began to interpret their lives according to these aims in their fight for sovereignty.

The New Afrikan Creed

Another important document in the canon of NAPS is the New Afrikan Creed, which reiterates the declaration's aims and builds on the pledge presented at the declaration's conclusion. In fact, the document is a set of guidelines for putting the principles of the declaration into daily practice. Written and approved shortly after the RNA's founders declared black people's right to seek independence from the United States, the New Afrikan Creed contains fifteen personal commitments to which New Afrikans agree when they became conscious citizens. Written as I-statements, they emphasize individual and collective spirituality, moral aptitude, revolutionary discipline, and the pursuit of global liberation. For example, point number ten states: "I will give my life, if that is necessary. I will give my time, my mind, my strength and my wealth because this IS necessary."[13] As such, this and other statements form the foundation for New Afrikans' collective identity and lifestyle politics.

The creed closes with a pledge that coherently summarizes its fifteen points of commitment. Like the declaration's closing pledge, it communicates an ideal matching the models put forth by New Afrikans' revolutionary forebears and many of their contemporaries. It posits a hopeful vision of a world free from oppression. In the original version, New Afrikans declare: "Now, freely and on my own will, i pledge this creed, for the sake of freedom for my people and a better world, on pain and disgrace and banishment if i prove false. For, i am no longer deaf, dumb or blind. I am—by the grace of Malcolm—a New Afrikan." The creed's authors borrowed the phrase "deaf, dumb or blind" from Elijah Muhammad, who used it to describe "so-called Negroes" who accepted European cultural, spiritual, and political domination.[14] By reciting "i am no longer deaf, dumb or blind," the speaker or reader reiterated a New Afrikan identity that is directly opposed to European hegemony, ignorance of black people's African heritage, and reluctance to struggle for self-determination. Rejecting the political impediments that the phrase signals also speaks to what it meant to actively construct New Afrikan political identity. In speaking these words, each person indicates a willingness to overcome the obstacles that maintain, and even facilitate, oppression. Therefore, one agrees to develop a political consciousness in service to the project of nation building.

Malcolm X's figurative prominence at the pledge's closing is apropos considering his influence in the lives of the Obadele brothers and many other Black Power activists. When the RNA developed the creed, Malcolm X's spirit endured as one of the preeminent forces behind various ideological trends of the period.[15] However, his distinction in the creed became subtler when on May 5, 1993, the RNA revised the pledge to state: "I am, by inspiration of the ancestors and grace of the Creator, a New Afrikan."[16] It is likely that with the aging and passing of several important activists whose work preceded and inspired the creation of the RNA, the PG-RNA sought to show gratitude to more than just this one ideological parent. That is not to suggest, however, that the importance of Malcolm X diminished. Since the 1970s, some New Afrikans have gone so far as to base their calendar around the physical departure of their patron saint, dating moments following his assassination as "adm," or after the death of Malcolm.[17]

Finally, the New Afrikan Creed, as a statement of principles, helped give more specific shape to the foundation of what later cohered as New Afrikan Political Science. The practice of reciting the full list of I-statements at gatherings helped solidify a collective New Afrikan identity based on struggle. New Afrikans' abilities to uphold the I-statements in various aspects of their lives became the essence of lifestyle politics because the statements guided how they interpreted their everyday actions and life choices. Coupled with the RNA's Declaration of Independence, the New Afrikan Creed imparts a basic understanding of how New Afrikans have constructed their identity and potentially structured their lives.

The New Afrikan Oath and "Black Power" Revisited

New Afrikan theorists distilled the New Afrikan Creed into a concise New Afrikan Oath. Through the oath, New Afrikans promise to devote their lives to New Afrikan independence.

For the fruition of Black Power,
For the triumph of Black nationhood,
I pledge to the Republic of New Africa
and to the building of a better people
and a better world, my total devotion,
my total resources and the total power
of my mortal life.[18]

Because the oath begins with a vow to bring Black Power to fruition through "the triumph of Black nationhood," it forces us to carefully reconsider some of the prevailing assumptions about the concept of "Black Power." Here, we can assess where and how ideas overlapped and departed.

According to a flyer produced by New Afrikans in New York City, "Black [P]ower means more than wearing Afros, dashikis, taking or teaching a course in Afro-American history, using traditional names and calling each other brother and sister." Instead, "Black [P]ower means having your own nation. But in order to build a nation [black people] must begin by controlling the institutions in [their] communities." The author of the flyer's text emphasizes controlling schools and supporting "real black political candidates, black community organizations such as the Welfare Rights Groups, and all Black revolutionary organizations."[19] Such goals were congruent with the more prevalent emphases of many Black Power–era organizations and initiatives. Yet, in articulating the end goal as the creation of a black nation-state, activists transformed seemingly reformist practices into revolutionary tactics for New Afrikan independence.

Though never given one single definition, Black Power always called for African Americans to exercise self-determination through their ability to make choices that reflected their best interests. Whether they endorsed changing one's name and donning an afro, fighting for the right to live in decent housing, or selecting people who would best represent black people's interests in institutional politics, activists discussed their goals and decisions in terms of "doing for self" or "controlling our own destiny." Because New Afrikans defined Black Power as the complete liberation of their people through attaining an independent nation-state and securing reparations, they complicated commonly understood articulations of the slogan and concept.[20]

Some New Afrikans held membership with the Black Panther Party, the single most studied Black Power–era organization. New Afrikans in the BPP tended to accentuate point number ten in the party's Ten Point Program, which originally stated that a "major political objective" of the party was to get "a United Nations—supervised plebiscite to be held throughout the black colony in which only black colonial subjects will be allowed to participate, for the purpose of determining the will of black people as to their national destiny."[21] When pressed about this matter, however, Huey Newton wrote to Robert Williams indicating that the BPP could not support the independence movement. His reasoning was that it would not be in black people's best interest to seek independence while the United States, "a capitalistic imperialist country," remained intact. He argued that by seceding, black Americans risked facing a colonial situation worse than those experienced by various African and Asian countries that had recently gained their political independence. Newton stated,

> In other words we're not really handling this question at this time because we feel that for us that it is somewhat premature, that I realize the physiological value of fighting for territory. But at this time the Black Panther Party feels that we don't have to be in an enclave type situation where we would be more isolated than we already are now. . . . And again I think that it would be perfectly justified if the Blacks decided that they wanted to secede the union [*sic*], but I think the question should be left up to the popular masses, the popular majority. So this is it in a nutshell.[22]

It was not unlikely that independence could leave the RNA as an isolated political entity within an ocean of hostility. Considering the examples of Texas, postrevolutionary Haiti and Cuba, and numerous other examples, independence without significant political power, or formidable allies in lieu of power, a liberated RNA might have caved or experienced extreme isolation. Although PG-RNA leadership hoped to develop strategic alliances, none had developed by the time Newton penned his letter to Williams. Newton's position represented a practical analysis of the geopolitical context.[23]

In 1970, after significant changes to his analysis of local and geopolitical conditions, Newton restated his position on the Provisional Government. Instead of considering it premature, he put forth that any land under PG control was "the people's liberated territory" that "represent[ed] a community liberated." However, for Newton, having liberated territory was not in itself a sufficient goal in a broader struggle for revolutionary intercommunalism. He insisted, "It is only ground for preparation for the liberation of the world, seizing of the wealth from the ruling circle and equal distribution and proportional representation in the intercommunal framework."[24]

Although Newton signaled some ideological support for the RNA, he maintained his disagreements with New Afrikan independence because of ideological differences between the PG and BPP. By arguing for intercommunalism, he also critiqued the major goal of New Afrikan independence activism, statehood.

According to Assata Shakur, many Panthers either did not understand or disagreed with Newton's arguments for intercommunalism. Perhaps this lack of comprehension and/or difference of opinion helps explain why some Panthers and Black Liberation Army cadres continued to promote point number ten of the BPP's program and platform. New York Panthers Safiya Bukhari and Bilal Sunni Ali pledged their allegiance to the Provisional Government as they carried out their duties for the party. As former Panthers, Shakur and her comrade Sundiata Acoli also swore loyalty to the PG-RNA toward the end of the 1970s.[25]

The Congress of African Peoples (CAP) also exhibited fidelity to New Afrikan independence in 1970. In a five-point resolution, it decided the following: First, CAP recognized that black people in the United States had a right to territory in the Black Belt. They had the right to "support the efforts of the Republic of New Africa to establish on this landmass an independent, progressive, technically and spiritually excellent nation for those black people who want it." Second, CAP recognized "the right of the Republic of New Africa [to] organize a peaceful plebiscite among the people living in the national territory and to secede the territory and the people peacefully from the United States should the plebiscite so decide, and the Congress explicitly opposes and condemns any efforts of the United States or its political sub-divisions to interfere with the peaceful organization of such a plebiscite or the peaceful execution of its results." Third, CAP urged "the Nixon Administration and a joint Committee of the U.S. Congress to meet individually or jointly with Representatives of the Republic to discuss terms of a peaceful settlement of the land secession question, and with representatives of the Republic and of the Congress of African Peoples to arrive at the details of a reparations settlement." Fourth, CAP emphasized the need to provide African Americans with reparations and resettle those who desired independence. Fifth and finally, CAP advised black troops fighting for the United States against Vietnam to enter a cease-fire agreement with the Democratic Republic of Vietnam.[26] Again, as an articulation of Black Power, land and independence qualitatively distinguished the New Afrikan project from many others of that era.

The oath, therefore, provided another opportunity for New Afrikans to align their individual lifestyles to the collective pursuit of territorial nationalism while using the rhetoric and symbols of Black Power. Theoretically aligning themselves with the Southern African concept of *ubuntu*, which bonds the individual to the larger collective, they considered each New Afrikan an important part of the Black Nation.[27] The fine line New Afrikans drew between the individual and the group served as the basis for the development of their lifestyle politics. This line also shaped theorizations about how the New Afrikan economy could function.

The New African Ujamaa: The Economics of the Republic of New Africa (1970)

The RNA Declaration of Independence, New Afrikan Creed, and New Afrikan Oath all sketch the broad ideological outline of NAPS, providing a basis from which New Afrikans could begin thinking about liberation. The booklet titled *The New African Ujamaa* irradiates some essential components of New Afrikan independence, specifically in the realm of economics. In concurrence with the aims written in the RNA Declaration of Independence, the document communicates New Afrikans' conviction that an economy based on the principle of *ujamaa* would best serve them in a global society. Onetime minister of culture Maulana Karenga's definition of *ujamaa* roughly translates it as "cooperative economics." However, the Kiswahili word literally means "family-hood."[28]

The *New African Ujamaa* outlines a plan that, if implemented, could be the economic foundation for a society that nurtures in its citizens the characteristics and personality traits explicated in the creed and oath. In fact, the *New African Ujamaa* expressly committed RNA citizens to the creation of the "New Community" that they envisioned in many ways as the antithesis of U.S. society. Seeking a productive and cooperative—as opposed to strictly consumerist and individualistic—way of life, the New Community would serve the basic needs of the New Afrikan people. In turn, once freed from poverty and oppression, New Afrikans would dedicate their work and leisure time to building and maintaining their nation. Or as written in the document, "those whom [RNA citizens] bring into the New Community will be New Africans: Black people already trained to live with one another as brothers and sisters and willing [to put] and capable of putting the New African Creed into practice."[29] New Afrikans' capabilities to live cooperatively in line with the creed "as brothers and sisters" would prove pivotal in making this economic philosophy and system successful.

The *New African Ujamaa* has eight sections, the first of which is a preamble that defines nation building and black liberation as sacred duties.[30] "Our supreme purpose in life—our reason for being," the author writes, "must remain a companion-guide, eternally with us, full bodied, and well formed." The author implores citizens to be mindful of "the world revolution until all people everywhere are so free," as she or he deems the end of worldwide oppression as part and parcel to black liberation from U.S. domination. Further, she or he posits the "supreme purpose of the nation" as akin to economic production, which under the proper system was supposed to ensure that each citizen's basic needs were taken care of. The author outlines such necessities in the preamble as the six basic principles of ujamaa: food, housing, clothing, health services, education, and the element of defense.[31]

The remaining sections of the *New African Ujamaa* explain the nuts and bolts of providing for citizens' basic needs and managing manufacturing, industry, trade, recreation, cultural production, and New Afrikans' personal incomes. One part states, "The principle involved is simple. All the wealth—the Gross National product (the GNP)—created by the work of the Nation shall belong to the people as a whole, to the Nation. . . . Every 'dollar' of the GNP would thus be divided in accordance with a calculated decision of the Government, designed to efficiently achieve national goals."[32] As described by the *New African Ujamaa*, the national economy would secure the nation's needs and protect each New Afrikan. After the fulfillment of those essentials, any possible surplus would be distributed as personal income for spending and saving. In this way, the architects of the plan hoped to furnish a better standard of living for the New Afrikan people than they believed most experienced in the United States. The RNA system of cooperative economics would also support many of the goals found in the previously mentioned foundational documents, including eliminating class disparity.

As students of the emerging modern nations, New Afrikans based much of their *New African Ujamaa* on the example set by Julius K. Nyerere and his political party, the Tanzania African National Union (TANU).[33] With a strong sense of Pan-Africanism and Third World solidarity during the mid- to late 1960s, some activists regarded Tanzania as an influential model for revolutionary achievement.[34] Black nationalists, students, and Black Peace Corps participants of all stripes from the United States began flocking to the unified republic, partially in response to President Nyerere's call to African Americans for assistance in TANU's nation-building project.[35] Furthermore, black activists such as Pete and Charlotte O'Neal found political asylum there in the early 1970s after fleeing the United States. Nyerere and Tanzania tremendously influenced the U.S. Black Power movement and the enterprises of African-descended revolutionaries across the globe. New Afrikan independence activists were just a few of the many individuals and organizations galvanized by President Nyerere's authority and significance.[36]

New Afrikans at times borrowed Nyerere's ideas. For example, Nyerere regarded the accumulation of personal wealth as a symptom of a troubled society. He claimed, "Apart from the anti-social effects of the accumulation of personal wealth, the very desire to accumulate it must be interpreted as a vote of 'no confidence' in the social system." On that premise, he forcefully argued that a healthy society was responsible for each individual and that no one should ever "worry about what will happen to him tomorrow if he does not hoard wealth today. Society itself should look after him, or his widow, or his orphans. This is exactly what traditional African society succeeded in doing. . . . That is socialism."[37] From the president's vantage point, each individual stood equally responsible for the well-being of the broader society. Again, Nyerere aptly summarizes the citizen's responsibility when he writes: "In traditional African society everybody was a worker. . . . But it is too often forgotten, nowadays, that the basis of this great socialistic achievement was this: that it was taken for granted that every member of society—barring only the children and the infirm—contributed his fair share of efforts towards the production of its wealth."[38] Following Nyerere, the *New African Ujamaa* predicates the RNA's success on similar ideals. New Afrikans' work, whether in civil engineering, in teaching, or as ministers in the Provisional Government, would go toward the betterment of the New Society they were trying to build. The reward for contributing one's time, skills, and labor-property to the RNA would include luxuries such as leisure time to nurture one's intellectual, artistic, and spiritual desires, as well as the accommodations to vacation at waterfront resorts financed by the Provisional Government with the surplus created by the hard work of its people.[39]

History shows that Tanzania, for various reasons, did not achieve the economic and political goals that Nyerere and TANU sought during the 1960s and 1970s. One explanation provided by Nyerere maintains, "Our ambitions do outrun our competence at times. . . . But we are aware of our goals, and we are conscious of the socialist philosophy which we have chosen as the path to them."[40] According to A. R. Mohamed Babu, TANU's failure resulted from its inability to learn from former colonies in Asia that, in previous decades, attempted to develop their own brands of socialism in an overwhelmingly capitalist world. In addition, Tanzania's socialist philosophy earned serious opposition from the United States and other nation-states hostile to the African country's policy of "non-alignment."[41]

Though the Republic of New Afrika has yet to gain political independence, New Afrikans have based the projected success of their economy on their ability to gain income from reparations, a national bank funded by Malcolm X Land Certificates, self-generating wealth, taxes paid by citizens, and donations.[42] Such logic assumed two things: first, that the United States will eventually pay reparations to the African people whose ancestors European Americans enslaved; and second, that black people, even conscious New Afrikans, were able to and would willingly purchase land certificates, pay taxes, make monetary donations, and contribute their labor to building a physical New Afrikan infrastructure. Although the *New African Ujamaa* expresses skepticism regarding the United States' willingness to pay what the New Afrikans demanded, the document conveys more confidence in the possibility that African Americans, once educated, would vindicate the second assumption.[43] Ultimately, however, the RNA's ambitions have seemed to outrun what has been realistically achievable. The duality of being consciously New Afrikan and paper-citizens of the United States compromised RNA citizens' ability to live their ideology.

The RNA Constitution and the
Organizational Structure of the PG-RNA

The Code of Umoja (the RNA constitution) was first approved in March 1970. Its ratification occurred during the convention at which Brother Imari won the presidency through what he argued was a popular election, though several prominent New Afrikans, including Brother Gaidi, Queen Mother Moore, and Betty Shabazz, boycotted both the convention and the vote. The Code of Umoja explains in detail the RNA's various government offices and describes the duties specific to each position. It also delineates the Provisional Government's plans for funding its operations, running the economy, and recruiting and retaining New Afrikan citizens as active workers. The publication of this early document marked an important step in the RNA's efforts to codify its various ideas presented in previous publications, including Brother Imari's *War in America: The Malcolm X Doctrine*. It also further demonstrates how the PG-RNA's goals and strategies departed from those of its Black Power contemporaries and offered ideas upon which adherents could build their lives and develop their lifestyles.

Founders set up the PG-RNA as a governmental body rather than as a social movement organization. A published booklet titled *Government Administration* that likely predated the Code of Umoja explains various government positions and their functions, the chain of command, the duties of RNA citizens, how to pay taxes, and many other legal and functional dictates that govern the nation.[44] The founders consciously framed the Black Government Convention as an opportunity for black people in the United States to formally declare independence and set up a nation-state separate from what they viewed as an oppressive colonizer. Because they wanted to create an entity that adhered to post–World War II understandings of a "state," they created space for a president, vice presidents, ministers, consuls, judges, and other officials. Unlike other Black Power–era formations, the PG-RNA did not intend to create these positions in name only. Instead, the PG-RNA fully expected to operate as a government with sovereignty eventually recognized by the United Nations and the United States.[45] When, in May 1968, Brother Imari delivered the PG's letter to Secretary of State Dean Rusk seeking negotiations, he did so both to demonstrate to black people that the PG-RNA was not a group of "armchair" revolutionaries and to begin the process of gaining sovereignty in compliance with international law.

Thus, the PG-RNA originally organized itself as follows: a president, first and second vice presidents, and several ministers and deputy ministers. An all-star cast of black nationalists filled the original Provisional Government's ranks, including Robert F. Williams, Betty Shabazz, Jamil Al-Amin (then H. Rap Brown), Maulana Karenga, Amiri Baraka, Akbar Muhammad Ahmad/Maxwell Stanford Jr., and Queen Mother Audley Moore. It seemed as if some RNA leaders, including Baraka, Brown, and Williams, only lent their names to the government and did not actually perform the duties of their positions to any significant degree. Others, including Queen Mother Moore, became lifelong ministers and consultants.[46]

Even though New Afrikans organized a government structure, some activists argue that the RNA initially functioned much like other Black Power organizations insofar as it conducted political education classes and promoted community-organizing rhetoric.[47] However, the RNA founders' initial and enduring intention to constitute and maintain an independent government distinguishes New Afrikan activism from that of their contemporaries. Not only did this aspiration set them apart from most other Black Power formations; it also developed among New Afrikan ranks a nuanced understanding of black people's relationship to the United States. Their advocacy of political independence and territorial autonomy as the only solutions to black Americans' problems attests to New Afrikans' profound departure from the objectives endorsed by the more popular Black Power organizations. Yet, although RNA's founders stated and agreed upon their desires for independence, disagreements over the path to that end goal caused internal dissention that led to notable changes in the government structure.

The first change occurred in 1969 following the New Bethel Incident. During that year, acting president Brother Gaidi reorganized the Provisional Government so that there were four regional vice presidents as opposed to first and second vice presidents. Within one year, as a result of the constitutional crisis and Brother Imari's usurpation of power, more changes took place. The Black Legion officially became the New Afrikan Security Forces, a change that seemed more nominal than substantial. However, over the next decade the PG-RNA grew and evolved to fit its changing program initiatives as well as the changing circumstances in which it found itself operating. Most important among those alterations were several revisions of the Code of Umoja, the creations of the People's Center Council (PCC) and the People's Revolutionary Leadership Council (PRLC), and the expansion of ministries such as those concerned with judicial and international affairs. Regarding these developments, it is important to mention that the PCC functioned as the top decision-making body in the RNA, followed by the president. Moreover, local PRLCs began replacing the consulates established in the late 1960s and early 1970s.[48]

The RNA's evolution through conflict, repression, and growth contributed to its desire to take steps toward being recognized by the United Nations. Political scientist James C. Roberts writes that in order for any "political community to be sovereign," it must adhere in some degree to the following principles: it must have territory and a population; it must demonstrate "effective rule over that territory and population"; and it must garner the "recognition of other nation-states."[49] Well versed in international law and trying to gain the recognition New Afrikans argued was due to the captive black nation, the New Afrikans began trying to live up to these criteria with their creation of the PG in 1968.

The codification of New Afrikan law was necessary for the creation of a national political structure and culture by which New Afrikan citizens began to develop a unique lifestyle. The intellectual paradigm expressed therein guided, and continues to shape, New Afrikans' understandings of their role in the pursuit of black liberation in the United States and global revolution. That paradigm defies the typical categories within which scholars tend to place black liberation groups and individuals and thus complicates prevailing understandings of black nationalism, black revolutionary activism, and Black Power in the United States. Further, a fuller comprehension of New Afrikans' ideological base reveals how difficult it has been for people to match their actual practice with their ideals, especially when those ideals run counter to the structure of the larger society of which they are a part. The concept of citizenship encompasses one important site for investigating Black Power activists' attempts to match their practice with their ideology. Citizenship, or the exclusive and contentious nature of it, formed the basis of the NAIM's founding. The founder's perception of it guided the republic's conceptualization of the New Afrikan and New Afrikans' attempts to develop solidarity with other oppressed nations.

RNA Citizenship

Considering themselves "an African Nation in the Western Hemisphere Struggling for Complete Independence," New Afrikans challenged the legitimacy of black people's forced incorporation into the United States.[50] The objection formed the basis of the PG-RNA's program for liberation and animated the decision to frame their actions using rhetoric befitting a government rather than an activist organization or a political party. Developments in international law also helped guide their course of action. In demanding liberation as a self-proclaimed government, the PG-RNA expected the United Nations to provide its people with certain protections guaranteed in documents like the UN Charter and UN Universal Declaration of Human Rights. Yet creating a provisional government and demanding that African Americans had the right to choose whether to remain as U.S. citizens did not immunize the nation builders from many troubles. New Afrikans had to negotiate being RNA citizens while inhabiting and being legally bound by the United States of America. Although there were some limitations imposed on them, choosing to become a citizen of the Republic of New Afrika also empowered activists to rethink their relationship with the United States and with other oppressed peoples around the world.

New Afrikans predicated their contest to liberate a land base in the South on the idea that African-descended people in the United States were, historically, not willing U.S. citizens. Their reading of economist Robert S. Browne's work led them to insist that the legacy of white supremacy troubled black people's citizenship in the United States. First, enslaved Africans were prisoners of warfare that resulted in their forced and brutal transport to the Western Hemisphere, where they and their descendants labored as chattel with no rights to the protections and privileges that accompanied political belonging.[51] Second, the ratification of the Fourteenth Amendment folded emancipated Africans into the U.S. body politic without their consent. In the PG-RNA's own words, "We are all born citizens of the Black Nation. This is the only legal citizenship We have. We are not legally citizens of the United States, because We were never given the chance to vote yes or no on American citizenship when it was *offered* to us after We became free."[52] Third, even with U.S. membership "offered" to them, African Americans never have enjoyed the full benefits of their association with the U.S. nation-state. Instead, violence and terrorism have characterized their experiences, and the United States has refused to adequately protect them or at least fully extend the means of legal redress that is supposedly guaranteed to U.S. citizens.[53] Although independence activists attempted to resolve the problems African Americans continued to experience after the destruction of some legal barriers to "first-class citizenship," the New Afrikan approach to those dilemmas contained its own set of limitations. In the production of a self-determined citizenship, New Afrikans could not completely ignore the benefits, responsibilities, and laws of U.S. society. As "captives" of and within the United States, they operated with a Du Boisian–like duality of being consciously New Afrikan, while simultaneously de facto, if not legal, U.S. citizens.[54]

New Afrikans were not the first group of people to struggle over the theory and praxis of citizenship. National belonging has long been a contested concept in the United States, especially for Africans and their descendants. When European settlers first arrived and began waging war against and displacing indigenous inhabitants, they brought with them the notion that people whose status was less than royalty were subject to the will of those in power. By the time they rebelled against England, the founders of the incipient American nation-state had significantly rethought previous notions of citizenship and subjectivity. The French Revolution helped them develop their thinking in this regard by substantiating among Anglo-Americans the notion of republican citizenship, a form of national membership based on responsible participation in the daily functioning of the state by every eligible person. It is important to note that prevailing ideas about who belonged in the pool of "eligible" persons was flexible and applied unevenly so that it served the best interests of individual new states, the federal body, and the propertied white men who occupied most, if not all, of the new positions of power.[55]

Because of this malleable and selective bestowal of U.S. citizenship, several collectivities posed immediate threats to these white men's exclusive conceptualization of national belonging. First, though they expected white women to help build their nation, they claimed that white women were entitled to limited citizenship that would become available gradually. Next, Anglo male citizens mainly considered Native Americans a natural part of the "frontier" environment and, therefore, beyond consideration for both citizenship and humane treatment. Various political leaders challenged and complicated this simple conception, demanding that Native groups receive more nuanced attention. The third group of concern was enslaved Africans, whose very existence posed a serious contradiction to the foundation of the newly created American state. In relegating enslaved Africans to perpetual servitude and claiming human chattel as the legal property of their owners, white male citizens cast them as beyond consideration for citizenship in legislative and judicial discourses and practices.[56]

A fourth group, legally free black men, presented the most complications to the praxis of U.S. citizenship, especially since many of these men participated on equal footing with white men in the carnage that won independence for the thirteen colonies. Some legally free black men possessed the lawful ability to meet the requirements of citizenship during the postindependence and antebellum eras; they were biologically male, owned property, and practiced responsible public and private duties for the individual states. In northern courts, case after case affirmed nominally free black men's citizenship and legal rights, but those supposed entitlements often went unenforced. Southern courts continually ruled legally free black men as "subjects," "quasi citizens or at least denizens," "wards," and "third class." In both the North and the South, this class of black men occupied positions of legal ambiguity and social liminality.[57] As discussions of black men's status proliferated at all levels of the ever-evolving local, state, and national politics, the combination of the era's racial and gender conventions facilitated a near erasure of black women as subjects in (or perhaps objects of) social and legal debates respecting U.S. citizenship.[58]

The *Dred Scott* decision of 1857 seemed to clarify, once and for all, black people's political status when it determined that those of African ancestry were not protected by the U.S. Constitution and could not be full members of the nation. While they could be residents in and citizens of individual states which determined their status and well-being, as noncitizens of the Union, black people ultimately had no rights that white men were bound to respect. In the aftermath of *Dred Scott*, black folks who before were skeptical of emigration began packing their bags and looking for homes in Liberia, Canada, and elsewhere. Even Frederick Douglass for a short time gave "qualified support" to black people's emigration to Haiti.[59]

The Civil War and Reconstruction soon revitalized black men's pursuit of U.S. citizenship rights and spawned national debates concerning membership in the body politic. The question of citizenship seemed to be settled with some enslaved Africans' legal emancipation beginning in 1862 and the ratification of the Thirteenth, Fourteenth, and Fifteenth Amendments of the U.S. Constitution. The Thirteenth Amendment abolished involuntary servitude except as punishment for a crime; the Fourteenth Amendment provided provisions for people to become U.S. citizens, and it promised citizens equal protection under the law; and the Fifteenth Amendment protected male citizens' right to vote.[60] Yet African Americans still would not enjoy the rights and privileges accorded to citizens of the United States. Instead, they entered a nadir during which racial terrorism, Black Codes, and discriminatory laws violently infringed on the rights those aforementioned pieces of legislation supposedly guaranteed to citizens.[61]

The revocation of black constitutional rights following Reconstruction clarifies the meaning of "paper-citizens," as articulated by RNA theorists in the RNA's Declaration of Independence. The term recognizes how people of African descent have formed the "constitutive outside" of normalized American citizenship.[62] White citizens in all parts of the expanding U.S. territory associated African people with enslavement, moral decrepitude, and intellectual debility. Historian Gerald Horne demonstrates that they were, over time, constructed as criminals, traitors, and enemies, especially as the thirteen colonies emerged as a new nation-state. These ideas carried over into what legal scholar Guyora Binder terms "the slavery of emancipation." In Binder's analysis, the long-standing ideas about African peoples and their descendants were made anew following the Civil War and were written into the Thirteenth Amendment. When New Afrikans complicate the Fourteenth Amendment and its impact, they reveal this complex historical relationship. Therefore, the term "paper-citizen" enlarges the arbitrary nature of black belonging.[63] Being constructed as commodities for the American market disallowed newly made black Americans from taking advantage of an opportunity to decide on and stand firm in their self-determined status as citizens. Simultaneously, this historical positioning permitted white Americans to define African peoples in opposition to their own *true* citizen status. In doing so, white Americans policed the boundaries of citizen and subject/commodity with brutal violence, unmerciful economic reprisals, and innovations in psychological terror.[64]

Prompted by violent provocations, the unfulfilled promises of freedom, and the desire to self-govern, African Americans attempted to gain and exercise their rights through a variety of actions. One tendency pursued the creation of black states and homesteads in places such as Texas and Mound Bayou, Mississippi, and in Kansas, Oklahoma, and Illinois.[65] The tendency persisted and evolved during the twentieth century through the National Movement for the Establishment of a 49th State, a Chicago-based effort that advocated for a U.S. state to be set aside for African Americans. Oscar Brown Sr. and Bindley C. Cyrus claimed that doing so would provide their people with the only significant means for becoming industrious, self-reliant, and self-sustaining. History had proven to them that white Americans would prevent African Americans from achieving their full potential when they were forced to live together under white political leadership.[66] The Revolutionary Action Movement and African Nationalist Independence Movement (organized by Oba Oseijeman Adefunmi and Queen Mother Audley Moore) maintained the idea, even as the New Afrikan Independence Movement was beginning to cohere.[67] Alongside these endorsements of territorial nationalism, black activists' various efforts to win reparations and, after the founding of the United Nations, the movement to charge the U.S. government with the genocide of African people in North America all challenged the assumption that the arena of civil rights could yield equality to all human beings.[68]

Another black movement tradition that wrestled with the concept of citizenship, though from a different perspective, included various exertions aimed at obtaining and securing full civil rights for African Americans. The visionaries of and participants in such endeavors often framed the struggle in terms of gaining "first-class citizenship." That rhetoric assumed that one of the major problems African Americans faced was exclusion from access to the rights and privileges guaranteed by the U.S. Constitution. Civil rights activists achieved their legal goals by 1965 when the Civil Rights and Voting Rights Acts criminalized, to some degree, discrimination in public accommodations and preventing eligible adults from exercising the right to vote.[69]

Based on these and other historical lessons and examples of black political agency, the Obadele Brothers, Queen Mother Moore, and other RNA theorists argued that African Americans had needed to exercise the right to choose where they wanted to place their consent of citizenship. According to the RNA Declaration of Independence, they could be citizens of the Republic of New Afrika. By the time New Afrikans began advocating this position in the 1960s, they learned how to utilize international law and recent legal precedents within the United States to argue their case.[70] For example, they cited the UN Universal Declaration of Human Rights, Article 15, which states: "(1) Everyone has the right to a nationality" and "(2) No one shall be arbitrarily deprived of his nationality nor denied the right to change his [or her] nationality."[71] Black people in the United States were indeed deprived of their original means of self- and community identification; after several decades of enduring life in what became the United States of America, they had forged new identities.[72] For these reasons, the Provisional Government claimed African descendants in the United States have since constituted a colonized "nation within a nation," the Republic of New Afrika. The RNA could enact its right to independence under United Nations Resolution 1514 (XV), which guarantees a people's right to self-determination and protects them from unwarranted "armed action or repressive measures of all kinds . . . in order to enable them to exercise peacefully and freely their right to complete independence."[73] When Brother Imari moved the RNA headquarters to Mississippi, he believed that he was acting on this internationally guaranteed right in earnest.

As they made gestures toward political independence, New Afrikans were more consumed with building membership and bringing their "president in exile," Robert F. Williams, home. Those activities earned the RNA plenty of government surveillance and routine attempts to discredit them and prevent them from gaining a large following. New Afrikans' resulting difficulties demonstrate the realities of being paper-citizens. Brother Gaidi's dispute with a Michigan judge is exemplary. An article published in the *Detroit News* on May 1, 1969, underscored what its author perceived as a contradiction between the Michigan lawyer's rhetoric and his tendency to make "full use of the rights, privileges and immunities of the system he detests," including "the privilege of practicing law in a Michigan court" and "practicing the constitutional right of free speech by declaring, as he so often had before, that he is not a citizen of the United States." Considering Obadele inconsistent, District Judge James Smelt reasoned that since the New Afrikan "was not . . . a citizen—how could he hold membership in the State Bar of Michigan?" Smelt stopped the lawyer during his defense of a client "and barred him from practicing in [Smelt's] court." Obadele responded to the judge's condemnation by asking, "How could the judge say I am not a citizen when the law of the land says I am, despite what I might think?" Smelt admitted to the *Detroit News* that he knew Brother Gaidi would not be prevented from practicing law in Michigan. The judge just wanted to make the point that the New Afrikan lawyer's rhetoric was problematic because it seemed to run counter to his actual practice. Certainly, the judge also wanted to flex his muscles in that situation to let Brother Gaidi know who was boss.[74]

U.S. state and federal agents demonstrated their power with deadlier effects in response to RNA citizens' attempts to match their bold rhetoric of nation building with corresponding actions. Just one year after the Provisional Government's founding, the presence of the RNA army, the Black Legion, caused alarm among authorities and residents in Detroit, and resulted in the New Bethel Incident.[75] A similar violent reaction occurred when Imari Obadele moved the RNA headquarters south. With a presumed "propensity for violence"—a reputation associated with New Afrikans purportedly because of the New Bethel Incident—the tone of RNA work posed a novel kind of threat to the United States' local, state, and federal governments.[76] In Mississippi, only about thirty New Afrikans regularly worked with the Jackson headquarters, and Brother Imari tried to "'make it perfectly clear [to local officials] that [they were] coming in peace.'"[77] Yet, because New Afrikans attempted to match their practice with the language of "revolution and nation-building," they challenged U.S. governing bodies' ability to exercise sovereignty over the RNA. For that reason, local officials and the FBI continued their efforts to monitor and "disrupt" RNA activity. Those efforts culminated in the August 18, 1971, raids on the RNA headquarters and residence—incursions that challenged New Afrikans' ability to exercise self-determination and unbind themselves from the United States.[78]

New Afrikans' entanglement in the shootout brought them charges "ranging from murder and levy of war against the state of Mississippi to possession of stolen property." Juries found three RNA activists guilty of murder, and Brother Imari was "convicted of conspiracy to commit offenses of assault and of unlawfully possessing unregistered firearms."[79] Those convictions stand to this day. In a pretrial attempt to protect the "RNA-11," the eleven men and women who survived the two raids, defense lawyers unsuccessfully filed "an Article Three challenge to U.S. jurisdiction over Afrikan people in North America. This motion argued that the RNA . . . is a nation separate from, though held captive by, the United States of America."[80] Making a clear connection between the RNA and people such as Martin Delaney, the RNA-11 and their lawyers attempted to articulate before a hostile audience a theory that had long been marginalized by the U.S. government and African Americans who never fully subscribed to idea that they were members of a "captive" nation.

The raid on the RNA headquarters, the charges brought against the RNA-11, and the fact that the state government indicted and convicted New Afrikans as U.S. citizens all magnified a duality New Afrikans faced in their simultaneous positioning as RNA citizens and "captives" under U.S. sovereignty. For New Afrikans, these happenings also signaled the outright refusal of the U.S. government to consider the legality (or morality) of African American citizenship. Finally, the charges and convictions demonstrate a fundamental problem with New Afrikans' project to construct their own citizenship. As a selectively imposed though ardently defended concept, citizenship only mattered as much as the forces in power dictated. Therefore, conscious New Afrikans' "dual citizenship" demonstrates the unbalanced personal and group application of such ideals, as well as the uneven persecution they faced because of their reconceptualization of national belonging.

Such complications are visible when considering the New Afrikans who associated with the Black Liberation Army (BLA). The BLA was an underground amalgamation of several autonomous military cells, some of which pledged allegiance to the Republic of New Afrika. Some of them faced violent repression that exposed the limits of their expressed RNA citizenship in U.S. courts. New Afrikan citizen Safiya Asya Bukhari joined the BLA after local and federal authorities forced her underground because of her activities as a Black Panther in New York City. In 1975, police apprehended her and convicted her of felony murder following a shootout in Virginia that resulted in the death of her comrade Kombozi.[81] Bukhari and her codefendant Masai Ehehosi claimed that because they were New Afrikans, the Commonwealth of Virginia had no jurisdiction over them. Brother Imari agreed, stating, "Sister Safiya and Brother Masai have lawfully chosen their citizenship of birth, in the Republic of New Africa, as that to which they owe their exclusive allegiance." That choice, the RNA leader argued, should be protected by the Emancipation Proclamation, the Thirteenth Amendment, and Article Fifteen of the UN Universal Declaration of Human Rights, "to which the United States is signatory." Therefore, Brother Imari insisted, the defendants could legally demand their release because they were prisoners of war and not common criminals. But, like the RNA-11, Sister Safiya and Brother Masai "were charged under civilian criminal statutes of the Commonwealth of Virginia and—despite their refusal to participate— were tried" and sentenced to forty years in prison each.[82]

Brother Gaidi's dispute with Judge Smelt and the trials of the RNA-11, Bukhari, and Masai are only a few examples of the formidable conflicts occasioned by New Afrikans' status as theoretical RNA citizens but physical inhabitants of the United States and legal subjects of the U.S. government's authority. Even though New Afrikans attempted to create an independent nation based on their reading of history and legal theory, as a captive nation, they were unable to exercise their beliefs as fully as they desired. This inability stems from the United States' and other nations' failure—if not outright refusal—to back the Republic of New Afrika and recognize it as a legitimate nation. Such refusal has affected the ways that activists have been able implement New Afrikan Political Science in their personal lives.

The Praxis of Being New Afrikan in the United States

Since its inception, the provisional New Afrikan government has struggled to protect New Afrikans' rights to choose their citizenship. Even as Brother Imari, Safiya Bukhari, and many others attempted to give legitimacy to their self-determined formulation of citizenship, New Afrikans' overall practice mirrored what Brother Imari prescribed in his solicitation of support for the "People's Revolt against Poverty." He instructed that "black people live in two worlds politically. You must vote in the United States elections, and We must support our black mayors and Congresspersons and other officials in the U.S. system. This is a matter of self-defense. But We must vote for and support the officials of our black nation, the Republic of New Afrika, also. Both things are necessary at the present time."[83] Nevertheless, the PG-RNA took steps soon after its founding to demonstrate to the world that the Republic of New Afrika was worthy of sovereignty and independence. One step involved the creation of the Black/New Afrikan Legion (or the New Afrikan Security Forces). Most, if not all, conscious citizens were required to serve in the army at some point.

Beginning with the Black Government Convention, PG-RNA founders took seriously the necessity of a strong military for the nation-building process. In fact, several paramilitary organizations represented a large number of participants in the convention for and signatories to the RNA Declaration of Independence.[84] The PG-RNA also later developed rules stating that no conscious citizen should ever serve in the United States Armed Forces. However, previous service did not cause suspicion. Brother Gaidi served as a fighter pilot in World War II, the U.S. Army hired Brother Imari as a contracted employee until 1968, and U.S. armed forces veterans filled the RNA's ranks.[85] Point number ten of the New Afrikan Creed illustrates the RNA's insistence on fostering among its citizens a willingness to sacrifice. In reciting it, New Afrikans claim, "I will give my life, if that is necessary. I will give my time, my mind, my strength and my wealth because this IS necessary." New Afrikans expected their comrades to give these aspects of their lives in order to achieve the republic's sovereignty and "a better condition than the world has yet known."[86] Service in the New Afrikan Legion created just one opportunity for New Afrikans to demonstrate their devotion.

The service of General Kuratibisha Ali X Rashid aptly exemplifies how some New Afrikans demonstrated their commitment to the Black Nation through participation in the Legion. Rashid involved himself with the Black Government Convention and was the ninety-ninth signer of the RNA Declaration of Independence. From that moment, he served in various soldierly positions under Minister of Defense John Taylor/Mweusi Chui, and another military leader, Alajo Adegbalola. General Rashid emphasizes the importance of leaders like Chui who were able to instill discipline in Legionnaires. As he reveals, "John Chui told us two things about weapons. He said 'guns are made to kill people.' He said, 'if you're not willing to kill people, leave your damn gun at home. . . . If you got a knife and you get so mad you pull it out, if there's nobody to cut, you cut yourself.' He don't want you to come back with a knife that you done pulled out of the holster and ain't no blood on it. That's pretty much how he controlled us with that weapon thing."[87] General Rashid's testimony indicates that Legionnaires had to be ready to give their lives and, if necessary, take the lives of others for the revolution. However, that dedication could not be based in reckless bellicosity that would give the U.S. government justification to further repress the NAIM. New Afrikans had to maintain discipline and discernment with regard to their use of military force. Therefore, crude suggestions likely made Legionnaires think carefully about the potential power and danger that came with wielding weapons for the movement.

Even though some New Afrikans emphasized the potential for combat, the RNA was never just a military apparatus (despite what the FBI and police might have stated). The Legion constituted one aspect of the Provisional Government. The PG-RNA also established several consulates that served as local governing bodies. The chief officer in each city, or the consul, was elected by local New Afrikans and approved by the RNA president. The consul spoke for the Provisional Government, coordinated RNA programming, and ran local RNA activity, including member recruitment, nation-building classes, and tax collection.[88] In fact, before a person could become a New Afrikan citizen, the RNA required that she or he go through nation-building classes.

Brother Bokeba Trice described nation-building classes as sessions that "explained the relationship between land and power. . . . How the land basically produced all of the resources that [New Afrikans] needed to be in control of—to survive as a people." He insisted until "We could get control of the land then We would always be dependent on outside sources for our power."[89] According to Sister Aneb Kgositsile, they also taught attendees who they were as an African people.[90] The *Government Administration* handbook contains more detail about what likely took place during nation-building sessions. First, class facilitators gave prospective citizens an orientation in which they learned about the Provisional Government and the founding documents. Next, potential New Afrikans learned the "history of white atrocities against black people in the modern era," as narrated by texts like W. E. B. Du Bois's *The World and Africa*, Herbert Aptheker's *A Documentary History of the Negro People in the United States*, and Ralph Ginzburg's *100 Years of Lynching*.[91] Taken together, such texts provided potential citizens with a historical and theoretical grounding in the circumstances African people faced in the United States and the world. The use of primary documents, as seen in Aptheker's and Ginzburg's edited volumes, indicates that New Afrikan leaders likely wanted recruits to learn to think critically about history by engaging directly with the voices of the oppressor and oppressed. Considering the documents included in those texts, it is conceivable that instructors highlighted their ancestors' multiple attempts to gain the rights of citizenship, but to no avail. Instead, they saw kidnappings and (re)enslavement, harsh Black Codes and slave laws, brutal and spectacular lynchings, sexual assault, and more. Such institutionalized viciousness reinforced Anglo-Americans' attitudes toward the prospect of black citizenship and inclusion. Further, Du Bois's research indicated that although the specific conditions of African Americans may have been distinct, they were not significantly different from what African people throughout the world faced under European and American domination.

Although nation-building classes were critical of white supremacy and the actions of European people, the use of scholars such as Aptheker and Ginzburg, both Jewish, may have allowed participants to focus their major critiques on systems of oppression. Consequently, they would have placed the actions and ideologies of specific individuals and groups within this broader context. The Apthekers and Ginzburgs may have reminded them that some people of European descent made useful and enduring allies. In doing so, they created space for participants to develop their own analyses about the historical trajectory of black people leading up to the 1968 Black Government Convention.

After becoming oriented to the need for New Afrikan liberation, aspiring citizens delved deeper into RNA doctrine and philosophy. They studied and discussed Imari Obadele's books *Revolution and Nation Building* and *War in America* and Malcolm X's "Message to the Grassroots." Students also read texts "dealing specifically with the emergence of modern nations (including white racist nations), Algeria, Ghana, Guinea, Tanzania, the Congo-Kinshasa, Australia, Cyprus, Israel, Rhodesia, Union of South Africa, Canada, India, China, and Cuba."[92] Matching such a comprehensive study of contemporary nationalisms with guided investigation of African people's condition in the United States prepared students to think critically about U.S. citizenship and determine their collective destiny.

Finally, instructors taught would-be citizens about how to define "New Afrikan." The RNA constitution provided that all African-descended peoples in the United States "are deemed to be citizens of the Republic of New Africa unless and until their actions or explicit statements indicate otherwise." Because most African-descended peoples in the United States did not (either by choice or through ignorance about the RNA) self-identify as New Afrikans, conscious citizens had to find a way to distinguish New Afrikan independence advocates from the black masses. Conscious New Afrikans, or "Citizens of Record," went "through the Government Center's or Consulate's Nation-Building and Orientation Courses." The *Government Administration* handbook delineates a list of behaviors and actions to aid further in this identification process and provide RNA citizens with guidelines for their daily practice. The sections titled "A Clear Understanding of What All Citizens Must Do" and "A Clear Understanding of What the Individual Must Do" list nine responsibilities that include paying taxes, studying RNA literature and current world events, selling and distributing RNA newspapers, and being *"a missionary"* who carries out "the basic, simple RNA message to all Black people with whom one come[s] in contact." The document stipulates that a missionary "must set an example in living up to the New African Creed and in industriousness, perseverance, constancy, and revolutionary fervor which [the missionary] may then rightly expect from other citizens."[93] In sum, nation-building classes provided an opportunity for potential New Afrikans to educate themselves about a range of historical, legal, and sociological topics and to think critically about their status in the United States.

Although New Afrikan belonging was based primarily on being of African descent, it at times expanded to include non-African people. As the case of Japanese-descended Yuri Kochiyama illustrates, New Afrikan citizenship should also be understood as a revolutionary identity that sought to include a broad array of oppressed people of color. Sister Yuri became a citizen of record in 1969. Prior to then, she was known in activist circles due to her relationship to Malcolm X—she cradled his head after assassins shot him—along with her activism in Harlem, her participation in the Organization for Afro-American Unity's liberation school, and her family's wildly popular open houses. An ardent supporter of the RNA almost from the moment they declared independence, she agreed with the nation's conceptualization of citizenship as well as its goal of creating an independent nation. She took the oath of citizenship shortly after that right was extended to non-Africans, and she died never renouncing her pledge to the Republic. Sister Yuri's identification as a New Afrikan and other New Afrikans' acceptance of her helps to illuminate how the flexibility of the "captive" black nation's conception of RNA citizenship accommodated other oppressed groups and individual non-black activists committed to liberation.[94]

If Sister Yuri's RNA citizenship stands as an exception, then Brother Imari Obadele embodied the quintessential New Afrikan. He served the PG-RNA first as minister of information and then as a regional vice president before assuming the presidency in 1970. Brother Imari used his various positions during the 1960s and 1970s to pursue RNA independence full time. He became a "New Afrikan Prisoner of War" following the August 18, 1971, shootout in Jackson, Mississippi, and due to the nature of the appeals process, he was incarcerated at different times from then until 1981. Within various penitentiaries, Brother Imari modeled intellectual curiosity and academic rigor, studying international law, U.S. and world history, and current events, even as he maintained communication with New Afrikans, RNA allies, and U.S. government officials. He dedicated his time and energy to building an independent black nation and to freeing the RNA-11 and many other black, Latina/o, and Native American radicals imprisoned for their political activities. During the intermittent periods when he was not in prison, Brother Imari traveled across the country raising funds for the RNA-11 and other RNA projects that he worked hard to maintain.[95] One of those projects involved the creation of Municipal Councils, the models that the PG-RNA borrowed from Native Americans, including the Navajo. New Afrikans reasoned that by developing the councils, they could qualify for and demand "millions of dollars in *Revenue Sharing* funds and in *Community Development* funds."[96]

Chokwe Lumumba, Esq., was another exemplary New Afrikan. He became a conscious New Afrikan citizen in 1969 while still a student at Kalamazoo College in Michigan. During his first year of service to the RNA, Lumumba functioned as one of three judges whom Brother Imari credited with preventing the PG from falling into shambles during the first constitutional crisis. He also served as minister of justice, and in 1970 constituents elected him vice president of the PG-RNA, a position he held until 1984 when he became chairperson of the newly created New Afrikan Peoples Organization. From the moment he committed himself to the RNA until his death in 2014, Brother Chokwe dedicated his legal expertise to serving the NAIM. He helped with the RNA-11 legal case; defended Mutulu Shakur, Fulani Sunni-Ali, and Bilal Sunni-Ali in the infamous Brinks expropriation case; and served as legal counsel for others. Lumumba later cofounded the Malcolm X Grassroots Movement, was elected to the Jackson City Council in 2009, and served as mayor of the city briefly before passing in February 2014.[97] Lumumba maintained that he ran for political office at the behest of his organization, and not for his own political aspirations. Despite his expressed reluctance to serve as councilperson and then mayor, his elections to those posts fit squarely with the long-term strategy developed by Brother Imari and others during the Provisional Government's formation.[98]

Kochiyama, Obadele, and Lumumba would have been considered model citizens because they dedicated their lives and careers to New Afrikan Political Science. But as one may imagine, they and other New Afrikans found it difficult to function purely as citizens of the RNA because they remained captives in the United States. That perceived captivity, like the imposition of citizenship, provoked a range of reactions from New Afrikans. For example, in May 1975, Brother Imari wrote, "The United States Government has continued to hold me under an illegal parole, restricting my travel, speech, and associations, and threatening me with re-imprisonment despite my station as a popularly elected Chief of State, lawfully on the territory claimed by the United States."[99] Even as he projected himself as a head of state, his legal status as an American citizen hindered his ability to fully exercise his perceived political and legal powers.

Sekou Owusu demonstrates how blurred the line between New Afrikan and U.S. citizen becomes in practice. Owusu became a conscious citizen of the Republic of New Afrika in 1970 and held several local and national positions. He even served as president of the RNA from 2008 to 2011. Before becoming a citizen of record, Owusu labored as a draft counselor. In that position, he educated young men about how the U.S. military's draft process worked and encouraged them to avoid fighting for the United States in the Vietnam War. In the process, Brother Sekou also learned how to protect himself from forced military service. When called before the U.S. draft board, he successfully stayed out of the military by using a student deferment.

In conversation, Owusu cited his abstention from U.S. military service as demonstrative of the many choices New Afrikans must make on a regular basis as dual citizens of the Republic of New Afrika and the United States.[100] From his vantage point, prospective New Afrikans already operate with that sense of duality by the time they pledge allegiance to the RNA. Some folks, regardless of citizenship allegiance, found ways to completely "drop off the grid" and live outside most U.S. legal boundaries and responsibilities. Brother Sekou, on the other hand, refrained from taking that freedom for himself, though he was able. He stated, "i cannot just disregard everything according to U.S. citizenship" because "i have no power to exercise . . . RNA citizenship [fully]." Further, the PG-RNA never acquired the power to offer him complete protection, even as former president and a conscious citizen of the RNA.[101] However, this state of affairs did not prohibit Owusu from pushing the boundaries that confined him as a dual RNA-U.S. citizen. As concerns an instructive model for circumventing the restrictions of U.S. citizenship, Brother Sekou offered the examples of Brother Imari and a delegation of New Afrikans who, he claimed, visited Libya several years earlier by traveling across state borders using RNA-issued passports.[102]

Another example of testing the boundaries of New Afrikan and U.S. citizenship involved a New Afrikan from Detroit. At the time of the incident, the citizen was driving one car in a caravan of New Afrikans traveling through rural Mississippi when they all were pulled over at a police checkpoint. The New Afrikan apparently did not have a state-issued driver's license. Instead, he presented authorities with his RNA-issued one. The black police officers at the checkpoint could have given him a hard time for failing to produce "proper" identification. Instead, they chatted briefly with the occupants of the New Afrikan's car and their fellow travelers. Then after a few intense minutes, everyone passed without further interference or reprimand.[103]

Brother-D.B. Aammaa Nubyahn provides a counterpoint to the aforementioned enactments of New Afrikan–African American duality. In proclaiming "[I am] a United States citizen, but i'm an African," he distinguishes between his legal citizenship and his racial identity. Brother-D, as he is called, argues that some New Afrikan independence rhetoric is empty because the Provisional Government and its affiliated organizations have not built institutions that provide enough power to protect its citizens' sovereignty. He considers New Afrikans "delusional to think [they're] free based on declaration alone." By his own admission, he uses U.S. licenses and certificates for legal matters and, when traveling abroad, "will quickly play that [U.S. citizen] card" if necessary. Even within U.S. borders, he has had to "play that card" because of the benefits at his disposal. Those benefits include ambulance service in case he needs to be rushed to the hospital in an emergency. "Where is the New Afrikan ambulance?" he asks, insisting that before New Afrikans can talk honestly about independence, they need to take into account all the benefits associated with being "enslaved" by the world's richest slave master.[104] Brother-D's contentions highlight the fact that such societal advantages impact how most conscious New Afrikans negotiate U.S. society, and they also influence how others view New Afrikans.

Some social movement theorists discuss how social movement outsiders construct the identities of movement participants in terms of "alter versions." Alter versions are "identity constructions of a movement that develop among those outside of a movement, including movement opponents, movement targets, and would-be movement participants."[105] Local newspapers—the RNA's most vocal enemies—proffered unforgiving alter versions of New Afrikan identity. With the blessings and encouragement of the federal government, the *Mississippi Clarion Ledger* strategically challenged every possible aspect of New Afrikan culture, including the use of chosen names, New Afrikans' marital status, and self-determined citizenship. For example, when Hekima Ana stood trial for the murder of the police officer who died in the August 18 shootout, *Clarion Ledger* staff writers often referred to him as "Thomas Edward Norman who prefers his adopted Swahili name of Hekima Ana."[106] Every time they mentioned his partner,

Tamu Ana, they referred to her as his "common-law wife" because, though recognized by the RNA, their marriage lacked the legal authorization of a U.S. state government.[107]

On the other hand, some white progressives and leftists offered qualified support to New Afrikans' attempts at exercising self-determination and respected the idea of New Afrikan citizenship. Following the Black Legion's shootout with Detroit police during the New Bethel Incident, a group of white Detroiters created a Black Legal Defense Fund "to provide funds for the defense of citizens of the Republic of New Africa." However, Black Legal Defense Fund members did not expect everyone interested in helping their cause to recognize and respect New Afrikan autonomy. They claimed that group membership "does not imply agreement with the political ideas or program of the defendants."[108]

The malleability and uneven application and/or imposition of U.S. citizenship demonstrates at least two basic problems that New Afrikans have yet to resolve fully. First, the conceptualizations and practices of U.S. citizenship are not static, but evolve based on several interdependent factors, including domestic and international politics, U.S. constitutional amendments, demographic shifts, and changing priorities of the national government.[109] For Africans in the United States, economic factors weave a major cord that tethers them to their ever-changing-same status over time. More specifically, their enslavement, the denial of their citizenship rights, and the legal and de facto social proscriptions on their full participation and protection under the law have all been intimately entangled with their oppressor's ability to earn a profit.

Second, New Afrikans' theoretical foundation exhibits marked limitations due to the RNA's exclusive focus on Africans enslaved in the South, elision of Africans enslaved in the North, and notable omission of legally free, though politically liminal, black men and women in both regions. Including this precariously situated "quasi-free" group in their analysis would permit them to better theorize the deep-running racism at the root of U.S. citizenship, and may prompt New Afrikan intellectuals to question the various ways that the very concept of citizenship itself may operate as a tool of oppression. As the citizenship of Yuri Kochiyama demonstrates, the PG-RNA has already taken practical steps toward redefining citizenship in broader terms than their theory and rhetoric suggest. In fact, their creation of a revolutionary/Third World identity has allowed New Afrikans to empower themselves in important ways, including building solidarity with other oppressed people of color.

New Afrikan Identity and Third World Liberation

The RNA's identification as a colonized nation has prompted its citizens to form alliances with peoples who claim their land was stolen or unjustly occupied by an imperial force, thereby compelling them to seek sovereignty, restitution, and/or independence. The PG-RNA states in its Code of Umoja, "It shall be the policy of the Provisional Government to recognize the just *claims* of the American Indian nations and other oppressed nations for land in North America. It shall be the policy of the [P]rovisional Government to negotiate with the American Indian Nations the claims which conflict with the claims of the New Afrikan nation and to resolve these claims in the spirit of justice, brotherhood, and mutual revolutionary commitment to the human and natural rights of all oppressed nations in North America."[110] Given New Afrikans' self-identification as paper-citizens of the United States, it comes as no surprise that the RNA Declaration of Independence, creed, and other such documents emphasize New Afrikans' respect for and support of other oppressed groups' rights to self-determination and struggles for liberation in the United States and abroad. As indicated in the passage cited from the Code of Umoja, New Afrikans were especially pressed to make negotiations with indigenous nations whose claims to land precede those of the RNA.

As part of their recognition of American Indians' struggles and just demands, the RNA has often used precedents set by treaties between Native Americans and the United States to argue for New Afrikan liberation and to strategize ways to create New Communities within the bounds of U.S. law.[111] Also, periodicals like the *New Afrikan Journal* occasionally ran sympathetic articles reporting on the historical and contemporary struggles Native Americans have faced. In one notable article, the author detailed various ways that the Bureau of Indian Affairs curtailed the sovereignty and self-determination of Native Americans through its policies on elections, education, and reservations. Characterizing their struggles as "war," the author sought to draw parallels between Native American and New Afrikan battles against their common oppressor.[112] The D.C. Unit of the PG issued a statement supporting "the Liberation Struggle of the indigenous peoples of North America" and proclaiming New Afrikan and Native people "shall dwell on the land in prosperity and harmony."[113] A public display reinforced such messaging. During a demonstration marking the bicentennial of the United States of America, black liberation forces and Native American activists agreed to demonstrate their solidarity by marching side by side holding visual markers of their common goals while parading through a North Philadelphia neighborhood. Further, there is some evidence that PG-RNA officers initiated concrete dialogues and negotiations with Native Americans as New Afrikans anticipated acquisition of land in the five states. One letter from former PG minister of foreign affairs Kwame-Osagyefo Kalimara to Robert Robideau of the Leonard Peltier Defense Committee exemplifies ongoing engagement between representatives of both movements. Robideau also wrote a statement of support for the NAIM, which the *New Afrikan* published.[114]

Similarly, RNA activists and Puerto Rican liberation fighters have had some contact and shows of solidarity. In mutually amicable statements, Rafael Cancel Miranda and Imari Obadele identified the rights of New Afrikans and Puerto Ricans to land and independence.[115] RNA articles exclaiming "Free Puerto Rico!" and praising the actions of people such as Marie Torres, Oscar Collazo, and Lolita Lebron litter New Afrikan publications. One article lists the various actions Puerto Ricans carried out in the name of independence. What is more, the article expresses solidarity by detailing the repressive actions committed against Puerto Rican liberationists and, once again, drawing parallels between New Afrikan liberation and global revolution against forces of imperialism. Ahmed Obafemi articulated this point in 1981. After explaining some of the history of comradeship between various oppressed groups in the United States, he called for them to continue working together toward their common goals. He explained that the New Afrikan effort to "free the land" was interconnected with the claims of their Native American, "ChicanoMexicano," and Puerto Rican comrades. It was a goal that these oppressed nations would work toward in partnership and solidarity.[116]

As noncitizens of the United States, New Afrikans vocally supported many other struggles for self-determination and independence since its founding in 1968. Even though New Afrikans' penchant for thinking of their own liberation in terms of global revolution fit neatly with the mood of the Black Power era, this tendency's nuances distinguished New Afrikans' objectives from those of their contemporaries. New Afrikans argued that a worldwide revolution against colonialism, imperialism, and white supremacy would shift both the world economic structure and the very organization of U.S. society. Though their solutions to race relations, poverty, education, and many other issues fell within the spectrum of socialist perspectives popular at the time, New Afrikans diverged from their contemporaries insofar as they problematized inclusion within American society. Instead, they argued that Black Power and socialism could be achieved only when New Afrikan people controlled their own sovereign and independent territory, the Republic of New Afrika.

· · · · · ·

Building on an international tradition of black struggle against racism and colonialism, RNA activists framed their movement as one that sought to overthrow oppression wherever it existed. In doing so, they put forth an alternate interpretation of the Black Power slogan and concept. Alongside the rhetoric of community control and socialist revolution, New Afrikans engaged in serious discussions about their very place in society, including whether African-descended people in the United States should fight for "first-class" citizenship or pursue self-determination. The New Afrikan perspective on that issue guided and justified their struggle for independence, influenced with whom they formed alliances, and determined to a major degree how they approached the attainment of their goals. Indeed, New Afrikans' conviction that the actualization of their revolution depended on their ability to gain recognition within the United Nations highlights a dimension of the Black Power movement that continues to hold relevance for modern-day activists.[117]

New Afrikans' determination to attain Black Power guided the practice of their theory. However, living according to NAPS presented limitations due to the RNA's long-standing and ongoing captivity. In other words, New Afrikan citizens' attempts to enact political autonomy were bound by the laws of the United States. Although they could not fully exercise RNA citizenship, New Afrikans found other ways to empower themselves. They identified as a diasporic African nation that existed as part of a revolutionary Third World. This identification encouraged New Afrikans to forge alliances with other oppressed groups. In addition to the efforts aimed at securing independence, New Afrikans operationalized more personal tactics to empower themselves.

3 Revolutionary Name Choices

Self-Definition and Self-Determination

· ·

It seems that the Afro-American tradition of bestowing meaningful
names on children has gone full circle. Original African names that
were taken away by slavemasters [*sic*] are returning in increasing
numbers with the conscious reaffirmation of Afro-American culture,
the result of Black people's newly revived pride in their genetic and
cultural roots.

—Sheila S. Walker, *Ebony*, 1977

The naming ceremony in which Richard Trice participated began with a li-
bation. To perform this rite, Imari Obadele spoke the names of powerful
predecessors and probably invited other participants to call on the names
of their forebears. Brother Imari then poured water either onto the ground
or into a plant between the chanting of each name and at other points in
the procedure. After the completion of this ritual, he bequeathed Trice and
others newly pledging allegiance to the RNA with a name. Leaders selected
names for recently enlisted New Afrikans based on the qualities they noticed in the students who were completing nation-building classes. At fifteen years old, Trice became Bokeba Wantu Enjuenti, an appellation that
signifies "one who struggled for a beautiful nation." By accepting it, Trice
acknowledged his symbolic departure from his former existence and his
commitment to the new life "of an African revolutionary." To end the ceremony, Trice and his cohort sipped from a unity cup and chanted "Harambee" (Swahili for "let's all pull together") in unison seven times, thus
signifying the importance of pulling individuals together in service to their
larger group. At the conclusion of the formal service, drummers sent rhyth-
mic messages to participants and guests who enjoyed food and fellowship
in celebration of this newly committed group of New Afrikan freedom
fighters.[1]

New Afrikan Political Science (NAPS) stipulates that before the Black Nation can achieve statehood, black people must become true and conscious
New Afrikans. Part of that transformation included internalizing New

Afrikan ideas and theories and developing a mindset that embraced self-determination rather than assimilation into the dominant society. The revolutionary praxis of being New Afrikan presented itself in various aspects of RNA activists' daily lives, including name choices. A name adoption, like that described by Trice, served as an outward display of the internal metamorphosis that many people experienced when they committed themselves to the mission of black liberation. The naming ceremony was a public graduation of sorts that the Provisional Government–Republic of New Afrika (PG-RNA) hosted periodically to celebrate its growing cadres and to present them to the broader black community.

During the 1960s and 1970s, black people across the United States engaged in discourses about their African heritage and debated whether or how their ancestry should inform their present lives. Along with clothing, hair, and relationships within families and communities, the topic of nomenclature proved popular, as it was an aspect of life in which black folks could easily exercise control. Following a long tradition of choosing designations that provided African-descended people with a means of self-definition, Black Power–era naming practices sought to empower them. Through their name choices, they sought to reconcile their African heritages with "new world" realities. New Afrikans who shed their "slave names" exhibited a consciousness that recognized the ancestral connections and (neo)colonial conditions they shared, to some extent, with Africans worldwide, all while remaining attentive to the specificities of their local political conditions.[2] For New Afrikans, then, name choices were among the most basic displays of self-determination and lifestyle politics.

It is important to ask how and why some New Afrikans perceived assuming an Afrikan name as an external manifestation of internal, cognitive liberation from American hegemony.[3] Here, the term "Afrikan name" denotes identifiers that activists adapted from a range of African languages and cultures and/or from Arabic. In some cases, an Afrikan name may be made up, but inspired by what an individual learned about Africa. At the same time, many New Afrikans maintained their slave names, in part or in full. The term "slave name" typically indicates an appellation given to an enslaved person by the enslaver and/or in the tradition of the slaveholder's culture. Slave names intentionally cut their bearers off from ancestral lands and kin ties. Many slaveholders denigrated enslaved people through naming, either by the nature and process in which designations were given or because actual names themselves were intended as invectives for the dehumanized.[4] In this context, slave names refer to European designations originally forced upon bonded Africans or taken by them in their attempts to assimilate or protect themselves from violence and discrimination during and after chattel slavery.[5]

Even if some New Afrikans decided not to take on a new name or alter the names accorded them at birth, they accepted the group moniker "New Afrikan." This collective designation, along with many activists' personal names, conveyed the idea that RNA citizens constituted a nation distinct from, though connected with, African-descended people in other regions of the world. Conscious citizens saw their struggle for independence as part of a broader revolution that would liberate African people and the Third World more broadly. Put differently, name choices made up one of the most basic and mundane aspects of lifestyle politics, and it confirmed that revolutionary activism was a comprehensive process that transformed individual people even as they struggled to bring to fruition their vision of a postcolonial futurity.

Although the logic behind name changes seems simple—black people wanted to psychologically rid themselves of their oppressors' cultural practices and identify more closely with their ancestors—this brief survey of New Afrikans' resolutions to alter or maintain their names demonstrates the complexity of naming. Choosing one's name comprised one act of self-determination in a broader process of mental decolonization. Even when cloaked in religious ideals and symbolism, name choices indicated a deep-seated disapproval of the *Maafa* which placed many Africans in the United States, where they experienced superexploitation, first through the international system of enslavement, then through anti-black terrorism, and, even after the advent of legal equality with the dominant racial group, through continued political and economic oppression. Though not the sole indicator of, or a necessary step toward, New Afrikan liberation, the adoption of Afrikan names represents the most obvious manifestation of that process and provides a gateway into the complexities of lifestyle politics. Denominating is one of the most basic and fundamental actions carried out by New Afrikans in their broader pursuit of individual and group self-determination through revolutionary activism.

What's in a Name? Onomastics and African History in the United States

The literature on naming practices forms a dynamic and useful field of study that provides scholars an opportunity to explore activism using avenues that heretofore remained underinvestigated. In addition to attracting the attention of scholars from across several disciplines, onomastic studies cover an impressive range of issues. Several texts focus on the appellations people choose for themselves and their children, the various reasons people select certain designations, and where and how specific adopted names originated. These texts discuss the conscious and unconscious motives behind naming and whether or how the names influence bearers' personalities and ambitions.[6] Some studies focus on African Americans' history and the correlation between enslavement and African descendants' names. Such analyses highlight how enslavers deployed nomenclature that attempted to cut Africans off from their ancestral lands, kin ties, and cultural knowledge, as well as to assert control over their human property.[7] They also pinpoint ways that Africans used naming from their earliest moments in the Western world both to assimilate into the dominant culture and to create unique designations that emphasized individuality and Africanity while establishing new kinship bonds.[8] Some scholarly literature on black naming traditions emphasizes African cultural retentions in American culture.[9] Further, some scholars have begun researching the large numbers of African Americans who consciously looked toward Africa for inspiration in their naming practices during the 1960s and 1970s.[10] Taken together, these studies help contextualize New Afrikan practices of naming during the Black Power era.

The sheer volume of scholarship that analyzes names from myriad cultures of various times and places indicates that human beings value names. More than just labels that identify one individual from another, names often represent a "verbal signal of [a person's] whole identity, his [or her] being-in-the-world as a distinct person."[11] A name may identify one's class status, region of origin, and date of birth. It also potentially equates to a person's spiritual essence and connects each person to ancestors. On a psychological level, personal designations communicate affirming and detrimental connotations that may affect self-esteem and personal development.[12]

In political struggles for black liberation, names garnered particular importance because of the context in which most African Americans came to inherit their personal and family names. Human traffickers brought captive Africans to what is now the United States. After being stolen from their ancestral lands, alienated from their families, sold and shipped like cargo across the Atlantic Ocean, and sometimes held over in the Caribbean, the enslaved endured the process of someone marking them as subhuman partially through denaming and renaming. Europeans may have sold an individual repeatedly, renaming that person with each sale. Historian Sterling Stuckey argues that the acts of stripping enslaved people of their personal names and saddling them with unfamiliar and often denigrating ones produced traumatic psychological changes and revealed the absolute spite with which European enslavers viewed them. In discussing the implications of denying an entire people their group names, Stuckey claims that "the act of denying a whole people their names and giving them new ones in a new language—and only partial names at that [as they did not typically receive last names]—must be regarded as a serious act of aggression, as a reflection of their subordinate state."[13] Both enslaved and "free" Africans were acutely aware of this violent arrangement.

The U.S. black population combated this forced renaming through a variety of self-determined onomastic practices. Some enslaved people were known to use secret names and pet names when away from the presence of authorities, and many of them gave their children dignified names that they associated with powerful people and religious figures. Africans who were not enslaved but who lived in legal and social liminality that could easily lead to (re)enslavement enacted a more formal process of onomastic resistance. Often given abbreviated versions of common European names such as Will and Tom for men and Jen and Sari for women, they frequently changed their names to William and Thomas or Jennifer and Sarah, upon manumission. Historian Ira Berlin suggests that in such situations renaming symbolized "personal liberation and political defiance; it reversed the enslavement process and confirmed the free Negro's newly won liberty just as the loss of an African name had earlier symbolized enslavement." Further, many among the emancipated adopted last names that they deemed significant, including "Freeman," "Washington," and others.[14] Interestingly, some African names (especially Sambo) reminded them of derisive slave names. With the exception of Cuffee (in all of its various spellings), African names waned as black people sought political empowerment within the dominant system. However, African appellations and naming practices did not lose their significance altogether. Instead, Africans in the United States have applied their traditional customs to European nomenclature.[15]

For black activists during the 1960s and 1970s, these lessons made several issues clear. First, Africans and people from various racial and cultural groups believed that a name embodied the very essence of one's being and aligned a person with his or her ancestors. Europeans intentionally stripped enslaved Africans of their ancestral names in order to render them into dehumanized and depersonalized chattel detached from meaningful genealogies and with hopes of controlling their thoughts and actions.

Second, Black Power activists comprehended this process of dehumanization, depersonalization, and domination as an act of aggression and thus one aspect of the war in which they engaged as soldiers. Third, as part of their strategy to combat filial estrangement and oppression, African-descended people's name choices were central to how they affirmed their humanity and maintained ancestral ties and diasporic connections.[16]

During the Black Power era when African Americans sought to renew their relationship with Africa and consciously chose to embrace various aspects of African cultures rather than assimilate into mainstream America, reconsidering names empowered both individuals and the larger collective. For many New Afrikans and other Black Power activists, the process of abandoning a European name for one of their choosing occasioned a critical juncture in the development of their black racial identity and indicated their acceptance of a nationalist or Pan-Africanist political ideology. However, the move was not without precedent. The Nation of Islam (NOI) helped bridge the gap between black people's conditions under American apartheid and quotidian terror and their use of names with European origins.

Prodigal Children: The NOI's Influence on Name Choices during the Black Power Era

> Your number in prison became a part of you. You never hear your name, only your number. On all of your clothing, every item, was your number, stenciled. It grew stenciled on your brain.
>
> —El-Hajj Malik El-Shabazz

Shabazz's statement about his prison number parallels how many of his contemporaries understood their own personal and family names.[17] The process of programming prison inmates—slaves according to the Thirteenth Amendment of the U.S. Constitution—to identify with their prison number corresponded with the seasoning enslaved Africans underwent during their transformation into legal chattel. After realizing that anti-black oppression facilitated his path to prison and obtaining that number, Malcolm Little rejected his mental enslavement and embraced the teachings of the Honorable Elijah Muhammad. In *Message to the Blackman in America*, Muhammad urged that so-called Negroes "be given names of [their] forefathers whose names are the most Holy and Righteous Names of Allah" and insisted "that resolving [their] identity is one of the first and most important truths to be established by God, Himself."[18] Malcolm X sought his "Holy and Righteous Name" as he worked tirelessly to help other African Americans understand and overcome their mental enslavement. The Nation of Islam was the most influential black organization to draw clear connections between the political and spiritual properties of names and to call for a rejection of slave names. During the 1950s and early 1960s, Malcolm X played a pivotal role in the transformation of black political consciousness and activism because of the sheer number of people who considered themselves disciples of his praxis. His own personal transformations, as recollected in his speeches and in his posthumously published *Autobiography,* provided his political progeny a model of evolutionary change to identify with as they underwent their own self-transformations.

In 1952, Malcolm Little exchanged his surname for the letter "X" to symbolize his transition from a self-hating Negro to a self-defined black man. His adoption of the X signified a dual recognition of his unknown ancestral name and his departure from a life of criminality. At the time, he had just finished a prison sentence for a number of robbery convictions compounded by his sexual relationship with a white woman. His decision to drop his slave name indicated that he gave up the lifestyle that led to his incarceration. Instead of engaging in theft, gambling, and drugs, Malcolm X pursued knowledge of self and served Allah's will through his commitment to the Honorable Elijah Muhammad and the NOI. Perhaps more important, he adhered to the belief that his slave name, like his previous lifestyle, rendered him subservient to the will of "the white man," which was antithetical to the teachings of the NOI. Attaining an X, then, symbolized his decision to become an independent thinker who would help black people gain their liberation.[19]

Malcolm's experience with naming encompassed much more time and space than his incarceration or experience in the Nation of Islam. As a child growing up in Michigan, he remembered being called "nigger" and "Rastus" by his white teachers and classmates. As a hustler in Boston and Harlem, he earned such nicknames as "Detroit Red." While in Charlestown State Prison, other prisoners referred to the malevolent inmate as "Satan" before he underwent his personal transformation and flirted with calling himself "Malachi Shabazz." Even though his X endures in history and public memory, some of his Nigerian associates endowed him with the name "Omowale," and he finally accepted the name El-Hajj Malik El-Shabazz before assassins took his life.[20] All of the names mentioned here marked important phases of personal transformation. They took on even more significance due to

Shabazz's iconic status and representation as someone from a historically oppressed group who decided to reclaim and redefine his identity on his own terms.

A mixture of politics and spirituality provided compelling reasons for rethinking a name. Whether they searched through the Hebrew Scriptures or studied with the NOI, people altered their personal designations and rejected their surnames in response to what they interpreted through their religious faith and/or spiritual intuition as a higher calling.[21] Their calling was typically tied to an important sociopolitical objective. Shabazz provides an interesting example of this tendency. Although the various monikers he assumed or received during different stages of his life signified his growth and evolution, the name he assumed as an NOI convert is exceptional, primarily because of the ideology on which it rests. Reiterating Elijah Muhammad's assertion, the NOI believed that maintaining slave names kept African people as psychological captives to white supremacy. Such people could not determine their best cultural, political, and socioeconomic interest.[22] In their attempts to undermine the arrangement, the NOI required prospective members to submit letters to Muhammad expressing their desire to reclaim their heritage and religion. The correspondent requested that Muhammad give him or her an "Original name." Members of the NOI scrutinized these letters and, upon approval, furnished the person requesting membership with an X. The X stood in for the person's unidentified Original name, which the person could receive only from Allah. Therefore, the X represented a transitional space between one's former slave name and Original name.[23]

Many black people also adopted new appellations in an attempt to reunite with any obtainable portions of their African ancestry. According to Minister Malcolm, "The devil white man cut [enslaved Africans] off from any knowledge of their own language, religion, and past culture until the black man in America was the earth's only race who had absolutely no knowledge of their true identity" and "that no longer even knew their true family names."[24] If the loss of people's knowledge of their past symbolized and reified dehumanization and oppression, then regaining that knowledge accomplished a crucial aspect of empowerment and a significant step in the process of liberation.

The transformation of El-Hajj Malik El-Shabazz and others followed what psychologist William C. Cross identified in 1971 as the "Negro-to-Black Conversion Experience." In Cross's original model and its various revisions, he claimed African Americans underwent various evolutionary phases (or fit into various identity clusters), each representing a stage of psychological development in their progression toward embracing their blackness. One phase, the pre-encounter, included the total acceptance of everything European and the denial of racism's impact on African Americans. In contrast, the internalization identity cluster involved a nuanced analysis of European/Western hegemony. In between the two aforementioned stages was what Cross termed the immersion/emersion identity cluster. This juncture was particularly important because it constituted the point when a "convert" underwent an extreme identity change and embraced all things African or black. People in this identity cluster often decided to take on a new name as they attempted to disassociate from European culture. In this context, name changes represent that critical moment in the Negro-to-Black Conversion Experience during which individuals accepted fully an identity they had determined for themselves.[25]

Several Black Power activists, including many who considered themselves disciples of Shabazz, rationalized name changes according to a logic that paralleled Cross's explanatory model. As one member of the Us Organization told a *Newsweek* reporter, although "'with some people it's just a fad . . . with most it's a step along the way to consciousness and understanding of self.'"[26] That reasoning resonated with more than just activists; African people in the United States and abroad found it important to reject the monikers they received in the context of oppression in favor of sobriquets (and often legally changed names) that projected their connections with their real and/or imagined ancestors. Ghanaian novelist and critical essayist Ayi Kwei Armah articulated such logic behind shedding European names. In his renowned novel *Two Thousand Seasons*, he wrote:

> It is the white men's wish to take us from our way—ah, we ourselves
> are so far already from our way—to move us on to their road; to
> void us of our soul and put their spirit, the worship of their creature
> god, in us. . . . They say it will be reward enough when we have lost
> our way completely, lost even our names; when you will call your
> brother not Olu but John, not Kofi but Paul; and our sisters will no
> longer be Ama, Naita, Idawa and Ningome but creatures called
> Cecilia, Esther, Mary, Elizabeth and Christina. . . . The white men
> want us to obliterate our remembrance of our way, the way, and in
> its place to follow their road, road of destruction.[27]

The ideas expressed by Armah, the NOI, and Shabazz found their way into the rhetoric and lived experiences of Black Power movement activists who sought to liberate black people from all vestiges of Euro-American cultural and political domination. Understanding themselves as African peoples rather than Negroes or simply Americans, these women and men carried on the legacy of resistance that their ancestors first put into practice.

New Afrikan Name Stories

In 1969, Imari Obadele gave fourteen-year-old Bernadette Taliaferro the name Shushanna during a naming ceremony. She found that the name, which means "rose," was in use among some Native Americans and has roots in Hebrew. Around that same time, her oldest brother chose the name Shakur, which they understand as "one who directs the way," for himself, Shushanna, and their sister. They soon learned that another family member, Chokwe, had already chosen the name Lumumba for himself. When the family's youngest siblings became RNA cadres, they took on that name. When explaining why she took on her new names, she recited the claims about African people losing their original names when Europeans enslaved them. She explained, "i could see someone who is fighting for liberation of their people and their selves, and their identity to take on a new name." Because it was impossible to find out and take on the exact identity and names lost through violence, the next best option was to re-create one's self. The name symbolized that new creation.[28]

Resistance to cultural and political domination through name choices reveals one aspect of New Afrikan lifestyle politics. Some people embraced Afrikan names to confirm an African identity that was complicated by the unique history of captivity and resistance in North America. Though altering one's name might seem minute, for New Afrikans, such modifications echoed larger arguments regarding black people's right to choose their own nationality after being properly informed about why and how to make that choice. In this sense, New Afrikan name choices signified activists' pride in their ancestral heritage and their desire to obtain New Afrikan liberation. However, some people decided not to replace their slave names. The rationale behind such decisions further complicates the connection between identity, self-determination, and liberation in ways that resist one-dimensional understandings of Black Power–era nomenclature. Finally, some activists who did change their names discarded them or had them revoked. These various situations clarify the matrix of self-determination and power, along with the significance of gender norms as they and other social constructs intersect with the different views activists held about their legitimacy as revolutionaries.

During the Black Power era, various individuals and groups contemplated the proper identity African Americans should assume. Among these activists, Stokely Carmichael considered all black people Africans who should seek a land base on the continent of Africa. During the early 1970s, he took on the first name Kwame in honor of Ghanaian former head of state Kwame Nkrumah. He adapted Ture from the last name of Guinea president Sékou Touré.[29] Although some people shared Ture's opinion on African American identity and Pan-Africanism, the people who gave life to the NAIM contended that African Americans were no longer "African" in the geographic and strict cultural sense of the term. Because they considered themselves a captive nation within a hegemonic state, whose ancestors developed practices and outlooks formed through an amalgamation of African cultural retentions, acculturation under European domination, and life in a new land, it was difficult for successive generations to identify completely with the diversity of continental African societies. Nations and cultures in Africa had evolved between the sixteenth and nineteenth centuries, due in part to the changes that occurred through greater contact with Europeans and Asians, including the global traffic in Africans and the forces of colonialism.[30] In contrast to activists like Ture, RNA leaders argued that African Americans should identify as New Afrikans, a people who, though racially black or African, embodied a republic distinct from other African nations, and certainly different from the body politic constituted by their white American counterparts.[31] As part of this understanding of New Afrikan identity and their global political positioning, RNA citizens often shed their slave names in favor of Afrikan ones.

RNA documentation contains an array of ideas that illustrate the PG-RNA's flexibility on formal designations. In a letter to citizens during the constitutional crisis of 1970, Brother Gaidi requested that people reply and provided spaces for respondents to provide both their "slave names" and "Traditional Names."[32] In addition, the "Adult Application for the R.N.A." furnished lines for one's "Assumed Name" as well as "Slave Name."[33] RNA citizens considered changing their names as symbols of their commitment to New Afrikan liberation, and many of them did. However, some New Afrikans chose to hold on to birth names for legal and sentimental purposes, and others concluded that assuming an Afrikan name was not necessary. That the PG-RNA made space in printed documents for both kinds of names underscores the varying opinions among New Afrikans on the topic of nomenclature.

Although taking on a new name was not a requirement for New Afrikans, plenty of them decided to adopt one. Such people found, or were given, their names in situations and processes as multifaceted and diverse as New Afrikans themselves. Many received their names, as did Shushanna Shakur and Bokeba Trice, from elders or respected community members. Some found their names in books created for that purpose, and others came to them from studying African history and cultures. In at least one case, a New Afrikan developed his name through years of careful consideration and internal exploration. Iyaluua Ferguson, like many other New Afrikans from the 1960s, received her name from Nana Oseijeman Adefunmi, a Yoruba priest and cofounder of the Provisional Government. The religious leader presented her with the name during a naming ceremony. Iyaluua means "mother of the people." The two-term People's Center Council (PCC) chair explained, "My greatest honor is that Baba gave me that name, and that Queen Mother Moore also was Iyaluua, and i really feel that was a great honor to me."[34]

The theme of honor in receiving an Afrikan name found its way into the name story of Dr. Njeri Jackson. She recalled with sentimental delight the day a group of children named her during a Kwanzaa festival. The children were concerned that she lacked an Afrikan name. After being prompted by their teacher, they "talked about who i was and how i was the wife of" Michael Finney, "a warrior" who helped hijack a plane to Cuba one month prior. "And so the kids had been studying a lot of—there were a lot of naming books out in the late '60s. And so the children . . . said, 'We want her to be Njeri, one deserving of a warrior.'" Because the children "named me, i took it, and i kept it. . . . So i'm Njeri, that's it. I *take* my name."[35] That the children gave Jackson a name that she used for the remainder of her life speaks to the communal significance of names for some of the people who were entrenched in the New Afrikan community. People like Jackson believed that by taking on an Afrikan name, they connected with their immediate communities and their global counterparts, past and present.

However, not everyone who became a conscious RNA citizen or who established intimate relationships with New Afrikans found it necessary to change their name, although to some, "it was pretty much customary."[36] Whereas Iyaluua Ferguson decided to use her Afrikan name regularly, her husband, Herman, felt that he should refrain from employing his. Like Mama Iyaluua, Nana Oseijeman gave him his name, Adekoye Akinwole, during a naming ceremony. However, Ferguson developed some reservations about using the name, and about the practice of renaming more generally. He recalled: "I felt that there was a wave of name changes. A lot of things were happening back in those days that were culturally nationalism. And i didn't consider myself a cultural nationalist. My idea of a nationalist was purely and fully political." Further, he believed that one should receive a new name after they had proven themselves politically. He maintained "that the person who took that name had achieved a certain status. . . . They had earned that right."[37]

Baba Herman's distinction between cultural nationalism and political nationalism illustrates a point of contention black activists debated during the late 1960s, as various groups and individuals, including David Hilliard and Maulana Karenga, made similar differentiations between their theories and strategies for black liberation. The distinctions represented fundamentally divergent views about the best methods for achieving their goals. On the one hand, cultural nationalists who are often represented by Karenga and the Us Organization argued, "We must free ourselves culturally before we can succeed politically." In other words, African-descended people in the United States had to undergo a process of mental decolonization before they could wage a successful revolution against white supremacy and oppression. Because ideological leaders, such as Karenga, claimed "the cultural revolution gives identity, purpose and direction," some of their contemporaries perceived cultural nationalists as neglecting grassroots organizing. Historian Scot Brown suggests that the relatively small membership of Us contributed to that perception but also points out that many cultural nationalists did indeed participate in the more visible aspects of political organizing.[38]

On the other hand, the BPP typically represented political (or revolutionary) nationalists and claimed to be more concerned with addressing the concrete political conditions that left black people susceptible to oppression. Former Panther David Hilliard wrote, "We call our position 'revolutionary nationalism,' as opposed to 'cultural nationalism,' which limits the struggle for self-determination to appearances—dashikis, African names, talk about 'new nationhood' and the black nation." He distinguished between "steeping ourselves in an African past and folklore" as a goal, claiming instead that revolutionaries aligned themselves with other liberation fighters, or those movements that waged armed political struggle against oppressive capitalists. "We are about gaining economic and political freedom," he added; "after that, worry about what you call yourself."[39] Hilliard's comrade Huey P. Newton maintained a similar position. He argued that cultural, or "pork chop," nationalism was insufficient because he did not see it as being rooted in a socialist perspective; and anything other than a socialist perspective would cause potential revolutionaries to be reactionary, thus prompting them to replace one oppressive regime with another. Newton used Haiti's Papa Doc as an example of someone who was pro-black, "which on the surface seems very good, but for him it is only to mislead the people. He merely kicked out the racists and replaced them with himself as the oppressor." With that situation unfolding as black nationalists were developing their liberation movement, he feared that many of his contemporaries in the United States were pursuing similar goals.[40]

Such differences in theoretical perspective sometimes led people from opposing viewpoints to enmity and violence, even as others seemed to negotiate the positions. The Black Panther Party–Us rivalry is instructive, as it culminated in the deaths of Panthers Alprentice "Bunchy" Carter and John Huggins, as well as the arrests and convictions of Us members George and Larry Watani Stiner. Of course, political differences alone were not enough to cause this bout of violence or to provoke other brutal episodes. FBI instigation, preexisting turf battles between members within the organizations, and many other elements contributed to the severe deterioration of the Us-Panther relationship.[41] Some Black Power–era activists deemed it wise to combine the tactics and ideologies of cultural and political nationalism. The House of Umoja, the New York Black Panther Party, the Afrikan Peoples Party, and Amiri Baraka's Congress of African People, among other formations, either argued explicitly for or practiced elements from both tendencies. In fact, as Langston Hughes, W. E. B. Du Bois, Angela Davis, Larry Neal, and others contended before and during the Black Power era, culture, especially as operationalized by an oppressed group to undermine its oppressor (and the reverse is also true), is inherently political.[42]

Herman Ferguson's stance on who deserved to use an Afrikan name evidences another important dimension of the nomenclature issue. During the 1960s and 1970s, black people of all political persuasions took on names that signified their connections with their ancestors, reflected their sociopolitical ideals, and/or illustrated some aspects of their spiritualities. Although one may like to believe that everyone active in political struggle remained steadfast in their beliefs, there were certainly activists who stood in an insincere, and sometimes outright fraudulent, relation to the ideals put forth by the groups and organizations in which they participated. Some men and women may have been attracted solely to the style and infamy associated with Black Power politics and culture. Others became involved as informants at the behest of local and national legal authorities. In fact, one of the people to whom Yoruba priest Nana Oseijeman gave a name supplied information about Herman Ferguson to the FBI and testified against him in court. Therefore, it should not come as too much of a surprise that Ferguson deemed it necessary for participants to prove their dedication to the movement before using Afrikan names. Yet, given Ferguson's close association with El-Hajj Malik El-Shabazz, involvement with the Revolutionary Action Movement and the PG-RNA, and his experiences as a target of several repressive actions from the 1960s into the 1990s, it is difficult to understand why he did not think he had "earned" the right to use Adekoye, which indicates that one has valor or courage.[43]

While people like Herman Ferguson believed it pertinent to fulfill some prerequisite conditions in order to earn an Afrikan name, others simply remained content with the designations their parents gave them at birth. In fact, former PCC chair Marilyn Killingham refused to get rid of her birth name. She opined, "Marilyn is a derivative of Mary and my mother's name was Mary. And she changed the 'y' to 'i' and added -lyn. She's an African warrior and i'm named after her. And i guess . . . if Jesus was black then i guess [his mother] Mary would have to be too."[44] However, her justification for holding on to her given name is significant because it highlights the reasoning of activists who valued their inheritance of appellations shared by people who made significant contributions to the lives of others despite having names identified with their former slave masters. Killingham considered her mother an African warrior whose name she proudly bore. Further, her name held great spiritual significance for her, too. As a devout Christian, she associated the name Mary with one of the most important figures in her faith. Even though the RNA never mandated that New Afrikans shed their slave names, Killingham explained that she had to defend her decision to keep hers. In a culture that sought to disassociate itself from any vestiges of oppression, people probably placed great pressure on her and others to take on an Afrikan name.[45]

Killingham's possession of an "African warrior" name is significant because her inheritance seemed to contradict what some perceived as the prevailing gender conventions. Assata Shakur wrote, "Women's names were nothing like the men's names, which meant things like strong, warrior, man of iron, brave, etc."[46] The proliferation among black women of names like Amina and Marini, which respectively mean "peaceful" and "charming," presumably confirms Assata's assertion. In addition, some women's appellations denoted generally heteronormative features of femininity, such as being a mother or wife.[47] However, at least some New Afrikan women adopted and gave their children "strong" names such as Fulani, Nefertiti, and Asantewa, designations shared by warriors and rulers. Nzingha, taken from the sixteenth-century military leader who successfully resisted the Portuguese occupation of her land and enslavement of her people for over thirty years, may have also gained popularity among black women of the era.[48] Yet dominant gender conventions persisted insofar as more men than women seemed to take on "warrior" names or sobriquets that held great military significance. Names associated with soldiers and hunters, including Balogun and Chaka (in all of their various spellings), as well as Kamau, Odinga, and Sundiata enjoyed prominence in an era during which some black men strove to overturn what they considered historic emasculation.[49]

Strong military names also garnered heightened significance because they suggested a willingness to engage in warfare. Because black people are a historically oppressed group, black people's assumption of qualities associated with predecessors whose acumen on the battlefield gained them great respect and fear constituted another important aspect of cognitive liberation. Such honorable appellations endowed bearers with a responsibility to live up to the characteristics of their names in the war against white supremacy, the battle for land and reparations, and the contest for independence. Having a name associated with an African warrior gave Killingham that sense of responsibility.

Like Mama Killingham, some men selected warrior names with a similar sense of responsibility to uphold the characteristics imbedded in them. One such man was Hannibal Tirus Afrik, a highly respected New Afrikan. Born in the mid-1930s, Afrik came from a poor family, earned scholarships to get him through Central State University in Wilberforce, Ohio, and climbed the U.S. military's ranks to the position of officer. In the process of attaining middle-class American comfort, he decided that African people in the United States could not be free until they achieved political independence and destroyed white supremacy and capitalist hegemony. This belief inspired him to get involved with the PG-RNA. When explaining his reasons for accepting his current name, he mentioned that Hannibal the Annihilator's "exploits are legendary." He was "but the greatest military strategizer in the history of warfare." The New Afrikan reported Tirus Afrik "was reputedly the head of the Zingha ten thousand years ago. The UNIA [Universal Negro Improvement Association] documented that that's where the red, black, and green first flew ten thousand years ago in the area of Northwest Africa which is now northern Mauritania." Because his valued students named him, he took pride in it and lived his life trying to fulfill the expectations that came with the name.[50]

Baba Hannibal's full name instilled in him the responsibilities to be militarily adroit and to embody great leadership. Further, his name placed him in a succession of mighty men beginning with ancestors from a time far gone up to participants in the twentieth-century Garvey movement. Afrik's full name did not originate in a single region of Africa; instead, it connected him with Africans from the Mediterranean world and West Africa, in addition to Marcus Garvey, the Jamaican-born organizer who built one of the world's largest black organizations to date. Living up to the reputations associated with his name was a tall order that Baba Hannibal proudly worked to fulfill in his personal life, in his public activities, and through his spiritual practice.

Well-known and widely respected New Afrikan Chokwe Lumumba began his association with the PG-RNA during his summer break from Kalamazoo College in Michigan. His name, like Afrik's, associated him with Afrikan military history and leadership. Regarding this association, he explained that Chokwe means "hunter," and it was the name of an "African nation—what white folks would call a tribe—which existed during the slave trade." They opposed and fought valiantly against human traffickers in the northeast region of present-day Angola. The Chokwe were also known for their arts. "They were one of the ones who started performances where they'd hold up masks to be different characters. A lot of people think the Greeks started that, but it was the Chokwe." Next, "Lumumba means 'gifted'" and was inspired by Patrice Lumumba, the assassinated leader who helped the Democratic Republic of Congo transition to independence. "So my name's significant because i've chosen a name which represents . . . some of the last resistance to the slave trade before the slave trade pretty much overtook Africa. And then Lumumba which is one of the first revolutionaries . . . who began to bring Africa back to its independence." Taken together, one may translate Chokwe Lumumba as "gifted hunter." But the name "also represents the nation and the brother that had important roles in our liberation struggle against white supremacy and for independence."[51]

As with Afrik, Lumumba's explanation of his Afrikan name contains the themes of military significance and leadership and hunting skills. Interestingly, he was not necessarily concerned with the military success or failure of the nation whose name he bears. Rather, he lauded their *resistance* against human trafficking. Further, the Chokwe gained a reputation for hunting elephants, trading in ivory, and their artistic contributions to the world. This combination of features demonstrates the well-rounded nature of that nation's culture. Finally, Lumumba's desire to embody traits affiliated with the person and icon of Patrice Lumumba originated from his aspiration to help the RNA achieve political independence from the United States in much the same way the Congo leader attempted to do so for his own country. The African leader enjoyed wide admiration from African Americans during the 1960s and 1970s, partly because he attempted to build a postcolonial Congo without the intervention of Western nations, and because his enemies overthrew him with the help of the CIA.[52]

Alongside this tendency to elect designations loaded with gender specificity, many New Afrikan women and men took on names with gender-neutral connotations that signified one's relationship with the Creator and reminded the individual of her or his life's purpose. Some names conveyed New Afrikan bearers' willingness to struggle for their goals, in this case those of New Afrikan independence and the destruction of white supremacist oppression worldwide. Assata Shakur's name is instructive. As she explained, her married name, Chesimard, constantly reminded her of the pain Europeans inflicted upon her ex-husband's ancestors. She recalled thinking about the name's origins and how a Chesimard in Martinique beat and raped his human property. She wondered "how many Black babies he had fathered, and how many Black people he had been responsible for killing," before deciding to relinquish the name.[53] At some point, the still–JoAnne Chesimard requested an Afrikan name while attending a festival hosted by New Afrikans. She received Ybumi Oladele. In Shakur's recollection, "I liked the way it sounded. Soft and musical, kinda happy-sounding." However, though she requested an Afrikan name and initially felt content with what she was given, she "promptly forgot about it" after a few days because she never felt any particular connection with it.[54]

As she came closer to obtaining her present name, Assata Olugbala Shakur, she decided that she wanted a strong name that aptly described her and her purpose. She insisted that it have "something to do with the liberation of our people. I decided on Assata Olugbala Shakur. Assata means, 'She who struggles,' Olugbala means 'Love for the people,' and i took the name Shakur out of respect for Zayd and Zayd's family. Shakur means 'the thankful.'" In Shakur's case, the significance of her chosen name is multifaceted. On the one hand, Assata found a name that embraced what she believed to be her purpose, namely, to struggle for her people. On the other hand, it encompassed her connection to a particular political family with whom she developed a strong bond.[55] Although she did not do so in her autobiography, one could read her entire name in a manner similar to how Chokwe Lu-mumba interpreted his own. That is to say, Shakur's full name may indi-cate her thankfulness for being given the responsibility of struggling for the people whom she loves. Her dedication to that struggle ultimately led to her violent arrest and imprisonment, torture, and exile to another country away from her family, comrades, and daughter.

Assata's experience of receiving a name during a ceremony or ritual was not uncommon. Bokeba Trice pointed out that the PG-RNA regularly pre-sented new cadres with Afrikan names at various events and celebrations. He recalled that in his experience, it was a popular thing to do: "Particu-larly for the young folks that were coming into the movement back then and even some of the young adults, it was pretty much customary shedding [their] slave names and adopting [their] Afrikan names." At first glance, Trice's comments may reflect a lack of political consciousness on the part of RNA recruits who assumed Afrikan names and suggest that adopting Af-rikan names was simply a popular or trendy activity. As obtaining an Afri-kan name exhibited a certain fashionableness at the time (or could be classified as a fad, according to Herman Ferguson), it is possible that the young Bokeba did not situate the act of taking on an Afrikan name within the full context of black people's struggles for liberation. However, his state-ment provokes several questions: For *whom* was adopting Afrikan names popular? In what context was the practice of taking on an Afrikan name customary? Trice began to answer such questions when he stated that "nam-ing ceremonies were big things back then in the late '60s and early '70s." They were a regular part of Kwanzaa programming and would occur during Malcolm X Day celebrations and other cultural and political gatherings.[56]

Trice's account suggests that black nationalists who collectively partici-pated in activities aimed at re-Africanizing (or perhaps *new*-Africanizing) Detroit's black population helped popularize the practice of acquiring an Afrikan name. In that context, even if Trice initially failed to understand the full significance of assuming his Afrikan name, his participation in black nationalist activities and intentional engagement with elders and peers who actively pursued liberation demonstrate that acquiring an Afrikan name represented more than just a trend. Further, the meaning of his acquired name signified his desire to contribute to the black revolution. Joining the RNA's Black Legion was an additional gesture that confirmed his develop-ing consciousness.

Another Legionnaire, Balogun Anderson, first received his Afrikan name in the late 1960s from a friend who found it in a book. He divulged that

Balogun "in West Africa pretty much means warlord. That's the meaning of it. Warlord. In the Republic, man i was just a . . . citizen soldier."[57] In addition to reflecting the gender norms undergirding Black Power–era New Afrikan name choices, Anderson's contemplation of his name also reveals the salient practice of obtaining appellations that identified bearers as both individuals and members of a larger community. Further, because community played a pivotal role in the giving, receiving, and accepting of names, Anderson's later participation in a naming ceremony befitted his alignment with a broader collective. Coincidentally, during the naming ceremony, he received his name a second time, this time from Nana Oseijeman Adefunmi. He remembered, "We were having a conference and Baba Oseijeman Adefunmi who was a Yoruba priest had gave [sic] . . . me a reading. And I didn't tell him that somebody had already selected a name for me and he told me that that was my name . . . through the readings."[58] Unlike Shakur, who could not connect with her given name, Anderson and Trice felt attached to theirs and used them regularly.

As the experiences of Trice and Anderson illustrate, some New Afrikans took on new names for reasons other than needing to disconnect from the oppressor's culture. They and others acquired Afrikan appellations in the spirit of building communal relationships and developing their evolving political identities. Therefore, their motives were as sentimental as they were political. What is more, some RNA citizens who received new names held on, in part or in whole, to their slave names. For example, Trice did not use his Afrikan middle and last names for long, nor did he completely stop using his birth name, Richard. The fact that some New Afrikans did not rid themselves of every nominal vestige of slavery is as significant as attempts at total disassociation.

General Kuratibisha Ali X Rashid provides a useful example of this tendency, albeit with some qualifications. He maintained his X, a stand-in for the unknown aspects of his heritage, which had become part of his identity. It was something that he felt he had earned because of his experiences within the NOI. He further explained that Kuratibisha is Swahili and equates with "'servant of the people.' Ali means . . . 'servant of Allah' [and] Rashid says that i'm supposed to be wise."[59] Even though he compiled several African and Arabic names that spoke to his political and religious ideals, he indicated, "I don't own my slave name, but i don't deny it either." Rashid never felt the need to completely drop his slave name, although he stopped using it. For him, the slave name is just as much a part of him as the X he assumed when he joined the NOI and his Kiswahili and Arabic names that project his purpose and personal attributes. All of his names reveal the identity he bore since birth and illuminate the qualities he strove to embody as he learned more about himself and his decided purpose. Or, as RNA citizen Jumaani Mweusi stated very simply, with regard to one's name, "Everything that We were, We still are."[60] In other words, even as people grow and evolve, they cannot dismiss the personal history that preceded their revolutionary activism and acquisition of Afrikan names. For that reason, New Afrikans like General Rashid refused to deny those aspects of their lives. Evolving and learning from their past lives and histories remained most important to such revolutionaries as they continued to struggle for liberation.

The theme of maintaining a sense of personal history presents itself in the name story told by New Afrikan lawyer Nkechi Taifa, Esq. The child of two educators and named Anita Caldwell at birth, Taifa found the Igbo appellation Nkechi (which means "gift of God") in a book when she was sixteen years old. As the president of her high school's Black Student Union, she thought that the development of her black consciousness necessitated her adoption of an Afrikan name. A few years later, after involving herself with the PG-RNA, she also took on the surname Ajanaku, which she defined as "struggling for the liberation of all African people until victory or death." However, she discovered that a polygamous family in Tennessee also employed that name, and because she disagreed with polygamy, she decided to discontinue using it. At one point, she married a man whose last name was Owusu. However, she never took his or anyone else's name through marriage. Finally, she settled on using the name Taifa, which means "nation" in Swahili. Over the several years during which she underwent this evolution, Taifa, like Trice, Anderson, Rashid, and others, never completely rejected the name she received at birth. Instead, she legalized her Afrikan name in order to use it in her professional endeavors.[61]

Brother-D.B. Aammaa Nubyahn identified himself with different names at different moments in his life, although for different reasons than those explained earlier. As a youth, he temporarily adopted the name Aa Menis Shaka Arungu. He adopted Menis from the "first pharaoh credited with uniting Upper and Lower Egypt, right." The legendary nineteenth-century Zulu warrior from current-day South Africa inspired him to take on Shaka. Finally, "Arungu's a Swahili word for organizer." Brother-D recalled that an acquaintance who was in the Five Percent Nation of Gods and Earths understood the names to mean the "first and last who sets in order."[62] No one regarded him by that name.

After more thought and self-reflection, Brother-D "felt the need to have a chosen name." However, he felt attracted to denominations other than those with strict African origins. Instead, he confers,

> If someone who had never spoken was to open their mouth to utter a sound that would stand for everything, "aa" is a sound that you don't have to do anything with your tongue, your mouth, you know. You just open your mouth and let that out. But i was like, you can't just be "aa." So i was like okay well if you were to open your mouth and then shut it and then open it again you get "aammaa." Then i went through some spelling changes before coming up with the name "Aammaa." So that's where Aammaa came from. . . . Using this sound as meaning everything, i [originally] put forward "one who has a basic understanding of the universe" and then modified that in years to follow. So i was using that as my last name. So i was Darryl B. Aammaa. So that's late '76. In '79 when i got married, We didn't agree with the idea of the woman taking the man's last name, so We chose a family name. That was Nubyahn. And so Aammaa became my middle name. Darryl Aammaa Nubyahn. And somewhere over the years i began putting the B. back in there. I was Darryl B. Davis and then Darryl B. Aammaa. And then Darryl Aammaa Nubyahn. And i was like, resurrecting my middle initial, and so D.B. Aammaa Nubyahn.[63]

Although he did not initially connect his name with Africa, Brother-D eventually learned that the Dogon of modern-day Mali use the name Amma to signify the Creator. This insight struck him as particularly significant because even though Malians spell the name differently, he developed an admiration for their intellectual achievements and spirituality. Also of importance was Brother-D's willingness to ignore, if not circumvent, the gender conventions surrounding the last names of married couples. He and his then-wife agreed in the 1970s not to force the man's name on the woman, which is an arrangement that, even in the twenty-first century, has not gained much traction in the United States. Further, Brother-D acknowledged that throughout the world, Aammaa, regardless of its spellings, often correlates with "a mother concept, which [he's] cool with." Finally, the Five Percent Nation of Gods and Earths influenced much of Brother-D's understanding of Aammaa. The Five Percenters are a group of black nationalists whose founder, Father Allah, broke away from the NOI during the mid-1960s to start his offshoot. One of their central beliefs is that God is not a spirit that exists outside the realm of human understanding; instead, God is embodied by black men. His reconciliation of that knowledge with his growth since he first assumed Aammaa eventually led him to modify his name's meaning to "one who *seeks* a basic understanding of the universe."[64] Even as they challenge traditional gender norms, Brother-D's names demonstrate another way that the NOI, in this case through the Five Percenters, could influence New Afrikan revolutionaries on a personal level.

Just as RNA activists gave designations to demonstrate a comrade's belonging in and worth to the black nationalist and/or New Afrikan community, they also revoked some people's names. Though relatively rare, on the occasion that someone "sold out" and became (or was exposed as) an informant, their former community banished the use of their Afrikan name, sometimes publicly. In one situation, New Afrikans discovered that a trusted comrade worked with the federal government to locate and arrest Mutulu Shakur and others who participated in the 1981 Brinks expropriation. As former House of Umoja/Afrikan Peoples Party member Dr. Akinyele Omowale Umoja explained, his name was Kamau, but movement publications referred to him as "Peter Middleton" after he cooperated with prosecutors against his former comrades. As Kamau was someone whom Shakur befriended and treated at his drug rehabilitation clinic, the federal government was able to use the man's dependency to convince him to cooperate with their plan to apprehend movement activists. The movement that gave him the name Kamau decided to revoke it: "Once he turned and became a snitch. . . . We called him by his slave name."[65] This may endorse Herman Ferguson's logic. If a person proved incapable of living up to the responsibilities required of a New Afrikan revolutionary, that person forfeited the right to be recognized by an Afrikan name.

Personal name choices played formative and foundational roles in individual New Afrikans' quests for self-determination. First, the practice of denominating symbolized New Afrikans' diasporic African consciousness, their desire to connect with their African ancestry, and the political objectives of their black and Third World contemporaries. That consciousness also fostered in them, or sustained, a sense of responsibility to serve their people. If an individual failed to live up to the responsibilities demanded of a New Afrikan revolutionary, other comrades may have chosen to abstain from calling that delinquent by his or her Afrikan name. Next, New Afrikan name choices arose from RNA citizens' relationships within their immediate communities. Such affinities are significant because they help reveal why activists dedicated so much energy to rethinking names and how various individuals understood their names as an aspect of their commitment to communally based goals and objectives. The interviews illuminate another theme, the entanglement of political and mental decolonization and how the various meanings individual New Afrikans associated with their names facilitated those dual processes. Finally, most of the New Afrikans cited previously continued using their slave names, even when they took on other ones. Although deemed slave names by some, appellations given at birth were not easily disregarded by many activists, even as they came into New Afrikan consciousness.

Taken together, New Afrikan name choices demonstrate that the Black Power–era project of identity reconstruction was much more complicated than the desire of black people to present themselves in ways that made them feel empowered. The focus on identity helped them analyze their sociopolitical positioning within the global white power structure. They reframed conversations about their place in the world and the potential political power they could exercise once they better developed their relationships with other black people in the United States and Third World comrades internationally. In other words, "identity politics" helped create a path for New Afrikan independence advocates to develop a complicated and potentially powerful reframing of a global order that minimized the ability of historically oppressed peoples to act in their own interests. The group designation, New Afrikan, helps explicate their vision and strategy.

The New Afrikan Nationality

If personal names constituted one important aspect of resistance for African people and their descendants, then group designations, orthography, place names, and honorable titles mapped out the ideological terrain on which they could exercise self-determination over their collective identity and, potentially, their political outcomes. Whereas a personal name gave an individual a chance to rethink one's relationship to power and social positioning, the group name, place designations, and other nominal markers clarified the larger goals of the movement. They indicated that such seemingly individualistic pursuits were part of the broader process for overcoming centuries of degradation. Taken together with personal names, then, these mass onomastic objectives contributed to the psychological decolonization of New Afrikans struggling against the U.S. empire from within its political territory.

The long-standing historical struggle of African people to develop a name with which to identify themselves based on their unique experiences in the United States has persisted since at least the seventeenth century. According to scholars Bettye Collier-Thomas and James Turner, black people initially insisted on identifying themselves as Africans. They used "African" in organization names, religious institutions, and many other group-centered social assemblages. However, as distinct African ethnicities merged and Africans produced offspring by force or by choice with Europeans and Native Americans, black people in the United States reconsidered the best names to represent their collectivity.

During the 1830s, many black folks began using "Colored" in order to avoid any association with the American Colonization Society and other deportation and emigration schemes that threatened free Negroes' ability to remain in the United States. Over time, "Afro-American" and "Tan American" (among other titles) provoked considerable debate across the spectrum of African-descended people depending on social position, class, and skin color. By the late nineteenth and early twentieth centuries, "Negro" thrived as a popular group label. Its advocates argued that the designation resonated with the overwhelming majority of African Americans and connected them with black people the world over. In fact, W. E. B. Du Bois, Marcus Garvey, and many other prominent figures championed its use, and it held widespread currency until the mid- to late 1960s.[66]

At the same time, since the late nineteenth century, several detractors of "Negro" also weighed in on the naming debate. *New York Age* editor T. Thomas Fortune and lawyer Everett J. Waring championed the use of "Afro-American," claiming that the appellation took into account bearers' African descent and acknowledged their non-African parentage.[67] By 1948, Richard B. Moore concluded that "Negro" was a vile and inherently oppressive label. In 1960, he argued that it racialized African people and marked them "for a special condition of oppression, degradation, exploitation, and annihilation. . . . If you are willing to accept the slave master's vile appellation 'negro,' [*sic*] you are also willing to accept segregated slums at double rentals and all the disabilities that go with tenth-class citizenship."[68] Moore's charge posited the word as an invention in service of hegemony. In many ways, his claim paralleled that of the NOI.

Just as they did with personal slave names, the NOI played an expansive role in proliferating, through print and television media, dialogue challenging the use of "Negro" as the group designation for African-descended people. According to the NOI, "so-called Negroes" were those people who feared white people so much that they reduced themselves to lackeys of their oppressors at the expense of their own group interests. They worshipped the gods Europeans forced on them and acted contrary to their own well-being. Put simply, the NOI claimed that Negroes lacked knowledge of self.[69]

Viewing the term as a device for European dominance, NOI leaders used "Negro" to critique and deride those black people whom they considered mentally colonized. Minister Malik Shabazz's "The Black Revolution" exemplifies this usage. In the speech, he asked rhetorically, "How can the so-called Negroes who call themselves enlightened leaders expect the poor black sheep to integrate into a society of bloodthirsty white wolves, white wolves who have already been sucking on our blood for over four hundred years here in America?"[70] In contradistinction to Negroes, Shabazz posited "the black masses" as a potential force that could secure liberation. However, he indicated that even though black people in the United States possessed the capacity to gain liberation, they still had a choice to make. He inquired, "Since the black masses here in America are now in open revolt against the American system of segregation, will these same black masses turn toward integration or will they turn toward complete separation?" He questioned further, "Will these awakened black masses truly revolt and separate themselves completely from this wicked race that has enslaved us?"[71] The contrast Shabazz drew between "the black masses" and "the so-called Negroes" is stark. He envisioned the black masses as those people who unmistakably revolted against white supremacy and, in his estimation, theretofore remained unimpressed by the potential of full inclusion into the U.S. sociopolitical system. He believed that because they remained ambivalent about admittance into it, they formed a powerful and dangerous force that, once organized, could potentially help create a separate society in which they could live free from oppression and exploitation.

As Shabazz evolved intellectually and politically, he continued to review and revise how he referred to African people in the United States. Because the NOI was not the only nationalist group challenging the names used to identify black Americans, Shabazz also benefited from the influence of people like Queen Mother Moore, John Henrik Clarke, and many others who strove to identify themselves in ways that reflected self-definition, empowerment, and their connections with continental Africans and African descendants across the diaspora. Possibly inspired by these intellectuals and activists, Shabazz eventually employed "Afro-American" and sometimes "African-American" as his appellations of choice. He also created the Organization of Afro-American Unity and "patterned [it] after the letter and spirit of the Organization of African Unity (OAU)." In addition to reflecting his commitment to Pan-African solidarity, "Afro-" and "African-" signified his desire to participate in the global revolution waged by people of color across the Third World.[72] Shabazz, his comrades, and his self-described disciples shifted their nomenclature throughout the 1960s and beyond. Many of his followers found resonance with the terms "black," "African," and "Afrikan" to describe themselves and their global kindred. Even though they varied on what to call themselves, they all agreed on the problematic nature of "Negro" as a name. For example, Maulana Karenga was quoted as saying, "'Negroes', [sic] still suffer from America's first concept of us—3/5 of a man."[73] The term lost its currency by the end of the 1960s.

NAIM activists joined the chorus of voices debating the name controversy when the organization reconsidered black people's nationality. Along with the question of citizenship—specifically as it concerned black people's right to decide with whom they should give their consent of citizenship—independence activists regarded renaming black people "New Afrikans" more pivotal to the process of psychological liberation than changing one's personal name. According to Milton Henry/Gaidi Obadele (who continued to use his birth name until his death in 2006), the brutal separation of black people from their homelands forced an evolution that prevented them from being Africans in the geographic and strictly cultural sense. Distinguishing the Provisional Government and its advocates from their emigrationist predecessors, he argued that it was practically impossible to migrate back to Africa. Instead, he and the other PG-RNA founders urged that black people in the United States consider themselves a *new* African nation whose home lay in the southern portion of the United States. Queen Mother Moore heavily influenced the endorsement. Having participated in the U.S. Communist Party from the 1930s until the 1950s when they dropped their Black Belt Thesis, she labored as one of the major architects of the renewed plan to acquire land in the South for African Americans.[74] RNA documentation contends that all African-descended people born in the United States are New Afrikans. Again, the title "New Afrikan" distinguishes Africans in America from their kin of other nations and signifies their rootedness in the land that New Afrikans claimed as theirs since 1968.[75]

Of course, one could also advance the thesis that becoming New Afrikan constituted a process in and of itself. As concerns such a process, Brother

Imari regarded being a New Afrikan as largely predicated upon developing a revolutionary mindset. Accordingly, he commented to Black Power activists, "If you are a black nationalist revolutionary, the Republic of New Africa is YOUR Government." Aside from having theorized that all African people in the United States who were the descendants of the enslaved were New Afrikans, his claim depended on the multiple pronouncements by activists that they were carrying forward the mission of Malcolm X. Because Obadele and other New Afrikan intellectuals argued that the fallen leader founded his nationalism on the struggle for land, they could use the claim to align their peers with that aspect of his approach to liberation. There were self-proclaimed nationalists who touted New Afrikan citizenship but who simultaneously pursued goals that compromised the RNA's success. Brother Imari maligned them as *"Negro,"* "unreconstructed niggers," *"comfortable* slaves," and the like.[76] As activists struggled for their versions of liberation, invectives alleging that they were undedicated, misguided by an incorrect assessment or ideology, or—and this was the worst of all charges— working with the white supremacist power structure to undermine the movement were probably the greatest insults. The decades of linguistic work and struggles for self-identification that had taken place within black communities were concentrated and, perhaps, overactive when embedded in these terms. They indicate that the power of words and names was to be harnessed for the development of a given interest group's ideology and objectives. For activists pursuing the creation of a Black Power nation-state, the ability to command language, shape perceptions, and direct conversations was an important tool in the construction of their contemporary reality and future ambitions.

New Afrikan Orthography and Cartography

As part of the larger effort to shape perceptions and exercise self-determination, Black Power–era New Afrikan activists devoted some of their attention to orthography and cartography. The Provisional Government, agreeing with Zimbabwean writer Ruwa Chiri's argument on the matter, decided in the mid-1970s to spell Afrika with a *k* rather than a *c*, because Chiri deemed the spelling more consistent with precolonial African languages. The PG-RNA announced the change in their spelling on November 30, 1975. New Afrikans were not alone in their concern with issues of language, translation, orthography, and cartography. Black nationalists of all stripes participated in this attempt to relearn their ancestors' tongues, and decolonizing nations debated the merits of European languages and externally imposed boundaries. New Afrikans based their spellings on Kiswahili because the popular notion during that historical moment was that the language would become the Pan-African lingua franca for continental and diasporic Africans.[77] But some RNA citizens also endorsed the spelling change due to their pressing desires to distinguish themselves from their oppressor's culture and linguistic norms. Trice recalled someone arguing that the original spelling of the African continent used a *k* instead of *c*. "Now i've never seen any evidence of that," he admitted, "but i do know that it became customary right around that time." Part of his reasoning was that black nationalists wanted to distinguish their orthography from that which they considered as colonial. "So it was more of a protest statement than any actual fact, i think."[78] As a protest statement, New Afrikans participated in a broader discussion among territorially and linguistically dominated peoples. Finding African languages from which to adopt and adapt words and spellings attempted to create revolutionary "linguistic and cultural ecologies" that would help move their black nationalist project forward.[79]

Another way to begin asserting New Afrikans' autonomy and decolonizing black minds was to invert the traditional logic of American liberalism, which posits the individual as the societal unit of greatest importance.[80] The New Afrikan challenge formed around the very simple consideration of personal and group pronouns, spelling "i" in the lower case to mean the first person singular and capitalizing the first letter in "We." Brother Imari seemed to be one of the chief architects of that move as he employed the uppercase "We" and lowercase "i" in his early books.[81] New Afrikans utilized such orthographic practices to promote a group-centered consciousness among RNA citizens; however, the significance may be greater. As residents in, if not members of, one of the world's most powerful nation-states, subsuming the individual to the collective represented a willingness to challenge a larger global order that suppressed the interests of colonized and oppressed populations throughout the world, hence the various overtures to potential interracial allies. Even as many African Americans, some who no doubt were black nationalists and Pan-Africanists, practiced political and economic liberalism in their attempts to find benefits within the American political system, New Afrikans explicitly rejected and attempted to undermine that arrangement.[82]

These decisions corresponded to their land claims and the various ways in which they attempted to name and act upon them. That independence activists chose five states in the U.S. South and sought to rename them the

Republic of New Afrika is of immediate significance. The PG founders followed a tradition in which African-descended people sought land and, very often, autonomy in the areas where they and their ancestors had labored and died. As an amalgamation of people from varying lands, cultures, and political units in Africa, they built upon numerous understandings of the importance of identifying and living on ancestral land. This may help explain why, even in the face of quotidian terror, so many African-descended people refused to leave the South and why others returned after living and working in other parts of the country. For many early NAIM participants, that retention or memory may have combined with romantic notions about rurality as factors in their decision to head south as opposed to remaining in cities like Detroit, which some of their contemporaries deemed the "black man's land."[83]

In their attempts to free the land, Brother Imari and the New Afrikans who agreed with his decision to move into Mississippi combined naming with reimagined mappings to claim the territory as they tried to convince other black people that the South was their ancestral home in America. Therein lies the significance of using the name El Malik to christen the property they intended to purchase from a black landowner named Lofton Mason. Following the tradition of attaching one's self, and in this case important spaces, to recognizable and respected forebears, these self-proclaimed Malcolmites wanted to identify themselves and their territory with a name that many white Americans despised, and which black nationalists revered. Beyond name recognition, calling on the name of this ancestor sought to overlay an area that many black people associated with violence and fear with one of the most valiant African warriors of their generation. Finally, the name El Malik sought to demystify what for many was an inevitable relationship between African Americans and the Deep South. That a sizable group of armed New Afrikans could fly the RNA flag in rural Mississippi unharmed surely signaled to onlookers that black revolutionaries could empower themselves anywhere in a country that imposed the conditions of internal colonization.[84]

El Malik stood just outside what New Afrikans named the Kush District, a collection of majority black counties in Mississippi "running for three hundred miles along the Great River [the Mississippi] from Memphis to the Louisiana border." According to Brother Imari, it contained "nearly sixteen thousand square miles, including the fertile Delta—an area almost twice the size of Israel and quite acceptable as the initial target for the independent

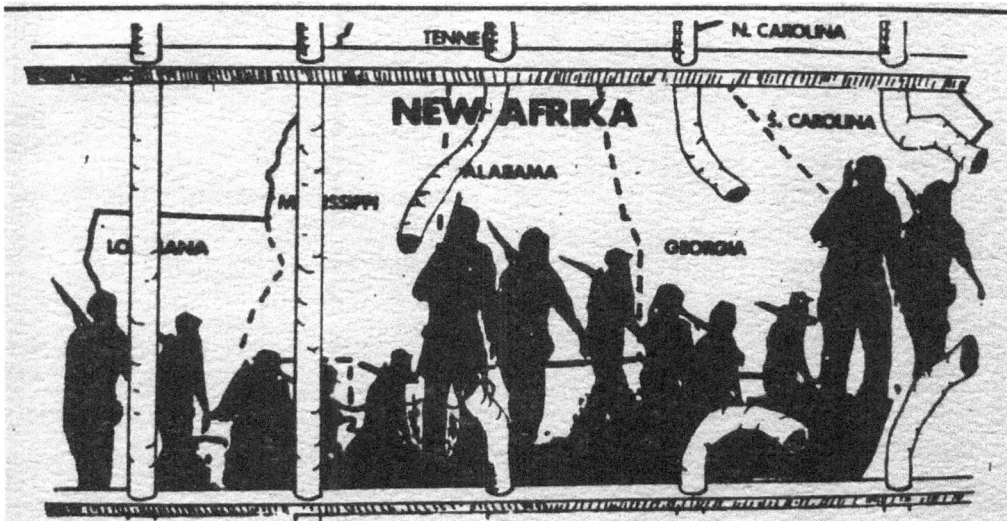

New Afrikan territory behind bars, *The New Afrikan Journal* 3, no. 2, ca. 1982.
Courtesy of Nkechi Taifa.

land mass of our nation."[85] The name Kush, like personal names and the group title New Afrikan, attempted to psychologically connect African-descended peoples in the United States with the continent of Africa. Reframing the area in the image of a revered portion of ancient Africa also sought to remind them of a mighty precolonial black civilization, a project that scholars and activists valued as they challenged American and European political dominance.[86]

The various mappings of New Afrikan claims to land and power, though within the bounds of U.S. and specific state laws, pending a plebiscite, helped concretize their vision for liberation. Early Republic of New Afrika maps highlighted the five states by isolating them from the continental United States. In doing so, the artists embedded the breadth of NAPS in one single visual image. Importantly, the isolation from other states, including Florida, implied that New Afrikan independence was indeed possible. Therefore, cutting off the U.S. nation-state would yield political power. In conceptualizing this arrangement, New Afrikans anticipated and responded to critiques, such as the ones put forth by Huey Newton, which (intentionally and unintentionally) placed socialist revolution in opposition to territorial nationalism. The image of the five states attempted to place New Afrikan independence within an international revolution that would dethrone hegemonic capitalist nations. Future iterations of the RNA map would clarify this relationship.[87]

One version of the New Afrikan territory appeared in the *New Afrikan Journal* in the early 1980s. The image depicts what geographer Priscilla McCutcheon terms a "landscape of liberation" by situating New Afrikan territory behind prison bars. Even as the image reinforces the claim that New Afrikans constitute a captive nation, it also reframes that captivity in terms of possibility. A dozen or so armed silhouettes march across the captive land and push through a section of broken bars. Most of the figures march eastward from Louisiana, but others seem to move southward as if coming from Tennessee and North Carolina, the only other states to appear in this version of the map. Perhaps this signified the charge for New Afrikans outside the National Territory to return "home" and help bring New Afrikan independence to fruition. Further, some New Afrikans prided themselves on being descendants of infamous and unnamed African warriors who never ceased to revolt against enslavement and violence, even at the expense of death. This visual representation of the Deep South claims space for the NAIM with such people in mind. The artist's reimagining of that space considers it the locus of black liberation in the tradition of Denmark Vesey and Harriet Tubman. Finally, it reinforces the potential that the liberation of New Afrika would have significant consequences for the United States, which developed its economic and political power, in part, because of its control over African people's bodies and labor through enslavement, convict leasing, and, by the 1980s, the cohering prison industrial complex. This New Afrikan rendering of the Deep South proclaims that America will not profit in these ways once New Afrikans achieve their goals.[88]

Titles and Respect

Another onomastic matter is that of titles. Though not used by New Afrikans exclusively, "Sister," "Brother," "Baba," and "Mama" constitute some of the common titles RNA comrades in struggle used to refer to one another. More than just signifying a familial bond, which revolutionaries attempted to create and maintain during their involvement with the movement, such titles stood as representative of the society they envisioned. Like other names, these titles were intended to help them overcome any alienation that existed among New Afrikans and between Africans in the United States and black people in other parts of the world. Also, the use of familial and courteous titles provided activists with chances to respect and revere elders, leaders in the movement, and each other in ways that white Americans historically denied black people. "Mama" and "Baba," for example, reminded activists that the movement's elders labored as their teachers and merited respect for the paths they attempted to forge for younger comrades and future generations. Within the PG-RNA, the practice of employing position titles such as "President" and "General" served to create a political culture that corresponded with those of other nation-states and fulfilled some of the requisites the United Nations set for collectivities seeking political autonomy and/or territorial sovereignty.

Taken together, New Afrikan onomastics sought to create a comprehensive revolutionary identity and culture that would facilitate the transition from internal colonization to New Afrikan and Third World liberation. Like personal names, group and place designations began with individuals in a unique collectivity but connected them with similarly positioned peoples throughout the world. These naming practices explicitly rejected the known sociopolitical order in favor of a postcolonial futurity of New Afrikan making. They aligned with NAPS to mobilize a revolution that would remake individuals and the world order. The specific names that they chose were both generative and reflexive in that they imagined new realities even as they responded to the material conditions and historic processes through which they lived.

· · · · · ·

Black people in general and New Afrikans in particular demonstrated their cognitive liberation by taking on Afrikan names in record numbers during the Black Power era.[89] These adopted designations reflected each bearer's need to find mental and spiritual emancipation from a historical and contemporaneous existence rife with oppression as the larger group collectively developed a new society and culture. Although assuming new appellations during the Black Power era appeared popular or trendy, this practice enabled personal and group self-determination that yielded significant political and psychological impacts. When New Afrikans renamed themselves and their children, when they chose a name for their nation and their territory, and when they reimagined the potential of themselves and their geographies, they shaped identity around a political culture that was invested with the power and responsibility to create a new society. Therefore, New Afrikans' onomastic acts demonstrate the most basic and profound examples of decolonized mentalities and capture the essence of lifestyle politics. Naming comprised a mundane yet substantial way for New Afrikans to empower themselves and to bring about a postcolonial futurity through the daily practice of NAPS. Naming, however, was only one aspect of lifestyle politics. For New Afrikans, family, work, and spirituality were also important.

New Afrikan Lifestyle Politics

Personal Histories of Political Struggle

· ·

As the everyday practice of political ideology, lifestyle politics involves the constant interpretation, negotiation, and reproduction of ideas shared between activists, allowing New Afrikans to seek empowerment in the most quotidian aspects of their lives in the movement. Therefore, the concept of lifestyle politics finds expression in some of the most intimate aspects of people's lives, including their weddings. Although there is not one set way of conducting nuptial ceremonies, New Afrikans consciously attempt to bring together varying ideas and customs from across the African diaspora. When Dr. Akinyele Omowale Umoja officiates weddings, they include an Eight Bowl Ceremony, a practice developed in the House of Umoja. Every bowl contains ingestible materials, each representing an ideal that a newlywed couple should seek to exhibit, or an occasion or trial that most people encounter as they build their lives together. The process of explaining and tasting each element casts the matrimonial journey in distinctly political terms that place African and African-descended communities and their cultural expressions at the center of the union. An otherwise commonplace occurrence, such a marriage becomes one indicator of how people may create distinct cultural traditions based in New Afrikan politics.[1]

Inspired by African practices and ideas, and infused with elements of New Afrikan Political Science (NAPS), the Eight Bowl Ceremony demonstrates the dialectic of lifestyle politics as empowering practices and displays the views and beliefs that fill the interstices of New Afrikan daily life. The ceremony reminds us that being New Afrikan in America has been a process, one that constantly negotiates NAPS with elements of Western cultures, and in the cases of people from other countries, their respective customs. A wedding may bring together, for example, people from different countries or religious backgrounds and/or with different cultural understandings. Umoja offers the example of someone with generations of ancestors from the United States marrying a Panamanian. Weddings, like New Afrikans' name choices, also remind us that no two people understand NAPS exactly the same way; or as Umoja states, being New Afrikan is not dependent on "one set ideology."[2] Each New Afrikan had to negotiate distinct daily actions and long-term choices about employment, their perspectives on the New Afrikan family, and spiritual worldview with a unique interpretation of NAPS.

One way to determine how people entered daily negotiations and in what ways such decisions influenced their lives is to provide a life course analysis. Yet, productive as they may be, such studies tend to focus on activists' lives since participation in social movements. Any changes in the lives of participants in a social movement are largely assumed based on self-reporting through questionnaires.[3] A life course analysis that considers life before and during social movement participation offers a fuller explanation of a movement's biographical impact. In-depth interviews concerning various aspects of New Afrikans' lives reveal the rationale for involvement in the New Afrikan Independence Movement (NAIM) and convey the multiple ways in which participation in the movement influenced individual lives.[4] For New Afrikans, the earlier life experience compelled them to seek self-determination and independence as the best remedies for racist oppression. The specific expression of NAPS was based on each activist's political ideals and wisdom gained from past life experiences of being gendered and racialized in the United States of America.

The stories of individual New Afrikans provide details of the forces that drove them into the independence movement, including their experiences with education, family, religious upbringing, and political awareness and activism in their youth. They had varying encounters with racism and developed a range of tools to resist violence and humiliation. Next, they describe their entry into social movement activism and how they became involved in the New Afrikan activism. Those who became conscious citizens of the Republic of New Afrika (RNA) developed a desire to struggle for independence based on what they learned from previous life and organizing experiences. They each had some (and sometimes extensive) contact with people already active within the independence movement by the time they decided to join those efforts. Finally, the New Afrikans featured in this chapter provide a sense of how movement activism shaped their lives. Just as they had a range of distinct personal experiences prior to joining the movement, participation in it yielded a variety of results in their personal lives.[5] Despite important differences in upbringing and encounters with U.S. social and political norms, coming-of-age experiences taught the people under study here to embrace black liberation through self-determination and independence. Once in the movement, their ways of thinking about and making decisions regarding family, education and occupation, and religion reflected their political allegiances and goals.

Pre-RNA Gestation: Childhood and Youth Experiences

The people who became New Afrikans observed and experienced racism and other forms of oppression embedded in U.S. society and interwoven through every aspect of their lives, namely, their socialization in schools, their early religious associations and training, family upbringings, and other social interactions. Their experiences led them to critique racism, question the authority of the U.S. government, and study the various ways that oppressed people could find redress for their problems. Therefore, exploring New Afrikans' backgrounds helps contextualize their decisions to become activists, making visible some factors that incited various individuals to advocate for New Afrikan independence instead of only seeking full citizenship rights within the American body politic.

Early Educational Experiences

School was an important space for socialization. As a site of major social and political indoctrination, it brought children and youth into direct contact with the official ideologies of the United States and those ideas that contradicted them. School forced would-be New Afrikan citizens into situations with racial—and for some, gender—oppression, and provided several of them with opportunities to interact with white Americans. For black children, formal schooling was filled with culturally irrelevant and sometimes anti-black course material. Such encounters occurred in the actual curriculum, through both traditional and rogue teachers, through carceral agents, and in their co-curricular activities. The presence or absence of white peers and teachers complicated their experiences, either through providing alternatives to blatant white supremacy or by maintaining the status quo. Such contact helped inform these black children's future decisions.[6]

Marilyn Preston Killingham was born and spent her childhood in Nashville, Tennessee, in the 1940s. During the 1950s she lived in Gary, Indiana, where she was dedicated to her local church and proved to be a bright student. As a young woman, her major aspirations in life were "to marry [a man] and have twelve children." She "wasn't interested in a career." But, because she took pleasure defying the status quo and challenging the broader society's assigned place for women, Killingham decided to become involved in business and destabilize the mostly male composition of that aspect of society. That being the case, Killingham joined Roosevelt High School's Future Business Leaders of America (FBLA), which led her to encounter segregation that left a lasting impression. Killingham explained that when she and another black student attended an FBLA conference in Muncie, Indiana, the conference hotel refused to let them sleep there. As she explained, "It was 1951. And the head of the business—Dr. Studebaker, i shall never forget him—he arranged for me and [the other young lady] to stay in the boys' dormitory at Ball State University. And then We could come and attend the conference at the hotel, but We could not sleep there . . . I don't know how i lived before. I was so busy trying to be accepted in some majority culture that didn't want to deal with me."[7] As a youth, Killingham believed that she could live a life that was congruent with the American dream. She desired marriage, children, and comfort, even as she sought to defy the gender norms that came along with that lifestyle. However, as she tried to assert herself as an independent black woman, she recognized the multiple obstacles that would make attaining her conflicting desires difficult.

Other areas of Killingham's school experience in Gary were defined by racial discrimination. She recalled that most of the schools, the local swimming pools, and Marquette Park Beach were all segregated. Although she did not indicate whether this segregation was legal or de facto, the results were the same: societal norms maligned and treated as subhuman the people who were excluded from the full rights and benefits of American membership. Because of her experiences with northern racism, Killingham came to believe that "anybody that wasn't conscious . . . was crazy."[8] Her racial consciousness and the decision to rebel against patriarchy were indicative of the critiques she would later develop.

Similarly, Khalil Mustafa's childhood educational experiences brought him into direct contact with racial oppression. His parents involved him in a civil rights struggle challenging school segregation. They leveraged their children's lack of access to quality facilities to bring the New Rochelle Board of Education to trial. Mustafa explained that the case "became the focal [point] of the first desegregation case in the North, the New Rochelle school system, the Lincoln School. That's what they called it, the Lincoln School. And the case went all the way to the Supreme Court. The name of the case was *Taylor v. The Board of Education*. The plaintiff section of the suit, my sister was named co-plaintiff. My mother and father, being the next of kin, represented her on the suit. So that's how my education started out."[9] Similar to other plaintiffs across the country, Mustafa's family won their case and helped desegregate New Rochelle's school system. A victory that surely made many proud, the case lent itself to the national effort to provide black children with quality education. However, Mustafa became a "guinea pig" in the desegregation experiment that soon followed. As such, he faced some extreme racism and enforced patriotism within public schools. His responses led him into the penal system and set the course his life would take into his adulthood.

News about the brutal murder of Emmett Till reached the young Mustafa around the time he integrated one of New Rochelle's public schools. In response to the murder, he rebelled against the system by refusing to salute the American flag and recite the American Pledge of Allegiance. His infractions against these rituals in a space that already seemed hostile to his very presence, Mustafa insisted, earned him expulsion and forced him to continue his education in a state reformatory. His school-to-prison experience only exacerbated the pain he felt when dealing with authorities of the United States. While in the reformatory, he experienced—and helped organize other youth to challenge—inhumane living conditions and humiliating forms of torture.[10] Unlike stories of Southern youth, such that of as the Little Rock Nine, who received significant media coverage and public outcry when they were abused, Mustafa's integration story in the North did not garner such attention. It seems that because people expected hostility in places like Arkansas, they were able to see it more clearly there than in a relatively more liberal state like New York.[11]

If the abovementioned experiences were to be expected, Aneb Kgositsile and Ukali Mwendo demonstrate how complicated educational socialization was, depending on the place where and time when one lived. Mwendo began his public education in the mid-1950s, after the *Brown* decision and following the brutal murder of Till. However, because Leonard C. Jones Elementary School was located in an all-black neighborhood, Mwendo did not directly associate with white students and teachers. Nor did he experience the hostility that Mustafa recounted. Instead, he recalled with fondness the ways that his teachers recognized and nourished his intellectual gifts.[12] Kgositsile's experience was more complex due to regular relocations at the behest of the U.S. Air Force, which employed her stepfather. She first attended a segregated school in Tampa, Florida (her birthplace), during the late 1940s. Then, upon moving to Salina, Kansas, she was "very conscious of racism" due to how her teachers and the white children with whom she played treated her. However, she also attended schools in Bermuda and England where segregation and anti-black hostility did not shape her experience. When her family later moved back to the United States, she attended school in Springfield, Massachusetts, before graduating from high school in Sacramento, California, in 1959. A white teacher at Sacramento's McClathy High School noticed her intellectual promise and mentored her. He encouraged her to attend the University of California, Berkeley, where she earned her bachelor's and master's degrees.[13]

The experiences of would-be conscious New Afrikans were complex. Some of them experienced hostility and aggression from white teachers and peers. Integration in their local schools brought them into close contact with white students and teachers, who helped shape their understanding of racism and other forms of oppression. Others, like Mwendo, suffered indirectly from the broader system of racial oppression, which ensured that he and his peers did not have resources equal to their white counterparts, but spared them from the antiblack hostility from teachers and schoolmates. Still others did not recall encountering harmful or painful attitudes and actions in their schooling environments.

Bilal Sunni-Ali grew up mainly in the South and North Bronx in New York City. As a child in the South Bronx, he went to school with mostly black children. But when a series of organized tenement building fires forced his family to relocate to the North Bronx, his contact with other school children changed drastically. He went from being part of the majority to becoming a minority student in a mostly white environment. Although he recalled being uncomfortable with that arrangement, what he found more important was the leftist curriculum of his social studies teacher. Going against the grain of the typical Cold War–era approaches to pedagogy, the Irish American social studies teacher helped Sunni-Ali begin to articulate his thoughts about class and economic inequalities. The teacher's curriculum included "the Communist Manifesto, and he made us study about the French Revolution." Although Sunni-Ali did not realize it then, the texts and teaching helped shaped his political views. He explained that he "thought it was good when i heard it [because] i had listened to my father and his friends talk about their job." He was able to use the revolutionary ideas about which he was reading to better understand why working-class power was so important for people like his father. With the help of his left-oriented teacher, Sunni-Ali deepened his critique of the oppressive conditions he experienced outside of school and those that he learned about from others. He was receiving these history lessons at school as he was gaining exposure to African culture, Islam, and black liberation activities around New York City and as he began his path to becoming an accomplished musician.[14]

Njeri Jackson's experiences in the San Francisco school system of the 1950s and 1960s would also influence her later in life. Beginning in first grade with Miss Duncan, an African American teacher, she was groomed to attend college, something no one else in her family had done.[15] The inspiration to pursue higher education stayed with Jackson through high school, where she began to live what she considered her mission as a Christian to fight for social justice and the human rights of all people. Accordingly, Jackson was the president of her junior high school's student government, and during high school she participated with the Student Interracial Relations Society. Her positions in such political groups allowed her to access the inner workings of the local government, brought her into close contact with the Black Panther Party, and prepared her for the organizing she would do at the University of California, Berkeley.[16]

Out of the twenty-nine New Afrikans who shared their experiences, nineteen of them indicated that they participated in some political organizing or group activity as youth and/or young adults due to their experiences in public, private, and religious schools. For example, Bokeba Trice was chairman of the Black Student Action Movement at Kettering High School, and Nkechi Taifa was president of her D.C. high school's Black Student Union. Taking another route, Khalid Abdur-Rasheed belonged to gangs in North Philadelphia. As his political consciousness developed, he began organizing them to serve and protect their communities. Even those who did not organize understood their educational experience as helping to shape their political consciousness. For Iyaluua Ferguson, it meant "you had to be better than that white guy." But what was more common was that they had complicated experiences with integration, because they came into contact with a range of ideas that pervaded the larger society and guided the policies of the nation's leaders. So, more than just jaded members of a minority group, some of the people who would become revolutionaries were women and men who at an early age determined that they did not have to accept the world as it was. They decided that they could empower themselves and others, and they began searching for ways to do just that. They gained similar lessons from their religious experiences and social activities.

Childhood and Youth Contact with Religion

Religious spaces, like schools, exposed young people to prevailing ideas about class, race, and gender. Future New Afrikans were overwhelmingly raised by Christians, and their contact with both affirming and denigrating religious beliefs resulted in critiques that guided them. One, Njeri Jackson, grew up in the Mormon Church during the 1950s and 1960s. Her impoverished family received food from the local Mormon group on the condition that Jackson and her sister attend their religious programs and services. As young mixed-race girls in the Mormon Church at that time, they were among the first children of African ancestry to be baptized by a religious organization that throughout most of its history preached that African people were "cursed" with the "mark of Cain." That belief, and several personal experiences with the church's racism and sexism, led Jackson to reject religion when she was in her youth.[17] In her own words,

Mormons are pretty sexist in addition to being pretty racist—and i did a speech about women being equal to men. And that there was no justification in scripture or law—now this is how i'm arguing it now, but you know it wasn't in that kind of language—for women to be treated differently and that people should not have any expectations that women should just be mothers, [and] wives, and obey their husbands and stuff. They didn't know . . .'cause i had always been a good little girl and gave my little speeches—and they didn't know that fire was in me. And the bishop came up to me afterward and was trying—came up after i spoke and said "Well, you know, some of our young [laughter], they don't know what they talking about." And that was it for me. Like do *you* know what i'm talking about? What do you mean, i don't know what i'm talking about? And i had talked about gender out of the experience of race. And i said for instance that Mormons believe that blacks are inferior to whites. But i dare any among to say that i'm inferior to any of you. . . . This white man came over and sat down next to me and turn[ed] and looked at me and said, "Wow, i never knew you were a nigger." So you have those kind of experiences in life . . . and so my position was "i never have been one. And i always suspected you were a bigot, but thanks for clarifying." And for me that was kind of it. It was like wow, this is some—and a couple whose names i can't remember overheard him and they were outraged. And they came up to me and said, "Don't listen to that man; what he said was wrong and totally insensitive." *Insensitive?* What do you mean insensitive? That was bigoted and racist . . .'cause they thought i was going to be damaged and marked for life. But i was angry. They tried to clean it up, but there was no cleaning it up after that.[18]

Jackson and her sister were the products of a recently legalized union between a black man and a white woman. Although they never tried to hide that fact, and Jackson openly identified as black, some people chose to overlook it until they were forced to confront her mixed parentage. Because the religious leadership and congregation taught that she was inferior and subordinate for being black and a woman, Jackson decided that she could not hold on to her religious affiliation.

However, not all of her experiences with religion were adverse. Jackson credits the Mormon Church with instilling in her several political and social values that guided her through the course of her youth and became the basis for her political activism and self-empowerment. For example, she decided to embrace vegetarianism in the late 1960s because the Mormon Church emphasized living a healthy lifestyle. "I also took seriously some of the tenets of Christianity," she said. "You know, do good, treat people nice. . . . They say be honest. Share, be loving. I understand at its core what Christianity, Jesus Christ, and the whole crew was about. And i thought those things made good sense." Although she claimed that the Mormon Church mistreated people of African descent, Jackson gained the courage to stand up for herself and her principles in that environment. Her religious experiences also taught her the importance of careful research. She stated, "I had a big mouth. And to have a big mouth you had to back your stuff up, you have to read a lot. And the more you read and learn about the world, the bigger your mouth gets, especially around matters of injustice."[19]

Unlike Jackson, Bokeba Trice did not recall having any positive experiences with religion as a child. Growing up in his mother's house in Detroit necessitated that he and his younger brother attend Catholic church services regularly and attend a recently integrated parochial school where he felt that the religion was being "shoved down [his] throat" by racist nuns whose disdain of African peoples traumatized him. Consider the following:

> I remember probably being in the second grade. We were in catechism class. We were on a chapter about angels. I was thumbing through the book and [i] was maybe six or seven years old. Then i raised my hand and i asked the teacher, i said, "I don't see any pictures in here of it, but can black people be angels?" And she told me, "No." And i'm like, wait a minute—if we obey the Bible and obey the Ten Commandments, get our lives right, aren't we supposed to go to heaven? She was like, "No." I said, "Well, if we don't go to heaven, we don't go to hell if we're good?" She said, "No." I said,

"Well, then, where do we go? We don't go to purgatory if we've been good." She said, "No, there's a place for black people that's like between purgatory and heaven." I'm like, this ain't making no sense. I'm steadily trying to question her and she finally lost it and she leaned over and said, "You dirty little heathen, you dare question the word of God?" And this is a nun with a full habit on. . . . I mean the nuns were very racist. They had this attitude because "this was such a nice quiet place before y'all [African Americans] came here. Since y'all came here, it's been nothing but trouble."[20]

Like Jackson, Trice's early contact with religion included the attempts by some to dehumanize him, in this instance by suggesting that he was not capable of receiving the same salvation that the nuns promised his white peers, assuming they met certain conditions. His mother's participation in a fight to integrate their church compounded his scorn. "And at the time— this was in the late [19]50s—black folks had been allowed to come into the service, but they had to go sit up in the balcony; they couldn't sit on the main floor. So my mother and some other folks led a big struggle against that and finally they decided they were gonna integrate Sunday service." After they succeeded, "half of the white families left." Trice's experience likely mirrored that of many black Catholic children at the time, as there was a nationwide effort of black families and white sympathizers to desegregate their churches and schools. Through his vulnerable position in this struggle, Trice learned early in life that racism had a significant impact on religion. He eventually rejected Christianity.[21]

However, religious spaces eventually opened up an opportunity to do some of the political work about which he was passionate. As chairman of the Black Student Action Movement at Kettering High School and as an active RNA citizen, he decided to use his attendance of Catholic services to spread the good news of the New Afrikan Independence Movement. "We'd come to church a half hour early and We'd be out in front of the church selling *The New African* as all the white folks and some black folks was coming into the church. And there was another brother who had been one of the original young black folks when We had integrated the school years before that."[22] Even though he neither believed in Catholicism nor found many positive lessons in the doctrine that he learned as a child, Trice and some other black youth found ways to empower themselves in the face of opposition.

Sekou Owusu and other New Afrikans had neutral, if not positive, experiences with religion as children and youth. Owusu also grew up attending a Catholic church, where he served at one point as an altar boy. Yet he was never really "gung-ho" about religion, although he remembered voluntarily reading the catechism and other religious material at home. "I believed that stuff, you know, you not supposed to work on Sunday or God is gonna punish you." Owusu also gained exposure to a Protestant version of the Christian religion where he remembered learning the doctrine through songs and Bible stories. However, he never developed a preference for either and eventually stopped participating in Christianity altogether because of the contradictions he noticed between the religion's written principles and the church's positions on sociopolitical issues. "When the Vietnam war came i was saying shoot, well, God said thou shall not kill, and the Catholic Church could just excommunicate everybody. It should say you're outta the church if you go fight that war. But they wouldn't do that, so i said everybody's connected here somehow. I don't understand how, but this is all bogus. So i stopped going to church then."[23] Because Owusu was able to notice a direct connection between the Catholic Church and the war in Vietnam, he decided to let go of the Christian religion. His decision came as the result of accepting new schemas through which he interpreted the war, the religion, and his own experiences. Like Jackson and Trice, these new mental frames helped him rethink his life and how he would live it.

Iyaluua Ferguson also had extensive experience with Catholicism. She grew up in Brooklyn, New York, and was the youngest of five children born to a longshoreman and a stay-at-home mother who sometimes did domestic work outside of their home. Both of her parents were immigrants. Her father was Trinidadian and her mother Austrian. They raised her as a Roman Catholic and instilled in her an obligation to attend services every Sunday. "We went to church and whatever Sunday school We did, We did in preparation for the sacraments or whatever." However, she continued, "church wasn't an integral part of my life." Instead, it was an obligation and a social opportunity. "I had friends in church, and sometimes there was something happening." Even though she entered her first marriage in the Catholic Church, she did not subscribe to the official doctrine regarding issues like birth control. Ferguson also developed dissatisfaction with what she viewed as "a tremendous shackle around people's minds, particularly black folks." And because she never felt a strong spiritual connection to it, she found it easy to let go of the religion later in life.[24]

Bilal Sunni-Ali's mother was Presbyterian, but he never developed any strong connection with Christianity; instead, Islam earned his devotion. The

Sankori Nubian workshop, a "West African, Islamic Institute" that used music, dance, and theater to teach about African culture, first exposed Sunni-Ali to the religion. Chief among the influential people with whom he connected in that workshop were the Shakurs, a group of families and friends who developed a strong relationship through spirituality, culture, and black liberation activism.[25] Sunni-Ali did not relate any stories of negative experiences with the Christian religion. Instead he questioned why, even as they participated in what Sunni-Ali viewed as Islamic practices through their affiliations with Masonic organizations, his parents could continue to reject the religion in other aspects of their lives. "I didn't consider my family backwards, but just on that part of religion and spirituality, i thought there was a contradiction there. I didn't hate my family for it; i just found a family that i could relate to on a different level."[26] Religion bonded him with a new a cultural and political "family" and would impact him in just about every aspect of his life.

Sunni-Ali also gained exposure to African religion as a youth through what he called the Damballah Hwedo African temple. Nana Oseijeman's Order of Damballah Hwedo Ancestor Priests maintained a presence in Harlem and provided people like Sunni-Ali with a mixture of West African and diasporic religious traditions. "And that religious identification with studying about ancestors, studying about Orisas, it was all part of growing up at that point to a lot of us. It was more learning about the world, but learning about it through elders who had identified—who disassociated themselves with the status quo—with society here."[27] This statement and Sunni-Ali's road to Islam suggest that he valued a spirituality that allowed him to continue developing the critique that began with his father's experiences and his exposure to leftist political ideologies, even as it strengthened his connection to African culture.

Similarly, Khalid Abdur-Rasheed and Gwendolyn Zoharah Simmons grew up in Christian households, but eventually each embraced Islam. Each developed questions that went unanswered and each lost, or perhaps never developed, faith in the religion. In Abdur-Rasheed's mostly Baptist family, the questions that Abdur-Rasheed had "would always get stifled. 'You not supposed to ask those questions.' So i wasn't really inclined toward religion as a child." Simmons also developed questions about Christianity, but her grandparents and her Baptist church largely discouraged her from exploring possible answers. One minister in her church did try to respond to her inquiries in what Simmons considered a rational manner. But she was also reading the Bible and found it, especially the Hebrew scriptures, "shocking."

These early experiences with unanswered questions and dissatisfaction opened paths for them to embrace Islam later in life.

Unlike most of the other New Afrikans presented here, Killingham never questioned the Christian religion over the course of her life. She was baptized into Our Memorial United Church, a Methodist congregation in Nashville, as an infant. At the age of thirteen she received her "confirmation," indicating that she understood Christianity, and she remained a Methodist all of her life. Killingham, like many of the black liberation theologians of the 1960s and 1970s, learned to negotiate Christianity with her desire to create a "new society" instead of allowing the apparent conflicts between Christianity and political work to detour her from her faith as it did others. For example, she believed that Jesus was black. "We know that Jesus was not white. He was black. . . . i know that he was black and i know that there was scripture to back that up." For Mama Killingham, there was no contradiction between her religious beliefs and disgust for the political and economic systems of the United States. She stated, "i see no problem with Christianity and the revolution. I do see a problem with Christianity and capitalism. They cannot coexist. Christianity is sharing and capitalism is greed . . . and as a business major, i truly understand it."[28] Similarly, Gaidi Obadele was an ordained Christian minister, and Baba Hannibal Tirus Afrik never gave up his belief in and support of the African Methodist Episcopal Church, even after he embraced Akan spiritual practice.

Yet religion (especially Christianity) exposed many young black people to the pervasiveness of racism in American society. Some experienced racial hatred and societal oppression in their supposedly sacred spaces. Others saw contradictions between the stated doctrine and the actual practice of religious leaders. On the other hand, religious training instilled some principles that even atheists, such as Herman Ferguson, credited with developing revolutionary values. Accordingly, "The schooling, the religious activity, all of that—that was part of my development and growing up and making me who i am."[29] For others, the religious doctrine of their upbringing became a tool for advocating revolution and independence. Regardless of whether they embraced Christianity, early encounters with religion helped many of them develop a critique of societal oppression.

Family Socialization

New Afrikans' immediate family life had a tremendous effect on how the activists came to understand their place in the world. Regardless of whether they were raised in single-parent homes, within "nuclear" families, or in extended family structures, what New Afrikans learned from their parents and other family members was enduring. Their actions, advice, and affiliations guided the choices made by those who would become New Afrikans.

Sekou Owusu and Nkechi Taifa grew up in "nuclear" families. Owusu came up in a working-class family in which his father worked constantly at a liquor store and then as an employee with New York City's transit authority. His mother stayed at home to raise her children and tend to the household before she eventually worked for the local social security office. Taifa was the product of a middle-class upbringing in which both parents held master's degrees and worked in education. From their parents, both New Afrikan citizens learned the value of hard work, self-efficacy, and working toward goals that could improve the lives of themselves and others. Owusu also learned from his father the value of being independent, something that he believed led him to support the NAIM.[30]

Khalil Mustafa also grew up in a two-parent household, but he indicated that his mother, especially, had a tremendous impact on the development of his political consciousness. She was "something like a Pan-Africanist" who encouraged her children to wear their hair natural "like Kwame Nkrumah" and who made sure that the entire household learned about African freedom fighters, including Julius Nyerere and Patrice Lumumba. Lumumba, in particular, was a name that Mustafa heard often in his youth because his mother was involved with a coalition that formed after the assassination of Patrice Lumumba. Through her organizing, Mustafa's mother developed relationships with Clarence 13x (or Father Allah, founder of the Five Percent Nation of Gods and Earths) and Stokely Carmichael (later Kwame Ture) of the Student Nonviolent Coordinating Committee (SNCC). Her participation in African independence activism and the relationships she formed with black nationalists and revolutionaries surely had a lasting impact on Mustafa, who refused throughout his youth to condone oppression and later determined that black people in the United States would gain true liberation only if they secured independent statehood.[31]

Bokeba Trice's mother was also influential. She was a single parent and "an NAACP [National Association for the Advancement of Colored People] activist. And so early in life we were always involved in integrating something. So We were like the second black family to move on the block over in northwest Detroit." As studies of civil rights struggles throughout the country demonstrate, neighborhood integration was never an easy transition.[32] For Trice, it became another early lesson in the power of anti-blackness and northern racism.

> In [19]58 when We first moved on the block that my mother stayed
> on for years—and i was probably about five years old—and i remem-
> ber coming outside to play one Saturday morning and looked up and
> down the block and there were about twenty moving vans up and
> down the street. All the white folks were moving on the same day.
> And i went back in and asked my mother, i said, "Mama, i don't
> know what's wrong with this block, but everybody's leaving. Is there
> something you ain't telling me?" [laughter] You know how mothers
> do, "Baby, when you get older you'll understand." But i ain't ever
> seen anything like that before.[33]

One may interpret Trice's recollection of this experience as childish hy-perbole and dismiss it because of that. However, regardless of the accuracy of his recollection, his telling conforms to studies of racism in the North, which demonstrate that even if white people in places like Detroit supported integration in the U.S. South, when African Americans attempted integra-tion in *their* neighborhoods, many white people exchanged their interest in social justice for hostility, fear, and violence.[34] Trice's story also provides insight into what led him to become involved with the Provisional Govern-ment. Not everyone who witnessed or experienced personally this type of oppression decided to be active in liberation struggle. However, Trice learned from his mother's example at an early age that one way to resist and overcome oppression was to organize against it.

Killingham found inspiration in a great-grandmother who had been en-slaved until she was about sixteen years old. When Killingham was a child, her great-grandmother was a Garveyite whose meetings took place in their home, providing the young girl with her first exposure to political organ-izing. But what stuck with her more were the elder's stories.

> She would tell me and my sister . . . stories around the fireplace
> about—one of the most graphic ones was when [enslaved black]
> girls would reach puberty and these white men would gather, and
> go and select one nice fresh girl from the camp—this was before she
> was freed—and take them and they would pour what she called
> witch hazel—they'd take the young girl that just reached puberty,
> and pour this—granny would say in spread eagle—and pour this

and the girls would be screaming and you could hear them back in the camp. And then these men would run trains on them. And she told that story over and over again. Sometimes more graphic than others. But she would always end, "Don't you eeeever let a white man tech you." She didn't say "touch." "Tech." And it always ended that way because there had been so much exploitation of—and that never left me. Even to this day.[35]

As Killingham indicated, her great-grandmother taught her two major lessons early in life. The first was that black people must organize, and the other was to never to allow white men to use her body for exploitation. That the great-grandmother emphasized brutal gang rape and other forms of sexual violence is significant because she was the product of an encounter between a white man and an enslaved African woman. After emancipation, Killingham's great-grandmother was forced into a marriage with a seventy-year-old white man from which Killingham's grandmother was born. Sexual exploitation, therefore, was something the great-grandmother witnessed and experienced during critical times in her life. With a traumatic family history and the stories of brutal sexual violence, the elder likely explained some of Garvey's political positions about interracial unions in terms that helped the great-granddaughter connect interracial sex with political oppression.

Herman Ferguson grew up in a large, archetypal family with his brother and three sisters in Fayetteville, North Carolina. Both of his parents were religious; his mother was a Baptist, and his father was the superintendent of Sunday school in the African Methodist Episcopal Zion Church. Besides the Christian religion, Ferguson's parents valued education and insisted that Baba Herman and his siblings use their education to get as far in life as possible. Baba Herman and three of his siblings graduated from high school and college. The other sibling died before graduating from high school. Ferguson's father was employed as a mail carrier with the local post office, and his mother stayed at home tending to the children and the house. The Ferguson family observed "aaallll the Christian holidays. All of the non-Christian holidays. All of the political holidays. All of the presidents' birthdays. Whenever there was a day off from school, We observed it, because that meant We didn't have to go to school. And my parents, they would support that. That was the only time We didn't go to school." Given this seemingly "normal" upbringing, what led Baba Herman to struggle for black liberation? According to the New Afrikan, "Being born in the South, i experienced a more in-your-face kind of segregation, discrimination, and outright dislike of you. And they made no bones about it. You lived around them, but you weren't a part of them. You didn't go to school with them. You played with them until a certain age. By the time you started going to school, they would go to their separate schools, you go to your school."[36] Growing up during the 1930s and 1940s in segregated society could have led to a belief in white superiority. However, Ferguson chose to fight against black subordination, ideologically and even physically, during his youth.

Ferguson did not indicate whether his parents encouraged him to struggle against oppression. Instead, he explained that they, in line with the customs of his community, dictated that he comport himself as a respectable young man so that he would not bring shame or embarrassment to his family. Therefore, even as he clearly challenged racial oppression when the opportunity arose, he still participated in "all the church groups, and i sang in the choir, and all of that stuff. So i would say that my politics developed in the black church." Such activities were considered the attributes of a good child.[37] Eventually, though, Ferguson rejected the religion and associated thinking that shaped him during his formative years.

Importantly, not all had the resources to protect their children. Kuratibisha X Ali Rashid explained that he experienced sexual abuse throughout his childhood. Besides teaching him that women were sexual objects, it taught him how white supremacy, sexual exploitation, and even ageism operated in tandem. He also was well aware of lynching. Rashid recalled that when he was about seven, he saw the burning remains of two black men whom local white residents had brutally tortured to death. "They was hanging; they were burning; their penises were in their mouths," he stated. Although he claimed to already have grown somewhat accustomed to terrorism and brutality, he still was not prepared to smell and see the mutilated remains of those men. He ran home in a panic and but was unable to tell anyone. Silence, not communication about and resistance to white supremacist terrorism, was his only available recourse. When the young boy asked whether white people would go to heaven, his mother explained that "all of God's children" can go to heaven. In response, Rashid indicated that he'd rather go to hell than to spend eternity with people whom he learned to associate with violence and inhumanity. For that, his mother severely punished him. At the intersections of his various social positions in society and within his family, Rashid was absolutely powerless. The feeling of powerlessness left a lasting impression on one of the last surviving signers of the RNA Declaration of Independence.[38]

Societal Awareness

Family life, education, and religious experiences are all important realms of socialization in the early development of people who embraced NAPS. These aspects of their private and public lives provided the practitioners of the burgeoning movement with political awareness that led them to seek self-determination as the best method for remedying black people's problems in the United States and abroad. As important were the moments when, as youth, these New Afrikans learned about society away from their immediate families, their schools, or religious authorities. For some New Afrikans, it included being victimized by de jure and de facto segregation. Others learned these lessons through their positive interactions with elders and peers. Still others began developing their political consciousness by keeping up with the civil rights struggles taking place throughout the country. Collectively, New Afrikans' various experiences led them to question the practicality of seeking full inclusion in U.S. society.

Khalil Mustafa learned at a young age to rebel against oppression because of his experiences in school and based on the influence of his mother. Some of his actions earned him time in state and federal detention centers, like the New York State Agriculture and Industrial School, where he claimed to have witnessed and experienced brutality and torture at the hands of those in power over him and other black youth.

> I mean, they used to do things like put dog excrement, or shit, in our hair. And they used to bury us in holes; they would put us—i forgot what they call them things—but they would put us like in a shallow grave and it had a door on there and they would lock us in there. Sometimes they would put us in a hole where they disposed of dead chickens. Yeah, it was very brutal. . . . A lot of people, when you talk about these things, they say that couldn't have really happened, right. But it started from the first day that We were incarcerated at the place. And our people had to come up and threaten to go to authorities to try to quell that action. But it went on anyway.[39]

Mustafa explained that he refused to accept such treatment, so he organized other incarcerated youth in an attempt to put an end to the facility's abusive treatment. More specifically, he "advocated like a boycott of recreation, boycott of eating . . . boycott of work because that was the first time [he] really understood the machinations of slavery." He also notified his parents of the treatment, and they waged a legal battle against the facility on behalf of their son and the other incarcerated youth. Further, Mustafa organized his fellow inmates to protest police brutality taking place outside of the correctional facilities in which he was imprisoned. Therefore, by the time he became interested in participating in the efforts of the Black Panther Party and the Provisional Government–Republic of New Afrika (PG-RNA), he had already gained a wealth of experience with organizing for the needs of his people.[40]

Iyaluua Ferguson never spent any time as prison, but as a youth growing up in Brooklyn, New York, she recognized that society was set up in ways that were oppressive to black folks. She recalled that white store owners were always cheating their black patrons, and that even when sifting through ads to find a place to live, black people had "to figure out whether they took black folk—this was Brooklyn, New York—whether you could move from one area to the other. You couldn't, but We were aware of that." Housing discrimination and hostile relationships with local white business owners were just two ways that Mama Iyaluua learned about America's racial structure. "And so, that consciousness was, i think, a part of all of our lives. People reacted differently. As i became older, i became more militant. More outspoken—i was always outspoken about it. But [i became] even *more* outspoken." Even in her childhood and youth, she was constantly "prepared not to take any crap from anybody," because any given white New Yorker "was always ready to put his foot in your neck if he could." Perpetually primed for combat, Ferguson learned to challenge the forces that victimized her. She emphasizes educating one's self as a key to fighting back. "One of the reasons that you went to school, you knew that you needed that education to beat him [the white guy] back. The other thing though was that in everything you did, even in school, you had to be better than that white guy. . . . You knew you were a black kid, and you had to do more than that white kid did in order to get" ahead in life.[41] Acquiring information and developing her intellectual proficiency provided Ferguson with the tools she needed to resist and survive racial oppression.

Preparedness was a theme in other New Afrikans' recollections of their childhood, especially when the individual was away from the relative safety of a predominately black community. But not everyone insisted on lashing out against each act of racism. Sometimes the struggle manifested as a subtler, though no less important, defense of one's sense of humanity. For example, Baba Hannibal Tirus Afrik lived in Newport, Rhode Island, during part of his early development. There, he learned to resist on a daily basis a similar "in-your-face kind of" racism as that described by Herman Ferguson and which was infused in just about every aspect of the city's structure. He felt that people did everything they could "toward making you white nationalist." Further, "People [were] talking about integration. I suffered from integration. So ain't nobody gon' tell me nothing about white folks. . . . i had to work two jobs, working . . . at the golf course during the day . . . [and] the bowling alley at night. . . . Had white folks calling me all types of names, but i had to take it cause i had to come up with at least some kind of resources to keep myself going." Some of Afrik's other memories of Newport included having to read the book *Little Black Sambo* as part of his elementary school curriculum, and never having one black teacher the entire time he lived there. To further demonstrate the saturation of white supremacy, he maintained that to be considered dark skinned and called "black" was an insult. "Wasn't nothing beautiful about being black," he insisted. In these hostile surroundings, Afrik's family and the AME Church were his only sources of affirmation as an African until he moved to Ohio to attend Central State University. Those black spaces likely provided him with glimpses of black autonomy and helped shape his future desires for New Afrikan independence and statehood.[42]

Ukali Mwendo "never had to deal up front, close, and personal, with white folks" when he was growing up in New Orleans. Therefore, he did not see the personal face of racism until after he graduated from high school. He did, however, experience poverty and a level of deprivation that he began to recognize early on in life. His mother worked as a custodian in Hines Elementary, one of the white schools, which exposed him to the educational inequalities built into American segregation. She regularly supplied her children with hand-me-down "supplies, books, [and] magazines that the school was getting rid of." Although he derived some minor benefits from this arrangement, it added to his experience of seemingly indirect, though wholly systemic, racial oppression.[43]

Mwendo's first encounter with "up front" racism and its mechanics occurred when he joined the integrated military in 1968. As a member of the armed forces, and as a black man who was smart enough to take on the jobs from which white servicemen attempted to exclude African Americans, he experienced sabotage at the hands of superior officers. He recalled that they gave him "special assignments" that kept him away from the rest of the company and away from the instruction and education his peers were receiving. "But because i stayed in touch with the brothers in my company, i was able to keep up with what they were doing. . . . But i could see that they were trying to keep me from doing well on the exams that we had to take."

Because Mwendo's first encounters with such treatment came in his young adulthood, he did not know how to handle it. "I learned how much the cards are stacked against you because the very people you are supposed to go [to] and deal with your grievances . . . are some of the same people who are trying to undermine you."[44] Considering the options before him, Mwendo learned that one cannot appeal to the source of one's problems in hopes of developing a solution. Instead, he began to critique the system that prevented him and others from obtaining substantial redress. The best solutions were to be found beyond the reach of U.S. sovereignty.

Like Mwendo, all of the men and women who became politically active in the NAIM at some point in their lives did so because their early experiences made the pursuit of independent land and statehood palatable. Before fully recognizing the systemic nature of racial oppression, they learned in integrated spaces that white people viewed them as inferior and would use any means in their power to contain them, socially and politically if not geographically, in the "proper" place. Whether they encountered hostility from white people, recognized the nuances of systemic injustice, or simply developed dissatisfaction with the options they saw growing up, they all determined at some point that self-determination was worthiest of their political energies. By weighing what they were being taught and what they experienced in various spaces against their individual goals and ideals, they developed perspectives that opened them up to alternative schemas and, therefore, political goals, such as the unique aspirations of the NAIM.

Rebirth: On Becoming a New Afrikan

As a teenager at the height of the civil rights movement, Ukali Mwendo was developing alternative ideas about how to create a peaceful society. An intelligent young man whose favorite places in New Orleans were Dooky Chase's Restaurant and the public library, he was developing independent and critical thought that found expression in his concept of "a city within a city." In Mwendo's conversations with a neighborhood friend, the only peer with whom he could discuss politics and philosophy, the two came to believe "that the only way to change the world was to start locally. And we needed a place where there wasn't any racial discrimination. Everybody could get a good education. Where food was shared." They imagined that "once that city was established, everyone else would see how good it was and they would want one too. Everybody would get on board with this idea and, before you know it, the whole country and the whole world would be a much better place to live in."[45] Such ideas suggest dissatisfaction with the state of politics and black progress on the eve of the Black Power movement. It also suggests that Mwendo and his comrade were attempting to think critically about the problems they saw and traditional solutions offered. They may also express nascent ideas about independence, though not in the same exact ways that Mwendo would express them from the vantage point of the NAPS in the following decade.

The Black Power era experienced no shortage of formations seeking the liberation of African and African-descended peoples. Locally and nationally, in neighborhoods and at primary and secondary educational institutions, in prisons, in religious spaces, and in cultural hubs, Black Power efforts found diverse homes and expressions. With so many options available, why did some, like Mwendo, choose to pursue independent statehood? How did activists find their ways into the NAIM? Although the former question is difficult to answer with certainty, the latter question has a clear answer. There were a variety of routes to taking on New Afrikan consciousness, though acquaintances and relatives in the movement were a significant factor for many.[46] Sekou Owusu may help us begin to understand what distinguished New Afrikans from other black revolutionaries of their time. He stated, "I really figure that people with a particular bent get involved in this. You know, meaning that you have a . . . certain way of looking at things that are different from other people's perspectives."[47] That "way of looking at things" includes at its foundation the belief that independence, not full inclusion, was necessary for black liberation.

People like Marilyn Killingham may confirm the idea put forward by Owusu. She considered herself defiant as a young woman whose insubordination against social norms partially influenced her to take up business administration, a path that was encouraged for young men, as her undergraduate major in college. Her personal rebellion positioned her to become a trusted adviser to students who participated in demonstrations through the Revolutionary Action Movement (RAM) at Central State University during the early to mid-1960s.[48] However, defiance is not an adequate explanation for what motivated her to join the NAIM instead of an effort that sought remedy within the United States. One important factor may be her relationship with her great-grandmother, a woman who lived through enslavement and who was forced to marry an elderly white man. The stories that she told reinforced what the young Killingham saw with regard to Universal Negro Improvement Association organizing and what she experienced as a black woman in a segregated and patriarchal society. That socialization and her experiences as an adviser to RAM members revealed to her the strengths and weakness of seeking rights within the U.S. body politic. Such experiences helped prepare her to accept the idea of New Afrikan independence. The people she met through RAM facilitated a connection with activists who would later found the Provisional Government (PG), which she thought offered the optimal prospect for attaining true black empowerment.

Killingham became active in the RNA in the early 1970s after living in Maine for about twelve years. In Maine, she "was a minister in the largest Women's Job Corps Center in the nation." The corps "had taken these urban Hispanics and blacks from New York, Detroit, Chicago and put them way out in the middle of nowhere, Poland Spring, Maine, where they [bottle] the water." There, she felt isolated because she was becoming "blacker and blacker" as the Black Power movement was growing. When she was able, Killingham moved to Chicago, where she would have closer contact with her political comrades. "So when We formed in 1968, March 31st, it was very turbulent time. And at that time i was in Maine, so i certainly wasn't in Detroit. I'm not one of the original signers of the Declaration of Independence. . . . But i knew quite a few of them. And of course . . . the Battle of New Bethel took place the following year. In [19]69, everybody knew someone who was in the independence movement."[49] The idea that "everybody knew someone who was in the independence movement" was not limited to Killingham. Among the people interviewed for this study, everyone already had exposure to the idea of independence or to people who were directly involved in the NAIM prior to their decisions to became involved in the movement.

Richard Bokeba Trice, Michael Balogun Anderson, and Shushanna Shakur all maintained close associations during their youth and young adulthood with Detroiters who were directly connected to the PG. Trice lived about two blocks away from Imari Obadele and his family in 1968. Trice had already "started getting into a little bit of activism if you will, probably about a year before that. Some young brothers in my neighborhood came together. We just started doing some thangs in the neighborhood." At the time, he considered himself to be "following Martin Luther King's philosophy of non-violence." After being introduced to the PG-RNA by Imari Obadele II, Trice began interacting "with some people from the Nation and got actively involved and joined." He soon became the minister of information in Detroit, a Legionnaire, and a martial arts instructor. Being a childhood friend of the son of a PG-RNA founder allowed Trice to place himself in a position to achieve various ranks in the Detroit consulate between the ages of fifteen and nineteen.[50]

Anderson became involved with the PG-RNA during the summer of 1968. He had already been undergoing a process of becoming a revolutionary after hearing Malcolm X speak, learning of his assassination, experiencing the devastation of the 1967 rebellion, and then learning of the assassination of Dr. Martin Luther King Jr. Those bookmarks in his life compelled him to cut off his chemical "process," begin developing a Pan-Africanist consciousness, and seek out formations through which he could bring about the changes he thought were necessary for the liberation of black people. He felt that the NAIM provided the most opportunity. Other factors in Anderson's life contributed to his attraction to New Afrikan independence. For example, he attended New Bethel Baptist Church as a child. There, he came into contact with Gaidi Obadele, who regularly visited the church. Brother Gaidi had a reputation among "street brothers" like Anderson, because the lawyer consistently defended them in court. Anderson was also a supporter of the Shrine of the Black Madonna, where a liberation-oriented theology guided the message and work of the Shrine's leading minister, Reverend Albert Cleage. In other words, once Anderson had made the decision to devote his resources to black liberation, there were enough people and organizations in Detroit to provide him with opportunities to explore his left-evolving politics. Meeting and developing a cordial relationship with Imari Obadele provided Anderson with the specific route to the NAIM as a Legionnaire and as a part of Brother Imari's security team.[51]

Shushanna Shakur learned about the RNA on several separate occasions before she became involved. The first was in 1968 when a peer whom she respected spoke enthusiastically about the independence movement. Shakur admitted that she believed New Afrikan independence was a crazy idea. However, her oldest sibling, Reggie, soon spoke approvingly of the movement. Her second oldest sibling, Edwin (now Chokwe Lumumba), similarly praised the concept and the people pursuing it after returning to Detroit for his summer break from Kalamazoo College. The brothers took their younger siblings to RNA meetings and even hosted one in their home when their parents were out of town. The meetings gave Shakur the opportunity to meet Imari Obadele, who impressed her deeply and helped move her into the independence struggle. Interactions with her lifelong friend and mentor, Aneb Kgositsile, kept Shakur involved until she married and began having children. It did not hurt that Lumumba and Obadele advised black students at her Mumford High School and other area schools when they began demonstrating, sleeping in, and walking out of class to bring a black history curriculum, more black teachers, and black authors' texts into their schools.[52]

Nkechi Taifa actively sought out the PG-RNA before she met any activists with a direct connection to the NAIM. Her journey began when she was a politically active youth who decided to utilize U.S. law as one method of serving in the struggle for black liberation. Brutal attacks on the Black Panther Party (BPP) and the trials, incarcerations, and assassinations of those activists convinced her that the black liberation movement needed more lawyers. As a college student, Taifa became interested in the idea of creating an independent all-black nation after hearing a man speak on the topic. A year later, she learned about the Provisional Government and shortly thereafter sent the imprisoned Imari Obadele a letter expressing her interest in the independence movement. Because of his incarceration and relative isolation from the PG, Brother Imari replied to Taifa "with a whole laundry list of tasks he needed done." Significantly, he placed her in charge of creating the Committee to Free the RNA-11, those people who, like Obadele, remained under some form of state supervision as a result of the August 18, 1971, shootout in Jackson.[53]

Like Taifa, Owusu also learned of the NAIM during his college years. He had just completed his first year at City College of New York, where an English professor helped him realize how ignorant he was of black culture and history. Feeling ashamed of his ignorance, Owusu resolved to learn about his history and involve himself with anything political. He recalled, "The first time i heard about the Republic of New Afrika was in 1968—was during the summer—and might have been in the dorm or at City College . . . so it might have been in September. And i think it was the brother who was the minister of culture. He had a place that was on 116th Street . . . but they were talking about [how] We just declared ourselves independent, and We have this nation, the Republic of New Afrika."[54] Owusu soon met Baba Herman Ferguson, who was one of the signers of the New Afrikan Declaration of Independence; and he met Mutulu Shakur, a young New Afrikan activist who participated in a program called Black Concern. Owusu began volunteering with Black Concern, as well as with a campaign to elect Ferguson for U.S. senator on the Freedom and Peace ticket. Through the connections he had made from that point on, he gained a lot of exposure to the RNA and turmoil centered around the 1969 New Bethel Incident. He explained that he "became a citizen in [19]70" after the New Bethel trials finished. "What i liked mostly about them," he continued, "was that they didn't [complain] about white folks. . . . It was about what We're gonna build and what We can do."[55] Finding the New Afrikan focus on action attractive, Owusu took the oath of citizenship. Since becoming a conscious New Afrikan, Owusu held many positions within the PG-RNA, including the presidency from 2008 to 2011.

Mustafa became interested in the PG-RNA after seeing the Obadeles on William Buckley's television show *Firing Line*.[56] Mustafa had just been released from a sentence at Woodburn Prison, and Gaidi Obadele's arguments for an independent black nation compelled Mustafa to want to "get down" with the PG-RNA. Mustafa had already considered himself a separatist and had been politically active in various carceral facilities. Further, he "had been down with the Black Liberator's Party" and sought membership with the BPP. A sister he knew suggested he contact Fulani Sunni-Ali, daughter of then–RNA minister of defense Alajo Adegbalola and a respected New Afrikan in her own right. "So i called Fulani up and said 'What's happening with the Party?' She said, 'Well i'm not in the Party anymore, i'm with the Republic of New Afrika, that's what's happening.'" What Sunni-Ali emphasized in her conversation with Baba Khalil was that the RNA sought independent land. As Mustafa was a self-styled separatist, talk of land appealed to him. He decided to get involved and took the Oath of Allegiance later that year at the PG's Eastern Regional Conference. From the moment Mustafa took the oath in 1969, he never reneged on his RNA citizenship. Even though he has spent much of his time in various New York State carceral facilities, he found ways to serve the Provisional Government.[57]

Like Killingham and Taifa, Mustafa was interested in the idea of black independence from the U.S. government before he found his way into the movement. Because he knew some of the people already involved, he was proactive about finding ways to participate in the effort. He and many of the others presented here reaffirm Owusu's argument about having developed an inclination toward independence. For Mustafa in particular, his continual confrontations since childhood with the U.S. penal system taught him not to trust the government to properly care for him and his people. Therefore, the PG-RNA allowed people like him to act on their preexisting desire to develop solutions on their own terms and in their own interests. Others, including Anderson, Shushanna Shakur, and Trice, did not necessarily express any strong affinity with the idea of independence before they met people directly involved. But their critiques of their situations and knowledge about other formations led them to believe, once invited to participate with independence efforts, that it was a better option than seeking inclusion in the United States.

New Life: Lifestyle Politics as Everyday Assertions of Self-Determination

The PG-RNA provided a platform calling for a total restructuring of society and reorganization of their daily lives based on NAPS. Documents and statements that outline NAPS charge participants with becoming new people who live by liberation-oriented ideals, creating the ideological foundation for the development of New Afrikans' lifestyle politics. Brother Imari and other prominent people, such as Queen Mother Moore and Chokwe Lumumba, were, at various moments, highly visible manifestations of such lived expressions of their ideas. However, they and lesser-known individuals within this collective effort found various ways to embody NAPS, in how they negotiated their personal work and family commitments and in their spirituality as they embraced black nationalism and made commitments to struggle for liberation.

Education and Employment

The New Afrikan Oath charges pledgees to devote all of their resources, as well as "the total power of my mortal life," to the pursuit of black liberation and independence. Further, the New Afrikan Creed reminds citizens that community is more important than the individual because the New Afrikan community is synonymous with family.[58] The New Afrikans in this study believed that, at least during certain moments if not for their entire lives. Therefore, they made adjustments, including some that affected their educational and career goals as they learned, and attempted to live by, the principles of NAPS. They were, in varying degrees, able to live as New Afrikan citizens in American society. The example of Hannibal Tirus Afrik helps us dig deeper into their struggles and opportunities.

After completing high school, Afrik moved to Ohio, where he attended Central State University, eventually graduating with a bachelor of science degree in biology. He also received military training at Fort Knox, and he was employed by the U.S. Army for thirteen years. He indicated that he "was a company commander [of] over 220 men we took in the streets when the rebellion occurred in '68. And then my final assignment was intelligence, battalion intelligence office. I was on the fast track; they were gonna make a Colin Powell out of me. I would have been a colonel in another 20 years. But [with] the racism in the National Guard . . . i had to change my loyalties and resign my commission after thirteen years in '69." That change of loyalties, specifically, was Afrik's decision to dedicate his efforts to support, as opposed to quash, black rebellion and liberation activities. By the time he was sent to help contain the urban uprisings, he had already decided that he wanted to be a full-time revolutionary. An educator at Farragut High School (now Farragut Career Academy) in Chicago, Baba Hannibal learned before he became involved with the PG-RNA that he needed to help educate black children and youth about their African heritage, as well as their contemporary needs in pursuit of self-determination. He established and ran an independent African-centered school, Shule ya Watoto. Further, he maintained that African people needed to become proficient in science and math so that they could be useful to black liberation efforts in the future, particularly with regard to being able to help the Republic of New Afrika become self-sustainable after independence. Baba Hannibal, since the mid-1960s, worked in the field of education teaching life science and military science until he retired in the 1990s and eventually moved to Mississippi.[59]

Chokwe Lumumba chose his career path before he became a New Afrikan independence activist. Like Taifa, he knew that the movement needed lawyers. The NAIM played a major role in helping him determine how to use his chosen career in service to black people. Lumumba's political leanings had a major impact on his professional career, because he took up cases such as those stemming from the 1981 Brinks Expropriation. Defending supposed terrorists and criminals earned him the contempt of judges and others within the legal community who tried, on at least one occasion, to have his admittance to the bar revoked. Even when facing these possibilities, Lumumba continued to use to the law to New Afrikans' advantage.[60]

Former Legionnaire Balogun Anderson began his career in computers as a direct result of his participation in the NAIM. He stated, "i actually was a prisoner of war during the early part of the [19]70s" because of an "independent action," or an activity that the Provisional Government neither publicly nor officially sanctioned. In this case, he participated in a gun battle that resulted in the wounding of some Detroit police officers. While incarcerated at Michigan State Prison in Jackson, he recalled "getting into computers when i got locked up. . . . i started getting into computers at Jackson Community College; i will never forget it. They used to take you downtown to Jackson, Michigan, at night to the computer classes." When he was paroled in 1973, Anderson moved to New York City because he did not want to be in contact with the same police officers with whom he engaged in warfare, a choice he based partially on the murder of Chaka Fuller. While in the Big Apple, he enrolled at New York University, where he "got into a work-training program. . . . I was working for them as a computer operator in the evening part-time and then going to school and driving a cab and working in music."[61] Relocating to New York may have saved Anderson's life. The movement unintentionally gave him access to a profession that he enjoyed, and the move east allowed him to develop his newfound passion into a career.

Shushanna Shakur decided her career path based on her experiences as a youth participant in the Detroit consulate. There she was a mentee of former SNCC activist Aneb Kgositsile, who worked with others to create cultural programming for Detroit youth. Kgositsile and a brother named Carlice Collins "had us doing drama and developing our knowledge of black poetry and literature." In 2014, Shakur told Kgositsile that such study and practice of black creativity inspired her to similarly teach young people at various points in her life. She took the lessons she learned from the two PG workers and used them to help children and youth develop their own poetic and dramatic skills in the high school English courses she taught and during after-school programs. In addition, Shakur has written and performed short works through the Malcolm X Grassroots Movement (MXGM), a grassroots community organization that grew directly from the New Afrikan People's Organization (NAPO) in 1990. In addition, Shakur gained a great deal of legal education and experience because of the work she did with her older brother, Chokwe Lumumba, and his associates. Although she never completed her formal legal training, she used what she learned to help young people when she was a juvenile probation officer and then a probation parole agent.[62]

Nkechi Taifa worked full time at the African-centered Watoto School from 1977 to 1980. Then from 1980 to 1984, she attended law school at night while working full time during the day at the Washington Office on Africa. Although her interest in law preceded her participation in the NAIM, it was her interactions with Imari Obadele that helped her determine her focus. "I always wanted to be a lawyer [but] i didn't know much about international law or anything like that. That was definitely the RNA. In fact, the reason i'm so sensitized to international human rights . . . is because of my early underpinnings back then learning about the Geneva Convention." Taifa gained such knowledge because in addition to her full-time job and coursework, she was the primary organizer for the Committee to Free the RNA-11, a significant job in itself. She labored tirelessly alongside Reverend Ishakamusa Barashango, a preacher at the Temple of the Black Messiah in Washington, D.C., and a printer by night. The two scripted letters that included the now-iconic picture of the half-naked RNA-11 as the committee's logo. Further, Sister Nkechi spoke on behalf of the imprisoned New Afrikans. Those speaking engagements taught her to develop her public speaking style, which she claimed was in imitation of Brother Imari. When asked whether she was ever paid for the work she did for the Provisional Government, she laughed and answered no. However, the work brought her into contact with "luminaries," including John Conyers, Sonia Sanchez, and Haki Madhubuti, and required her to communicate with Fidel Castro. Although her political work did not begin with the NAIM, working on behalf of the captive Black Nation nurtured her and contributed to the maturation of her political and legal work.[63]

Bokeba Trice indicated that some New Afrikans in Detroit did receive pay for the work they did, though not through the PG-RNA. "I think it was maybe the summer of 1970 when the city had a program called the Neighborhood Youth Corps. It was basically the youth summer job program. And We managed to plug into that and so our youth—the young folks back then—We were actually getting paid to organize and you know the nation-building classes and the whole thang. It was amazing 'cause i remember . . . i was getting paid like $37.50 a week. To us that was big money." Even though he was employed by the city at that point and beginning to rethink his participation with the Provisional Government, the RNA and the things that he learned about nation-building "were really the foundation for everything" that he got into the rest of his life. His employment choices and his conception of family were two major manifestations of the lessons he learned through the practice of nation building.[64]

Trice left the PG-RNA in 1970 after the birth of his first son. Having a child forced him to find a way to support the new life that he helped bring into the world. That need became more critical when the child's mother left, making Trice the sole caretaker of that child and two others who soon followed. However, Trice never relented in his desire to work on behalf of black people, even if not through the PG. He continued "to advocate for the community, to fight for resources—i had a lot of jobs where i had influence or access to major funding that was coming into the city of Detroit and my whole philosophy was to make sure that it got to our people. And i was successful at being able to do that for over a lot of years." He attributed the things he learned as a youth in the movement as being "the motivating factor" behind his future decisions. Some of his work allowed him to organize youth and homeless folks in Detroit through organizations like Project

Lead, which he headed for several years, and through the Hunger Action Coalition of Michigan.[65]

Regardless of whether they received pay for their work in the NAIM, all found some type of personal fulfillment in movement activism. Killingham went so far as to refuse to even consider her role in the NAIM as work. "I don't consider the movement to be work. It's a duty. It's an obligation. You owe it to yourself to get respect. . . . As far as involvement, i participated, i did both sides. I did the civil rights stuff, the freedom rides."[66] Killingham fulfilled her obligations by serving the Provisional Government until her death in December 2009. For some, dedicating one's life to the struggle was far more important than earning a salary.

With regard to educational and career options, these New Afrikans made choices that allowed them to align their career goals with the independence movement. Elder Balogun, like others, made his career choice because of the circumstances in which he was placed due to his participation with the Black Legion. That reciprocal interaction between activists and the movement is an important aspect of lifestyle politics in that it demonstrates how activism influenced participants' life courses. But there are other aspects of New Afrikan Political Science that impacted people's lives, including family life.

The New Afrikan Family

Black nationalists of diverse perspectives developed ideas about the black family during the 1960s and 1970s. Among them, the Nation of Islam, Maulana Karenga and the Us Organization, and the Black Panther Party (insomuch as they were nationalists) have been the subjects of study.[67] The scholarship on these organizations demonstrates that although there were some distinctions between the organizations depending on their political and cultural emphasis, many of them had the same core tenets about family, which included the following: at their foundation, families were heteronormative and consisted of a man, a woman (or women), and especially children. A family may have included immediate relatives, very close friends, and/or comrades in the movement. Next, *strong* black families were vital in the overall success of black liberation struggle. Finally, black families were discouraged from looking to Euro-American and/or capitalist models of family as inspiration in building their own. Independence theorists worked these conceptions of family into NAPS.[68]

Republic of New Afrika

An Afrikan Nation in the Western Hemisphere
Struggling for Complete Independence

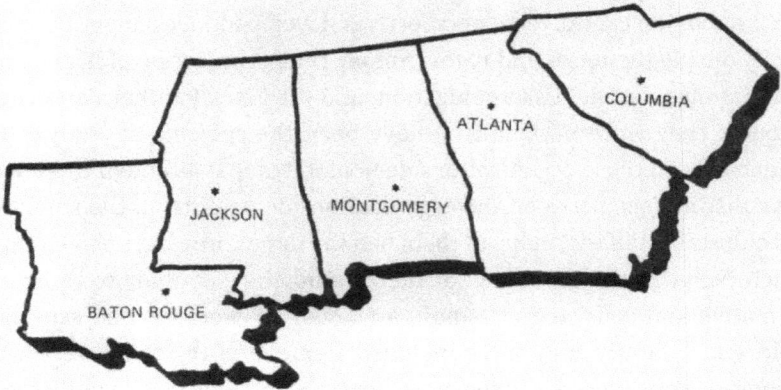

COLUMBIA

ATLANTA

JACKSON   MONTGOMERY

BATON ROUGE

The New Afrikan couple, *Suggested Guidelines for the Land Development Cooperatives*, no date. Courtesy of Nkechi Taifa.

Gaidi and Imari Obadele developed ideas that fit with the broader black nationalist trends of their time and attempted to reimage black marriage. Looking first to "African tradition," as well as their contemporary sociopolitical needs and values for the black nation, the People's Center Council approved the new marriage as an opportunity to build New Afrikan families in ways that would be distinct from American and European models and norms. Because, they argued, the Creator had established the sexes with the explicit purpose of creating new life, and due to the slightly greater proportion of women to men, polygamy was acceptable in the nation, once independent. Besides, polygamy would ensure that each woman had access to a man and no woman would be "forced" to "resort" to same-sex intimacy. Yet Brother Imari attempted to distinguish New Afrikan marriages from traditional marriages of this sort. He argued that the New Afrikan version would respect women's rights to be as free as men if they wanted to maintain multiple intimate relationships outside of marriage. He also claimed that the *New African Ujamaa* would ensure women's economic survival independent of a husband or another patriarch. In these ways, he hoped that marriage and New Afrikan families would conform to the antisexist aspects of the RNA Declaration of Independence and other founding documents.[69]

The Obadeles' approach to marriage was more about permission than it was a mandate to which everyone had to adhere. Yet the concept of polygamy and the aspects of "free love" that also found a home in NAPS became ideas with which New Afrikans had to negotiate. Most people did not seem openly interested in participating in these arrangements. Taifa decided against using the name Ajanaku because of its connection with a polygamous family in Tennessee. For Jackson, the RNA stance on polygamy was one of the factors that prevented her from becoming a citizen of record. However, other women, like Queen Mother Moore, responded favorably to men's having multiple wives. Afeni Shakur, a Black Panther and conscious New Afrikan, entered into a polygamous relationship, which was based more on her husband's religion—he was Muslim—than on any black nationalist ideologies. She stated in her biography that the arrangement was problematic for her because of the pain it caused the other woman, not because she disagreed with the principle. Further, men like Afrik and Abdur-Rasheed built families, each with one woman at a time, and seemed to value one-on-one marriages. And although he initially saw it as his right to be in an open marriage, Chokwe Lumumba came to realize that his embrace of free love caused more pain to his wife than it was worth.[70]

One New Afrikan man, General Rashid, agreed with the idea that a man should be allowed to take more than one wife. He explained that during the 1970s, two of his wives were security personnel.

> I will talk about one of them 'cause she's a major figure [in that we were] trying to make her some kinda like Queen Mother Moore of the military. . . . She was highly skilled. She was—in that group she was the oldest wife and she was older than most of the females [in the] military. . . . She was one of the first national trainers that We had—i'm talking about that was a female that had both male and females under her command. She solved the problems herself. If a brother did something to disobey her rule, she told him to go get his gear. She got beat up a lot of times, but she got the respect.[71]

The reference to Queen Mother Moore is important, because it indicates how much respect Rashid's wife had earned within the security structure of the RNA. Even as he acknowledged that he held many sexist views in his lifetime, Rashid never doubted that women could serve in military positions with men. His emphasis on his Legionnaire wives is instructive of how he tried to negotiate his admitted sexism with the needs of the movement.

Next, Rashid argued that having multiple wives was consistent with his religion, Islam. He stated: "I'm Muslim. I believe in polygamy, but i don't believe in pimpin'. You understand? And one reason i don't practice [polygamy] now is 'cause it can get expensive, 'cause if you do it according to the Qur'an, you have to take care of them. Whatever that family is that she brings, you have to take care of 'em. So that can get expensive." Rashid distinguishes his practice of polygamy from sexual exploitation and argues that he was never interested in running around with several women simply for the sake of controlling their sexuality and reproductive labor. Instead, his relationships with his wives included the responsibility of providing for each woman and whatever "she brings" to that arrangement—more specifically, her children. General Rashid explained that he had twenty children, and "seven or eight" of them were his biologically. The remainder came into his family through his wives. In addition to the potential expense, he claimed that polygamy is not a practice accepted by the larger society, and he would not want to do anything to bring disharmony into the community. Therefore, he stopped entering such unions.[72]

In some ways, Rashid's comments are in line with the patriarchal views and concomitant structures that various feminists challenged vigorously during the 1960s and 1970s.[73] Yet there are some aspects of his outlook that depart from traditional sexist logic. Even in some of his most sexist moments during the 1960s and 1970s, he always advocated for what black feminist Linda La Rue called "role integration." He believed in giving women the same responsibilities, protections, and promotions within the PG-RNA that were guaranteed for men.[74] Supporting this take, Marilyn Killingham credited Rashid with being the most vocal advocate and supporter of her unsuccessful run for the presidency of the PG-RNA in the 1980s.[75] During our conversations, he was adamant about giving both men and women credit for the contributions they made to the NAIM and the PG-RNA. Considering Rashid's belief in the RNA Declaration of Independence and his participation in the Legion, he likely came to admit and attempt to modify his sexism based on edicts demanding that men respect women as their equals in revolutionary struggle and combat.

But one must keep in mind that Rashid's antisexist stance pertained to the struggle for black liberation, not to his personal or home life. "We had the government," he explained, "and We had business to take care of, and We was pretty disciplined in terms of leaving the baggage at the door when We was entering the arena [of liberation struggle]. And We got to be pretty good at that. So i never had no problem with none of my wives."[76] The baggage they left at the door included disputes that occurred within their household. That General Rashid believed they were able to prevent such tension from getting in the way of their liberation struggle responsibilities suggests that they valued New Afrikan independence enough to try to keep their family strife "at the door." Rashid's comments apparently challenge the concept of the personal being political. His advocacy of separating his public and private spheres makes it seem as though he applied two different philosophies depending on whether he was at work or at home, including with regard to the wife of whom he spoke so highly. She still ranked lower than he did. She ultimately had to follow his orders, not the reverse. As he did in their home arrangement, he maintained a dominant position in their political relationship. Importantly, some New Afrikans have critiqued the Provisional Government for a broader trend of male dominance and the dismissal of women's ideas, especially when they were critical of the PG or the movement.[77]

Baba Hannibal Afrik also maintained a traditional patriarchal family. Although he did not have multiple wives (apparently, very few men did), during mid-twentieth century he insisted on building his family according to the conventional "breadwinner" and "housewife" paradigm. He was the sole head of his household who instituted the family's migration from semicontented liberal Americans to black revolutionary nationalists. When he became active in the movement and began to strongly identify as African, his wife and children did the same. In particular, once he and his comrades created an independent school, Afrik's wife "saw the benefits, [and] she began to become more supportive." From there, he and his family changed their names, began to dress differently, and exchanged European traditions for African-inspired ones. As he explained, "I told my kids We ain't celebrating Christmas no more, and when people would say 'Merry Christmas, what do you want for Christmas' . . . they had enough strength to say 'We don't celebrate Christmas, We celebrate Kwanzaa.' But that was because the reinforcement, my wife and i being on the agreement and the chillun following our examples. And when they saw they could get Kwanzaa gifts, that made it more palatable."[78] In some ways, Afrik's dedication to the movement and his views allowed for harmony within his family.

Still, discord periodically caused havoc within the Afrik family because of the large amount of energy Baba Hannibal placed in the liberation movement, the transitions the family underwent because of their rapidly changing views, and the dangers of being a black revolutionary in the 1960s and 1970s.[79] Even though his wife respected him enough to allow him to lead the family into that turbulent arena, Afrik admitted that he "made a whole lot of mistakes trying to be [a revolutionary]—jeopardized my family, my job, and my health. . . . But in retrospect i spent eighteen years doing double duty at working at school and at Shule [the African-centered independent school]. Almost destroyed [my] marriage and my family, resources and all that."[80] Many would probably considered Baba Hannibal and his family a model for others to follow in the movement. Consistent with the New Afrikan Oath, he dedicated most of his resources to the movement, both in the independent school he was helping to run and because of the roles he served within the Provisional Government. His family seemed to adapt as his views evolved, and even though they went through many transitions, they were able to maintain their family unit.

Sekou Owusu described his ideal New Afrikan family as fully embracing yet going beyond the specific guidelines in NAPS. He indicated, "You have the creation of the new man, the new woman. So the whole thing was a rebirth about New Afrika; that's why it's the Republic of *New* Afrika. So during the whole movement thing that goes beyond just the creation of the Republic of New Afrika is that idea that We gotta be new people, new birth, We gotta take new values, We gotta get the slave master's stuff off. That's always been in the theme of the movement of black nationalism."[81] The

"Educate to Liberate," *The New Afrikan Journal*, ca. 1980. Courtesy of Nkechi Taifa.

newness of which Owusu spoke sought to be comprehensive and inclusive, instead of choosing, say, economic nationalism as the singular path to self-determination, something that the New Afrikan family was supposed to embody and reflect.

Owusu emphasized the importance of independence in the everyday life of New Afrikan families. The household should be "that place where you're supposed to value what is more African as far as your motif. . . . You're supposed to read a certain type of way; you're supposed to try new values in the sense that you're not supposed to bring all that stuff from off the street, running around with other women and that type of stuff." This includes celebrating Kwanzaa "or some other holidays that are relevant to you" instead of, or in addition to, Christmas. His ideal New Afrikan family dressed differently, rejected slave names, educated the children in independent schools, and was involved in political organizations that helped the community. In other words, "you're no longer European, so that's that kind of stepping out the box, being independent. I guess that's the sense of the whole movement in general. You gotta be independent. Separate yourself from white America."[82] Although the practices that Owusu mentioned were not unique among New Afrikans, the conscious desire to perform them in concert with achieving statehood distinguished New Afrikans from other Black Power formations. As a nation, the RNA presented independence activists with opportunities to openly embrace a variety of nationalist tenets while still pursuing their distinctive territorial objectives.

New Afrikans have had varying degrees of success in achieving this ideal, especially when assessing their children's acceptance of NAPS. Bokeba Trice suggested that his children demonstrated in various aspects of their lives that they have embraced NAPS, or at least black nationalism, more broadly. "All of my children have Afrikan names. I have four children. Seven grandchildren. Many of my grandchildren have Afrikan names. So they were raised in a New Afrikan household. And as youngsters they traveled with me to conferences and conventions around the country. So, We didn't celebrate Christmas in our household; We celebrated Kwanzaa. They were raised in a very cultural African surrounding."[83] His oldest son, especially, has shown interest in and agreement with Bokeba's political beliefs by giving his children Afrikan names, deciding to wear African clothing, and remaining intellectually and socially engaged with the black community and its struggles. Trice's other children accepted these ideals in subtler ways, such as by giving their children Afrikan names.

Aneb Kgositsile did all that she could to raise her son in black liberation and African-oriented spaces. It was important that he be educated outside of the American mainstream, so she and several comrade educators created an African-centered school. Originally named Alexander Crummell Center, it became Aisha Shule/DuBois Preparatory Academy and functioned from 1974 to 2013. After high school at Cass, the young man attended the historically black Tuskegee Institute, now Tuskegee University, where he studied physics and created a technology company, Motown Wireless. According to Kgositsile, he has used his expertise to set up technology hubs in black neighborhoods whereby community members could learn technology while accessing resources that benefited their communities. The company states that it would like to bring "low cost internet access, hardware and digital education to" Detroiters. He has also volunteered at African-centered schools and has enrolled his daughter into one. "So he's one of the Babas and [is] on the Baba team" there. Kgositsile explained with pride that her son is "very happy to have been brought up in the culture and to have that kind of grounding."[84]

However, passing on the knowledge of NAPS could not guarantee that the recipients would accept, internalize, and apply it in the ways their parents may have hoped. Killingham, for example, tried to raise her son as a New Afrikan. However, he rejected the overt aspects of the NAPS, especially its positions on racial solidarity, New Afrikan self-determination, and the war against white supremacy, which he considered racist. He preferred liberal notions of multiculturalism, which he thought was more in line with his Muslim faith. Killingham's only child converted to Islam as a college student during the 1980s. He came to understand any type of racial pride as contrary to the will and purpose of Allah. On the other hand, he embraced the idea that capitalism is destructive. Again, he couched his reasons in Islam as opposed to New Afrikan Political Science.[85]

For Khalid Abdur-Rasheed, the ability to raise his children was complicated, despite having a wife and a father-in-law who both pledged allegiance to the RNA and lived according to NAPS. Abdur-Rasheed raised his children to be proud New Afrikan citizens, even though they did not embrace it in the ways that he originally imagined. A revolutionary nationalist, he met and married a cultural nationalist woman named Daima, Reverend Barashango Ishakamusa's daughter. They met when her group, Pure Black Poets, performed at an event Baba Khalid helped organize. He courted her through a series of letters he sent her when he was jailed following a demonstration that blocked Girard Avenue in North Philadelphia. He recalled, "When i came home she said, 'You coming over?'" He exclaimed, "I'll be right there." Then confirming the depths of his Philadelphia upbringing and his excitement, he added, "I walked." Together they sought to bring the cultural nationalists and revolutionary nationalists together for the cause of New Afrikan independence. The two gave their four children names such as Lumumba, Najashi, Naima, and Ishakamusa, which were inspired by religious figures and loved ones in the liberation struggle. They also participated in New Afrikan independence activities, such as meetings, physical fitness routines, and military training. But Baba Khalid and his children point out that he did much more. He was a peacemaker in his D.C. and Philadelphia communities. He was (and continues to be) "Baba" to dozens of children and their parents.[86]

Baba Khalid's children grew up in the movement, and the younger ones seemed to attract their peers. Because they were doing physical fitness training, orienteering, and learning self-defense (something that Alajo Adegbalola loved doing with the Abdur-Rasheed children), other children in the neighborhood were exposed to the teaching and training. It did not hurt that at least one of Abdur-Rasheed's children had a reputation as "Karate Kid" because of his ability to handle himself in scuffles. Whenever the New Afrikan parent learned about such violent interactions, he attempted to use them to build friendships between "brothers" instead of allowing young people to fight against one another. When considering what he did for his family and community, Abdur-Rasheed referenced duty and obligation: "This is what we supposed to be doing as black men, you know." He also expressed deep love for and inspiration from his comrades. His community and family were his strength.[87]

Dr. Njeri Jackson recalled that her young family did not have a chance to mature in NAPS. The August 18, 1971, shootout in Jackson took place when her daughter was only two. Two months later, her husband, Michael Finney, and two comrades made their way to Jackson, Mississippi, under the auspices of helping the Provisional Government. Jackson did not learn until years later that the mission may have included liberating Imari Obadele from detention. "You know that saying, 'The old make the wars, the young fight them,'" she stated—pain still in her voice four decades later. It was partly this experience that dissuaded the "wife of the bro-tha" who hijacked the plane to Cuba from taking the oath of citizenship. That decision also came from her critiques of patriarchy and sexism, the feeling of abandonment by the Provisional Government during her time of great need, and her growing distaste for pledging allegiance to any entity, whether it be the United States of America, the Mormon Church, or the RNA. This is not to say that Jackson viewed everyone who worked toward New Afrikan independence disapprovingly. In fact, she was lifelong friends with people who went out of their way to take care of her and her toddler, emotionally and economically, while Finney was sitting in a Cuban prison awaiting a decision on his fate. People like Yusufu Sonebeyatta, Akbar and Kristen Cleage Williams (Reverend Cleage's daughter)—"these are at the heart, i think, of . . . a fundamental quest for a better world." When her family was suffering in the aftermath of an act that some considered criminal and others heroic, these were the people who helped her navigate the tumult of the time.[88]

New Afrikan Spirituality

Unlike the New Afrikan family, there are no stipulations or precepts that guided people toward a singular entity called New Afrikan spirituality. The preamble to the *New African Ujamaa* states, "The supreme purpose of all of our activity, economic and non-economic—in short, the purpose of life—shall be to solve the mysteries of life and death."[89] The claim echoes the RNA's Declaration of Independence and the New Afrikan Creed and finds complementary references to biblical scriptures at the opening of some of Imari Obadele's published texts.[90] Brother Imari and others had, at one point, likened nation building to a larger divine purpose of relieving humans of oppression and hunger so they could more fully pursue spiritual enlightenment and elevation, but they never restricted individuals' spirituality to any one approach or religion. Instead, they embraced people's right to choose their own religious ideologies. Therefore, people brought Christianity, Islam, Yoruba, Akan, other religious systems, and atheism into the movement. Doing so made sense because activists envisioned the RNA as a revolutionary socialist republic, not a theocracy, which allowed people with a range of spiritual worldviews to bring their varying perspectives together in relative harmony.

Afrik stated that he was "involved with African spirituality from a large ecumenical vein. But i'm still in AME Church 'cause i believe that there's hope." Claiming that he appreciated the work King and other preachers did to make the Christian church useful to the black community, Afrik stated, "I'm not gonna turn the other cheek and that kind of stuff. I respected him for what he believed, what he lived, and what he was prepared to die for."

Speaking as a lifelong member of the AME Church, Afrik argued, "That to me is where AME Church has failed 'cause we still in the church" as opposed to feeding and clothing people out in the community. "You talk about Christ, Christ was a revolutionary; he was an activist. He was out there with the people." When he was still based in Chicago, Baba Hannibal was able to take some of his community programs to the AME Church. "Had i not brought programs to the church in Chicago, they wouldn't have been accomplished if i were outside the church." Afrik made full use of Christianity as a tool for the New Afrikan revolution. Although he remained a member of the AME Church and believed that revolutionaries must be more involved with the church in order to accomplish some of their goals, he also came to embrace African spirituality, especially that practiced by the Akan. In these ways, he maintained a connection with an institution through which he believed he could create programs and propagate the ideas of the NAIM. Further, he could nourish his spiritual connection with his ancestors and bond with other Africans across the world.[91]

Other New Afrikans have also learned to embrace African spirituality, sometimes along with Christianity and other times by itself. For example, Sister Nkechi Taifa claimed that she attended Sunday school in her childhood and youth but came to practice African spirituality in her adulthood. Not restricted to any one spiritual outlook, she participated in both the Yoruba and Akan Temples. On the other hand, Sekou Owusu never got into any religions after he left the Catholic Church. He never embraced Islam, which was popular among many of his associates, and he did not look for any other forms of Christianity. He had had enough religion and did not want any more. Instead, he was drawn to ideas that emphasize the power and divinity of each individual. "You know, ancient Kemet talked about becoming gods and you worked on your internal stuff to raise your consciousness. I'm kind of on that bent." He also expressed some openness toward West African religious traditions that his comrades embraced.[92]

The Fergusons, Jackson, and Trice also had their fill of Christianity, although to varying degrees and with different outcomes. Whereas Baba Herman claimed not to know anything about an almighty God, Mama Iyaluua and Jackson did not completely discredit the idea of serving the purpose of a higher power. Instead, both described themselves as agnostic, with Jackson finding spiritual power and fulfillment through Yoga, meditation, and holistic health.[93] Finally, Trice stayed away from Christianity for a significant portion of his adult life because of his painful childhood experiences with Catholicism. However, he did try to find ways to "develop spiritual understanding" by reading various religious and spiritual texts. Trice stated, "I read the Qur'an, i read the Bible, i read the Egyptian Book of the Dead, [and] the Kabalah" before becoming a Baptist in 2001. He eventually became a deacon, taught Sunday school, and ran several ministries in his church.[94]

Several others embraced Islam at various points in their lives. One of Abdur-Rasheed's favorite aunts affiliated with the Nation of Islam and offered him an alternative worldview. Though she never spoke directly to him about Islam, she left the NOI newspaper within his reach. He recalled being impressed by the brothers who worked for Your Cleaners, the NOI's cleaning service. He "found them to be kind of impressive, too, with their suits and their ties and their mannerisms." However, Khalid never joined NOI because he did not believe in some of the doctrine. But he "respected their mannerisms and courtesy."[95] Bilal Sunni-Ali embraced Islam as a youth, but Gwendolyn Zoharah Simmons learned about Sufism as an adult. Others accepted Islam through the Nation of Islam and found variations of the religion that suited their needs. Like many of those presented here, they were dissatisfied with Christianity because of perceived contradictions and unanswered questions. It is likely that some of them, similar to Iyaluua Ferguson and Sekou Owusu, just could not accept the religion but embraced Islam as a way to connect with something more meaningful and more consistent with their views of black liberation.[96]

Of the people interviewed for this study, only Elder Balogun claimed that his contacts within the NAIM aided in the development of his spirituality by exposing him to new ways of approaching religion. "Well you know at this time man i was really kinda experimenting. Like i said, Baba Oseijeman Adefunmi was a Yoruba priest. I was looking into Orisa, Voodoo, and some remnants of Islam, [and] Buddhism, and then like i said the Pan-African Christian Orthodox Church [was] getting started then, so i was looking into that." He learned through his interactions with these people and institutions that with "as many ways to the Creator as there are, you know, all roads eventually lead to him anyway." From that perspective, he came to believe that there was no reason to choose any one religious or spiritual worldview over another. "I don't consider myself a religious person. But i'm more spiritual now; that's becoming the acceptable thing. But i'm open-minded about all religious endeavors. I can't say that there was one that i favored above others. I still tap my foot to and shake my head and walk back and forth to a good gospel tune—you know what i'm saying. But i can also feel something when it's a call to prayer in Arabic."[97] Elder Balogun seems to approach religion and spirituality in a manner similar to the Provisional Government, which as the pregovernmental body for a *nation*, not a theocracy, never dictated that its citizens adhere to any one religious worldview. The belief in a racial-political nation is the dominant idea within the New Afrikan Independence Movement.

· · · · · ·

New Afrikans created new frames through which people would come to understand many aspects of their ideology and lifestyles, though lifestyle choices were not the single most important factor in their struggle for independence. Each person's experience as a racialized, gendered, and classed being in the United States prior to becoming involved in the NAIM helped shape how they understood everything, from education and spirituality to family and career paths. It was their understanding of their own life experiences, along with their observations about the broader society, that informed their decisions to become active in the NAIM. And it was based on that understanding that these activists then decided to reenvision their families, reimagined their life's work, and made other quotidian but significant choices about their lives. They took such ideas and attitudes into the movement, where they inevitably had a profound influence on the Provisional Government and on the NAIM.

For example, African American Studies scholar John Bracey recalled a moment at the Black Government Convention when Queen Mother Moore, Gaidi Obadele, and Oseijeman Adefunmi debated which religion would provide the most opportunity for New Afrikans.[98] Similarly, New Afrikans had conversations and debates about how culture, education, and many other aspects of human life could be potentially liberatory or oppressive. New Afrikans negotiated their preactivist orientations—those outlooks and principles that they developed through their experiences in a racist, sexist, and capitalist society—their worldviews as adults, and the daily challenge of being New Afrikan in the United States, which made for a dynamic process through which they developed new understandings that they then applied to their activism. It was a total, cyclical process, not a one-way cause (activism) and effect (biographical impact). That is where the power of lifestyle politics resides. How New Afrikans decided to live out the ideologies guiding their practice became an important site of tension and agency that allowed activists to begin exercising self-determination, even as they resisted the violence and domination of the American state and its citizens.

Another major influence on activists' lives was their relationship with the state agencies responsible for policing the country and stopping people and ideas that threatened to undermine the status quo. New Afrikans, much like their predecessors and peers, had to endure the routine and sometimes brutal repression that played no small part in preventing them from achieving their goals. Even though they were aware of and tried to anticipate a range of government actions, they did not fully theorize and prepare for the multifaceted onslaught that they ultimately experienced. To be sure, local and national policing agencies and their strategies and tactics for undermining New Afrikan independence efforts had an impact on the movement and on activists' lifestyle politics.

5 Cointel's Got Blacks in Hell

State Repression and Black Liberation

I didn't know about COINTELPRO then, but I knew something was
amiss.

  The United States of America would have you believe that i am
a criminal, that We are all criminals. That just isn't so.

—Geronimo ji Jaga

I am a New Afrikan soldier, and We have an absolute right to fight for
our freedom. . . . What is necessary to exercise that right is to stand up
like men and women and exercise it.

—Sekou Odinga

Fulani Sunni-Ali lived on a farmhouse in an area called Byrdtown (located
in Gallman, Mississippi) with her elderly father, Baba Alajo Adegbalola,
and Jerry Gaines, another New Afrikan woman. Together, they ran one of
the Provisional Government's education programs for children on their
property. On October 27, 1981, at approximately 6:00 A.M., about two hundred federal agents from several states, armed with tanks, machine guns,
and helicopters, raided the property. They handcuffed and arrested everyone (including the children, save two infants) at gunpoint. The suspicion
that Sunni-Ali had conspired with Black Liberation Army members in a
recent "expropriation" of an armored Brinks truck in upstate New York
inspired the raid and rough treatment. While justifying their actions to the
public, the FBI announced that they uncovered a cache of weapons at the
rural Mississippi home. That "cache" included "three .22 (squirrel) rifles
used to hunt small game, and two larger caliber rifles. Each gun was legally registered and none [had] been involved in any crimes."[1] The FBI labeled Sunni-Ali, as they had done with all of the expropriation suspects, a
terrorist.[2] Although the state soon had to drop its original conspiracy
charges against Sunni-Ali, the state decided to use another legal tactic to
harass and intimidate her; that December, it subpoenaed her to participate
in the grand jury investigation of the expropriation. Viewing the grand

jury as an attempt to intimidate her and other movement activists and as a method to place her at odds with her comrades, Sunni-Ali refused to cooperate. She determined that it was better to remain steadfast in her convictions and to maintain the trust of her comrades, even at the expense of her personal freedom. The federal government used her resistance as another opportunity to prosecute and jail her, taking her from her loved ones and educational work.[3]

FBI press releases and media coverage of the raid and the circumstances surrounding it signal some limits to self-definition and the complicated and interactive processes by which identity construction occurs. Although the methods by which New Afrikans organized and expressed their collective identity and lifestyles are important, forces outside of the movement also played an important role. Entities like the FBI, local policing agencies, and the press influenced collective identity through the development of "alter versions."[4] If those entities considered New Afrikans as criminals, black militants bent on destroying America, and as cop killers, then such images would partially influence New Afrikan collective identity construction, sociopolitical positioning, and daily life choices.[5] Alter versions helped justify repressive actions targeting New Afrikans and placed a range of limitations on them. Although New Afrikan responses and reactions to repression helped shape the New Afrikan Independence Movement (NAIM), such impediments were not strong enough to stop the movement.

To be sure, New Afrikans prefigured government repression in their strategy. Just months after the National Black Government Convention, Detroit citizen Warren Galloway reportedly believed that the Republic of New Afrika (RNA) was "completely infiltrated by representatives of the Federal Bureau of Investigation (FBI), the Central Intelligence Agency (CIA), the Michigan State Police, and the Detroit Police Department. He indicated that he personally was endeavoring to ascertain the identity of these informants." An unidentified FBI informant delivered this interpretation of Galloway's comments to the Detroit Bureau office without a hint of irony.[6] Galloway's statement and the reporting of it reflected the general security consciousness of New Afrikan independence activists. Although such forethought and its concomitant planning brought them relatively little ability to prevent or withstand state repression, the notion factored into the construction of New Afrikan ideology and identity. As a captive nation, New Afrikans used the reality of repression as a reminder of their condition and the need to change it through independence. They also used it to justify some of their military actions.

Both perceived and actual repression had an impact, psychological as well as physical, on people who were attempting to bring their goals of self-determination and a new society to fruition. In fact, that aspect of repression is important because it provides a glimpse into one of the many ways that social movement participation led to the detainment, injury, and death of activists and their loved ones. For example, one aim of government repression was to create fear and discord among targets. After the raid on the RNA home in Byrdtown, it is reasonable to assume that the children suffered in immeasurable ways due to the disruption that the raid caused in their lives and their treatment at the hands of law enforcement. Because one of the key adults was immediately taken from loved ones, the other adults were, no doubt, forced to reconsider their participation in the Provisional Government–Republic of New Afrika (PG-RNA).

The raid reminds us that black activists, including New Afrikans, were subject to a laundry list of repressive actions, including continual surveillance and harassment by police, media smearing, and even murder.[7] The primary reason New Afrikans' antagonists went to such great lengths to undermine activists was because the activists' ideas ran counter to the American status quo. Although those who opposed them labeled New Afrikans and others as violence-prone criminals and sometimes terrorists, the potential for violence mattered less than the threat of their ideas. That political alternatives to the status quo existed and sometimes gained traction made them worthy of neutralization. As one supporter stated: "The message is this: You cannot oppose the policies of the U.S. government, you cannot resist these governmental declarations of war, and if you do we will send an army to terrorize you, your family, and any of your supporters."[8] By the 1980s, the PG-RNA was able to determine, through the Freedom of Information Act, the full extent that they were targeted and attacked by "one of the most bizarre and sinister—and illegal—plots of the COINTELPRO era."[9] By that point, their efforts had stalled, supporters distanced themselves from black left activism, and several self-determined RNA citizens were wards of the state or recent parolees. Nevertheless, the independence movement would outlive the era that birthed it.

FBI Repression of Black Revolutionaries

From its inception in 1906, the Federal Bureau of Investigation (called the Bureau of Investigation until 1935) viewed the political Left as dangerous and, often, un-American. Along with anarchists and socialists from Europe, as well as striking factory workers, dissidents of African descent required special resources for control and neutralization, at least according to the FBI. Alleging that dissatisfied black women and men were the political dupes of the Soviets, the FBI took various actions against any efforts that challenged the racial and economic status quo. Included on the Bureau's radar were Marcus Garvey and the Universal Negro Improvement Association (UNIA), A. Philip Randolph, Dr. Martin Luther King Jr., the National Association for the Advancement of Colored People (NAACP), the *Chicago Defender*, and multiple other individuals and organizations. FBI Director J. Edgar Hoover and his agents initiated counterintelligence programs (or COINTELPROs) against them, even as the Bureau refused to investigate in earnest the rampant murders and other abuses that victimized black people across the nation. The director and his agents viewed black people as potential threats to the nation, not a group in need of protection. The purported inability to safeguard African Americans from savage terrorism, and its own repressive actions against those desiring equal rights within the U.S. political structure, revealed that the Bureau's agenda was to keep African people in a position of subjugation.[10]

The fear of the black self-activity led to the Bureau's formal launch of a COINTELPRO against black nationalist "hate type" individuals and groups in August 1967. Following several waves of urban rebellions in black communities, Hoover nearly doubled the FBI's activities. An extensive network of agents, informants, police, media personnel, utilities operators, pub owners, and market vendors helped surveil and neutralize civil rights and Black Power activists.[11] Hoover ordered his field offices to develop imaginative means to prevent the rise of a black "messiah" and to maintain the racial political order.[12] Agents' methods were effective in that their actions resulted in grave bodily harm, psychological trauma, imprisonment, and/or death for African Americans whose major crimes were their insistence on exercising their civil and human rights and self-determination, through peaceful or violent means.

Field offices in various locales worked together to spy, at one level, on high-profile targets such as Stokely Carmichael/Kwame Ture. The FBI and CIA surveilled Carmichael in the United States and monitored his activities abroad. In 1970, the Senate Subcommittee to Investigate the Administration of the Internal Security Act and Other Internal Security Laws summoned him to testify about his activities.[13] He and other public targets are representative of a much larger program of monitoring and policing of black bodies by Uncle Sam.[14] Yet such monitoring was not reserved only for known radicals; the FBI spied on entire black communities from Watts to Harlem and Bronzeville to the Ninth Ward, allegedly to identify the people who agitated for and participated in urban rebellions and other forms of dissent. This breadth made potential targets, their neighbors, and their families the subject of memos that landed on Hoover's Washington, D.C., desk. Reported surveillance even extended to black-owned bookstores, neighborhood social spaces, and cooperative businesses. Considering the scope of this COINTELPRO, it seems that the entirety of black America was a target.[15]

One such example is the African Students Association (ASA) in Pasadena, California. Members of the organization advocated for self-determination and boasted friendships with Jonathan Jackson and Angela Davis, potentially associated with the Us Organization, and expressed goals that aligned with the NAIM. Their willingness to consider New Afrikan programs and goals earned the organization attention in FBI documentation and made certain that people who lent meeting space became targets for deeper research.[16] Although the available documents do not detail how agents gathered further information about the people they added to their indexes, it is safe to assume that their methods included interviews with employers, friends and relatives, and even the target. Gathering intelligence on the ASA fell into what social scientists designate as "intelligence/covert actions." They also identify two other categories, including legal repression and violence. Some scholars also break repression down into "soft" and "hard" repression. The former is typically covert and includes regular monitoring and infiltration by informants and agents, bad-jacketing, defamation in the local and national press, and making targets the avatars and recipients of bogus mail. Hard, or overt, repression includes harassment, arrest, raids, and violence against intended targets.[17] As targets of many such actions by the state, New Afrikan Independence advocates lost opportunities to organize and experienced periods of strategic stagnation. Repression shaped, in part, the development of New Afrikan collective identity and, therefore, lifestyle politics.

FBI documents on the Henry brothers, the Group on Advanced Leadership (GOAL), and their affiliates provide ample evidence that even before they championed armed revolution, people who would become New Afrikan citizens were targets of state repression.[18] For example, the FBI monitored Betty Shabazz, whose life was of interest to the state since at least 1958. They kept tabs on where she lived, where she traveled on a daily basis, when she married Malcolm X, when she became pregnant with her children, and with whom she communicated (including the mayor of

New York City).[19] Because she was the wife of Malcolm X, one might expect (if with disgust) such a high level of surveillance on her, even down to such personal issues as her pregnancies. Perhaps it is to be expected that, like Sister Betty, GOAL and the Henry Brothers in Detroit were targets of FBI monitoring and infiltration. The Henrys had decades of experience challenging white supremacy. The feds took interest in these activists' public proclamations, the relationship between GOAL activists with the Revolutionary Action Movement (RAM) in Detroit and in Cleveland, and the formation of their aboveground self-defense clubs. The Bureau was especially on edge about the latter. In an "URGENT" memo, Hoover ordered field agents to get information not only to verify the formation of the Medgar Evers Rifle Club but also to conduct background checks on the informants and police officers monitoring GOAL.[20] Although these examples, as well as that of Betty Shabazz, did not include any recommendations for violence against these targets, they are indicative of how agents of the state constructed alter versions of activists and their families, even the unborn ones. In addition to identifying activists and assessing them as potential threats to national security, policing agencies framed any acquired information in ways that created fearsome images of activists. If they could convince the public that revolutionaries were violent black criminals, that would deter potential members and allies. Although it is impossible to accurately quantify the state's success, current scholarship agrees that surveillance was a necessary component of policing agencies' neutralization programs. By nurturing a culture of fear, they prepared for more obviously malicious forms of repression, including letter writing, rumor, legal repression, and eventually physical violence.[21]

FBI and police infiltration of New Afrikans in Detroit was indicative of the movement's compromised security. However, New Afrikans lived all over the country and were mobile. So, too, were agents of the state who followed Dr. Gwendolyn Zoharah Simmons, a onetime supporter of the Provisional Government and a citizen of record. Dr. Simmons recounted an experience during which she drove from Cleveland to Detroit for an RNA event. She and her three passengers, all New Afrikan citizens, noticed that someone was following them. The New Afrikans could not verify who their pursuers were. However, they "were white men in suits. . . . Every time we stopped to get gas, they stopped." Dr. Simmons was convinced the men wanted the travelers to know they were under surveillance. "I was terrified of what was going to happen," she explained. However, surveillance seemed to be the extent of their activity that day. Regardless of who the unidentified men were, Dr. Simmons perceived them as agents of the state assigned to monitor her and the other RNA citizens. Being surveilled so blatantly caused her distress, not least because her comrades were armed and prepared for the possibility of confrontation with their stalkers.[22]

Marilyn Killingham was surer of who was monitoring her, as well as their intentions. She claimed that the FBI "*wanted* you to know that they were following you. When they changed shifts with the cars that were following you, they made sure that you saw them. I mean, they *wanted* to run you crazy. They wanted to harass you; they wanted to hurt you or make you hurt yourself."[23] If, as Killingham and Dr. Simmons claimed, the state wanted activists to know that they were being followed and monitored, it raises the question, why? What did these agents hope to gain from such visibility? Ward Churchill and Jim Vander Wall indicate that the purpose was to induce paranoia in political activists, "making them aware they'd been selected for special treatment and that there was 'an FBI agent behind every mailbox.'"[24] Such paranoia would exacerbate inevitable personality conflict and would increase those tensions, straining already-fragile relationships.

One of the FBI's stated goals was to deter its targets from gaining the support of potential allies. Robert Williams's distrust of people like Imari Obadele and other key citizens confirmed that if people saw the signs of monitoring and infiltration, they would be more likely to stay away from compromised groups and individuals. And they had decades of experience to confirm the effects that great distress could bring about in their targets. Having knowledge that one was being watched, listened to, followed, and potentially targeted for violence increased the likelihood that that person would respond to the situation with actions that could easily justify greater repression.[25]

The arrests of Ahmed Obafemi and Tarik (misidentified in some sources as Malik) Sonebeyatta demonstrate how policing agencies used soft and hard repression simultaneously. In July 1972, Obafemi and Sonebeyatta attended the Miami Democratic National Convention as "official envoys of the RNA with orders to distribute literature to [Senator George] McGovern's headquarters." Specifically, they were circulating copies of the RNA Anti-Depression Program, which outlined a plan for reparations. At one point, Obafemi attempted to approach the presidential candidate from South Dakota but was apprehended by local authorities. It was rumored that Obafemi and Sonebeyatta had planned to harm McGovern and others after Secret Service agents found two handguns in their borrowed automobile. Fear of assassination attempts soon passed, but Obafemi and Sonebeyatta did not win their release. Instead, they were each tried and convicted on three firearms charges and sentenced to five years in prison.[26] Newspaper reports claimed matter-of-factly that the FBI agents, who had been surveilling Obafemi and Sonebeyatta, tipped off the Secret Service that the two New Afrikans were worthy of a special vehicle search. No one questioned why the two men were under FBI surveillance or why the agents decided to make the Secret Service aware of their presence after joining the convention instead of running interference and searching them before they could potentially place convention goers in danger. It seems that by the early 1970s, news media had accepted the idea that black nationalists were synonymous with criminals and, therefore, did not require any investigation into activist or FBI intentions. Another possibility is that certain papers and reporters were working with the FBI to develop and disseminate these ideas.[27]

Whatever the case, it is rather curious that the men were caught with concealed handguns at an event where there would surely be heightened security. The RNA minister of justice, Chokwe Lumumba, stated that "McGovern, Humphrey, and the convention Vice Chairwoman and several other political figures at this convention were apprized by letter prior to this convention that we would be here and what we would be about."[28] Assuming those individuals received the communication, Obafemi and Sonebeyatta would have expected that their presence as New Afrikans at a political convention, especially months after the Lewis Street shootout that resulted in their president's incarceration, would result in greater scrutiny. Also, Obafemi and Sonebeyatta's envoy assignment came just months after activists gained solid evidence that the FBI had played a major role in undermining their activities. Therefore, some extra precautions, such as inspecting a borrowed vehicle for any items that could possibly give state authorities just cause to apprehend and detain, were in order. Finding or even possibly planting two handguns in the New Afrikans' borrowed car allowed the state to achieve two goals simultaneously. First, in detaining their targets, policing agencies and media were able to build on their story of New Afrikans being criminals, possibly deterring potential allies from joining the independence effort. Second, by placing them on trial and in prison, the state effectively drained economic and human resources from the NAIM. For this reason, especially, legal repression was a fruitful method of disrupting black revolutionaries. The legal process was often lengthy, expensive, and in itself generated plenty of damning press releases against trial defendants, even if the charges were later changed or dropped or convictions overturned.

The mixture of covert repression, legal actions, and unfavorable media attention all provided the state with the elements they needed to create alter versions of New Afrikan collective identity. Mobilizing alter versions delegitimized New Afrikans and the goal of territorial liberation. Projecting them as dangerous criminals and even terrorists, the U.S. government sought to deter people who may have agreed with the RNA's goals from getting involved. The state simultaneously used the alter versions to justify violent actions against New Afrikans and their allies. Personal recollections, newspaper articles, police and FBI documents, and recent scholarship all confirm that the FBI was effective in its endeavors. Taken together, these sources paint a comprehensive picture of how activists' lifestyles were altered.[29]

Repressive Action and New Afrikan Collective Identity at War

New Afrikans claim that the United States has been waging war against African peoples for decades (if not centuries). "Warfare" is a useful framework for examining repressive action. War is a struggle between two or more groups that can be, and typically is, associated with a recognized state of armed conflict. Thus, we often frame it in ways that bring the carnage of U.S. soldiers in Vietnam or their combat in Afghanistan to mind. However, war is more expansive than the horrors of napalm and unmanned fighter drones. In many cases, such as the protracted battles between oppressed groups and their oppressors, war goes undeclared. As nothing more or less than active struggle or antagonism between two or more entities or competing forces, combatants develop various ways to wage struggle.[30] War can be blatantly physical like the examples mentioned earlier, or it may seem more as an ideological "cold war." Regardless, harm reaches out beyond those who are consciously participating to determine the fate of innocent children, noninvested captives, and those who may seek refuge from it. Its physical impact is always felt, even if not completely understood, as it undermines people's humanity and limits their chances at achieving the best possible life for themselves and their loved ones. Finally, war has a noticeable impact on the way future generations remember it. Even if the "winners" of the war choose not to tell the story, they regulate how the "losers" remember and disseminate that story. All of these characteristics of war are present in the history of the NAIM.

In the "Article 3 Briefs," Imari Obadele writes that the centuries-old "War in America" includes the kidnapping; brutal dominance through mental, physical, and sexual abuse; and theft of labor that came with enslavement. The war did not end with the promulgation of the Emancipation Proclamation and ratification of the Thirteenth Amendment. Instead, he argues, in the aftermath of those two legal acts, the U.S. government and its citizens actively fought to suppress any nationalistic self-activity in black communities. It "was, then, the consecration of a campaign of war and fraud by the American community against the new class [of recently emancipated Africans], wrongfully and illegally to prevent the new class from exercising the full range of political liberty that belonged to it. . . . Indeed, the Fourteenth Amendment attempted to *order* the new class into the American community." Worse still, "that membership would be limited politically and socially." He continues, "It is not too strong to say that all this was—and is—war."[31] So, too, were the various acts of resistance against the dominant nation.

Murders of human traffickers, slave owners, and overseers; organized rebellions; individual and collective escape attempts by enslaved peoples; and their volunteering to fight for the various military entities that promised freedom or improved conditions may factor into this framework, alongside attempts to emigrate and form homesteads and black towns and more recent efforts to protect black communities against lynchings, bombings, and police brutality. One may also include in this the creation of organizations, clubs, and protest movements, as well as the urban rebellions in locales such as Watts, Detroit, and Louisville, Kentucky. The shootouts at New Bethel and Lewis Street were two of the most famous New Afrikan skirmishes in this war, and for some, they were snapshots of the routine repression executed by the oppressive forces battling against the NAIM. Framing the movement in these terms allowed New Afrikans to include in their discussion New Afrikan political prisoners and prisoners of war. It legitimized the choice by some to dedicate their skills and resources to the military aspect of the movement. For the student of social movements, the conflict between the U.S. state and New Afrikans further reveals the consequences of attempting to live according to the values and goals of the NAIM.

Episodes of Violence

New Afrikans and law enforcement participated in several overtly violent interactions between the 1969 New Bethel Incident and the 1981 raid on the RNA home in Byrdtown. The FBI and police planned some, such as the raids in 1971 on the Lewis and Lynch Street houses. Others, like the New Bethel

Incident, seemed to be more spontaneous. Regardless of forethought, these occurrences demonstrate how covert repression and legal maneuvering such as traffic stops support deadly repressive actions. Both soft and hard repression also helped shape alter versions that figured into New Afrikan collective identity and became powerful, if undesired, aspects of lifestyle politics.

The New Bethel Incident is by far the best known event in New Afrikan independence history.[32] That fateful evening revealed the deep, long-held tensions between police and black communities. It reminded all involved that activist formations willing to challenge the status quo were especially vulnerable to violent encounters due to long-standing abuse and misgivings about armed representatives of the state. More concretely, many black Detroiters were distrustful of the police because of the violence local law enforcement inflicted in their neighborhoods. Police brutality, poor housing conditions, and the lack of substantive response to black Detroiters' needs fueled that tension, especially in the aftermath of the 1967 rebellion. Further, job and housing discrimination and illegal drugs wreaked havoc on many individuals and helped facilitate the "blighting" of many urban black communities. And Detroit is just one of the many cities that exemplify this problem. Various people from New York, for example, have given similar descriptions of the conditions that typified locales where black people became involved with RNA consulates.[33] Put simply, many New Afrikans who lived in such conditions and witnessed and/or experienced anti-black policing had a reasonable expectation that confrontations with policing agencies were not far off. Therefore, it is not surprising, especially in hindsight, that some were prepared to defend themselves in such an event.

The death of Chaka Fuller is perhaps also less surprising years after the shootout, trials, and subsequent acquittals. Policing agencies had been on guard against New Afrikans, partially due to the presence of the Black Legion. Within months of its founding convention, the Provisional Government began to organize an army with a chain of command, uniforms, regular training, and a recruitment strategy. As it organized, the Legion quickly caught the FBI's attention.[34] Although it no doubt caused concern, there was no strong directive indicating how to handle this army/security force. Assistant Attorney General J. Walter Yeagley wrote to Hoover, stating, "It would appear that the expressed intent of the captioned organization and some of its leaders would fall within the ambit of 18 Y.S.C. 2389. Section 2389 makes unlawful the recruiting of soldiers or sailors within the United States, or the establishment of recruiting stations for the enlistment of soldiers and sailors, to engage, or serve in any manner, in armed hostilities against the United States." However, his only recommendation was that Hoover notify him if the Bureau decided to take significant action, perhaps because the Legion seemed to operate more as a security group than as a regular army.[35] Regardless, local and federal law enforcement were on edge.

U.S. law enforcement also may have had reason to suspect that more violence would follow the New Bethel Incident. In one report, police officers claimed the doctors who treated a wounded police officer received threats of bodily harm. No details accompanied the report, but another claim had a little more substance. In this case, police expected "an uprising within the boundaries of the Tenth Precinct."[36] Whether that uprising was understood as a "riot" or a protest is not specified. However, an informant for the police claimed that New Afrikans planned to incite Detroit police to use their weapons to harm and kill participants at a support rally for Judge George Crockett, the black jurist who had released over one hundred New Bethel arrestees hours after the death of Officer Czapski.[37] Like many of the other reports, no substantial details accompany the allegation. If New Afrikans discussed having a demonstration in the aftermath of the New Bethel Incident, it is likely that they discussed the potential of police assaults on demonstrators, as well as the potential effect police brutality could have on people who constantly witnessed and were recipients of misconduct at the hands of lawmen. If, as the informant reported, some New Afrikans were indeed willing to provoke deadly violence against protesters, it would have been an attempt to demonstrate the consistency of police brutality against African people colonized in urban locales such as Detroit. Like their southern counterparts who dramatized the violence inherent in racial apartheid, opening one's self up to public police violence would have been intended to provoke moral outrage from witnesses while demanding what New Afrikans believed was the only solution to such problems: the creation of a black nation in the Deep South.

It is not likely, even if someone suggested provoking police violence against demonstrators, that many New Afrikans would have supported the idea. In fact, New Afrikans were attempting to be more cautious in the aftermath of the New Bethel Incident. Some Legionnaires, especially top-ranking members, were reportedly planning to go underground and even wear a different type of uniform than those who remained above ground.[38] One police memo stated that Brother Gaidi openly considered moving the RNA headquarters to Cleveland, where the situation was not as "hot" as Detroit.[39] Openly courting police violence also would have had a negative impact on the cases of Detroiters Chaka Fuller, Alfred Hibbit, and Rafael

Viera, a teacher from New York, all who eventually went to trial for their suspected involvement in the New Bethel Incident. Hibbit's charges included unlawful possession of weapons, but Fuller and Viera were charged with criminal assault and murder.[40]

Viera and Fuller arose victoriously from their trials by September 1970, after which Viera headed back home to New York City and Fuller remained in Detroit. Both New Afrikans had received death threats, and someone quickly made good on their threat to Fuller when an unidentified assailant stabbed him to death just outside of his home less than one month after his acquittal. New Afrikans and other communities' members claimed that the police committed the murder to avenge Officer Czapski's death.[41] The murder has yet to be solved, but Fuller's death confirmed many New Afrikans' fears that the police were willing to kill them in revenge, if not pure spite. According to former Legionnaire Balogun Anderson, "That's one of the reason[s] why when i got out [of prison] i didn't come back here [to Detroit]. 'Cause during the time that i was in [prison], one of the pigs that i had wounded [in a gun battle], they were talking about making him police chief. So i said, well i know i can't go back. Yeah, so that's why i paroled in New York when i got out."[42] As Elder Balogun's statement indicates, antagonism between "the law" and New Afrikans posed a serious threat for known citizens and paramilitary cadres. Not only did they have to fear police harassment, imprisonment, and even death; they also had to consider leaving their communities and families in search of safety because they remained targets, sometimes even after they discontinued participating in the political actions that originally placed them on the state's radar. In other words, the consequences of participation in the NAIM often extended beyond a person's actual involvement with the movement. It impacted their entire lives, forcing them to carefully consider their life choices.

FBI-backed headlines and hysteria about the New Bethel Incident spread across the nation, triggering a brief surge in covert repressive actions against New Afrikans. Monitoring New Afrikans as they traveled to and from meetings, police departments and federal agents took license plate numbers and recorded their home addresses, as well as the addresses of family and friends.[43] By the time New Afrikans made it to Jackson, Mississippi, where they established their headquarters, the U.S. government had gathered much intelligence on their activities across the nation.[44] The FBI continued its general surveillance, and beginning in August 1970, the Mississippi Sovereignty Commission placed a watchful eye on New Afrikans in its state. At least one FBI agent watched New Afrikans regularly.[45] And with the consent of Mississippi state leadership, the FBI participated in several overt actions, including sanctioning Ku Klux Klan harassment of New Afrikans, attempting to prevent the March 29, 1971, Land Dedication ceremony from taking place, pressuring black landowner Lofton Mason into nullifying his agreement to sell land to the Provisional Government, and attempting to provoke violence.[46] They may have succeeded when Larry Jackson, a Legionnaire, forcibly removed Davis Smith, a hostile white reporter, from a press meeting. Smith ended up accusing Obadele and Jackson with misdemeanor assault at the FBI's behest. Both New Afrikans were convicted and paid fines.[47]

Taken together, each of these hostile interactions placed New Afrikans in a state of psychological unease similar to that which Killingham and Simmons described. Like New Afrikans in Detroit surrounding the 1969 shootout, the tension caused many to become paranoid, some beyond—or perhaps within—reason. Consider the episode related by Sekou Owusu, who traveled with a group from New York to the Land Dedication ceremony at El Malik in 1971.

> We had meetings and the police were patrolling and following
> everybody. . . . And one guy from New York, he got recruited to
> come down and he was riding with this other brother. . . . And the
> cops were messing with them and they were messing with the cops,
> playing a cat and mouse game, whatever was going on. This brother
> that came down from New York, he couldn't handle it. He flipped
> out. And so, they took him to the hospital. I heard he was in the
> hospital, so i went to see him or visit him . . . [and] there he was
> [lying] in the hallway. He hadn't had a room yet, and he was
> pointing at the light bulb, [saying] "God is white, God is white,
> God is white."[48]

If what happened to this man was a serious case, one should expect that several other New Afrikans experienced some degree of psychological trauma related to their experiences with being continually followed and sometimes harassed and surviving intense interactions such as the one described. An atmosphere of group preparedness for an attack, along with the individual mental trauma of being harassed by various law enforcement and vigilante groups, created a mixture of combustible elements that was designed to explode with the correct trigger.

Brother Imari expressed concerns regarding the volatility surrounding New Afrikan citizens' presence. Although some local journalists and police considered their move to Jackson as an attempt to foment violence, he argued that New Afrikans were not interested in having "a shooting war over" the land. He claimed publicly that "the New African cadre [was] proselytizing, teaching, organizing" for a reparations vote. Peace, he claimed, "not shooting war," was the best way to proceed.[49] In fact, Obadele had been sensitive about the press response to the RNA for some time. A "reliable" informant for the Mississippi Sovereignty Commission reported as early as July 31 of the previous year that Obadele was upset about the *Jackson Daily News'* characterization of the RNA as having a "propensity toward violence."[50] He seemed shocked that they would characterize him and his cadres in such a manner.

For the historian, however, it comes as no surprise that the mainstream media would be hostile. After all, New Afrikans were struggling to remove five states from an established country. Even as they promoted an approach that utilized legal channels for pursuing their goals, they also prepared for armed revolution. Not only was Imari Obadele the leader of a nationalist movement with a reputation of antagonism toward police, but he also had a poor reputation *within* some segments of the NAIM. His brother Gaidi and the RNA's first president, among others, viewed him as reckless and unreasonably violent. Such a view from top leaders surely contributed to the belief that Brother Imari was a suicidal militant. Williams may have even expressed suspicions that Brother Imari was an agent provocateur. That Imari Obadele was accused of planting a bomb at the Detroit Metropolitan Airport caused some of his leading comrades to view him with disdain.[51] Because Obadele was a ranking leader of the independence movement, opponents of the Provisional Government also associated him with the New Bethel Incident. Some may have been aware of several underground actions in which New Afrikans participated (and sometimes initiated) in Detroit, Michigan; Cleveland, Ohio; and Cairo, Illinois. Although these actions did not garner the same attention as New Bethel, state and federal policing agencies likely notified political leaders in Mississippi of each occurrence. Finally, Obadele's public actions and statements sometimes betrayed his claims that his mission was a purely peaceful one. In the midst of Robert F. Williams's 1969 detainment in London, Obadele (then Midwest vice president) reportedly met with the British consul general in Detroit. During that meeting, newspapers and the FBI alleged, Obadele demanded a formal apology and threatened "'possible military reprisals' by the Black Legion . . . against countries flying the Union Jack in the Western Hemisphere." In a speech at Beloit College, Obadele indicated that the Provisional Government's move to Mississippi would be a violent one, because local whites, like their counterparts throughout Michigan, were organized into armed militias and had consistently used them against black people. Therefore, "we understand that from the moment we arrive there must be war. And so the [B]lack [L]egion is preparing in America."[52] Just as New Afrikan citizens were prepared for repressive action, policing agencies anticipated something like what took place in Jackson, Mississippi, on August 18, 1971.

The gunfire that would affect the course of RNA organizing for the remainder of the decade burst from New Afrikans' residence at 1138 Lewis Street at approximately 6:30 A.M. On that warm, sunny morning, four of the seven New Afrikans who were present responded to tear gas canisters crashing through the walls of their residence with rifle fire.[53] As they engaged in a decisive battle with the police and FBI in what they considered a desperate attempt to preserve their lives, three others searched in vain for a safe route of escape. After about twenty minutes of shooting and the fatal wounding of one police officer, the seven surrendered. Half-naked and handcuffed, the men and women were marched down Lewis Street by their police escorts. It was a sight that many compared to images of enslaved Africans being marched to market for sale. Nearby, at 1320 Lynch Street, Brother Imari and three others surrendered to police and federal agents who had surrounded their office. Not one bullet exited a New Afrikan's, agent's, or police officer's gun. However, the circumstances of that interaction were no more peaceful than the episode that occurred several blocks away. One by one, each person walked slowly from the residence with raised hands. At a certain point, law enforcement ordered them to lie face down on the morning concrete, where they were bound and thoroughly searched.[54] Aside from the humiliating method of arrest, the New Afrikans from Lynch Street reported receiving beatings once in police custody.[55] These arrests solidified the state of Mississippi's victory in its effort to prevent the captive black nation from achieving independence. In addition to capturing the PG-RNA president, that win diverted many resources away from nation building to legal defense efforts for the "RNA-11," again demonstrating the organizational and personal costs some social movement activists paid as they worked toward their goals.

The New Bethel Incident and the Jackson shootout were two of many violent interactions between the state and black revolutionaries during the Black Power era. The consequences of those battles included the loss of life and injury of New Afrikans, police officers, and FBI agents and many others. They included New Afrikans' imprisonment, destruction of activist and community property, and the stagnation of RNA growth and development, not to mention contributing to the general perception of New Afrikans as violent criminals. In many ways, the U.S. government achieved its objectives through its strategy of surveillance and repression. However, its program did not crush the PG-RNA or the NAIM; the program has not yet won the U.S. government the war. Some citizens continued pursuing independence from behind the walls of prisons across the United States. Those who remained on the outside utilized the images of their imprisoned comrades to organize and mobilize for New Afrikan liberation.

Political Prisoners and Prisoners of War

Popular recollections of black freedom activism associate arrest and incarceration with brave nonviolent actions that utilized the moral high ground to expose the shortcomings in what activists and their supporters considered a broken but salvageable system. We remember neatly-dressed men, women, and children as heroes who exposed openly bigoted police chiefs and shamed America for its hypocrisy. We hail them for forcing ignorant citizens to better align political and social practice with a virtuous American creed. Such a rendering of civil rights history, when left here, ignores the fraught relationship between people of African descent, captivity, and the law in the United States. Prominent thinkers throughout U.S. history equated blackness with a state of criminality and developed manifold images of black criminality to naturalize the bondage of African peoples and their descendants. When civil rights activists sought incarceration, they hoped to undermine that painfully created but effortlessly maintained equation. For their willingness to put their bodies in harm's way, they faced hardships that were endemic to captivity in the prison system. Carceral spaces then were sites where black activists challenged fear and fought the enduring stigma of the black criminal, even as they were defined by confinement, loss of autonomy, and torture.[56]

For self-proclaimed black revolutionaries, the hostility that characterized the relationship between the state and its challengers was as severe. However, the liberation efforts of those black revolutionaries did not earn the same perception of moral authority that people like Fannie Lou Hamer and Martin Luther King Jr. commanded. The nature of their challenge and a political culture that valued "law and order" above social justice made New Afrikan appeals to morality and righteous acceptance of incarceration less effective than the efforts of southern civil rights activists of the early 1960s. Therefore, by the end of the decade, administrators of federal and local governments worried very little about answering for the treatment of political radicals. Activists understood this enduring reality and built their strategies in line with it.

Citizens of the captive New Afrikan nation and their allies considered people such as the RNA-11, Dr. Mutulu Shakur, Geronimo ji Jaga, and Safiya Bukhari to be political prisoners (PP) and/or prisoners of war (POW). They received such status because they were conscious fighters of a people struggling against colonialism and for national self-determination and independent state power. According to imprisoned New Afrikan theorist Owusu Yaki Yakubu, "New Afrikan Political Prisoners and Prisoners of War have sworn a general allegiance to the nation and its objectives, and sworn a particular allegiance to one of the formations of New Afrikan Independence Movement."[57] Thus, all POWs were also considered PPs, but not all PPs are POWs. The distinction rests on how the individuals were apprehended as well as their activities prior to and during the course of their captures. POWs include imprisoned military participants of the New Afrikan nation. More specifically, New Afrikan POWs "are armed anti-colonial combatants; they are members of structured military arms of political organizations; they are commanded by persons responsible for their subordinates; they adhere to international humanitarian law, i.e., they meet all criteria of said law, and they should be accorded Prisoner of War status and treatment by the U.S."[58] For example, Dr. Shakur and ji Jaga became POWs because of their involvement with the underground military operations of the Black Liberation Army (BLA) and (for ji Jaga) the Panther Underground.[59] Safiya Bukhari's participation with the BLA, as well as her arrest and conviction following the convenience store shootout that led to her capture, qualified her as a POW. In other words, POWs had to be involved directly with some sort of military formation or had to be apprehended during a military action, whether planned or circumstantial, in order to be granted that status. On the other hand, PPs were individuals whose imprisonment was a result of state targeting, regardless of whether they participated in military actions.

PPs and POWs were important topics of discussion to participants in the 1968 convention that led to the founding of the PG-RNA. It occurred after several paramilitary formations had organized for the purposes of defending black communities and eventually fighting in armed warfare that some were certain would soon be upon them. With the goal of political independence, such formations could cohere into a national army and seek legitimacy under international law. That international recognition would theoretically give any defensive or offensive military actions the political standing they needed to protect individuals from criminal prosecution. However, it was (and remains) an unreliable strategy in U.S. courts. No New Afrikan PP or POW has received such status or protection from U.S. criminal prosecution.[60] Nor is there evidence to suggest that the people who invoked legal protection under international law convinced their juries to doubt the legitimacy of a given defendant's legal proceedings as a criminal. In fact, the United States continues to proclaim that it has no political prisoners.

Of the many PPs and POWs, two of the most recognizable among them are Sundiata Acoli and Assata Shakur. The two BLA cadres became POWs in 1973 when New Jersey police officers captured them. Although the full details of their encounter with law enforcement remain unclear, it began with a traffic stop and resulted in the deaths of Zayd Shakur and Officer Werner Foerster. During the melee that occurred, Assata was shot with her hands raised above her head and taken prisoner. Since her capture, Shakur has become an international symbol of anti-imperialist struggle against the United States. Her dedication to improving the conditions of black people while she was a Black Panther and her perceived status as the "Soul of the Black Liberation Army" contributed to her visibility. But because of her legendary escape from Clinton Correctional Facility and the bounty offered for her return—dead or alive—to New Jersey, Shakur's power as a former POW and symbol as someone who beat the system has grown exponentially.[61] Her status as a symbol has placed her in the likeness of George Jackson and others who gave momentum to the prison movement. For his part, Acoli fled, but authorities soon captured and imprisoned him. He has since become one of the most articulate theorists of prison struggle and architects of radical political organization bridging those on the "outside" and those within "the belly of the beast."

The prison experience became the impetus for Chokwe Lumumba, Safiya Bukhari, cadre from the Afrikan People's Party (APP), and many others to create International Solidarity Day for African Prisoners of War and the Jericho Movement. Solidarity Day activities took place on March 30–31, 1973, and boasted the involvement of the National Black Political Convention, political comedian Dick Gregory, Julian Bond, and several liberal and left-nationalist political organizations. Organizers articulated the stated purposes:

1. Expose the nature of the pseudo-legal political persecution of African liberation fighters in the courts of the United States of America, and other imperialists.
2. To provide an opportunity for all Political Prisoners of War Committees to raise money and support for their particular political prisoner, or prisoner of war.[62]

New Afrikans continued to carry on their demands for retrying and releasing PPs and POWs as they worked from behind and outside prison walls to support the incarcerated. Their efforts, and especially the dedication of long-held prisoner Jalil Muntaqim, led to the creation of Jericho '98, which evolved into the Jericho Movement (so called because New Afrikans and their allies marched around the White House). Activists seek to gain "recognition of the fact that political prisoners and prisoners of war exist inside of the United States, despite the United States' government's continued denial [*sic*] . . . and winning amnesty and freedom for these political prisoners."[63] Some activists in Jericho and elsewhere hope to use evidence of government misconduct from the COINTELPRO era and other illegal government tactics to vindicate Acoli and others whom activists argue were unjustly imprisoned or improperly sentenced. Some of them seek to eventually abolish prisons altogether.[64]

One may construe the continued fight for the release of New Afrikan prisoners and the struggle for the abolition of the current prison system as beneficial outcomes of Black Power–era liberation struggle. Because so many people remain behind bars for their beliefs and actions, younger generations are gaining a more sophisticated understanding of political repression and of the carceral system as a tool for sociopolitical control. Accompanying that educational outcome, however, is the devastating loss of many talented individuals who could have a more active role in the betterment of society if they were not locked away in the state-run and (ever increasing) private prisons. Like the situation Balogun Anderson described, incarcerated activists cannot maintain the same human relationships as their counterparts on the outside. However, in their positions, they are able to better expose the general conditions endured by criminalized persons across the spectrum of political belief. Reflecting on her own incarceration, Assata stated, "One of the most, i mean, just raging pains that i had, was being separated from my child, was being forbidden to hold her, to touch her, to breast feed her—the condition of women imprisoned in the United States is just unbearable."[65] The loss of parents, not to mention doctors, lawyers, chemists, musicians, scholars, and farmers who could help solve many of society's problems, was a bitter consequence of social movement activism seeking to remove territory that an existing state claims as its own. Their removal, however, could not diminish their love for their people, nor has it extinguished their dedication to humankind.

Humanity Intact: New Afrikan Responses to State Repression

New Afrikans anticipated some level of state repression and violent warfare with the United States government, and so they planned for it. Some may argue that they even instigated or courted conflict with the state. New Afrikans considered themselves revolutionaries who, in a struggle for self-determination, made calculated decisions that they believed would help them achieve their goals. Imari Obadele hoped that by the time violent struggle became a reality, the PG-RNA would have enough international backing and "Second Strike," or underground military, support to make any violent offensive by the United States costly in terms of human life, property, and international standing. However, because they did not develop either to a degree that would allow them to be militarily successful, New Afrikans had to find other ways to deal with violent repression, and how they did so helped them maintain their humanity.

Not long after the Lewis Street shootout, three New Afrikans began a trip to Jackson, Mississippi, in order to do "party work." Instead, it culminated with their arrival in Cuba as part of a larger phenomenon that began the previous decade. On November 8, 1971, Fela Olatunji (former slave name Charles Hill) and Michael "Macheo" Finney were journeying from Berkeley, California, where they were students, teachers, Vietnam veterans, parents, and revolutionaries. Somewhere near Albuquerque, they met with Ralph "Antar Ra" Goodwin. The three were working for the Provisional Government, and at least one (Finney) had also been a member of the Black Panther Party. They headed toward Jackson, Mississippi, with a cache of weapons and multiple other items that suggested they were prepared to be off the grid for a number of days. At some point, New Mexico state trooper Robert Rosenbloom pulled them over. The encounter ended with Rosenbloom dead from a gunshot wound. Police found the vehicle abandoned early the next morning. Nearby, "a cache was found in heavy weeds and brush." It "contained black militant literature, primarily of the Republic of New Africa" and an unspecified number of "semi-automatic rifles, shotguns, and home-made bombs," in addition to personal items. Among the personal items were pamphlets about Africa, Malcolm X quotes, utensils, and food, including one slice of pumpkin pie.[66]

The New Afrikans then spent almost three weeks figuring out how to avoid capture by authorities in what journalist Anthony Lappé called "the largest manhunt in New Mexico history." In the meantime, "all ghetto informants and black extremist sources, as well as all criminal informants, were contacted in regard to this case." Police maintained heavy surveillance, setting up roadblocks and conducting door-to-door investigations in neighborhoods along all possible routes of escape. On November 27, after waiting in sand dunes for an opportunity to flee their predators, the young soldiers forced a tow truck driver to take them to Albuquerque Airport, where they commandeered a Chicago-bound flight. The three New Afrikans detoured the plane to Tampa, where they allowed the flight's passengers to deplane. After refueling, they forced the plane and its six-member flight crew to Havana. Once in Cuba, "the men settled into quiet lives as guests of the revolution."[67]

During the 1960s and early 1970s, rerouting flights from various locales to Cuba became one popular method that revolutionaries and other self-made enemies of the United States used to avoid arrest, imprisonment, and death. In many of those cases, the Cuban government accepted the skyjackers while returning planes, pilots, and passengers to their destinations. Those whom the Castro regime did not accept found themselves jailed and then returned to U.S. custody.[68] Skyjacking became so popular during the late 1960s that the Castro and Nixon governments sought ways to deter both countries' exiles from seeking refuge in their respective countries. And after what appeared to be a "downward trend" in hijackings, Cuba reached out to the United States to negotiate a resolution to deal harshly with people who diverted planes and boats to either country with hopes of finding asylum.[69] Besides the three New Afrikans mentioned above, several Black Panthers also utilized the skyjacking-to-Cuba method when they were in a bind.[70]

It is unknown whether the three young men realized during their escape to Cuba that they would spend the remainder of their lives in the island country. However, for two of them, that was a considerable consequence of giving their lives, when necessary, in pursuit of an independent black nation-state. Not long after arriving in Cuba, Goodwin died during a heroic attempt to save two drowning beachgoers. Finney also died in Cuba, though two decades after arriving there. His cause of death was throat cancer. Olatunji remains in Cuba, seemingly bitter in his freedom in exile. Like famed Black

Panther Pete O'Neal, who has lived in Tanzania for several decades, Ola-tunji has expressed deep appreciation of the Cuban government's willingness to protect him. However, he has claimed on more than one occasion that he would rather be in the United States with his family and friends.[71]

Not everyone decided, or was able, to escape U.S. authorities' legal reach. Therefore, New Afrikans and BLA cadres sometimes had to fight the state on its own territory. One method of combat was to utilize U.S. courts. New Afrikan lawyers such as Chokwe Lumumba defended their comrades in the courtroom while demonstrating the political nature of defendants' cases to juries. However, that method often led to imprisonment. According to Assata Shakur, "We couldn't look to the kourts for freedom and justice any more than we could expect to gain our liberation by participating in the u.s. political system, and it was pure fantasy to think we could gain them by begging."[72] They had to consider other options. Because so many black revolutionaries became inmates in state and federal prisons after being convicted for criminal offenses, when faced with the option to either pursue legal respite or flee, many chose the latter option. For them, going underground was an important temporary, and sometimes long-term, alternative to whatever legal options they had available. Put another way, New Afrikans for an undetermined length of time sometimes found it important to drop off the state's, and oftentimes even their loved ones', radars. With the help of North American anti-imperialists (white revolutionaries), they created safe houses at various locales and devised ways to alter their appearances and change identities. Sometimes they did so to achieve a specific short-term goal such as securing money resources, as evidenced by the 1981 Brinks expropriation.[73] Otherwise, they sought to create a completely new life for themselves in the United States and/or abroad.

Assata Shakur provides a glimpse of what it was like to go underground. Although her autobiography does not describe the actual process or the people who helped her take that step before and after her capture and imprisonment, it provides readers with details of the heavy tolls associated with that life. She stated, "Sisters and brothers from just about every revolutionary or militant group in the country were either rotting away in prison or had been forced underground." The comparison between "rotting away in prison" and being "forced underground" invites readers to consider the lived experience of an underground revolutionary. Like being imprisoned (or exiled in another country), those who lived underground could not associate freely with their families and loved ones, contradicting many people's intuitive desires for contact with the people they valued most. Further, Assata said, "Like most of us back in those days, i was new at this, learning about clandestine struggle as i lived it." It was unstable and stressful partially because underground revolutionaries could not remain in one place consistently. Like the descriptions provided by many imprisoned revolutionaries who were constantly moved from prison to prison, Assata stated, "Over the next few years, home became a lot of places."[74] Eventually, the same repressive forces that led to Assata's clandestinity also led to her imprisonment. But after surviving years in dungeon-like holding facilities, Assata escaped with the help of her BLA comrades and some white anti-imperialists. She eventually fled the United States as well, and since the 1980s she has been living and working in Cuba.[75]

Mention of Shakur's capture and escape demands that we direct our attention to some of the underground activities in which New Afrikans and many other political radicals participated. Besides skyjacking planes and freeing political prisoners, they trained for guerilla warfare, gathered intelligence on federal and local policing agencies, and created and disseminated political propaganda.[76] Some even participated in "expropriations," or what the general public considered to be bank robberies. For New Afrikan freedom fighters like Shakur and Bukhari, going underground was a necessity if they wanted to survive. However, going underground and participating in an array of independent actions were simultaneously intended to chip away at their enemy's confidence and to build support for the revolutionary war for the independence of the black nation.

According to the Revolutionary Armed Task Force (RATF) of the BLA, "New Afrikan Freedom Fighters represent the first point of resistance for the Black nation." These freedom fighters were brothers and sisters in struggle who had developed an analysis and a critique of the oppressor's system, as well as their own resistance to it, through years of aboveground and underground activism. Their critique led them to believe in the need for an army that would secure independence for the black nation. They had given their lives to struggle for their ideals, had become the targets of government repression, and regardless of the costs, had refused to submit to their oppressor's will.[77] Although primarily composed of New Afrikans and other black revolutionaries, the RATF also included several white anti-imperialist allies, including Kathy Boudin, David Gilbert, and Judy Clark, formerly of the Weather Underground.

On October 20, 1981, a wing of the RATF—also known as "the Family"—participated in the armed "expropriation" of a Brinks truck as it made its scheduled cash pickup at a shopping mall in Nanuet, New York.

During the expropriation, the BLA soldiers exchanged gunfire with the vehicle's guards, leaving one fatally wounded. The soldiers then proceeded as planned to a location where they would meet with their white comrades who were supposed to drive them to safety. However, the group members bungled their escape, and a resident college student witnessed the soldiers connecting with their drivers. The witness alerted local authorities and described the group members and their U-Haul truck, which police soon stopped at a blockade. During the stop, the armed New Afrikans ambushed the police, killing two. Several of the expropriation participants, including Boudin, Clark, Gilbert, and Samuel "Sol" Brown, were captured at or near the scene of the shootout. In a series of raids and roundups, law enforcement captured more New Afrikans, and one—Mtayari Shabaka Sundiata—lost his life.[78] The raid on Sunni-Ali's residence was just one of those that took place.

By May 1988, all of the known participants had been tried and many sentenced (if still alive). Dr. Mutulu Shakur and Marilyn Buck were convicted on all of the various charges stemming from their involvement in the Brinks expropriation, another 1981 armored car expropriation, and their alleged involvement in Assata Shakur's November 2, 1979, escape from the Clinton Correctional Facility. "Part of their convictions included conspiracy to commit, and actually committing, a Racketeering Influenced and Corrupt Organization conspiracy enterprise and "participating in a RICO conspiracy." These latter charges are important because they demonstrate how the racially ethnically heterogeneous jury comprehended the Black Liberation "Family's" actions; they framed the "expropriations" as criminal, as opposed to political acts. The defendants and their lawyers failed in their attempts to change the jury's conceptualization that the radicals' activities were purely criminal.[79]

In a move similar to that of several black liberation activists before them, some of the Brinks defendants challenged the legality of their trials. As illegitimate citizens of the United States, the New Afrikans tried in vain to convince the court that the U.S. government had no jurisdiction over them because their actions were political, which theoretically protected them from criminal trial under international law. New Afrikan defendant Chui Ferguson problematized his treatment as a U.S. citizen and used his claim as a non-American to argue that his trial in U.S. criminal court was unlawful. Like the attempts of Brother Imari, Safiya Bukhari, and others, that tactic did not produce the desired results for any of the defendants.[80] Instead, all of the convicted soldiers spent at least some time in prison. Many of them, including Gilbert and Dr. Shakur, are still serving time.[81]

· · · · · ·

The consequences of political participation on the human beings cited above may seem dire, because they remind readers of the hell some revolutionaries paid for their dedication to New Afrikan liberation. Some people were overly naïve about the full power of United States to undermine their efforts to free the land. As Baba Khalid Abdur-Rasheed stated, "As young people we weren't prepared to go up against the country the way we did. We had no idea the kind of intelligence apparatus the United States had and put in place."[82] However, many of the persons mentioned earlier were aware of the risks involved when they decided to give their lives, if necessary, to the goals they deemed valuable. In fact, they had planned for such outcomes, even though they certainly did not want to face imprisonment, exile, or death. Careful planning and consideration of these outcomes were important for them as they strove to maintain their humanity during their struggle for liberation. Forethought and unintended consequence also helped shape New Afrikan lifestyle politics.

The situations described in this chapter were also some of the extreme cases. As we have seen, the experiences of those who did not participate in shootouts or who did not have to operate underground were much different, even if they were informed by such spectacular violence. They, too, likely made it into the numerous indexes of FBI agents and police officers. As people who were aware of being targeted but who might not have been able to say specifically when and how, they lived with the stress associated with the raids, shootouts, and removal of their comrades. Yet knowing that they, too, could be staring down the barrel of a lawman's gun during a raid or facing a grand jury to testify against their comrades did not deter all of them from participating in the movement for independence. Instead, they continued to pursue their goals and live, to the best of their abilities, within the contours of their political convictions. Even for those who eventually let go of the idea of independence, the struggle for reparations continued, at least immediately, to demand their attention, time, and resources.

6 For New Afrikan People's War

Lessons and Legacies of the New Afrikan
Independence Movement

· ·

During the last weekend of March 1983, the Provisional Government–
Republic of New Afrika (PG-RNA) celebrated its first New Afrikan Nation
Day. Held at Wayne State University and Hartford Memorial Baptist Church,
organizers welcomed over four thousand participants in the course of the
three-day event. As with the 1968 Black Government Convention, the organizers boasted "high quality participation," including key figures from
across the political spectrum of black leadership. Conference goers heard
from and exchanged ideas with Minister Louis Farrakhan, the Reverend Ben
Chavis, Amiri Baraka, and venerable movement elders Queen Mother Moore
and Anwar Pasha. Kwame Ture ran a workshop covering African liberation
movements, while other sessions focused on political prisoners and prisoners of war, community health, and organizing women and youth. The weekend of festivities concluded Sunday evening with an RNA Founders' Dinner,
which honored New Afrikan Freedom Fighters, prisoners of war (POWs),
and movement elders. Considered "an overwhelming success," it signaled to
some New Afrikan Independence Movement (NAIM) activists "that people
are ready to stand and fight right now" and that they were witnessing a
"resurgence of [RNA] national consciousness."[1]

That summer, New Afrikans from Detroit, New York, Washington, D.C.,
Philadelphia, New Orleans, Boston, and other locations met in Atlanta and
then Brooklyn to focus on how to reunify the PG-RNA, which had become
fragmented. PG-RNA copresidents Dara Abubakari and Imari Obadele both
called for mending the fractures that erupted and hampered the movement beginning in 1978 (if not sooner). Abubakari stated, "WE [sic] need
principled Unity first between Black individuals and organizations inside
the Nationalist Movement and also with Black people who have never
heard or thought about us having our own independent nation." Obadele
agreed, considering the gatherings rare opportunities for healing and reconciliation. Using tape recordings, New Afrikan comrades behind the
walls even had a chance to proclaim their continued commitment to the

struggle and update participants on the ongoing crisis of government repression. Both Jerry Gaines and Fulani Sunni-Ali spoke about harassment against them due to noncooperation in the grand jury investigation into the Brinks Expropriation. In response, meeting attendees proclaimed their dedication to all of their incarcerated freedom fighters. The meetings were highly spirited and gave NAIM activists a renewed sense of solidarity.[2]

Both 1983 meetings made clear the fractures within and hopes spawning from the NAIM. In reflecting on fifteen years of independence struggle, the meetings provided opportunities to learn from their collective efforts and assess how to pick up the remnants of the Black Power movement of the 1960s and 1970s. Holding on to the spirit of possibility, participants focused on their shared goals and their determination to prevent unavoidable differences from further impairing their efforts to secure victories. The meetings and the pronouncements that came out of them also highlight the diversity of New Afrikan strategies and groupings organized around them. For a decade or longer, a handful of the New Afrikan political organizations that formed apart from the PG-RNA and some individuals, such as Chokwe Lumumba, had been pursuing alternative approaches of preparing the black nation for revolution and statehood. Regardless, they have been aligned in their common mission and have, in many instances, embraced the pronouncements by Abubakari and Obadele at different points in their groups' existence.

Other efforts in which New Afrikans had influence also gained momentum in the 1980s. Most significant is the struggle for black reparations for centuries of extensive exploitation and injustice. The NAIM, although it was not the origin of calls for repair, helped determine the direction and tone of the movement that took hold. With Washington, D.C., as an epicenter, activists and lawyers connected the movement for New Afrikan independence with financial compensation from the U.S. government. New Afrikans viewed reparations, far from being separate demands by disparate groups, as essential to their ability to build and sustain their republic. That these developments occurred when they did speaks to the lasting impact of government repression and competing visions of the New Afrikan trajectory but also to the stubborn persistence of black liberation struggle. Even as people within social movements dealt with the strain of participating in and shaping their lives within a protracted revolutionary movement, their resilience and hard-earned political acumen taught them which issues to emphasize depending on the political opportunities.

The following pages tell the story of the latter years of the New Afrikan trajectory, through the many New Afrikan parties, formations, organizations, and units that formed in the 1970s and 1980s. Although the entire list of related organizations is worthy of detailed explanation, some groupings, such as the New Afrikan People's Organization (NAPO) and the Afrikan People's Party (APP), have (so far) made a significant visible impact on the landscape of black political activism in ways that demand immediate attention. More important, the movement for black reparations in the United States, a Black Power initiative that has far outlasted the Black Power movement, has been a key demand of the NAIM. The story of the development of that struggle shows also how New Afrikans helped make way for the National Coalition of Blacks for Reparations in America (N'COBRA). These legacies indicate not only what movement participants learned and how their participation shaped their own lives but also how each participant shaped the protracted struggle for liberation, even extending beyond the specific calls for independence. They reveal that black America's most promising and progressive goals and ideas reflect the contributions of New Afrikans.

A Union of Revolutionaries: Non-PG Formations in the New Afrikan Independence Movement

The NAIM and the concept of an independent black nation-state are not coterminous with the PG-RNA. During the mid-1960s, the Revolutionary Action Movement (RAM) was the leading organization that promoted the concept. Under the mentorship of Queen Mother Moore and participation of people like attorney Milton Henry, some members of the underground organization were coinitiators of the 1968 Black Government Convention in Detroit. Further, there are New Afrikan formations that were born in the aftermath of the Black Power movement. One of the most visible is the New Afrikan People's Organization and its mass organization, Malcolm X Grassroots Movement (MXGM). NAPO evolved from the efforts of many New Afrikan formations who wanted to consolidate their efforts for liberation while building a revolutionary black political party that could bring the mass struggles into a unified political program. Its birth and contributions to the black political landscape in the aftermath of the Black Power movement help demonstrate some of the ways that New Afrikan independence activists transferred ideas from one political moment to the next.

Afrikan People's Party

There were a variety of NAIM formations active before and during the Black Power movement. One was the APP. The APP grew in the fertile ground of black left organizing throughout the country, particularly by RAM and Black Guard cadres and affiliates after RAM's dissolution. Beginning as the African American Party of National Liberation, or Black Liberation Party, in 1968, it took on the name Afrikan People's Party in 1972.[3] The membership developed a Ten-Point Program, similar to the Black Panther Party's Ten-Point Program, that clarified their demands and rallying points. Their goals generally sought "self determination [sic] and independent nationhood." To that end, members demanded that the five-state territory in the Deep South be turned over, along with control over the planning of black communities throughout the United States. With that control, said communities would be able to create cooperative structures that would help them meet their self-defined needs. These revolutionary nationalists saw the importance of exempting black men from military service, retooling education so that it benefited black children and adults, and ending incarceration of black people in general and political prisoners and prisoners of war specifically. The party also articulated the necessity of ending "the racist war of genocide" against people "held in captive colonial bondage inside the United States." Finally, the party called for a Congress of African Peoples to help steer the liberation movement and, therefore, the destiny of black people in the United States.[4]

Even as they maintained their commitment to their broader, more ambitious goals, the members of the APP struggled at the local level for tenants' rights and greater black labor power in the factories, often where APP members worked. Anticipating the ideas and ideological positions that Dara Abubakari and Chokwe Lumumba developed through their activism in the PG-RNA, APP members found it essential to develop relationships with and demonstrate that they were struggling on behalf of their neighbors, former schoolmates and teachers, gang members, and drug addicts. In other words, they favored mass organization, viewing the PG-RNA as "a national liberation front that tied forces" from various wings of the independence movement together.[5] The grassroots orientation gave them the tools to rebuild former RAM chapters within the new nationwide APP network.

APP cadres were important organizers in key events during the 1970s. One was the 1973 International Solidarity Day for African Prisoners of

War. Preceding Solidarity Day, activists from across the nation had formed an African Prisoners of War Alliance. The alliance attempted to consolidate organizations and individuals that, to varying degrees, competed with one another for leadership and relevancy in campaigns to defend political prisoners. These same forces helped the African Liberation Support Committee organize African Liberation Day in 1972 and then, under the leadership of Lumumba, brought their cadres together to mobilize for Solidarity Day. According to Saladin Muhammad, their principled efforts helped solidify some of the cross-organizational activity that characterized their work and that would be key to the successes of future high-visibility mobilizations.[6]

APP cadres also played a central role in the protests around the United States' bicentennial celebration of its independence from Britain. Beginning in late 1975, the July 4th Coalition formed, aiming to promote a "people's" remembrance of the nation's two hundredth birthday.[7] The coalition included over one hundred left-leaning "peace activists, black, Native American, feminist and Puerto Rican groups" who had been planning to use the bicentennial celebrations in Philadelphia to demonstrate for a range of political causes. New Afrikan calls for such protests had begun by January 1973 when *Soulbook* cofounder and House of Umoja (HOU) and Afrikan People's Party (APP) member Mamadou Lumumba-Umoja encouraged agitation for self-determination. His organization began to develop messaging that utilized key phrases from Frederick Douglass's 1852 speech "What to the Slave Is the Fourth of July" to build support for protests and organizing work that moved the black masses toward revolutionary consciousness and organizing. One issue of *Soulbook* was dedicated to helping spread these ideas, as were other APP-affiliated publications.[8]

As with other efforts to challenge the state, the moments leading up to the bicentennial saw a countereffort against the leftist coalition. Philadelphia mayor Frank Rizzo and other hostile actors proclaimed that the march would provide the radical Left with opportunities to unleash terrorism in Liberty City. The infamous mayor denied a coalition calling itself Rich off Our Backs (formed in part by the Revolutionary Communist Party) a permit to march their desired route near the official bicentennial activities, even as he was denied the use of federal troops whom he requested for assistance in keeping the peace. The July 4th Coalition, however, planned to march in North Philadelphia through one of the city's black neighborhoods. APP members secured the route after hosting a community meeting with local residents at the Church of the Advocate at 1801 Diamond Street.[9]

As part of the Afro-American Anti-Bicentennial Committee, APP cadres used the meeting at the Church of the Advocate to express trust and solidarity with other historically oppressed nations through what they considered efforts by white antagonists and allies alike to undermine their expressions of self-determination. White coalition members revealed elements of paternalistic racism, in addition to the manufactured crises that Rizzo and others attempted to use to prevent leftist protest, when they attempted to define the goals of black activism. Whereas the APP and other New Afrikans attached their participation to the banner "National Independence for the Domestic Black Colony," some of their white comrades attempted to compare them to Crispus Attucks, indicating that the black struggle was for full inclusion within the United States. American Indian Movement leaders, such as lawyer Clyde Bellecourt, agreed with black liberation activists that they should use the march as a moment to display solidarity and mutual interest. According to Saladin Muhammad, "The Native American and the black liberation contingency, represented by several forces, we walked side-by-side with a little indigenous child, probably about eight-years-old, carrying a peace pipe with a kind of a small black, red, and green flag on it. So this was how the Anti-Bicentennial . . . unfolded."[10] Participation in the July 4th Coalition permitted the APP to build solidarity outside of the independence movement. It also placed them in a position to include New Afrikan independence politics within other left-leaning coalitions and efforts.

New Afrikan People's Organization and Malcolm X Grassroots Movement

During the summer of 1973, Imari Obadele visited Detroit. While there, he met up with Chokwe Lumumba, who was also in town. The two decided to make business cards advertising their positions within the PG-RNA; however, they disagreed on what specific wording to use to describe the leadership. According to Lumumba, Brother Imari favored "Provisional Government," while Lumumba advocated for "Provisional Revolutionary Government." In Lumumba's telling of the story, the differing views on wording revealed a deep disagreement between the two regarding the best strategy for achieving their stated goals. Although they both used the language of revolution and independence in public and private pronouncements, Lumumba became convinced that Obadele was a romantic nationalist and an autocrat, not a revolutionary.[11]

Although NAPO's history is broader than the internal disagreements of PG-RNA leadership, the second constitutional crisis helped push some PG members into the coalition that birthed the organization. Following the resolution of the second constitutional crisis, the Abubakari-Lumumba group worked with other NAIM forces to create a mechanism that would help bring about "a mass national movement of the people which resists colonial repression of the American Empire by protest, rebellion, boycotts, strikes, popular armed self-defense, various other acts of mass concerted action, and the application of revolutionary force" by the People's New Afrikan Liberation Army.[12] Seeing the Provisional Government as undermining the building of what they would eventually call "People's War," many within the Abubakari-Lumumba group opted to form a revolutionary party and to focus their efforts on mass organizing.

NAPO did not work in opposition to the PG-RNA. As a formation dedicated to the creation of an independent black nation-state, NAPO saw its own work as being complementary to the PG's efforts. Where NAPO and the PG-RNA differed was in NAPO's focus on developing cadres and building at the grass roots enough support to make pursuit of New Afrikan statehood a mass-based effort that utilized democratic centralism, as opposed to a top-down Pan-African nationalist niche isolated from the black communities they wanted to serve. As Lumumba put it, the PG and any other revolutionary nationalists should focus first on finding out what the masses need. "Outside of these struggles, we lack credibility as authorities on how to solve the overall problems," Lumumba claimed in a communication to the incarcerated RNA president. Lumumba hoped that through grassroots organizing, they could help key people in various communities develop the discipline and leadership needed to help make nation-building and independence palatable. Success would occur when the masses begin to clearly identify conscious New Afrikans as their leaders and begin to call for and support the programs coming out of the PG. To struggle for New Afrikan political goals any other way would make the independence movement at best ineffectual, and at worst subject to the manipulation of the white supremacist power structure and actively ignored by the black masses.[13]

As the factions within the PG were working through their dispute, some held important meetings with other New Afrikan organizations and carried out a human rights campaign and demonstration that reflected the shifts in strategy and focus for a variety of Pan-African nationalists during the late 1970s and into the 1980s. The APP, which had reorganized into a national organization, met with members of the PG-RNA to discuss points of agreement and the possibility of joining forces. During one meeting on New Year's Eve, 1978, Chokwe Lumumba and Akbar Muhammad Ahmad met to discuss the potential for consolidation, or merging their respective formations into one National Liberation Front. However, there were several obstacles that the two entities had to overcome before they could advance that conversation in any sustained and fruitful way. First, Lumumba himself had to take a back seat in that conversation. By late 1978, his name was being associated with the factional dispute with Imari Obadele. Considering Brother Imari's allegations that Lumumba was part of a "liquidationist" effort that would undermine the independence movement, Lumumba was not in a position to guide any such negotiations. Lumumba and Ahmad seemed to agree that Ahmed Obafemi was better positioned for the task.[14]

Still, there was mutual suspicion between the PG-RNA and the APP on top of significant ideological challenges and distinct priorities. Some people within the former believed that the party was attempting to submerge the PG while giving up too little. Although Lumumba and Ahmad seemed to understand socialism and its potential for New Afrikan people, Ahmad was not convinced that other PG leaders would agree with the party's framing of scientific socialism. Further, conversation seemed to take place at a time when the two formations saw different issues as priorities. While the PG expressed the need to develop its cadres, working on the RNA-11 cases, developing the human rights campaign, and generating sufficient capital for its operations, the APP was focusing on the development of revolutionary black "workers, women's, student & prisoners organizations," the development of a mass base (something which, in this case, Brother Imari disagreed), and the "U.N. effort."[15] Finally, some mistrust between the PG-RNA and the APP stemmed, at least partially, from "the matter of the abuse of Queen Mother by Walter Collins." In January 1980, Bilal Sunni-Ali submitted a position paper to the APP National Coordinating Committee, explaining that there was a serious wound in need of healing. There were concerns that the responsible party members and the PG had not investigated thoroughly.[16] The conversations never moved toward the act of consolidation.

Although they did not cohere as some intended, both formations joined in the Black Solidarity Day demonstration sponsored by the National Black Human Rights Coalition (NBHRC) at the UN headquarters on November 5, 1979. Organizers framed the demonstration as a general strike and boycott that would "sharpen the role of the black working class participation" and aid in building the NBHRC.[17] An estimated five thousand people participated, including respected elders, such as Queen Mother Audley

Moore, and a seemingly endless roster of speakers. Speakers included Chokwe Lumumba; Dr. Betty Shabazz; state representative and Philadelphia Black United Front member Dave Richardson; Dara Abubakari, Grenada's ambassador to the United Nations; "a deputy representative from the Palestinian Liberation Organization"; and NBHRC chair and APP member Muntu Matsimela.[18] Recurring themes of the day included "self-determination for the Black Nation, gaining international support for the Black Liberation Struggle[,] and the existence of POWs here in the US [*sic*]." Major goals sought ending "police murders of Third World people," stopping attacks by white supremacist organizations, demanding the freedom of PPs and POWs, and garnering clear international support for the liberation struggle.[19] Matsimela joined Moore and Lumumba to present a statement to Tanzanian diplomat and president of the UN General Assembly Salim Ahmed Salim.[20] The trio represented thousands when they charged the United States with violations of black people's human rights.

After making some brief remarks, Matsimela read a statement from Assata Shakur, whom the Black Liberation Army (BLA) had liberated from prison just three days earlier. Written for Black Solidarity Day prior to her escape, she educated her audience about the extent of American brutality taking place on its own soil and throughout the world. Drawing specific attention to the captivity of Third World U.S. peoples, she asked, "In a country that historically used Blacks, Hispanics, Orientals, and Native Americans as scapegoats, what do Black and Third World people have to look forward to in the [1980s]? And what does all this have to do with political prisoners and the Prison Movement?" She found the answers in history, using previous "Black Messiahs" Marcus Garvey, Martin Luther King Jr., and Malcolm X, as well as the accelerated construction of prisons and their increasingly inhumane conditions. To her, these were evidence that such people had no place, no *home*, in the United States of America. Calling upon X's "Message to the Grassroots Speech," she revisited his claim that the revolution needed to focus on land. To Shakur, black revolutionaries should devote their energy toward the liberation of the Republic of New Afrika's national territory in the South: "We'll be free as Afrikans," she claimed. "New Afrikans."[21] Her words and her newly earned status as a modern-day maroon electrified the crowd. She was a living example that the United States had not defeated the NAIM. Shakur's words captured the central ideas that helped bring organizers together, and the act of successfully liberating her prior to the UN mobilization helped demonstrate the symbiosis between the aboveground and underground units within the movement. In the midst of ongoing efforts to hold the U.S. government accountable for the illegal actions of the FBI, these various forces proved that the spirit of black liberation could survive even the direst of circumstances.[22]

Some of the people involved in the conversations about consolidation and the Black Solidarity Day mobilization cohered into the New Afrikan People's Organization on Black Power patron saint Malik Shabazz's fifty-ninth birthday, May 19, 1984. Acknowledging and embracing the principles of the PG-RNA's Declaration of Independence, the self-avowed New Afrikan revolutionaries promised to create a new society for their people, one that would be free of racist, classist, and sexist oppression.[23] Although their ideas were based in and, in essence, agreed with the PG-RNA under the leadership of Imari Obadele, the focus of their daily work and articulation of their goals learned from and amended the RNA Declaration of Independence and other foundational documents in the New Afrikan Political Science. According to Lumumba, the belief was, "Our role is not to be a government, but our role is to organize people."[24] Therefore, they placed a clear focus on developing cadres, educating and organizing the masses, working with children, and creating viable political opposition to the established American political system in "the National Territory" and throughout the country.

In 1990, NAPO created the Malcolm X Grassroots Movement (MXGM), a mass organization. Considered "the single most important political program in our work today," the founders wanted to use the new organization as a tool to introduce black people to an organized "People's War," which would lead to greater mass revolutionary struggle.[25] More specifically, they organized around six primary objectives: exercising self-determination as a captive nation, recognition that that nation has been the victim of genocidal war, securing the basic human rights that the black masses had been denied, securing the release of political prisoners and prisoners of war, securing reparations "in the form of money, technology and land," and ending sexist oppression.[26] As a source of information on these issues and as theorists in the development of strategy for addressing them, the national grassroots movement had the potential to catalyze the masses. One of their approaches was to use hip-hop music and culture. Beginning in 1998, New Afrikan exile and MXGM cofounder Mama Nehanda Isoke Abiodun helped organize the Black August Hip-Hop Festival in Cuba. Bringing Common, dead prez, The Roots, and other notable acts to the island nation and sending them to Brazil and South Africa, the approach helped create an important pathway for the young organization to recruit potential activists.[27]

These brief summaries do not do full justice to the APP or NAPO, and they fall far short of explaining the breadth of the NAIM. A partial list of significant New Afrikan formations and efforts includes the National Task Force for Cointelpro Litigation and Research, Ahidiana, House of Umoja, the New Afrikan Women's Organization, the New Afrikan Prisoners Organization, and the New Afrikan Liberation Front. Covering all regions of the United States from the West Coast, through the South, into the Midwest, and along the East Coast, the individuals and organizations that have given their allegiance to New Afrikan liberation struggle demonstrate the persistence of their central idea and begin to hint at the extent to which people, even those who did not say so openly, agreed with the original concepts around which the 1968 Black Government Convention formed. One persistent idea, which scholars and activists frequently consider outside of the NAIM, is the struggle for reparations. Although reparations were never a persuit that NAIM proponents could claim as theirs exclusively, the New Afrikan articulation of that goal lives on through current efforts to secure a range of accommodations as recompense for centuries of oppression against African and African-descended people in the United States.

"A Debt Due *without* Strings": The New Afrikan Struggle for Reparations and Self-Determination

When the New Afrikan founding parents announced the New Afrikan Nation's right to self-determination, they simultaneously stipulated the "right to damages, reparations, due us for the grievous injustices sustained by our ancestors and ourselves." They maintained that the United States of America owes the descendants of the enslaved monetary restitution for their ancestors' capture, brutal transport from Africa to the British colonies/American states, forced labor, and status as enslaved property. Further, oppression against African peoples and their descendants did not end with the collapse of formal slavery. Instead, lynching, Jim Crow, educational inequality, labor exploitation, sexual violence, housing discrimination, race riots, police brutality, and much more characterized a significant portion of black people's lived experiences when Queen Mother Moore and others signed the declaration in March 1968. They framed it as a requisite condition on which the pursuit of independence would be possible. Of course, neither the RNA's argument for territorial sovereignty nor its demand for reparations was a new political claim. Both of these ambitions preceded the RNA insofar as organizations like the National Ex-Slave Mutual Relief,

Bounty and Pension Association and the National Industrial Council and National Liberty Party and individuals including W. E. B. DuBois and Queen Mother Moore advocated for them prior to the NAIM. However, that the New Afrikan articulation of the goal influenced the direction of black politics outside of the movement speaks to another important legacy.[28]

Moore was the founder and president of the Reparations Committee for United States Slaves' Descendants, Inc., a direct forerunner of the RNA. On December 20, 1962, the committee filed a reparations claim with the U.S. government on behalf of "more than 25 million . . . members of the Black Race" and in commemoration of the one hundredth anniversary of the Emancipation Proclamation.[29] The Reparations Committee demanded monetary compensation for what it considered genocide against African Americans. Its members sought monetary payment to help "rehabilitate and [alleviate] the national poverty which the American citizens of African descent suffer as a result of chattel slavery." The committee also called for "preferential treatment" in job training and hiring to help elevate people "commonly known as Negroes" to economic parity with their Euro-American counterparts. An acceptable though less desirable alternative would "disfranchise white citizens, deprive them of their citizenship rights, deprive them of their education . . . or generally reduce them to the level of the Negro masses to equalize [American] citizenship."[30] In other words, the pursuit of equity did not necessarily require that black people's condition improve, only that they did not occupy a lower socioeconomic and political status than their white counterparts occupied.

Another reparations effort that fed directly into New Afrikan advocacy came from the African Descendants Nationalist Independence Partition Party (AD NIP), whose members declared their independence from the United States in 1962, established a provisional government, and demanded reparations from the U.S. government in the amount of "nineteen (19) of the fifty (50) states" and "five hundred trillion dollars." As the party explained, "This reparations payment is for the four hundred and fifty (450) years of enslavement of the African Descendants and their ancestors." In reviewing the AD NIP's declaration and the language used to issue the party's demands, it comes as no surprise that Queen Mother Audley Moore served as AD NIP's minister of foreign relations. Robert Williams held multiple positions in the AD NIP's politburo.[31]

The point here is not to analyze in depth the history of black people's enterprises for procuring reparations from the U.S. government, but instead to acknowledge the foundation on which the PG-RNA built its reparations platform.[32] The Black Government Convention and the formation of the NAIM initiated the process of bringing together a number of black nationalist forces, many that participated in struggles for reparations or demanded compensation absent a specific plan to obtain it. Therefore, what is significant is the pivotal role New Afrikans played in helping cohere various efforts for African American reparations into a solid movement.[33]

Since the founding of the PG, New Afrikans have worked consistently to research and make the case for reparations. In 1972, they released the Anti-Depression Program, a plan designed "to end poverty, dependence, cultural malnutrition, and crime" and to "promote inter-racial peace." Filed with the U.S. Congress the year it was published, the program posited three "legislative requests" and delineated how their fulfillment would help solve some of U.S. society's problems.[34] First, New Afrikans suggested an act that would authorize the peaceful release of land and sovereignty to the PG-RNA wherever black people vote for independence. Second, they pursued an act that would authorize a reparations payment to the PG-RNA as compensation for slavery and warfare against African and African-descended peoples in the United States. They suggested $300 billion as fair compensation. Finally, they recommended an act that would permit representatives of the United States and the Republic of New Afrika to negotiate the fine details of a reparations agreement between the two nations.[35] Each request contains an explanation that is worth explicating.

The first legislative request begins with an overview of the various methods by which the United States has acquired land. Conquest, mutual consent, and seizure were important avenues for American land acquisition besides acquisition by purchase and by treaty. Effectively, these various processes indicate that the U.S. Congress and the American president had exercised the power to direct the ownership of American land. In the instances of Texas and Florida, representatives of the U.S. federal government recognized the self-determination of people in those territories, then respectively under Spanish and Mexican control. Sometimes pronouncements of self-determination occurred through a plebiscite, a vote by specific groups of people who wanted to determine the future of their land and citizenship.[36] The point is that the RNA demand was not without precedent, though it was unique because New Afrikans were attempting to remove land and people from the United States, not add to it.

Considering their situation as an exercise in legal interpretation, New Afrikans reiterated their questions regarding the legality of their U.S. citizenship. Here, Obadele expands on the language from the RNA Declaration of

Independence and reiterates his major points from the Article Three Brief. Pointing out the absence of black consent and critical rereadings of the Thirteenth and Fourteenth Amendments, Obadele in particular charged that New Afrikan people needed to receive an opportunity to think carefully about and determine their status as U.S. citizens. He stated that "since the freed slave was deprived of the ability to exercise that right [to self-determination] by mis-information, fraud, and force, that right devolved upon his progeny, the New African." Both amendments included statements about the enforcement of the law. Obadele argued that the United States could enforce the law properly only by considering what African Americans determined as the best options for themselves. That choice should include fair compensation for the crimes committed against them.[37]

The second legislative request sought compensation for war, forced trafficking, and enslavement. As he did in the previous section, Obadele opened with the legal precedents that involved the United States either supporting or helping to secure remuneration for groups and nations that experienced injustice through war. Included as examples were American Indians, as well as nations victimized by Germany during World War I and World War II. Because Obadele framed such payments as an aftermath of war, it was important to follow his list of precedents with examples of warfare that the United States waged against African people in the United States, or "the new African nation." Included in his discussion were the most obvious examples of enslavement and infringement on black people's citizenship rights via the *Dred Scott* decision. These twin assaults placed African people in a state of rightlessness, one that transferred easily into the postbellum criminalization of blackness and African Americans, and which endured into the time when the Republic of New Afrika declared its goal of independence in 1968. Obadele included analysis of cultural war that the United States waged in tandem with the physical attacks and abjection, going so far as to consider this aspect of anti-black warfare as causing greater loss of black life than the various wars since the Civil War.[38]

Finally, the RNA program recommends that the United States of America pay $300 billion in compensation for the multifaceted war it waged against African and African-descended people from the seventeenth through twentieth centuries. If divvied up among the black population in 1972, it would have amounted to about $10,000 for each "descendant of African slaves" in the United States. How did the RNA program come to such a number? "The Republic of New Africa's formula for reparations involves an estimation of the amount due the slave for labor, augmented by six percent interest compounded annually through the present, added to a sum for damages resulting from unjust military warfare and cultural genocide, added to a sum for unlawful deprivation of property since 1868, all reduced to a realizable figure of 300-billion dollars . . . and the cession of sovereignty over a reasonable expanse of land."[39] Slavery and its afterlife of poverty and limited rights of citizenship constituted war to the New Afrikan theorists. As the United States had supported measures for other war-torn nations, Obadele and his peers demanded it do so for the RNA. The United States, according to the RNA, had the ability to create a commission that could meet with New Afrikan representatives in hopes of negotiating the details of the reparations payment to the New Afrikan nation. Like the other two requests, this final one included a list of precedents intended to demonstrate the viability of the RNA request. Commissions prior to the RNA request dealt specifically with the aftermath of wars, including World War I, World War II, and the long-term wars between indigenous peoples and white settlers. Once again, either Congress or the U.S. president would have been able to create such a commission.[40]

The theorists behind these proposals were convinced that if these proposals were carried out, New Afrikans could use the measures to solve the overwhelming majority of problems the authors identified, namely, un- and underemployment, economic and political dependence, poverty, inadequate health, subpar education, poor self-esteem, and antipathy among black people and between them and others, especially white Americans. Anticipating Ta-Nehisi Coates's popular 2014 article, "The Case for Reparations," they established the direct connection between these problems and the United States' predatory relationship with its black inhabitants. In establishing the connection between enslavement, limited rights and/or rightlessness, and everyday living conditions that endured through violence and abjection, New Afrikans helped refine the basic framework around which future reparations advocates could then base their own claims.[41]

The New Afrikan government hoped to obtain $57 billion shortly after negotiating with the U.S. commission. The money had several immediate purposes that, essentially, would help jumpstart the nation-building process in the South while improving the lives of black people who chose to remain outside the national territory. In Obadele's vision, the money would cover tangible expenses such as relocating thousands of southbound families and creating an infrastructure to sustain the RNA's "New Communities." But Obadele also anticipated several important intangible effects. One intended outcome was the concentration of political and economic power that would create space for new ways of living on a daily basis. "The New African life-style will certainly be different from the American, but the emphasis of the design is to benefit the New African, not to harm anyone else."[42] Considering the various ways that the American state and U.S. nationalism were predicated on racial slavery, war against indigenous peoples, and the accumulation of private capital, this "New African life-style" offered a stark contrast from what black people (and many other inhabitants of capitalist societies) experienced under U.S. political authority. Another intended outcome—and this may be most significant—was "the rise of self-esteem, the release of creativity." The assumption was that having a nation-state with which they could wholly identify would help New Afrikan citizens overcome some of the unhealthy psychological conditions that mired black communities in the United States.[43] The acquisition of reparations, therefore, was one very important thread in the tapestry of total liberation.

Ultimately, Obadele contended, addressing these issues by enacting the Anti-Depression Program's three juridical proposals would result in the "removal of the [United States'] hands" from the collective black body. In underscoring the necessity of abolishing white interference, the plan's originators divulged, "This may be, for whites, the most difficult part. Whites, so used to us as 'our Negroes,' must remove their hands from our culture, our economies, our schools, our government, our persons. . . . The essence of reparations is that reparations are given as a debt due, *without* strings."[44] By calling for a "removal of the hands," the architects of the Anti-Depression Program reinforced previous calls for independence as the solution to black people's problems while simultaneously attempting to hold white Americans responsible for their infractions against the U.S. black population.

On this point, New Afrikans were adequately informed by both history and the contemporary situation of African Americans. They learned from past and present events that the key point of the *Dred Scott* decision had not outlived its usefulness for U.S. economic and political interests. Moreover, the "slavery of emancipation" and political liminality induced by an economic system that was dependent on the captivity and forced labor of African people (i.e., racial slavery) created a situation where black human rights were omitted from full consideration at all levels of U.S. society when considering the interest of U.S. capital gain.[45] RNA theorists understood this and argued that the only way their people's human rights would become a significant factor of any conversation was if they had their own nation-state to enforce their full human rights. The rights of American citizenship proved insufficient.

It is not clear whether RNA leaders gained similar insights from the contemporary developments in Africa. If so, why did they continue to focus on UN enforcement of international human rights law? Racism and the war against African people had transformed in the decades following World War II. During this time, African (and other Third World) nation-states formed as the colonized broke free from Europeans. The victories were the partial results of diplomacy and the Western inability to maintain hands-on domination. Africans themselves also reignited fierce warfare against settlers and symbols of colonization when necessary to remove European rulers. New Afrikans and their peers were well aware of these developments and gained inspiration from them. However, inasmuch as they focused on the victories of decolonization, they apparently ignored the legacies of colonization that overdetermined the inability of newly freed African states to develop effective political leadership and economic independence in their own countries. At the forefront of "neocolonialism" were multiple economic organizations and policies that all but ensured that Europe and the United States would continue to dominate the global economic order. The World Bank and International Monetary Fund, created shortly after the close of World War II, often ensnared Third World countries in perpetual indebtedness. The concomitant use of Cold War political devices steered infant nations away from redistributive economic justice and nationalism, preventing them from taking adequate control over their economies or benefiting fully from their countries' natural resources.[46] Obadele and others did not indicate that they were taking these developments into consideration as they pursued their objectives. In fact, in 1977 Obadele indicated that he was still interested in working with the United Nations to obtain reparations and independence.

Over the next four years, the RNA created several subprograms aimed at gaining reparations and self-determination. Brother Imari subsumed these programs under a campaign called the "People's Revolt." Interestingly, he designed the People's Revolt as a major part of his campaign for reelection as RNA president during the time when he was imprisoned and feuding with the Abubakari-Lumumba group within the PG. Along with his vocal demands for reparations, the embattled president organized his bid for re-election around liberating the RNA-11 and other political prisoners and prisoners of war. Significantly, the concurrent operation of these and other efforts under one platform often drew the participation and/or endorsement of high-profile black religious leaders such as Louis Farrakhan, the legal scholar and fiction writer Derrick Bell, playwrights, poets, and others who eventually became influential in other political efforts—Amiri Baraka, Sonia Sanchez, and Dick Gregory, to name a few. These activities had a direct impact on the course of reparations advocacy to come.[47]

Three-time national N'COBRA cochair Dorothy Lewis demonstrates one of the direct connections between the PG-RNA's reparations efforts and those that followed their "Anti-Depression Program." Lewis's writing and activism around reparations have reached the consciousness of countless people who were involved with the movement for African American reparations. The influence of the NAIM on Lewis is clear when she writes: "Would reparations require an amendment to the U.S. Constitution? No, it would simply require putting the Thirteenth Amendment into effect. . . . Although the Thirteenth Amendment set no restrictions on the freedom of former slaves, the Fourteenth Amendment, passed several years later, robbed freed slaves of some of their hard won freedom. Citizenship was imposed upon them without their consent, without a vote, without any discussion of political alternatives."[48] Although Lewis questions the validity of African people's citizenship in the United States, here she stops short of calling for New Afrikan independence. Instead, she emphasizes that a reparations settlement should not replace any of the citizenship rights that African Americans deserved. According to Lewis, "An African born in America is entitled to the same benefits of citizenship as any other first generation or tenth generation American is entitled to." However, she does acknowledge African Americans' rights to exercise their self-determination by deciding whether they want to remain U.S. citizens or take their consent elsewhere. These political alternatives to U.S. citizenship included an independent black nation-state.[49]

Not everyone who acknowledged the problems with black citizenship in the United States called for a plebiscite. In some cases, activists staged large gatherings in order to educate African Americans about the need for reparations and to bring various interested parties together under a coalition. In 1982, Lewis and others held an International Tribunal on Reparations for Black People in the United States in Washington, D.C. New Afrikans and the African Peoples Socialist Party supported and participated in this event. The tribunal led to the creation of the African National Reparations Organization, which then sponsored another tribunal in November 1984. In between these two tribunals, Lewis participated in the PG-RNA reconciliation efforts and attended the 1983 inaugural New Afrikan Nation Day.[50] The New Afrikans in the PG-RNA, NAPO, and other formations joined Lewis and a range of reparations advocates in calling for a coalition that attempted to bring unity to the reparations struggle. Called for in 1987, Brother Imari, Chokwe Lumumba, Nkechi Taifa, the National Conference of Black Lawyers, and many other conscious New Afrikans formed N'COBRA in 1989, and most of these activists held high-ranking positions in the organization. Even though scholars tend to overlook the RNA for its role in helping bring about the current struggle for reparations, Brother Imari's death on January 18, 2010, brought him such acknowledgments. Obituaries ordained him the "Father of Reparations" and mentioned his role in the process of building the current efforts.[51]

Very little academic scholarship about reparations mentions the New Afrikans' Black Power–era dedication to securing reparations for black folks. That which does fails to engage readers in any thorough discussion or analysis of the RNA, or even James Forman's Black Economic Development Conference and his work for the Southern Black Land Bank.[52] What is more, academic literature associated with Black Power barely mentions reparations, except when listing the goals of certain Black Power–era organizations. There is much more to be said beyond what this brief history covered.

. . . . . .

In poetic verse, Brother Imari's son, Imari Obadele II, highlighted some of the major emphases of the New Afrikan argument for reparations. He wrote:

Seems to me there's a master plan
To keep me from getting some land.
That would be alright, [sic]
If i was white,
And it was me that was dealing this hand.
But the fact of the matter,
Is things getting sadder,
And it seems We're out of time.
You pay the other nations,
Their reparations,
But seems you dont [sic] wanna pay me mine.
So dig, white man,
I've got a plan,
And i'm sure you'll find it cool . . .
Pay me. . . . Dont [sic] delay me. . . .
And quit tryin to slay me.

Just give me my forty acres and my mule.
Now some folks will say that i shouldn't be paid,
Just cause my folks were slaves . . .
But, it's about more than that,
It's about war acts,
That are committee [*sic*] on Us every day.
So, may the Most High bless Us,
Whom We ask to peacefully let Us,
Make our Exit-Us . . . And be blessed with
Reparations Yes[53]

In his poem, Obadele II cogently outlines many of the arguments that advocates for African American reparations advance in scholarly articles, books, and anthologies. The first line indicts the author's muse—in this case, the "white man" (the typical stand-in for the United States of America)—for conspiring to prevent New Afrikans from acquiring the five-state territory they claimed as theirs in 1968. The poem proceeds by drawing attention to the various reparations payments the United States issued to other nations that appealed for the redress of past wrongs committed against them. Obadele II questions the validity of antireparations arguments built on the devaluation of racial slavery's effects. He argues that enslavement involved more than forced labor; the institution and its effects constituted "war acts" committed against the enslaved and their descendants. Instead of advocating an in-kind response to those war acts, Obadele II pleads to the Most High to enable New Afrikans' peaceful exercise of their self-determination as a nation supported with the financial restitution owed by the United States for its transgressions against them. The direct descendant of an N'COBRA co-founder and, no doubt, a student of Queen Mother Moore, Obadele II signifies in his poem the inherited legacy and ongoing struggle that his elders and ancestors took up in the midst of the Black Power movement.

The ideas and efforts that Obadele II honors in his poem have found renewed life in the twenty-first century. Although discussions of reparations for African descendants in the United States have been marginalized, now mainstream politicians, Internet advocates and social critics, and grassroots coalitions, among others, are working calls for reparations into their programs and policy proposals. Some examples include various Democrats running in the 2020 presidential primary; Yvette Carnell and Antonio Moore, founders of American Descendants of Slavery; and the Movement for Black Lives. Enjoying the embrace of people from multiple points across the U.S. political spectrum, the varying visions for reparations recall the challenges that proponents have navigated for decades. Questions of what constitutes repair, whether and how to honor indigenous land claims, who deserves restitution, and who is responsible to the victimized parties all compete in mainstream social and political spaces, as well as a multitude of counterpublics. Through it all, the New Afrikan vision of repair continues to contend for and negotiate within varying spaces where the conversation occurs.[54]

Epilogue

On Terrorism, Lingering Silences, and the
Inextinguishable Determination to Free the Land

· ·

Speaking on a C-SPAN-televised town hall in the wake of the 9/11 attacks, Marilyn Preston Killingham explained her understanding of terrorism. She described a force that had long preceded the Taliban's attacks on symbols of U.S. political and economic power. Calling upon the previous forty-plus years of Black Liberation movement history, she explained how she "learned of [her] vulnerability to terrorism in the United States of America." She detailed the coordinated assassinations of Mark Clark and Fred Hampton, the battle at New Bethel in 1969, the raid and shootout in Jackson, Mississippi, on August 18, 1971, and other notable attacks on black freedom fighters. Although death was a factor in the events she named, she explained that those who survived became more fully cognizant of their vulnerability. That, for her, was terrorism.

Killingham told portions of her own story as well. She described her arrest in the late 1960s by a plainclothes police officer in an unmarked car after she reported to Annandale High School, just outside of Washington, D.C., for work. She insinuated that the arrest came at the behest of the school principal, who just one day prior stated that his teachers were not going to be supervised by a "Negra." For the offense of attempting to do her job, she stated, the officer arrested her on the pretense of driving a stolen car. Once at the station, officers took her fingerprints and a mugshot. They held her overnight in what she described as a filthy jail cell. Indicating that there was something unspeakable about her encounters with state-sanctioned violence, Killingham asked rhetorically, "Or did i learn about terrorism in my own Good Friday [April 12], 1974 experience that i will not share with you?" Her noticeable volume reduction and the hardening of her voice let listeners know that significant trauma occurred on a day that held religious significance for her. Her intentional silence on the matter reflects many other unstated and undocumented aspects of the history.

From the assaults on black activists, including her own personal experience, Killingham shifted the focus from the coordinated attacks on symbols of U.S. empire to the country's violence against members of oppressed nations who challenged America's authority. "You see, i know terrorism," she reminded her audience. And she did not "learn about it nine-eleven oh one."[1]

Following decades of continual effort, Killingham's comments could be interpreted as signs of surrender. A stranger listening to these stories of trauma and tragedy might wonder if state repression had succeeded in terrorizing black revolutionaries into submission. The unfamiliar listener might begin to think that by the early moments of the twenty-first century, Killingham and her comrades had given up. However, Killingham's very presence demonstrated that the fight was not over. She spoke as a proponent of various local and national efforts to improve the material conditions of African descendants in the United States and to maintain the political struggle for New Afrikan independence and reparations. Her placement on the stage with an otherwise all-Muslim and male panel demonstrated her ability as a New Afrikan Christian woman to find common ground with the diverse membership of her community. Her words were proof that the New Afrikan Independence Movement (NAIM) had not ended—indeed, it was continuing to weigh in on issues that concern black people and other historically oppressed groups.

Since at least the 1960s, NAIM activists have been visible, and sometimes integral, to various local and national black political projects. Although their main interests have regularly brought them back to the primary goal of freeing the land, the issues through which they have worked alongside their communities have ranged widely. Even as NAIM activists continue to participate in the daily work of organizing in their various locales, the less visible project of molding their lifestyles to New African Political Science (NAPS) has also continued. Participating in the movement led the people like Killingham, whose lives and experiences undergo study in this book, to create lifelong practices and ways of being that would ideally lend themselves to life after the revolution. Although many of them are elders and several have joined the ancestors, their legacy continues. Ongoing advocacy for political prisoners and the broad push for reparations are just two examples of topics that New Afrikan activists helped to make mainstays within black political circles. Their inextinguishable determination to free the land continues through these and other issues.

This study has historicized the NAIM and demonstrated some of the impact of this social movement on people and ideas, yet there are numerous silences that it has not rectified. It has, at best, begun measuring the known silences and, in the process, exposed more.[2] Further research on the movement will need to consider local histories of NAIM forces. Not only are there deeper stories about Detroit and Jackson waiting for exposure, but the voices of New Afrikans in New York, Philadelphia, New Orleans, Houston, Oakland, Washington, D.C., Atlanta, Cleveland, Chicago, and numerous other urban and rural locales must be heard if we are to understand the full scope of the movement. It remains to be seen how and through what apparatuses the movement's adherents operated and the relationship between the movement and other organizations, such as the Black Panther Party, the Black Liberation Army, and a number of Pan-African nationalist formations. Only through further research will we be able to answer comprehensively the lingering question of how members of organizations such as Ahidiana in New Orleans and the multicity Black People's Topographical Research Center related to the NAIM, NAPS, and the concept of an independent New Afrikan nation-state.

Knowing the actors and organizations behind various ideas and actions, grasping their motives and goals, and struggling with the strengths and weaknesses of the movement will be vital to the development of new ideas and strategies to undermine oppression. Exposing and measuring the silences that still remain will require all of the intellectual tools at our disposal—not just the methods of history and sociology, but geography, performance and film theory, communication studies and rhetoric, economic theory, and more. To fully understand the complexity of liberation struggle in America, the story of the NAIM must not be silenced.

Notes

Archive Abbreviations

173/LNSR	Liberation News Service Records
396/CCCC	Contemporary Culture Collection Periodicals
Alston	Chris and Marti Alston Collection (at WPR)
CCCC	Contemporary Culture Collection Periodicals (at SCRC)
CDIC	City of Detroit Inter-Office Correspondence (at WPR)
CMSC	Charles Deering McCormick Library of Special Collections
Cockrel	Kenneth V. and Sheila M. Cockrel Papers (at WPR)
CRDP	Civil Rights Documentation Project (at the Moorland Spingarn Research Center, Howard University)
DCCR	Detroit Commission on Community Relations–Human Rights Department: Part 3 (at WPR)
FAO	Freedom Archives (Online)
FBI-BSH	FBI Records of Betty Shabazz 105-71196 (Online)
FBI-GOAL	FBI Records of the Group on Advanced Leadership 100-HQ-442379.
FBI-MRH	FBI Records of Milton Robinson Henry 100-HQ-412654
FBI-RNA HQ	FBI Records (HQ) of the Republic of New Afrika 100-HQ-444362
FBI-RNA LA	FBI Records (LA) of the Republic of New Afrika 100A-LA-87436
GRP	Personal Papers of General Kuratibisha X Ali Rashid
LNSR	Liberation News Service Records (at SCRC)
MDAH	Mississippi State Department of Archives and History
MSSCR	Mississippi Sovereignty Commission Records (at MDAH)
MSU	Special Collections, Michigan State University
NDI	New Detroit, Inc. (at WPR)
NTP	Personal Papers of Nkechi Taifa
RAM	John Bracey Jr. and Sharon Harley, eds., *The Black Power Movement Part 3: The Papers of the Revolutionary Action Movement, 1962–1996*
RIP	Radical Information Project
RNAC	T/027: Republic of New Africa Collection (at MDAH)
ROB	John Bracey Jr. and Sharon Harley, eds., *The Black Power Movement Part 2: The Papers of Robert F. Williams*
SBC	Sgt. Brown Collection, Tougaloo College
SCL	Special Collections Library, University of Michigan
SCRC	Special Collections Research Center, Temple University
SFRNA	SF/Republic of New Africa 1970–1971 (at MDAH)
TIN	*The Illustrated News*
WPR	Walter P. Reuther Library

Introduction

1. The Provisional Government decided on November 30, 1975, to spell Afrika with a *k* rather than a *c*. For coherence and because this has been their preferred spelling for most of their existence, I use the *k* spelling to refer to the land and movement to secure that land prior to the actual spelling change. Likewise, readers will see the personal pronoun *i* in lowercase (see chapter 3). When quoting New Afrikan documents, I honor the recorded spelling. Regarding the founding meeting, although it was originally called the Black Government Conference, Christian Davenport indicates that the RNA founders redefined the meeting as a convention shortly after it began "so that the actions of the participants could be directed toward black nationhood." Therefore, the RNA Declaration of Independence states that it was "Approved in Convention," and Imari Obadele referred to it as such in his published memoir of the RNA-11. The founders settled on the name "Republic of New Africa" after deciding against "Songhay Republic." For *k* spelling, see "Black Nation Day," *The New Afrikan*, March 1976, 2, NTP. For convention, see Davenport, *How Social Movements Die*, 165; "Founding Convention Schedule Draft," group 1, ser. 4, reel 10, frame 138, ROB; and Obadele, *Free the Land!*, 267.

2. Nkechi Taifa, "Tidbits for History of PG RNA," NTP; and Conversation with Abdul-Aziz et al.

3. Several scholars have written about and debated the merits of the internal colony thesis, a widely discussed concept during the 1960s. For example, see R. Allen, *Black Awakening*.

4. New Afrikans have used the slogan "free the land!" through most, if not all, of the movement's history.

5. Republic of New Africa, *Forming Municipal*, 3, box 1, ser. 1, bay 1, folder 1, MDAH; and Milton R. Henry and Brother Imari (Richard B. Henry) to Hon. George Romney, January 15, 1968, disk 1, sec. 4, FBI-MRH.

6. "Birth of Our Nation," RIP.

7. For news coverage and basic information about these independence efforts, see "South Sudan Referendum"; "Scottish Independence Referendum"; Gea and Suarez, "Human Tower Builders"; and Perreaux, "After 40 Years."

8. "Jair Bolsonaro"; Intergovernmental Panel on Climate Change, "Summary for Policymakers"; Markus, "Far-Right's Creeping Influence"; Palatino, "Philippines' Duterte"; Hunt and Wheeler, "Brexit"; B. Wolf, "Trump." At least one U.S. website tracks groups associated with the Far Right. See http://www.rightwingwatch.org /organizations/.

9. See Obadele, *War in America*; R. Hall, *Black Separatism*, 219–20.

10. Self-determination generally infers that a group has the liberty to determine its own social and political fate. For African Americans, it includes their rights to exercise political power, obtain land and wealth by their own efforts, acquire and control their education, and use available assets to further their own causes. For Marxists, self-determination for oppressed nations typically means the right to struggle for independence. New Afrikans understood it to ultimately include their right to decide whether they would create an independent nation. For discussions

on self-determination, see Forman, *Self-Determination*; Franklin, *Black Self-Determination*; Lenin, *Collected Works*, 393–455.

11. Bennett, "Branded Political Communication," 103. See also Evans, *Personal Politics*.

12. See, for example, Brisbane, *Black Activism*; R. Hall, *Black Separatism*; Joseph, *Waiting 'til the Midnight Hour*; Kelley, *Freedom Dreams*; Thompson, *Whose Detroit?*; Van Deburg, *New Day in Babylon*; R. Williams, *Concrete Demands*.

13. Giugni, "Political, Biographical, and Cultural Consequences"; Marwell and Aiken, "1960s Civil Rights Activists"; Sherkat et al., "Explaining the Political"; Van Dyke, McAdam, and Wilhelm, "Gendered Outcomes"; Wilhelm, "Changes in Cohabitation."

14. Sherkat and Blocker, "Explaining the Political," 1051–53.

15. Two exceptions are Sherkat and Blocker, "Explaining the Political"; and Whalen and Flacks, *Beyond the Barricades*.

16. And at an even more basic level, these studies tend to begin with the moment of activism. In other words, they do not evaluate the full life of their subjects. Though it is not framed as such, Diane C. Fujino's *Heartbeat of Struggle*, a biography of Japanese American activist Yuri Kochiyama, attends to the issues that sociologists seek to better understand.

17. Matthews, "No One Ever Asks"; Spencer, "Engendering the Black Freedom Struggle."

18. Other scholars help advance the ideas and analysis in the subsequent pages of this book. They include S. Brown, *Fighting for US*; S. Brown, "Politics of Culture"; Farmer, *Remaking Black Power*; Spencer, *Revolution Has Come*; Springer, *Living for the Revolution*; and Taylor, *Promise of Patriarchy*. For movement activists' perspectives on the interconnectedness of culture and social movements, see Cabral, *Return to the Source*, 39–56; Fanon, *Wretched*, 206–48; Neal, "Any Day Now"; and Franklin, *Black Self-Determination*.

19. Generally speaking, participant observation helped guide my understanding and interpretation of NAPS and New Afrikans' lived experiences.

20. For various perspectives on both approaches, see Cha-Jua and Lang, "'Long Movement' as Vampire"; Carson, *In Struggle*; J. Hall, "Long Civil Rights Movement"; and Theoharis and Woodard, *Freedom North*.

Chapter 1

1. On C. L. Franklin, see Reverend Albert B. Cleage Jr., "Freedom March," *TIN*, June 10, 1963, 3; and "Rev. Albert B. Cleage Resigns from DCHR," *TIN*, October 28, 1963, 3. See also A. Dillard, *Faith in the City*, 269–72.

A quick note on names and spelling: after introducing people using both their European and, where applicable, Afrikan names, I often refer to them by their Afrikan names and periodically utilize their preferred titles, including "Brother," "Sister," "Mama," and "Baba," to provide readers with a feel for the language and culture that New Afrikans and many other black nationalists have been creating since the 1960s. See chapter 3 for a fuller discussion of names and titles.

2. "Cops' Version," A3; "Policeman Killed," 1; "New Detroit to Probe Church Raid Charges," *Detroit News*, April 8, 1969, 2A, 4A, RIP; John Griffith, "Cavanaugh Defends Police Acts," *Free Press*, April 2, 1969, RIP; Al Stark, "'Shot on the Floor': Bethel Raid Victim Talks," *Detroit News*, April 4, 1969, 3A, RIP; Lee Winfrey, "Police Tell of Shooting in Church," *Free Press*, April 9, 1969, 1A, 8A, RIP; The Detroit Police Commissioner's *24th District Reporter: Del Rio—Reports*, box 188, folder 27, NDI. See also Georgakas and Surkins, *Detroit*, 55–56.

3. Lester's clever, albeit problematic, title played on the widely recognized fear that African Americans would exact revenge on white America for enslavement, racial violence, and discrimination by violently taking over the United States and sexually conquering white women. Although Lester's book seeks to undermine the mainstream perception of the Black Power movement, Lester does not apply equal criticism to the feminine metaphor for the nation. See Lester, *Look Out Whitey!* For and white fears about black domination, see Reguly, "Detroit," ROB group 1, ser. 4, reel 10, frame 26.

4. Regulay, "Detroit."

5. Katzman, *Before the Ghetto*; Lewis-Coleman, *Race against Liberalism*; Sugrue, *Origins*; Thomas, *Life for Us*, 1–19; Thompson, *Whose Detroit?*, 12; and Welch et al., *Race and Place*, 21–22.

6. Lewis-Coleman, *Race against Liberalism*, 1–24.

7. Geschwender, *Class, Race, and Worker Insurgency*; Sitkoff, "Detroit Race Riot of 1943"; Widick, *Detroit*, 5–22.

8. Historian Megan Taylor Shockley demonstrates how such women employed the rhetorical power of motherhood as a tool in many of these battles for what they considered to be full citizenship rights that challenged the apparently masculine norm. See Shockley, *"We, Too, Are Americans,"* 170–204.

9. Smethurst, *Black Arts Movement*, 184–85; Georgakas and Surkin, *Detroit*, 57; Thompson, *Whose Detroit?*, 22–23.

10. A. Dillard, *Faith in the City*; Meier and Rudwick, *Black Detroit*, 219; Smethurst, *Black Arts Movement*, 183. For a general characterization of the shift to direct action, see McAdam, *Political Process*; and Morris, *Origins*. See also McDuffie, *Sojourning for Freedom*.

11. Fine, *"Expanding the Frontiers,"* 9.

12. A. Dillard, *Faith in the City*, 210–20; P. Foner, *Organized Labor*, 296–311; and Meier and Rudwick, *Black Detroit*, 221.

13. Warrant, *Independent Black Political Action*, 17.

14. Grace Lee Boggs, a Chinese American woman who earned her PhD in philosophy in 1940, was a notable activist whose political ambitions, intellectual prowess, and marriage to James Boggs ranked her among the "who's who" of Detroit activists involved in the black liberation struggle. James Boggs was a southern-born revolutionary thinker and activist whose 1963 book, *The American Revolution: Pages from a Negro Worker's Notebook*, distinguished him from other Marxian thinkers of his time because of his emphasis on African Americans as a revolutionary class. Together the interracial couple developed important relationships with C. L. R. James, Kwame Nkrumah, and the Socialist Workers Party. By the early 1960s, they

were independent theorists whose home and ideas had become popular among young revolutionaries. Reverend Cleage was a "Christian Nationalist" minister who would later create the Shrine of the Black Madonna. His brand of liberation theology had, by the early 1960s, energized him to use a combination of grassroots and institutional politics to achieve black equality. Ahmad, *We Will Return*, 137–43; G. Boggs, *Living for Change*, 34; A. Dillard, *Faith in the City*; Joseph, *Waiting 'til the Midnight Hour*, 84–94; S. Smith, *Dancing in the Street*; Ward, *In Love and Struggle*.

15. James Geschwender and Judson Jeffries, "The League," in J. Jeffries, *Black Power*, 135–62. See also Georgakas and Surkins, *Detroit*; Geschwender, *Class, Race, and Worker Insurgency*, quote on xiii.

16. Ahmad, *We Will Return*, 159; Ahmad, "RAM," in J. Jeffries, *Black Power*, 270.

17. For connections between New Afrikans and the BPP, see Rahman, "Marching Blind." See also Austin, *Up against the Wall*.

18. Clegg, *Original Man*; Gomez, *Black Crescent*, especially chapter 7. For an interesting perspective on including the NOI more fully into the discussion of Black Power, see A. Muhammad, "'Black Power.'"

19. "'GOAL' Takes New Tack," *TIN*, November 13, 1961, quotes on page 3; "School Bias Fight: 'GOAL' President Defies Brownell," *TIN*, September 24, 1962; "Re-Thinking Integration," *TIN*, December 4, 1961, 4, 7, quote on page 4; "Subject: Milton Henry," August 17, 1964, sec. 1, FBI-MRH; Fine, *Violence in the Model City*, 26; Richard B. Henry, "'GOAL' Defines Position on Urban Renewal," *TIN*, March 5, 1962, 2, 6; Richard Henry, "Urban Renewal: Patrick and the Real Issues," *TIN*, April 2, 1962, 3; GOAL, "Key Questions and Answers on Urban Renewal by GOAL," *TIN*, April 9, 1962, 4–5; and "How Segregated Super Market Buying Keeps You from Enjoying Vicki's Bar-B-Q Sauce," *TIN*, November 12, 1962, 7.

20. In contrast with popular perceptions of Detroit, one of the city's police commissioners claimed that his predominately white police force was 90 percent bigoted. The black community was no stranger to overt hostility. In a survey study, 40 percent of black respondents revealed that police displayed an attitude of general disrespect. They referred to black men as "boy" and treated black women as if they were prostitutes. Additionally, the police's disproportionate arrest of black Detroiters, regular use of "stop-and-frisk," and physical violence convinced African Americans that their neighborhoods were occupied by a hostile army. In fact, between January 1, 1961, and July 23, 1967 (the first day of the Detroit rebellion), African Americans constituted 59 percent of those who complained that the police brutalized them. See Fine, *Violence in the Model City*, 97–115.

21. Ahmad, *We Will Return*, 122–23 and 151–52; Dunbar, "Making of a Militant," 25–32; SA William J. Winchester to Secret Service, Detroit, December 14, 1965, sec. 2, FBI-MRH; Sherrill, "Birth of a (Black) Nation"; and Malcolm X, "God's Judgment."

22. Obadele, *War*, 3–4; Van Deburg, *New Day*, 144–45; Lumumba, *Roots*, 9; Malcolm X, *Malcolm X*.

23. See "The Changing Image of the Negro," *TIN*, December 4, 1961, 2; "Re-Thinking Integration," *TIN*, December 4, 1961, 3, 7; Dunbar, "Making of a Militant," 29; and Obadele, *Revolution and Nation Building*.

24. Obadele, *War*, 1. Emphasis in the original.

25. Atty. Milton Henry and Imari (Richard B. Henry), "Statement of the Malcolm X Society to the Hudson Committee," n.d., box 135, folder 29, NDI; Obadele, *War*; Dunbar, "Making of a Militant," 29; and Sherrill, "Birth of a (Black) Nation," 72–73.

26. See, for example, Fine, *Violence in the Model City*; Widick, *Detroit*; United States Kerner Commission, U.S. National Advisory Commission on Civil Disorders, *Report*.

27. Henry and Imari, "Statement"; Ahmad, *We Will Return*, 151–52; Dunbar, "Making of a Militant," 31; Fine, *Violence in the Model City*; and Willis, *Second Civil War*, 128–33.

28. Henry and Imari, "Statement"; Obadele, *War*; Dunbar, "Making of a Militant," 29; and Sherrill, "Birth of a (Black) Nation," 72–73.

29. Lumumba, *Roots*, 37–38.

30. For details about the CP's take on black self-determination, see J. Allen, *Negro Question*, 195–203; Dawson, *Black Visions*, 196; Lumumba, *Roots*, 5–8, 38–39; and Ahmad, *We Will Return*, 10–11. For Queen Mother Moore's take on the CP's abandoning of black self-determination, see McDuffie, "I Wanted a Communist Philosophy," 185. For membership estimates of these various organizations, see Kuykendall, "African Blood Brotherhood," 17; Makalani, *In the Cause of Freedom*, 45; Vincent, *Voice of a Black Nation*, 123; and "Communist Party Membership."

31. Gary Blonston, "Group Linked to Shooting: RNA's Goal: Black Nation," *Detroit Free Press*, March 31, 1969, 1A, 10A, col. 3, box 21, folder 23, DCCR; Sherrill, "Birth of a (Black) Nation," 72. The convention took place at three different locations: The Shrine of the Black Madonna (7625 Linwood Ave), the 20 Grand Motel, and Wayne State University.

32. Kuratibisha Ali X Rashid, "The Military Story behind the Founding of the Republic of New Afrika," unpublished document, n.d., GRP; Lumumba, *Roots*, 9–10. Quote on page 10.

33. Brother Milton R. Henry to Unnamed Recipients, March 15, 1968, GRP.

34. "Congressional Hearing, 'Riots, Civil and Criminal Disorders,'" reel 16, ser. 12, frames 397–402, RAM.

35. Quote from Republic of New Afrika, "Declaration of Independence," GRP. Delegates signed the document in the Derby Room of the Twenty Grand Hotel. See also "Congressional Hearing," reel 16, ser. 12, frames 401–2, RAM; and reel 6, ser. 5, frames 692–93, RAM.

36. "Proposal: The Provisional Government," ROB, reel 10, group 1, ser. 4, frame 138; Provisional Government-Republic of New Afrika, "Code of Umoja," GRP; Gaidi Obadele, "Executive Order Number 1," ROB, reel 10, group 1, ser. 4, frame 162; "The Republic of New Africa" in C. Hamilton, *Black Experience in American Politics*, 61.

37. "Congressional Hearing"; "New Africans Push Black Legion, Tax, Popular Vote," *Ujamaa Newsletter* 1, no. 1 (June 15, 1968), 1, SCL; Obadele, *Free the Land!*, 90. For background on the PG-RNA's strategy, see Obadele, *War*.

38. Imari Obadele, "Freedom: The Eight Strategic Elements Necessary for Success of a Black Nation in America" (A Synopsis of a Speech by Brother Imari, September 1968), n.d., box 1, folder 1, RNAC.

39. Obadele, "Eight Strategic Elements"; Obadele, *Revolution and Nation Building*, 18–30; and Republic of New Africa, "Short Official Basic Documents," NTP.

40. Obadele, "Eight Strategic Elements"; Los Angeles to Director, "RNA Cabinet Meeting," August 23, 1968, "Subject: Republic of New Africa," sec. 3, FBI-RNA LA; and Ya Salaam, "We Are New Afrika," 62–71. For more on Williams's life, see Tyson, *Radio Free*.

41. Obadele, *Revolution and Nation Building*, 6–10, 30–31. See also Sherrill, "Birth of a (Black) Nation," 75; Obadele, *War*, 51–64.

42. There were two RNA offices on Puritan Street. The first was located at 2217 Puritan. They later moved the office to 2595 Puritan Street and then to 9823 Dexter Street. RNA meetings also took place in various homes, the local YMCA, the 20 Grand Motel, and Wayne State University. Michigan State Police, "Additional Complaint Report," May 14, 1969, RIP. See also "Black Army Seeking Recruits: Women Included," *Michigan Chronicle*, March 1, 1969, RIP; "Petition Campaign for 'Juridical Status' for Blacks, *Michigan Chronicle*, June 7, 1969, RIP; Detroit Police Department, "Surveillance of Stuart Williams House N/M/22, 16595 Baylis," January 2, 1969, RIP; Detroit Police Department, "Information Received from Special Investigation Bureau Source [deleted]," February 7, 1969, RIP; Detroit Police Department, "Information Received from Special Investigation Bureau Source # 718," November 12, 1969, reel 21, group 2, ser. 4, frames 977–90, ROB. Quote from Provisional Government–Republic of New Afrika, "The New Afrikan Creed: Fundamental Principles that Guide the New Afrikan Independence Movement," GRP.

43. "Williams Calls for Broad Foreign Aid to Africa," *Ujamaa Newsletter* 1, no. 1 (June 15, 1968), 1, SCL; and Ya Salaam, "We Are New Afrika," 67–69.

44. "1969," RIP; "Congressional Hearing," frame 345, 402, ROB; Ya Salaam, "We Are New Afrika," 68.

45. "Petition Drive on for Black Republic," *Jet*, September 12, 1968, reel 9, group 1, ser. 4, frame 210, ROB; "Reparations Drive Started," *The New African* 1, no. 1 (July 20, 1968), 1 ser. 10, reel 14, frame 11, RAM; "Williams Calls"; Imari Obadele to Robert Williams, November 28, 1968, reel 20, group 2, ser. 4, frames 770–71, ROB; and Ya Salaam, "We Are New Afrika." For media coverage of the Black Power Conference, see "Plan 'Separate Nation for U.S. Black People," *Journal and Guide*, September 11, 1968, reel 10, group 1, ser. 4, frame 28, ROB. For more detail on black college students, see "1969."

46. "Gunmen Out to Get Me, Says Bethel Defendant," *Detroit Free Press*, October 30, 1970, RIP; Sister Ayodele to Unnamed Recipients, n.d., RIP; Blonston, "Group Linked to Shooting," 1A; Douglas Glazier, "Bethel Trial to Be Heard by Circuit Judge Gilmore," *Detroit News*, September 9, 1970, RIP; Fred Manardo, "Fuller, Freed in Bethel Case, Is Slain by Knifer," *Detroit News*, October 20, 1970, 1A, 10A, RIP; and Special Investigation Bureau Memo, March 2, 1969. Quote in "New Africa Head Blasts Cahalan," *Michigan Chronicle*, July 4, 1970, box 21, folder 23, DCCR. For a full transcript of George Crockett's handling of arrestees and complaints about police conduct, see *24th District Reporter: Del Rio—Reports*, box 188, folder 27, NDI; Obadele, *Free the Land!*, 36; and Rahman, "Walking Blind," 189–90.

47. General Kuratibisha Ali X Rashid stated, "The Detroit shootout and this one here 'cause they scared hell outta people who were selling us land. They took it back—and made us the enemy." Conversation with Hannibal Tirus Afrik, March 29, 2009.

48. "Black United Front Lashes Police, Lauds Crockett," *Michigan Chronicle*, April 12, 1969. In author's possession. Detroit Police Department, "Information Received from Special Investigation Bureau Source [deleted]," RIP.

49. Ya Salaam, "We Are New Afrika," 68–69; Milton R. Henry to Prime Minister Harold Wilson, n.d., reel 10, group 1, frames 163–64, ROB; Williams Schmidt, "Black Separatists Awaited; Militants, Police Greet Wrong Williams," *Detroit Free Press*, September 8, 1969, DCCR.

50. Detroit (157-3161), "Richard Bullock Henry, aka.," December 22, 1969, RIP; Michigan State Police, Complaint Report, January 19, 1970, RIP; Michigan State Police Complaint Report, January 22, 1970, RIP; Michigan State Police Report, February 2, 1970, RIP.

51. Detroit Police Department Memo, February 25, 1969, RIP; Tom Ricke, "President of RNA Resigns," *Detroit Free Press*, December 4, 1969, box 21, folder 23, DCCR; SAC, Detroit to Director, FBI, "Re: Bureau Letter to Detroit to Detroit, dated 12/3/68, and Detroit Airtel to Bureau, Dated 1/18/69," February 6, 1969, RIP; SAC, Detroit to Director, FBI, "Re Detroit Airtel to Bureau, Dated 1/13/69, Captioned Above," RIP; Detroit Police Department, "Information from Special Investigation Bureau Source # [deleted], December 2, 1969, reel 21, frame 979, ROB; and Clarence M. Kelley, Director to Mr. Imari Abubakari Obadele, I, March 30, 1977, box 111, folder 4—Republic of New Africa, LNSR.

52. Imari Obadele to Gaidi Obadele and Robert Williams, November 21, 1969, in reel 4, group 1, ser. 1, frames 503–505, ROB; Michigan State Police, "Additional Complaint Report," November 13, 1969, RIP; Brogan, "Williams Quits"; Mary Kochiyama to Robert and Mabel Williams, December 13, 1969, reel 4, group 1, ser. 1, frames 515–16, ROB; Ahmad, "RAM," 270; and Ahmad, "Revolutionary Action Movement/Republic of New Afrika," Art & Power in Movement, University of Massachusetts Amherst, November 20, 2010.

53. "The Republic of New Africa," ser. 5, reel 6, frame 693, RAM; Henry E. Wittenberg, "Imari's Faction Picks a New Temporary Leader," *Detroit News*, January 26, 1970, RIP; "Henry's Split Is Denied," Detroit News, January 24, 1970, RIP; "Assassination, Bomb Scares Fizzle at RNA Convention," *Michigan Chronicle*, RIP; "Henry Brother's Rift Causes Split in RNA," *Detroit News*, November 16, 1969, 1, RIP; Brother Imari to Gaidi Obadele and Robert Williams, November 21, 1969, reel 4, group 1, ser. 1, frames 503–505, ROB; and Obadele, *Free the Land!*, 8–9. See also Detroit Police Department memos, reel 21, frames 977–1004, ROB.

54. Kwame-Osagyefo Kalimara and Chokwe Lumumba, "Chronological History of Constitutional Crisis in Provisional Government of Republic of New Afrika," December 13, 1980. In author's possession courtesy of Chokwe Lumumba.

55. Conversation with Lumumba, March 28, 2010; Osagyefo and Lumumba, "Chronological History," 1–2.

56. According to FBI surveillance, Sister Shabazz resigned just prior to the New Bethel Incident. Her role in the PG-RNA seemed more nominal in nature and was meant to inspire more African American interest in the RNA. See Bufile (105-71196) to NYfile (105-29845), February 2, 1969, pt. 2, FBI-BSH; and "Report of [deleted]" March 16, 1970, pt. 2, FBI-BSH.

57. Wittenberg, "Imari's Faction"; FBI Report, July 30, 1970, RIP; John Peterson, "Strife-Torn RNA Drafts Charter," *Detroit News*, January 25, 1970, RIP; John Peterson, "Richard Henry Claims RNA Victory over Milton," *Detroit News*, April 1, 1970, RIP; Edward Shanahan, "Weary of Revolution: Separatist Joins Suburbia," *Detroit Free Press*, July 2, 1970, DCCR; Gaidi Obadele to New Afrikans, January 19, 1970, reel 10, group 1, ser. 4, frame 158, ROB; Republic of New Africa, *Short Official Basic Documents*; Dunbar, "Making of a Militant," 31; "RNA Moves HQ South," *Detroit Free Press*, April 6, 1970, RIP; SAC, New Orleans to Director, FBI, May 26, 1970, RIP.

58. Johnson, *Revolutionaries to Race Leaders*, especially chapters 3–4.

59. For a first-person overview of the circumstances surrounding the August 18 shootout, see Obadele, *Free the Land*.

60. Conversation with Lumumba, March 28, 2010.

61. Conversation with Lumumba, March 28, 2010.

62. Conversation with Lumumba, March 28, 2010.

63. Conversation with Lumumba, March 28, 2010. For a detailed history of these groups, especially the House of Umoja, see Watani Sundai Umoja Tyehimba, "NAPO / MXGM ROOTS & CHRONOLOGY: 1960–1998." In author's possession courtesy of Dr. Akinyele Omowale Umoja.

64. Imari Abubakari Obadele, "Clarifying the Current Provisional Government Controversy," n.d., 1, box 6, folder 15, Alston; "Malcolm X Party Principles and Structure," n.d., box 111, folder 4—Republic of New Africa, LNSR.

65. On political taunting, see "Study Finds Congress."

66. The agreement occurred on March 13, just days before Black Nation Day in Detroit. "Agreement Brings Unity of RNA Government Near," *The New Afrikan Journal*, April 1983, 4, 24, NTP.

67. Conversation with Lumumba, March 31, 2009; Conversation with Umoja, March 20, 2010.

Chapter 2

1. "The Flag of Our Nation," n.d. (ca. 1970), RIP.

2. "CCAC" Leaflet, n.d. (ca. 1967), RIP; V. Stoner to Mr. Marks, November 30, 1967, "Subject: Meeting CCAC 11-29-67," box 18, folder 23, CDIC; and Vaughn, *RED BLACK and GREEN*. By the early 1980s, some versions of the New Afrikan flag included a phoenix placed at the center. The fiery bird itself gained frequent use in RNA periodicals such as *New Afrikan Notes*, a publication of the Malcolm X Party faction of the PG-RNA during that era. See *New Afrikan Notes* 1, no. 3 (August 1981), Alston; Imari Obadele, "Time to Play Our New Afrikan Card Part 3: Taking the First Step

for Economic Empowerment," *The New Afrikan Journal: The Official Voice of the Malcolm X Party*, n.d., 4, GRP.

3. One document states that NAPS is an "ideology for analyzing the historical condition of New Afrikan people and for devising means to improve that condition." Ukali Mwendo, "New Afrikan Political Science," n.d. In author's possession courtesy of Ukali Mwendo. Cultural scholar Stuart Hall defines ideology as "the mental frameworks—the languages, the concepts, categories, imagery of thought, and systems of representation—which different classes of social groups deploy in order to make sense of, define, figure out and render intelligible the way society works." S. Hall, "Problem of Ideology," 26.

4. Republic of New Afrika, "Declaration." For explanations of the term *Maafa*, see Marimba Ani, *Yurugu*, xxi, and 583-84; and Erriel D. Roberson, *Maafa & Beyond*, 6.

5. Republic of New Afrika, "Declaration." The RNA conception of ending global oppression may seem to recall Trotsky's theory of "Permanent Revolution." Therein, Trotsky states that revolution cannot be confined to national struggles, that socialist revolution must have an international character. However, there is a long-standing tendency in African American thought to argue that no African person in the United States could be free until Africans all over the world were free. This argument was manifest in the overwhelming black support of the Haitian revolution; it found resonance with David Walker and Maria Stewart, abolitionists and black activists such as Frederick Douglass, Martin Delaney, and Alexander Crummell. Black club women and Pan-Africanists of the late nineteenth and early twentieth centuries found ways to theorize about and act in accordance with the belief in a common oppression and therefore, liberation. And Garvey, the African Blood Brotherhood, and many more African-descended people in the twentieth century made similar claims. See Trotsky, "Permanent Revolution."

6. Republic of New Afrika, "Declaration."

7. Republic of New Afrika, "Declaration."

8. Guy-Sheftall, *Words of Fire*, 231–40; D. King, "Multiple Jeopardy"; and Springer, *Living for the Revolution*.

9. Young, *Soul Power*. A debate occurred in the 1970s around the idea of black Americans being aligned with the Third World. Even as the PG-RNA, Congress of African People, and Black Panther Party began to consider themselves as key players in, and in some instances as at the forefront of, global revolution, Haki Madhubuti, Shawna Maglangbayan, and others detested that African Americans should consider themselves the "vanguard" of such a movement. Their reasoning included that African people had a history of being put on the front lines of other people's struggles, without those people returning the favor for them. See Madhubuti, "Latest Purge"; and Maglangbayan, *Garvey, Lumumba and Malcolm*, 88.

10. Dubois and Garrigus, *Slave Revolution in the Caribbean*.

11. Geschwender and Jeffries, "League of Revolutionary Black Workers," in J. Jeffries, *Black Power*, 151.

12. Newton and Blake, *Revolutionary Suicide*, iv.

13. Provisional Government–Republic of New Afrika, "New Afrikan Creed," GRP.

14. As should be clear by now, the Nation of Islam was a significant influence in both the wording and the ultimate goals of the RNA declaration and broader program. The Honorable Elijah Muhammad explained "what the Muslims want" in 1965, outlining their demands for societal justice, a separate state or territory, and reparations. However, the New Afrikan Declaration of Independence proved more progressive in that it is more inclusive of varying religious practices, clearly calls for "equality of rights" regardless of sex, and supports revolution wherever oppression exists. Nevertheless, with some founding New Afrikans being current members (at least at the time of the founding convention), or former members of the NOI, and with others being admirers, the inspiration of the NOI on adherents of the NAIM is undeniable. See E. Muhammad, *Message*; Essien-Udom, *Black Nationalism*, 250–64; and Lincoln, *Black Muslims*, 87–97. Importantly, some New Afrikans have begun to point out the potentially ableist nature of the phrase. See "Thoughts on the Creed."

15. See, for example, Newton and Blake, *Revolutionary Suicide*; Joseph, *Waiting 'til the Midnight Hour*; Sales Jr., *From Civil Rights*; and Van Deburg, *New Day in Babylon*.

16. Provisional Government–Republic of New Afrika, "New Afrikan Creed," GRP; "Political and Philosophical Documents of the Independence Movement Which Guide the Work of the Provisional Government of the Republic of New Afrika," n.d., GRP; Provisional Government Republic of New Afrika, "The Republic of New Afrika: Land Independence, Self-Determination," n.d., NTP.

17. See, for example, Taifa, "The Spirit of Author McDuffie," *The New Afrikan Journal* (1980): 35, NTP.

18. See "Oath of Allegiance Issued at Chicago," *New African* 1, no. 1 (July 20, 1968), GRP; "The Oath," n.d., GRP; and Republic of New Africa, *Short Official Basic Documents*, 3.

19. "Message to Our Young Brothers and Sisters," reel 10, frames 671–72, RAM.

20. There has always been some tension about how advocates and opponents define "Black Power." See Carmichael and Hamilton, *Black Power*; Joseph, "Black Power Movement," 751–76; Martin Luther King Jr., *Where Do We Go from Here*; Van Deburg, *New Day in Babylon*.

21. Newton and Blake, *Revolutionary Suicide*, 118; Seale, *Seize the Time*, 68. For information about the introduction of the plebiscite, see Spencer, *Revolution Has Come*, 84–85; and 141–42.

22. Newton, "To the RNA," 72.

23. A few attempts for self-determination help make the potential problems to which Newton spoke clear. Besides Haiti and Cuba, which did not have the support of their powerful neighbors when they achieved independence and socialist revolution, respectively, Biafra and Cameroon provide useful case studies. See, for example, Atanga, *Anglophone Cameroon Predicament*; and Uzoigwe, "Background." For analysis of Haiti and Texas, see Bevill, *Paper Republic*; Dubois, *Avengers of the New World*; Miller, *New Orleans and the Texas Revolution*; Popkin, *Concise History of the Haitian Revolution*.

24. Newton, "Speech," 33.

25. See also Bukhari, *War Before*, 18–19; Shakur, *Assata*, 225–26; and Conversation with Sunni-Ali.

26. Congress of African Peoples, "Republic of New Africa: Proposed Resolutions for Political Liberation Workshop," n.d., box 159-11, folder 13, CRDP.

27. For an explanation of *ubuntu*, see Tutu, *No Future without Forgiveness*, 34–35.

28. For Karenga's popularization of the term, see Mayes, *Kwanzaa*, 142–43; Nyerere, *Freedom and Socialism*, 2. For a theoretical explanation and critique of this concept, see Nyerere, *Ujamaa*, 106–10.

29. Republic of New Africa, *New African Ujamaa*. (Note: this booklet contains no page numbers.)

30. The document's authors discuss them as though a human being—a revolutionary sage—on a spiritual journey fraught with obstacles challenging that person's ability to stay on his or her chosen path. In his unpublished autobiography, Imari Obadele uses strikingly similar wording to describe his views on New Afrikans' dedication to liberation. See Obadele, *Seize the Land!: The Autobiography of the Primary Apostle of Malcolm X Detailing How the Foundations Were Laid for a Black Struggle for Independent Land in the United States*, 24, NTP.

31. Republic of New Africa, *New African Ujamaa*.

32. Republic of New Africa, *New African Ujamaa*.

33. Republic of New Africa, "Government Administration," 18, n.d., box 1, ser. 1, bay 1, folder 1, RNAC.

34. Mazrui, "Tanzaphilia."

35. See Cobb, *African Notebook*; D. G. Du Bois, "Afro-American Militants in Africa"; Ladner, "Tanzanian Women"; Wilkins, "Black Power in the Belly of the Beast."

36. See, for example, K. N. Cleaver, "Back to Africa," 211–54. Haki Madhubuti, after having an opportunity to speak with Nyerere, decided that instead of seeking independence, it was more fruitful to develop black institutions in the United States that could then service African Americans and Africans in other countries. Conversation with Madhubuti.

37. Nyerere, *Ujamaa*, 3–4. Elsewhere, Nyerere claims that "it most certainly is wrong if we want the wealth and the power so that we can dominate somebody. . . . [To do so] is completely foreign to us, and it is incompatible with the socialist society we want to build here" (6).

38. Nyerere, *Ujamaa*, 4–5.

39. Republic of New Africa, *New African Ujamaa*.

40. Nyerere, "From Uhuru to Ujamaa," 3–8.

41. Babu, *African Socialism or Socialist Africa?*, xv and 111.

42. Republic of New Africa, *New African Ujamaa*.

43. Republic of New Africa, *New African Ujamaa*.

44. Republic of New Africa, "Government Administration," 32.

45. See McNeely, "Determination of Statehood."

46. Conversation with Rashid, March 30, 2009; and Lumumba, *Roots*, 9–11.

47. Conversation with Anderson.

48. Provisional Government–Republic of New Afrika, "The Code of Umoja" (December 2, 2017). In author's possession.

49. Roberts, "Sovereignty."

50. The quoted text appeared as a byline in some RNA publications. For example, see Imari Obadele, "Freedom: The Eight Strategic Elements Necessary for Success of a Black Nation in America" (A Synopsis of a Speech by Brother Imari, September 1968), n.d., box 1, folder 1, RNAC.

51. For examples, see Hartman, *Lose Your Mother*; J. Morgan, *Laboring Women*; Mustakeem, *Slavery at Sea*; and Rediker, *Slave Ship*.

52. Republic of New Africa, *Forming*, 3. Italics mine.

53. Browne, "Case for Separation"; Obadele, *People's Revolt*, 2.

54. W. E. B. Du Bois, *Souls of Black Folk*, 3.

55. Kettner, *Development*; R. Smith, *Civic Ideals*.

56. C. Holland, *Body Politic*; Kettner, *Development*, especially chapter 10; T. Miles, *Ties that Bind*; C. Mills, *Racial Contract*; Purdue, *Cherokee Women*; Ricci, *Good Citizenship*; Shklar, *American Citizenship*; R. Smith, *Civic Ideals*, especially chapter 9; Walzer, *What It Means*.

57. L. Alexander, *African or American?*; Berlin, *Slaves without Masters*; Kettner, *Development*, 288–333; R. Smith, *Civic Ideals*, 255–63.

58. See L. Alexander, *African or American?*; Bay et al., *Toward an Intellectual History*; Winch, *Philadelphia's Black Elite*.

59. Blight, *Frederick Douglass' Civil War*, 132; R. Smith, *Civic Ideals*, chapter 9; Kettner, *Development*, 324–33.

60. "The Constitution of the United States," Amendment 13; U.S. am. 14; and U.S. am. 15.

61. Logan, *Negro in the United States*.

62. Political theorist Kathy E. Ferguson writes that the constitutive outside is "the entity that must be excluded from the nation so that the 'inside' can remain familiar, clean, and safe. As is often the case with the 'outside,' it becomes paradoxically important to those still on the 'inside,' who need their outside so they can reject it, over and over again, in order to sustain their self-understanding." K. Ferguson, *Emma Goldman*, 22.

63. See Binder, "Slavery of Emancipation"; Horne, *Counter-Revolution of 1776*. These ideas receive sustained and nuanced treatment in Kendi, *Stamped*.

64. For post-Reconstruction, see Berry, *Black Resistance/White Law*, 69–107; Painter, *Standing at Armageddon*. This nadir included new legal mechanisms to criminalize African Americans. See Gross, *Colored Amazons*; K. Muhammad, *Condemnation of Blackness*.

65. E. Foner, *Short History of Reconstruction*, 180–98; Franklin, *Black Self-Determination*, 105–46. See also T. Hamilton, *Up from Canaan*.

66. Higgins, "Blacks Sought Separate State," 18–20; Llorens, "Black Separatism," 88, 93–94.

67. Cha-Jua, *America's First Black Town*; Carlisle, *Roots*; Draper, *Rediscovery*, 57–68, 132–47; Kelley, *Freedom Dreams*, 111–34; and Obadele, *Suggested Guidelines*, 20, NTP.

68. Civil Rights Congress, *We Charge Genocide*; Berry, *My Face Is Black*; Kelley, *Freedom Dreams*, 110–34; and Rabaka, "W.E.B. Du Bois," 81–111.

69. For documentation and firsthand accounts from the era, see Carson et al., *Eyes on the Prize*. For historical analysis and critiques of the civil rights movement, see Robnett, *How Long? How Long?*; Hogan, *Many Minds, One Heart*; Joseph, *Waiting 'til the Midnight Hour*; McAdam, *Political Process*; and Morris, *Origins*.

70. For example, Reparations and State of Israel as well as indigenous Alaskans. See Kelley, *Freedom Dreams*, 113. According to legal scholar Henry J. Richardson III, African people in the United States have a tradition of utilizing international law in their struggles for liberation that began in the seventeenth century. See Richardson, *Origins*, xxix.

71. UN General Assembly, Universal Declaration of Human Rights.

72. Gomez, *Exchanging Our Country Marks*.

73. UN General Assembly, Resolution 1514 (XV); Obadele, *De-Colonization*, 36–37.

74. "A Critic Who's Still a Citizen," *Detroit News*, May 1, 1969, box 21, folder 23, DCCR; and Chester Bulgier, "Full Oakland Circuit Bench to Mull Henry Citizenship," *Detroit News*, April 30, 1969, box 21, folder 23, DCCR.

75. "Cops' Version," A3; "Policeman Killed," 1; "New Detroit to Probe Church Raid Charges," *Detroit News*, April 8, 1969, 2A, 4A, RIP; John Griffith, "Cavanaugh Defends Police Acts," *Free Press*, April 2, 1969, RIP; Al Stark, "'Shot on the Floor': Bethel Raid Victim Talks," *Detroit News*, April 4, 1969, 3A, RIP; and Lee Winfrey, "Police Tell of Shooting in Church," *Free Press*, April 9, 1969, 1A, 8A, RIP.

76. Paul R. Alker, "Republic of New Africa," December 7, 1971, SCRID# 13-25-5 -99-13-1-1, MSSCR, http://www.mdah.state.ms.us/arrec/digital_archives/sovcom /result.php?image=/data/sov_commission/images/png/cd09/072889 .png&otherstuff=13|25|2|99|13|1|1|71955|; Obadele, "Struggle Is for Land," 32.

77. "'Nation' Plans Sites in Miss.," *Clarion Ledger*, April 3, 1970, 1, SFRNA; and Alker, "Republic of New Africa," SCRID# 13-25-5-99-7-1-1, MSSCR, http://www .mdah.state.ms.us/arrec/digital_archives/sovcom/result.php?image=/data/sov _commission/images/png/cd09/072882.png&otherstuff=13|25|2|99|7|1|1|71948|.

78. For examples of this surveillance, see Untitled Document, August 4, 1970, SCRID # 13-25-2-2-1-1-1, MSSCR, http://mdah.state.ms.us/arrec/digital_archives /sovcom/result.php?image=/data/sov_commission/images/png/cd09/072639 .png&otherstuff=13|25|2|2|1|1|1|71708|; Director, Sovereignty Commission to The Honorable Herman Glasier, August 5, 1970, SCRID# 13-25-2-3-1-1-1, MSSCR, http: //mdah.state.ms.us/arrec/digital_archives/sovcom/result.php?image=/data/sov _commission/images/png/cd09/072640.png&otherstuff=13|25|2|3|1|1|1|71709|; and Jack Smith to Chief J. D. Gardner, "Subjects Staying at Jackson Airport Travel Lodge," SCRID# 13-25-2-23-1-1-1, MSSCR, http://mdah.state.ms.us/arrec/digital _archives/sovcom/result.php?image=/data/sov_commission/images/png/cd09 /072685.png&otherstuff=13|25|2|23|1|1|1|71754|.

79. "Hearing Today for RNA Leader: Henry-Obadele Arrested in 1971 Shootout," *Times-Picayune*, April 2, 1973, SFRNA; "Sentence Meted to RNA Figure," *Times-Picayune*, April 3, 1973, SFRNA; Hollis Landrum, "RNA Member Pleads 'Guilty' to

Assault: Shillingord Given 2 10-Year Sentences; Some of Time Cut," *Jackson Daily News*, January 19, 1973, SFRNA; Obadele, *Free the Land!*; The Republic of New Africa, "Mississippi . . . Old and New," 1971, box 1, folder 4, RNAC; Obadele, *President to President.*

80. Lumumba, "Short History," 75.

81. "Interview with Safiya Bukhari."

82. Obadele, *De-Colonization U.S.A.*, 38–39. Quote on page 39.

83. Obadele, *People's Revolt*, 7–8.

84. Rashid, "The Military Story," GRP; Lumumba, *Roots*, 9–10.

85. Dunbar, "Making of a Militant," 25–32; Ya Salaam, "We Are New Afrika," 62–71; and Sherrill, "Birth of a (Black) Nation."

86. Provisional Government-Republic of New Afrika, "New Afrikan Creed."

87. Conversation with Rashid, November 1, 2009.

88. C. Hamilton, "Republic of New Africa," 64.

89. Conversation with Trice, March 2, 2009.

90. Conversation with Kgositsile.

91. Republic of New Africa, "Government Administration," 17–18.

92. Republic of New Africa, "Government Administration."

93. Republic of New Africa, "Government Administration," 18–20. If no consulate was established where one desired to become a citizen of record, that person could demonstrate to a PG official that he or she had educated himself or herself and then take the oath before such an official. Republic of New Africa, "Government Administration," 31.

94. Fujino, *Heartbeat of Struggle*, 110–233. The removal of the strict racial criterion confirms Communist Labor Party author Nelson Peery's argument that nations' being forced into being because of imperialism compels peoples to form solidarity although they might not see any other common interest between them. See Peery, *Negro National Colonial Question*, 102.

95. Obadele, *Free the Land!*; Conversation with Taifa.

96. Republic of New Afrika, *Forming*, 2; and "Municipal Councils?," *New Afrikan Brief: A Newsletter from the Black Nation* (March 1976), 2, box 1, ser. 2, bay 1, folder 2, RNAC.

97. For biographical information on Chokwe Lumumba, Esq., see Chokwe Lumumba, ed., *Selective Writings by and about Chokwe Lumumba*, unpublished, n.d., in author's possession courtesy of Chokwe Lumumba; Front Line Defenders, "Human Rights Defender Chokwe Lumumba." For information about Lumumba's political work in Jackson, see Mott, "Runoffs Provide Decisive Wins"; and Malcolm X Grassroots Movement, "Chokwe Lumumba's Election Victory."

98. For early RNA strategy, see Obadele, *War in America*; Obadele, *Revolution and Nation Building*; and Sherrill, "Birth of a (Black) Nation," 71–75, 176–78.

99. Obadele, *De-Colonization*, 59. Italics mine.

100. Conversation with Owusu, September 8, 2009.

101. Conversation with Owusu, September 8, 2009.

102. Conversation with Owusu, September 8, 2009. New Afrikans have not been the only group to attempt to circumvent nation-state-issued documentation as the

only legitimate means of moving across national boundaries. Some have attempted to use a "World Passport," which has contributed to legal troubles for the rapper and actor Yasiin Bey. See Garcia, "Yasiin Bey Arrest."

103. Participant observer, March 29, 2009.

104. Conversation with Nubyahn, September 20, 2009.

105. Holland, Fox, and Daro, "Social Movements and Collective Identity," 106.

106. David Smith, "Norman Confers with Attorneys," *Jackson Daily News*, April 29, 1972, 1, 8, SFRNA; George Whittington, "RNA Defense Uses Last Jury Challenge," *Clarion Ledger*, April 25, 1972, 1–2, SFRNA.

107. George Whittington, "Second RNA Trial Scheduled for July 17," *Clarion Ledger*, July 7, 1972, SFRNA. See chapter 3 for a discussion of Afrikan names.

108. "Whites Seek Funds for RNA Citizens' Defense," *Michigan Chronicle*, June 21, 1969, box 21, folder 23, DCCR.

109. L. Alexander, *African or American?*; Shklar, *American Citizenship*.

110. Provisional Government–Republic of New Afrika, "Code of Umoja," 10–11.

111. For example, see *Reparations Yes!*; Republic of New Afrika, *Forming*; and Provisional Government–Republic of New Afrika, *A People's Struggle: An Analytical Outline of the Struggle of Afrikans in North America* (Washington, D.C.: PG-RNA, 1986), NTP.

112. "Sovereignty for Native Americans," *The New Afrikan Journal* (ca. 1980), 19. See also "Free Leonard Peltier," *The New Afrikan Journal* Special Edition (1980), 20–21, NTP.

113. Republic of New Afrika, *Black Nation Day Commemorative Journal*, March 1986, NTP.

114. That representatives of the American Indian Movement participated in New Afrikan Nation Day in 1993 also speaks to concrete efforts between the two groups to work together. Conversation with Saladin Muhammad, September 2, 2018; and Kwame-Osagyefo Kalimara to Robert Robideau, September 7, 1983, NTP; Karolczyk, "Subjugated Territory," 338.

115. An image of both incarcerated men clasping hands accompanies the statements. See Rafael Cancel Miranda, "Solidarity Statement," July 6, 1979, and Imari Obadele, "Solidarity Statement Reply," both in *The New Afrikan Journal*, n.d. (ca. 1980), 15–16, GRP.

116. "Free Puerto Rico!," *The New Afrikan Journal* (ca. 1982), 20, 31; "Puerto Rican Liberation," *The New Afrikan Journal* Special Edition (1980), 21; "Re: The Puerto Rico Struggle," *The New Afrikan* 6, no. 2 (December 25, 1976), 9–10, NTP. Ahmed Obafemi, "Building Strategic Alliances and People's War: National Liberation Inside the U.S. Imperialist State," in New Afrikan Institute of Political Education, *Towards the Liberation of the Black Nation: Organize for New Afrikan People's War! Towards the Liberation of the Black Nation: Organize for New Afrikan People's War!*, 1981, 17–22, FAO. See also Lumumba, *Roots*, 14–20.

117. In 2014, several youth activists traveled to Geneva, Switzerland, to charge genocide against the United States due to police violence against African Americans. See http://wechargegenocide.org/; and Berlatsky, "At the United Nations."

Chapter 3

1. Conversation with Trice, February 8, 2012. Ukali Mwendo also informed this description of the naming ceremony. Conversation with Mwendo, February 4, 2012. For the meaning of Harambee, see Karenga, *Kwanzaa*, 93 and 96; and Mayes, *Kwanzaa*, 85.

2. Several scholars have explored the multiple African American efforts to rethink identity in terms that would empower them while connecting them to other African and Third World peoples. Historian Ashley Farmer shows how black women made use of African and Third World identification and existing gendered constructs to reconfigure their identities, to push the boundaries of those gendered constructs, and to challenge racial oppression. Similarly, Russell Rickford explains how the concept "We are an African people" informed identity formation even as it was central in initiatives for independent African-centered schooling during the 1960s and 1970s. Following Adolph Reed, Rickford questions the extent to which the bourgeois elements focused on "psychological fortification" instead of advancing concrete plans to transform society. While promoting the pragmatism of certain Pan-African nationalist objectives, Rickford cautiously embraces the aspects of nationalist identity that led activists to develop radical political ideologies and strategies that could potentially benefit broader black communities and oppressed peoples throughout the world. Cultural scholars Rychetta Watkins and Cynthia A. Young similarly emphasize the importance of developing revolutionary identities that matched activists' political objectives. See Farmer, *Remaking Black Power*; Reed, "Pan-Africanism"; Rickford, *We Are an African People*; Watkins, *Black Power, Yellow Power*; and Young, *Soul Power*.

3. The term "cognitive liberation" is adapted from Doug McAdam, who defines it as "the transformation from hopeless submission to oppressive conditions to an aroused readiness to challenge those conditions." McAdam, *Political Process*, 34.

4. Patterson, *Slavery and Social Death*, 55.

5. Essien-Udom, *Black Nationalism*, 203.

6. Leonard, "Changing Times and Changing Names"; Cameron, *Name Givers*; Nuessel, *Study of Names*; and Wilson, *Means of Naming*.

7. Berlin, *Slaves without Masters*, 50–52; Cody, "Naming, Kinship, and Estate Dispersal"; Puckett, "Names of American Negro Slaves"; Patterson, *Slavery and Social Death*, 54–58; Stuckey, *Slave Culture*; and Wood, *Black Majority*, 181–86.

8. Khatib, "Personal Names and Name Changes"; Pharr, "Onomastic Divergence"; Puckett, "American Negro Names"; Puckett, *Black Names in America*.

9. J. L. Dillard, *Black Names*; Paustian, "Evolution of Personal Naming Practices."

10. Obiagele Lake, as she argues for African Americans to reject European values and cultural norms, includes a brief explanation of the importance of black nationalist and Black Power organizations' emphasis on shedding slave names. And Scot Brown briefly discusses the politics of naming for the US Organization. See Brown, *Fighting for US*, especially chapter 3; Lake, *Blue Veins*, especially chapter 1.

11. Patterson, *Slavery and Social Death*, 54.

12. Cameron, *Name Givers*, 1–2, 42–48; and Fairchild, "Black, Negro, or Afro-American?," 48.

13. Puckett, "Names of American Negro Slaves," 484; Stuckey, *Slave Culture*, 195–99, quote on 198; and Wood, *Black Majority*, 181–86. For a firsthand account of this process, see Equiano, *Interesting Life of Olaudah Equiano*.

14. Berlin, *Slaves without Masters*, 51; Stuckey, *Slave Culture*; Lake, *Blue Veins*.

15. J. L. Dillard, *Black Names*, 22–29; and Smitherman, *Talkin and Testiyin*. These struggles also occurred at the level of group designations. See Smitherman *Talkin that Talk*, 41–56; Stuckey, *Slave Culture*, 198–244; and Thomas and Turner, "Race, Class, and Color."

16. Michael A. Gomez discusses the complexity of African acculturation within the plantation system. Gomez, *Exchanging Our Country Marks*.

17. Malcolm X and Haley, *Autobiography*, 152. Malcolm X forgot his prison numbers, possibly intentionally. His forgetfulness seems to suggest disgust with having his personal existence replaced with numerical anonymity. Besides, it would only make sense that for one who had evolved from a hustler to Muhammad's top minister, some sort of spiritual purification would have taken place, erasing that psychologically damaging part of his memory.

18. E. Muhammad, *Message to the Blackman*, 54.

19. Malcolm X and Haley, *Autobiography*, 199.

20. Evanzz, *Judas Factor*, 12–14; Malcolm X and Haley, *Autobiography*, 28–29, 343–63.

21. For example, Proverbs 22:1 states, "A good name is more desirable than great riches; to be esteemed is better than silver or gold" (New International Version [NIV]). A popular example of biblical figures undergoing a name change to symbolize their acceptance of their perceived purpose is Saul of Tarsus, who became Paul. See Acts 13:9 (NIV). Following similar logic, Isabella, an enslaved woman in New York, became Sojourner Truth after her escape. See Gilbert, *Narrative of Sojourner Truth*.

22. E. Muhammad, *Message to the Blackman*, 34–35, 41–43, 54–55.

23. Interestingly, it was customary for people to maintain their first names, even if they had European origins. Further, many NOI members continued using their slave names when handling such business as signing checks. Essien-Udom, *Black Nationalism*, 203–5; Lincoln, *Black Muslims*, 105; Marsh, *Lost-Found Nation of Islam*, 40.

24. Malcolm X and Haley, *Autobiography*, 162.

25. Cross, "Toward a Psychology," 18–21.

26. "Black Names," 88.

27. Armah, *Two Thousand Seasons*, 130–31. See also Nigerian singer Fela Kuti's "Upside Down" on *Upside Down*, Decca Afrodisia DWAPS2005; and "Mr. Grammar-ticalogylisationalism Is the Boss" on *Again, Excuse O*, Coconut PMLP1002.

28. Conversation with Shakur.

29. For Carmichael's arguments about African identity and a land base, see Carmichael, *Stokely Speaks*, 197–205; and Carmichael, "Pan-Africanism," 36–43. In his autobiography, Carmichael/Ture never stated exactly when he took on his Afrikan

name, nor did he state why he chose the variant of "Ture." Carmichael and Thelwell, *Ready for Revolution*, 627–28.

30. The scholarship explaining and analyzing such changes is vast. Some examples include Essien, *Brazilian-African Diaspora*; Kanogo, *African Womanhood in Colonial Kenya*, especially 81–84; Mbogoni, *Aspects of Colonial Tanzania History*; Mlambo, *History of Zimbabwe*; and Shelter, *Imagining Serengeti*.

31. The basis for New Afrikans' distinction from other nations may be found in various documents written by RNA theorists and intellectuals with whom they exchanged ideas. See, for example, Browne, "Case for Separation," 7–15; A. Moore, *Why Reparations?*; Obadele, *Revolution and Nation Building*, 18–30; and Republic of New Africa, *Short Official Basic Documents*.

32. Brother Gaidi Obadele to RNA Citizens, January 19, 1970, reel 10, group 1, series 4, frame 158, ROB.

33. Republic of New Africa, "Adult Application for the R.N.A," GRP.

34. Conversation with Ferguson and Ferguson. Baba Oseijeman Adefunmi was an influential priest in the Yoruba tradition, an author, the prime minster of the Harlem Peoples Parliament, and also the first minister of culture of the PG-RNA. Sometime after he helped cofound the PG, he moved to South Carolina, where he created the Oyotunji Village. Conversation with Sunni-Ali; Hucks, *Yoruba Traditions*.

35. Conversation with Jackson. It is important to note that before being named by the children, Jackson was content with her given name, Melanie. Although her mother of German and Irish ancestry did not know it at the time, "Melanie" is a Hebrew name that signifies "black." Emphasis is a reflection of Jackson's vocal inflection.

36. Conversation with Trice, March 2, 2009.

37. Conversation with Ferguson and Ferguson.

38. Karenga, *Quotable Karenga*, 4. See also S. Brown, *Fighting for US*, 23 and 107–30.

39. Hilliard and Cole, *This Side of Glory*, 163.

40. Hilliard and Cole, *This Side of Glory*, 169.

41. Stiner and Brown, "US-Panther Conflict."

42. Chrisman, "Formation"; A. Davis, "Art on the Frontline," 236–47; W. E. B. Du Bois, "Criteria of Negro Art," 100–105; Hughes, "Negro Artist," 91–95; John, "Complicity, Revolution"; Collins and Crawford, *New Thoughts*; Neal, "Black Art and Black Liberation"; Mkalimoto, "Cultural Arm"; Wright, "Blueprint for Negro Writing," 194–205; Ya Salaam, "African American Cultural Empowerment."

43. Conversation with Ferguson and Ferguson. The idea of meeting some unspecified criteria before taking an Afrikan name provokes several questions. First, for a people whose names were taken as part of a larger assault against their humanity, why did Baba Herman not consider taking an Afrikan name as a human right for those who chose to undergo that process? Next, several people—including many New Afrikans—gave their children Afrikan names. Should an organizational standard or criterion be imposed on children before their parents can give them the Afrikan name of their choosing? Also, there were many New Afrikans who, like

Herman Ferguson and Audley Moore, maintained their slave names in everyday use and within their political circles. Were they less dedicated to liberation struggle because they had not taken on Afrikan names? It is not likely that requiring people to fulfill certain expectations before they could use an Afrikan name would have enhanced efforts for black liberation. There were many informants who gained the trust of black liberation activists through years of seeming dedication to the struggle. Many of them were revealed as agents and informants only after they supplied important information about the groups and individuals who were the targets of state repression. Conversation with Umoja, March 20, 2010.

44. Conversation with Killingham.

45. Queen Mother Moore, one of the most respected icons of black liberation, never appeared to take on her given Afrikan name, "Iyaluua." Conversation with Ferguson and Ferguson.

46. Shakur, *Assata*, 184–85.

47. As literary scholar Margo Natalie Crawford mentions, black women were often expected to be mothers "first and foremost." However, many women fought against such ideas, and even gained many male allies. See Crawford, "Must Revolution Be a Family Affair?," 185–204.

48. Obadele, *Free the Land*, 26; Clarke, "African Warrior Queens."

49. Farmer, *Remaking Black Power*, 58–59; see also Cleaver, *Soul on Ice*; Jean Carey Bond and Patricia Peery, "Is the Black Male Castrated?," 141–48.

50. Conversation with Afrik, March 29, 2009.

51. Conversation with Lumumba, March 28, 2010.

52. Dworkin, *Congo Love Song*; Meriwether, *Proudly We Can Be Africans*, 224–40; Minter, Hovey, and Cobb, *No Easy Victories*.

53. Shakur, *Assata*, 185; and Clayton, "What's in a Name," 48–49.

54. Shakur, *Assata*, 184–85. Like the name, Shakur did not seem to feel connected with her New Afrikan citizenship when she first signed up.

55. Shakur, *Assata*, 186.

56. Conversation with Trice, March 2, 2009.

57. Conversation with Anderson, January 7, 2009.

58. Conversation with Anderson, January 7, 2009.

59. Conversation with Rashid, March 29, 2009.

60. Conversation with Afrik.

61. Conversation with Taifa.

62. Conversation with Nubyahn, October 10, 2009.

63. Conversation with Nubyahn, October 10, 2009.

64. Conversation with Nubyahn, October 10, 2009. For information and analysis regarding the Five Percent Nation of Gods and Earths, see E. Allen Jr., "Making the Strong Survive"; Miyakawa, *Five Percenter Rap*; and Onaci, "'I Can Be Your Sun.'"

65. "Revolutionary Nationalists' Vigilence [*sic*] against Traitors and Treason: The Lesson of Samuel (Solomon) Brown, Yvonne Thomas, Peter Middleton and Tyrone Rison," *New Afrikan Freedom Fighter* 2, no. 1 (March 1983): 3, box 303, folder—New Afrikan Freedom Fighter, CCCC; and Conversation with Umoja, March 20, 2010. After assuming the presidency, Imari Obadele barred his brother from using his

"free name." See "Richard Henry Puts Milton on Suspension," *Detroit News*, June 4, 1970, RIP.

66. Collier-Thomas and Turner, "Race, Class, and Color"; Mills, "'United States of Africa,'" 97–100; Stuckey, *Slave Culture*, 198–244.

67. Collier-Thomas and Turner, "Race, Class, and Color," 18.

68. R. Moore, *Richard B. Moore*, 223–39, quotes on 231 and 233.

69. E. Muhammad, *Supreme Wisdom*, 16–18.

70. Malcolm X, "Black Revolution."

71. Malcolm X, "Black Revolution."

72. Malcolm X, "Speech," 288–93, quote on 288; Ahmad, *We Will Return*, 26–33.

73. See, for example, Karenga, *Quotable Karenga*, 1.

74. Lumumba, *Roots*, 5–8.

75. See, for example, Provisional Government–Republic of New Afrika, *Code of Umoja*, 2007, 9, GRP. Longtime New Afrikan Bilal Sunni-Ali insists that African people in the Caribbean and other regions of the Western Hemisphere are also New Afrikans. Conversation with Sunni-Ali. The New Afrikan People's Organization also seems to agree with this notion. See New Afrikan People's Organization, "Why We Use New Afrikan."

76. Obadele, *Revolution and Nation Building*, 9, 65; Obadele, *Seize the Land!*, 35, 47, NTP; Obadele, *Free the Land*, 25. All emphasis from the original quotations.

77. "Black Nation Day," *The New Afrikan*, March 1976, 2, NTP. For critical discussion of African uses of European languages, see Ngugi, *Decolonizing the African Mind*; Achebe, "Politics of Language," 268–71. For Swahili, see Kijembe, "Swahili and Black Americans." For critical analysis of the rationale for and results of linguistic decolonization, see Rickford, *We Are an African People*, 150–51.

78. Conversation with Trice, March 2, 2009.

79. Kachru, "Alchemy of English," 275.

80. For an explanation of American liberalism, see Dawson, *Black Visions*, 29–33; see also Mills, *Racial Contract*.

81. Obadele, *Foundations of the Black Nation*.

82. For critiques of nationalists and Pan-Africanists who fully adhere to the logic of liberal capitalism, see Allen, *Black Awakening*; and Reed, "Pan-Africanism."

83. J. Boggs, *Racism and Class Struggle*, 39–50. For analysis of circular migration patterns of black southerners, see Gregory, *Southern Diaspora*, 38–40. For African concepts of ancestral land, see Gomez, *Exchanging Our Country Marks*, 94, 112–30; Kanogo, *African Womanhood*, 81–84; Shelter, *Imagining Serengeti*, especially chapter 3. For examinations of the broader import and discourse around land and its symbolism, see Brickell, "'Mapping' and 'Doing'"; Conn, "Back to the Garden"; Lowenthal, "Past Time, Present Place"; McCutcheon, "'Returning Home'"; Rickford, "'We Can't Grow'"; and R. Williams, *Country and the City*, 1–8.

84. Obadele, *Free the Land*, 27–28. New Afrikans were not the only ones who chose to challenge the power structure in Mississippi. See Umoja, *We Will Shoot Back*; Payne, *I've Got the Light*; C. K. Lee, *For Freedom's Sake*.

85. Obadele, *Free the Land!*, 28.

86. For example, see Diop, *African Origin of Civilization*.

87. For Newton's conceptualization of revolutionary struggle, see Dawson, *Black Visions*, 212–14.

88. Untitled Image, *New Afrikan Journal* 3, no. 2 (Summer ca. 1982), 1; New Afrikan People's Organization (booklet), http://urbanguerilla.org/new-afrikan -peoples-organization-napo-1989/ (accessed December 19, 2017). For the prison industrial complex, see Alexander, *New Jim Crow*.

89. Pharr, "Onomastic Divergence," 405–7.

Chapter 4

1. Conversation with Umoja, March 26, 2010; see also Akinyela, "Eight Bowls Full of Life."

2. Conversation with Umoja, March 26, 2010.

3. McAdam, "Biographical Consequences."

4. The interviews presented here follow the methods of journalist Leon Dash.

5. The life course scholarship tends to ignore black left nationalists, instead focusing on liberal civil rights and progressive students in SNCC and Students for a Democratic Society. Those studies are useful and clearly establish that activism has important consequences; however, by studying political radicals, we develop a more nuanced understanding of this process. New Afrikan activists, in particular, are important because there has not been one homogeneous black social movement that was fighting for fully agreed-upon goals. And the movement is ongoing. Therefore, NAIM activists provide a unique opportunity to trace people's interactions with ideas over the course of decades. Doing so helps us move away from cause-and-effect analyses, the approach that currently dominates the sociological scholarship, in favor of a more dynamic engagement with questions of biographical impact. It is clear that movements change people. However, people also shape movements by disagreeing with ideas and actions; by helping each other fine-tune ideas; by trying, failing, and succeeding to move forward with specific ideas and projects. The process of being an activist teaches us that ordinary people can make extraordinary contributions to social movements, even if they do not get the credit that high-profile participants receive.

6. For culturally relevant pedagogy, see Ladson-Billings, "Toward a Theory."

7. Conversation with Killingham. Considering the stories that Killingham's great-grandmother told about sexual violence at the hands of white males, staying in the boys' dormitory was probably traumatic in and of itself.

8. Conversation with Killingham.

9. Conversation with Mustafa. For more information on the desegregation case, see OpenJurist.org, "288 F. 2d 600."

10. Conversation with Mustafa. For information and analysis about the school-to-prison pipeline, see Meiners, "Ending the School-to-Prison Pipeline." For routine state violence in prisons, see Gilmore, *Golden Gulag*; and James, *Warfare in the Homeland*.

11. Routine and normalized violence also may have had a different impact on witnesses than did spectacular events, especially in places where mass violence was

expected. For example, violence in carceral spaces had been normalized through centuries of brutality against captives (regardless of the state or nation in question). Not only have carceral spaces been accepted as violent, but the cases Mustafa discussed also occurred outside of the South, where racial violence was notorious and othered, as opposed to in northeastern states like New York.

12. Conversation with Mwendo.

13. Conversation with Kgositsile.

14. Conversation with Sunni-Ali. For local battles with school segregation, see Back, "Exposing the 'Whole Segregation Myth,'" 65–91; Ferguson and Ferguson, *Unlikely Warrior*; Theoharis, "'I'd Rather," 125–51.

15. Conversation with Jackson.

16. Conversation with Jackson.

17. For the "mark of Cain," see Kendi, *Stamped from the Beginning*, especially chapters 1–9.

18. Conversation with Jackson.

19. Conversation with Jackson.

20. Conversation with Trice, March 2, 2009.

21. Conversation with Trice, March 2, 2009. The scholarship on Black Catholics is an expanding area of inquiry. See, for example, DeCuir, "'Nothing to Be Feared'"; Cressler, *Authentically Black and Truly Catholic*.

22. Conversation with Trice, March 2, 2009.

23. Conversation with Sekou Owusu, October 11, 2009.

24. Conversation with Ferguson and Ferguson.

25. Notable members of this "family" are Afeni Shakur, Assata Shakur, Lumumba Shakur, and Mutulu Shakur.

26. Conversation with Sunni-Ali.

27. Conversation with Sunni-Ali. For more explanation about the Order of Damballah Hwedo, see Hucks, *Yoruba Traditions*, 70–77. The Orisa are deities in West African, primarily Yoruba, and Yoruba-derived religions. For details, see Falola and Genova, *Orisa*.

28. Conversation with Killingham.

29. Conversation with Ferguson and Ferguson.

30. Conversation with Owusu, October 11, 2009; and conversation with Taifa.

31. Conversation with Mustafa. Black nationalists and community organizers gained significant attention in New York City on February 15, 1961, when they participated in demonstrations at the United Nations following Lumumba's assassination. See Joseph, *Waiting 'til the Midnight Hour*, 38–44; and Meriwether, *Proudly We Can Be Africans*, 229–40. For the Nation of Gods and Earths, see Onaci, "'I Can Be Your Sun.'"

32. Boyle, *Arc of Justice*; H. S. Lee, *Gentle Giant of Dynamite Hill*; McWhorter, *Carry Me Home*.

33. Conversation with Trice, March 2, 2009.

34. Eskew, "'Bombingham'"; Massey, *American Apartheid*; Sugrue, *Sweet Land of Liberty*.

35. Conversation with Killingham.

36. Conversation with Ferguson and Ferguson.

37. Conversation with Ferguson and Ferguson.

38. Conversation with Rashid, March 30, 2009; and conversation with Abdul-Aziz et al. For stories about and advocacy for childhood sexual abuse survivors, see Simmons, *Love with Accountability*.

39. Conversation with Mustafa.

40. Conversation with Mustafa.

41. Conversation with Ferguson and Ferguson.

42. Conversation with Afrik.

43. Conversation with Mwendo, April 2, 2017.

44. Conversation with Mwendo, April 2, 2017.

45. Conversation with Mwendo, April 2, 2017.

46. Payne, *I've Got the Light of Freedom*.

47. Conversation with Owusu, October 11, 2009.

48. Conversation with Killingham.

49. Conversation with Killingham.

50. Conversation with Trice, March 2, 2009.

51. Conversation with Anderson.

52. Conversation with Shakur.

53. Conversation with Taifa.

54. Conversation with Owusu, October 11, 2009.

55. Conversation with Owusu, October 11, 2009.

56. *Firing Line with William F. Buckley, Jr.*, Episode 126, "The Republic of New Africa," directed by Warren Steibel, aired November 18, 1968, on PBS.

57. Conversation with Mustafa. The "Black Liberator's Party" that Mustafa mentioned was probably the Black Liberation Party that formed as RAM was dissolving in 1968 (see chapter 6).

58. "The Oath," n.d., GRP; and Provisional Government–Republic of New Afrika, "New Afrikan Creed," GRP.

59. Conversation with Afrik. Baba Hannibal never specified the city or cities to which he was sent. Rebellions took place in Baltimore, Chicago, Washington, D.C., and many other places. He was living in Chicago during that time, so it is possible that he was involved with helping quell the rebellions in the Midwest.

60. Provisional Government, Republic of New Afrika, "RNA Lawyer Battles Contempt," October 28, 1983, NTP.

61. Conversation with Anderson.

62. Conversation with Shakur. Kgositsile eventually pursued her PhD at the University of Michigan, where, she says, she was "motivated by this question of land."

63. Conversation with Taifa.

64. Conversation with Trice, March 4, 2009.

65. Conversation with Trice, March 4, 2009.

66. Conversation with Killingham.

67. For example, see Hayes III and Jeffries, "Us Does Not," 82–85; Matthews, "No One Ever Asks"; Spencer, "Engendering the Black Freedom Struggle"; and Taylor, "Elijah Muhammad's Nation of Islam," 190–94.

68. For example, see "The Black Government Must Help Bring Family Stability." *New Afrikan Journal* (April 1983): 21–22, NTP.

69. Henry, "Independent Black Republic," 33; Obadele, *Foundations*, 42–48; Obadele, *Free the Land*, 110–11. In 1983, the People's Center Council revisited the discussion about marriage and family. See "Black Government Must Help."

70. Guy, *Afeni Shakur*, 70–72, 104–11, 126; and Buffalo, "Reclaiming Our Marriage," 118.

71. Conversation with Rashid, November 1, 2009.

72. Conversation with Rashid, March 29, 2009.

73. See, for example, Bambara, *Black Woman*; Beale, "Double Jeopardy," 146–61; La Rue, "Black Movement," 164–73; and White, "Africa on My Mind."

74. La Rue, "Black Movement," 167.

75. She ultimately became PCC chair. Conversation with Killingham.

76. Conversation with Rashid, March 29, 2009.

77. Conversation with Jackson; conversation with Kgositsile; conversation with Killingham; and conversation with Abdul-Aziz et al.

78. Conversation with Afrik.

79. In some ways, then, he was not living up to his patriarchal duties. But because he was fighting for the people, he was providing for his family in other ways—liberation.

80. Conversation with Afrik.

81. Conversation with Owusu, October 11, 2009. Emphasis added to match Owusu's verbal emphasis.

82. Conversation with Owusu, October 11, 2009. Dean E. Robinson strongly disagrees with this assertion, arguing that black nationalism is all but an imitation of American nationalism and a buttress for the politics of whiteness. See D. E. Robinson, *Black Nationalism*.

83. Conversation with Trice, March 2, 2009.

84. Conversation with Kgositsile. For a brief history, see the school's Facebook page, https://www.facebook.com/Aisha-ShuleDuBois-Academy-117525055009521/ (accessed November 9, 2017); for the school's closing, see http://www.wxyz.com/news/region/detroit/aisha-shuleweb-dubois-preparatory-academy-to-close-permanently-october-31st (accessed November 9, 2017). For Motown Wireless, see https://prezi.com/fsg8o3ps1dtb/motown-wireless/# (accessed November 9, 2017).

85. Conversation with Killingham; and conversation with Taifa.

86. Conversation with Abdur-Rasheed.

87. Conversation with Abdur-Rasheed.

88. Conversation with Jackson.

89. Republic of New Africa, *Short Official Basic Documents*. In the essay "And Went Their Ways," Obadele explains that the project of nation building is not an end in itself, but a means to help humans overcome the obstacles that prevent them from satisfying the human need enough to pursue spiritual enlightenment with greater dedication. See Obadele, *Foundations*, 49–56.

90. See, for example, Obadele, *Free the Land*; and Obadele, *Foundations*.

91. Conversation with Afrik.

92. Conversation with Owusu, October 11, 2009.

93. Conversation with Ferguson and Ferguson; and conversation with Jackson.

94. Conversation with Trice, March 2, 2009.

95. Conversation with Simmons; conversation with Abdur-Rasheed.

96. For Islam in America, see Essien-Udom, *Black Nationalism*; Gomez, *Black Crescent*; and Taylor, *Promise of Patriarchy*.

97. Conversation with Anderson.

98. John Bracey, "Revolutionary Action Movement/Republic of New Afrika," panel discussion, Art & Power in Movement, University of Massachusetts, Amherst, November 20, 2010.

Chapter 5

1. The Republic of New Afrika, "Statement by the Provisional Government of the Republic of New Afrika Regarding the Arrest of Fulani Sunni Ali, Chair Woman of the Peoples Center Council of the Republic of New Afrika," 2 November 1981, 1, NTP. The title quote comes from Nkechi Taifa, Untitled Poem, *The New Afrikan Journal: The Official Voice of the Malcolm X Party*, 1977, repr. 1980, 19, NTP. For the epigraphs, see ji Jaga, "Every Nation Struggling," 71; and "Fighting for Freedom Is Not a Crime," n.d., GRP.

2. See SAC [redacted], "Republic of New Africa," February 10, 1972, sec. 13, FBI-RNA LA. The FBI generally considered a wide range of black liberation activity, especially that which challenged policing agencies, as "terrorism." This character-ization has enjoyed support among scholars of terrorism in the United States and abroad because they often rely on police and newspaper reports for data. See, for example, Hewitt, *Understanding Terrorism in America*, 23–52; Horgan and Brad-dock, *Terrorism Studies*; Laqueur, *Terrorism*. For a challenge to this long-standing construct, see Berger, *Outlaws of America*, 283–86.

3. "Case against Fulani Ali Collapses," *The Mississippi Enterprise: A Positive New Service for Mississippi and the Nation*, November 14, 1981, 1, 4, NTP; "Grand Jury Jails Leftists for Silence," *Guardian*, December 16, 1981, 7, NTP; Republic of New Afrika, "Louis Farrakhan, Fulani Sunni Ali (Cynthia Boston) & Chokwe Lumumba to Speak at Rally for Freedom Fighters," box 6, folder 15, Alston; Wechsler, "Activ-ists Jailed," 3. See also Berger, *Outlaws of America*, 250–69. For detailed analysis of this event and Sunni-Ali's life, see Gaines, "Revolutionary Black Female."

4. Holland, Fox, and Daro, "Social Movements and Collective Identity," 106.

5. ji Jaga, "Every Nation Struggling," 71.

6. Director to Los Angeles, September 16, 1968, sec. 3, FBI-RNA LA.

7. Wolfe, *Seamy Side of Democracy*; J. Jeffries, "Black Radicalism and Political Repression"; and Jones, "Political Repression of the Black Panther Party."

8. Jill Nelson, "Terror by Association: The Case of Cynthia Boston," n.d., 34, NTP.

9. Howard, *Political Repression and Government Surveillance*, 2, NTP.

10. For examples, see Churchill and Vander Wall, *Agents of Repression*; K. Fergu-son, *Emma Goldman*; Gage, *Day Wall Street Exploded*; Garrow, *FBI and Martin Luther King, Jr.*; Kornweibel, *Seeing Red*; McDuffie, *Sojourning for Freedom*, espe-

cially chapters 1–2; Meriwether, *Proudly We Can Be Africans*; Ransby, *Eslanda*, 223–38; Von Eschen, *Race against Empire*; and Woodruff, *American Congo*.

11. It has been alleged that even the famed civil rights photographer Ernest C. Withers was an informant for the FBI. Perrusquia, *Spy in Canaan*; and Cahan and Williams, *Revolution in Black and White*.

12. Churchill and Vander Wall, *COINTELPRO Papers*, 106–10.

13. Senate Subcomm. to Investigate the Administration of the Internal Security Act and Other Internal Security Laws, *Testimony of Stokely Carmichael*.

14. For examples, see, H. Rap Brown/Jamil Al-Amin. H. Rap Brown, *Die Nigger Die!*; Levy, *Civil War on Race Street*. For Brown's/Al-Amin's more recent legal troubles, see Glanton, "Backers"; Muwakkil, "Echo." For a critical perspective, see Pipes, "Curious Case."

15. O'Reilly, *Racial Matters*, 261–92. For modern-day manifestations of black community surveillance, see Coleman and Brunton, "'You Might Not Know Her.'"

16. SAC [Redacted] to SAC Los Angeles, "Subject: African Students Association, RM," March 29, 1971, sec. 11, FBI-RNA LA.

17. Churchill and Vander Wall, *Agents of Repression*, 39–53; and Jones, "Political Repression."

18. "Subject: Group on Advanced Leadership," FBI-GOAL.

19. See, for example, FBI-BSH, June 30, 1958; and FBI-BSH, August 29, 1958.

20. Director, FBI to SAC, Detroit, "Medgar Evers Rifle Club, Detroit, Michigan, RM," August 3, 1964, sec. 1, FBI-GOAL.

21. Davenport, *How Social Movements Die*, 38–57; and Jones, "Political Repression," 416, 432–33.

22. Conversation with Simmons. She believes that one of the men riding with her from Cleveland to Detroit was Ahmed Evans, who was arrested shortly after the founding convention due to a shootout with police. For more information, see Masotti and Corsi, *Shootout in Cleveland*.

23. Killingham, "Marilyn Killingham."

24. Churchill and Vander Wall, *Agents of Repression*, 39.

25. Jones, "Political Repression," 421.

26. "2 ARRESTED"; "2 Held"; "Pair Termed Envoys"; "Pistol Packers Arrested"; "Separatists Jailed"; Wallace Turner, "2 With Guns."

27. Churchill and Vander Wall explain that Hoover was skilled at public relations and media manipulation. See Churchill and Vander Wall, *Agents of Repression*, 3–7. See also Churchill and Vander Wall, *COINTELPRO Papers*, 2.

28. "The RNA Anti-Depression Program Presented at the National Democratic Convention, Miami Beach, Florida," *The New African*, August 1972, 9.

29. Despite the critiques of using newspaper articles in research on governmental repression against dissidents, periodicals and other forms of print media are quite helpful in attempts to reconstruct the past. See C. Davenport, *Media Bias*.

30. www.merriam-webster.com/dictionary/war (accessed April 30, 2010). Several scholars agree that although the FBI stopped using the name COINTELPRO in 1971, just before Hoover's death, the practices that characterized it continue to this

day. See, for example, Churchill and Vander Wall, *Agents of Repression*, 62; Cunningham, *There's Something Happening Here*; and O'Reilly, *Racial Matters*, 9–47.

31. Imari Abubakari Obadele and Atty. Gaidi Obadele ([slave name] Milton R. Henry), *The Article Three Briefs: Establishing the Legal Case for the Existence of the Black Nation The Republic of New Africa in North America*, June 25, 1973. Much appreciation to Ukali Mwendo for making this document available to me.

32. See, for example, Davenport, *How Social Movements Die*, 213–44.

33. See, for example, Brown, *Manchild*; Ferguson, *Unlikely Warrior*; Guy, *Afeni Shakur*; Shakur, *Assata*.

34. According to one FBI informant, First Vice President Gaidi Obadele disagreed with the Legion's structure, which contributed to tension with Brother Imari. SAC Detroit to Director, September 13, 1968, sec. 3, FBI-RNA LA.

35. J. Walter Yeagley to Director, Federal Bureau of Investigation, September 13, 1968, sec. 3, FBI-RNA LA.

36. Detroit Police Department Memo, April 1, 19669, RIP for quote; Detroit Police Department Phone Call Report, April 2, 1969 for phone call about doctor threat, RIP.

37. Detroit Police Department Memo, April 4, 1969, RIP.

38. Special Investigations Bureau Memo, April 4, 1969, RIP; and Report of Detroit SAC [redacted], November 24, 1969, sec. 9, FBI-RNA LA.

39. For example, see Special Investigations Bureau Memo, April 2, 1969, RIP; and Special Investigations Bureau Memo, March 3, 1969, RIP.

40. For personal details about each of the defendants, see *24th District Reporter: Del Rio—Reports*, box 188, folder 27, NDI; "Teacher Arraigned."

41. "Gunmen Out to Get Me, Says Bethel Defendant," *Detroit Free Press*, October 30, 1970, RIP; "RNA Calls Fuller Murder the 'Insane Work of a Mania[c],'" *Michigan Chronicle*, November 7, 1970, RIP; "Survival & Defense: We Must Survive America," box 18, folder 26, Cockrel; Nadine Brown, "Says Fullers Sister: 'There Was Contract Out on My Brother,'" *Michigan Chronicle*, November 7, 1970, RIP; and Fred Manardo, "Fuller Freed in Bethel Case, Is Slain by Knifer," *Detroit News*, October 20, 1970, RIP.

42. Conversation with Anderson; and LA to Detroit, September 30, 1968, sec. 3, FBI-RNA LA.

43. Special Investigations Bureau Memo, January 3, 1969, RIP. For analysis of media response to RNA, see Gaines, "Race, Power, and Representation." For a comparison with the Black Panther Party, see Austin, *Up against the Wall*; Davenport, *Media Bias*; E. Morgan, "Media Culture"; Rhodes, *Framing the Panthers*.

44. I have fifteen sections of FBI documents and have seen thousands of pages' worth of police surveillance reports. Considering that these are only the documents that have been declassified, one should suspect that there is much more.

45. Obadele, *Free the Land*, 81–83. The Mississippi Sovereignty Commission files are available online. See Mississippi Department of Archives and History, http://www.mdah.ms.gov/arrec/digital_archives/sovcom/. For information on the Mississippi State Sovereignty Commission, see Katagiri, *Mississippi State Sovereignty Commission*.

46. For details, see Obadele, *Free the Land*, 76–78; Davis Smith, "Local Cops Arrest Armed Militants: Weapons, Grass Seized in Arrests," *Jackson Daily News*, March 24, 1971, MDAH; Davis Smith, "New Africa State Dedicates Acreage: Couple Married; Officials Say to Record Future Ties, Births," *Jackson Daily News*, March 29, 1971, MDAH. See also Churchill and Vander Wall, *Agents of Repression*, 59–60.

47. Jackson (157-9599) to Director (157-9097), sec. 6, FBI-RNA HQ; see also Obadele, *Free the Land*.

48. Conversation with Owusu, October 11, 2009.

49. Obadele, *Free the Land*, 73.

50. "Director, Sovereignty Commission to The Honorable Herman Glasier, Executive Assistant to the Governor," August 5, 1970, ser. 2515, MSSCR, http://mdah .state.ms.us/arrec/digital_archives/sovcom/result.php?image=/data/sov _commission/images/png/cd09/072640.png&otherstuff=13|25|2|3|1|1|1|71709|.

51. Detroit (157-3161), "Richard Bullock Henry, aka," December 22, 1969, sec. 5, FBI-RNA HQ.

52. Director (157-9079), "Re: Richard Bullock Henry" September 16, 1969, sec. 5, FBI-RNA HQ; John Peterson, RNA's Henry Vows Revenge on Britain," *Detroit News*, September 12, 1969, sec. 5, FBI-RNA HQ.

53. "Weather History for Jackson, Mississippi," http://www.almanac.com /weather/history/MS/Jackson/1971-08-18 (accessed May 10, 2010).

54. Report of SAC, Detroit (157-2413) Report, February 10, 1972, sec. 13, FBI-RNA LA.

55. See Obadele, *Free the Land*, 135–44.

56. Chana Kai Lee's retelling of Fannie Lou Hamer's torture is especially instructive here, because it considers the permanent suffering the torture caused Mrs. Hamer. It also demonstrates the abject conditions of other incarcerated African Americans who, at the mercy of their captives, were forced to participate in the brutal assaults of other black people. C. K. Lee, *For Freedom's Sake*, 49–55. For analysis of civil rights activists' carceral experiences, see Berger, *Captive Nation*, especially 20–48. For information and analysis about the image of the black criminal, see Kendi, *Stamped from the Beginning*, 248–60. For the endurance of the image as a form of racial control, see M. Alexander, *New Jim Crow*.

57. Yakubu, Owusu Yaki. "Who Are New Afrikan Political Prisoners and Prisoners of War?" *Crossroad* 4, no. 3 (Winter 1992). Reprinted in *New Afrikan Political Prisoners & Prisoners of War Profiles* (Chicago: Spear & Shield, 1998), 5. In author's possession courtesy of Hondo T'chikwa. See also Bukhari, *War Before*, 105–7; and Killingham, "Marilyn Killingham." Some scholars of social movements in the United States have explored the definitions and distinctions between PPs, POWs, and the general prison population. See Berger, *Outlaws of America*, 252–63; and Fujino, *Heartbeat of Struggle*, 205–9. It is worth restating that the founders of the PG-RNA went into the Black Government Convention with the intention of gaining prisoner of war status for freedom fighters. The rationale rested on the assumption that because the United States had been assaulting African people with the consistency and intensity of warfare, those who were captured as they worked to defend themselves and their people were legitimate prisoners of war. See "Justice Ministry

Bulletin—Republic of New Africa: RNA-11 Still Await Appeal of U.S. Federal Conspiracy Convictions!," ROB, reel 10, ser. 7, frames 677–78.

58. Yakubu, "Who Are," 5.

59. Umoja, "Black Liberation Army," 228–31.

60. For example, see Berger, *Outlaws of America*, 252–63.

61. Castellucci, *Big Dance*; and Shakur, *Assata*.

62. Minutes of the International Solidarity Day for African Prisoners of War Meeting, December 15, 1972, in SAC Jackson (157-9599) January 4, 1972, sec. 13, FBI-RNA LA.

63. "About."

64. For example, Muntaqim, "Jalil A. Muntaqim." For a powerful explanation of prison abolition, see Berger, Kaba, and Stein, "What Abolitionists Do." See also Davis, *Are Prisons Obsolete?*

65. Dorsey Nunn interview with Assata Shakur, https://youtu.be/bTD-5KuzilU (accessed July 1, 2017). Shakur's reflection is especially important at a moment with increasing rate of women's imprisonment. See Gross, *Colored Amazons*, 3.

66. Conversation with Jackson. For the contents of the vehicle, Albuquerque Report, "Police Killings, NFA—Harboring; UFAP—Murder; Crime aboard Aircraft—Air Piracy, Conspiracy," December 10, 1971, sec. 13, FBI-RNA LA.

67. "3 Slaying Suspects"; "3 Suspects in Slaying"; "Stewardess Says"; and conversation with Jackson. Quote from Lappé, "Fugitive from Time," SM54.

68. See, for example, "Havana for First Time Sends Back Hijack Suspect," *Los Angeles Times (1923-Current File)*, 25 September 1970, ProQuest Historical Newspapers *Los Angeles Times*, 1; and Paul W. Ward, "Cuba Returns Airliner Hijacker to U.S.," *The Sun (1837-1985)*, September 25, 1970, ProQuest Historical Newspapers *Baltimore Sun*, A7.

69. "Cuba Offers"; M. Miles, "U.S. Skyjackings"; and United States House of Representatives, House Committee on Foreign Affairs, *Hijacking Accord*.

70. Conversation with Jackson; Brent, *Long Time Gone*; Rohter, "25 Years and Exile"; Latner, *Cuban Revolution in America*, 123–51.

71. Conversation with Jackson; and Rohter, "25 Years and Exile."

72. Shakur, *Assata*, 243.

73. See Castellucci, *Big Dance*.

74. Shakur, *Assata*, 241-42.

75. Shakur, *Assata*, 267-74.

76. See *Black Liberation Army Communique: A Message from the Underground*, n.d., NTP.

77. Black Liberation Army, "Messages from Clandestinity: Communique from Revolutionary Armed Task Force of the Black Liberation Army," *Arm the Spirit: A Revolutionary Prison Newspaper*, Fall 1982, 6, 16, NTP.

78. For details of the actual expropriation and background about the connection between the BLA and white radicals, see Castellucci, *Big Dance*; Black Entertainment Television, "Mutulu Shakur."

79. Lena Sherrod, "Mixed Jury Convicts 2 Revolutionaries," *New York Amsterdam News*, May 21, 1988, 4, NTP.

80. Judith A. Clark and David Gilbert James also challenged the criminal proceedings on the grounds that they, too, were political, not criminal, defendants. James Feron, "Hearings Begin in Brink's Case amid Protesters." *New York Times,* September 14, 1982, B3, NTP; and Berger, *Outlaws of America,* 252–56.

81. Collection of Biographies, *Can't Jail the Spirit.*

82. Conversation with Abdur-Rasheed.

Chapter 6

1. Part of the title comes from New Afrikan Institute of Political Education, *Towards the Liberation of the Black Nation,* n.d., 8, FAO. New Afrikan Nation Day was originally called "Black Nation Day." For the 1983 Black Nation Day celebration, see "4,000 Come Together!: BND Conference Considered Overwhelming Success," *The New Afrikan,* December 1983, 9, GRP; "Black Nation Day" (flyer), box 6, folder 15, Alston.

2. "Re-Unification Meeting Held for Black Nation." *The New Afrikan,* December 1983, 9.

3. Watani Sundai Umoja Tyehimba, "NAPO / MXGM ROOTS & CHRONOLOGY: 1960–1998," 42. In author's possession courtesy of Dr. Akinyele Omowale Umoja.

4. African People's Party, "A Brief History of the Early Development of the African People's Party: 1968 to 1972." In author's possession courtesy of Dr. Muhammad Ahmad. There is an important locally focused history that has yet to gain scholarly attention. Such a focus would detail the histories of cadres in Atlanta, Georgia; California; New York; and Philadelphia, Pennsylvania, among other places.

5. Conversation with Muhammad.

6. Conversation with Muhammad.

7. "People's 76," *Common Sense: Philadelphia Action Report,* July 1–15, 1975, 1, box 119, CCCC.

8. Tyehimba, "NAPO / MXGM Root," 46, 50.

9. Ellen Goldensohn and Tom Doerr, "July Fourth March," *Common Sense: Philadelphia Action Report,* Summer 1976, back cover, CCCC.

10. "Crispus Attucks." *Common Sense: Philadelphia Action Report,* July 1–15, 1975, 2–3, box 119, CCCC; New Afrikan Institute of Political Education, *Toward the Liberation,* 2, FAO; and conversation with Muhammad.

11. Lumumba, "Revolutionary Provisional Government," November 2, 1978, 2–3, 20–33. In author's possession courtesy of Chokwe Lumumba.

12. New Afrikan Peoples Organization, "Peoples War," 7, n.d. In author's possession courtesy of Dr. Akinyele Omowale Umoja. See also Chokwe Lumumba to Imari Obadele, July 1, 1977, 4, 7. In author's possession courtesy of Chokwe Lumumba.

13. Lumumba, "Revolutionary Provisional Government," 12–18. See also Chokwe Lumumba to Imari Obadele, July 1, 1977, 1–8, quote on 5. In author's possession courtesy of Chokwe Lumumba; New Afrikan People's Organization, "Profile of the New Afrikan People's Organization (NAPO)," n.d., FAO; New Afrikan Institute of Political Education, *Towards the Liberation,*" n.d., 5, FAO; and Executive Council, Provisional Government of the Republic of New Afrika to The New Afrikan People's Court, 1–6, 4 October 1980. In author's possession courtesy of Chokwe Lumumba. For a

scholarly critique of Pan-African nationalists' insularity from their wider communities, see Rickford, *We Are an African People.*

14. "The Development of the Contemporary New Afrikan Liberation Movement and the Origins of NAPO: Roots, Achievements, and Struggles," n.d., 18. In author's possession courtesy of Dr. Akinyele Omowale Umoja. This may not have been the first time such a merger had been on the table. According to an informant for the FBI, Tony Dotson, a New Afrikan cadre member from Philadelphia, had suggested that the PCC seriously consider merging with the APP as early as October 1974. See FBI Memo, October 12, 1974, 12, box 6, folder 15, Alston.

15. "CL & AMA re: Consolidation," December 31, 1978, reel 2, frame 692, RAM; Imari Abubakari Obadele I, "A Letter to All Cadre," September 12, 1978, box 6, folder 15, Alston; and Imari Abubakari Obadele, "Clarifying the Current Provisional Government Controversy," n.d., 1, box 6, folder 15, Alston.

16. Bilal Sunni-Ali to All members NCC, "Ongoing Work of Rectification Campaign: 'Healing a Wound,'" January 30, 1980, reel 3, frame 465, RAM; conversation with Muhammad.

17. "Build the National Black Human Rights Campaign!," *The Fuse*, October 12, 1979, 3, FAO.

18. "Global Acclaim."

19. "Black Nation Charges Genocide: U.N. Rally Demands Human Rights and Self-Determination," *Update: Committee for the Suit against Government Misconduct* (October/November, 1979): 1, FAO; "Assata Shakur Liberated!!," *Update* (December/January, 1979–80): 2, FAO.

20. "Global Acclaim"; "The Brownstone Movement and the Ku Klux Klan: A Forum against Urban Genocide," *Update*, December/January 1979–80, 10, FAO.

21. Assata Shakur, "U.N. Human Rights Campaign—Statement from Assata Shakur," November 5, 1979, 3, FAO.

22. "Assata Shakur Liberated," 9; New Afrikan Institute of Political Education, *Towards the Liberation*, 2, FAO.

23. "Development of the Contemporary New Afrikan Liberation Movement," 1.

24. Conversation with Lumumba, March 31, 2009.

25. NAPO, "People's War, 16."

26. Prairie Fire Organizing Committee, "War & Racism: Interview with the Malcolm X Grassroots Movement," *Breakthrough*, Summer 1991, 16, FAO.

27. For more information about Abiodun, see New Afrikan People's Organization, "Statement"; hampton, *Black August Hip Hop*; Latner, *Cuban Revolution in America*, 242–51.

28. Davidson, "Encountering the Ex-Slave Reparations Movement"; Rabaka, "W.E.B. Du Bois."

29. Moore, *Why Reparations?*, 7.

30. Moore, *Why Reparations?*, 11.

31. African Descendants Nationalist Independence Partition Party, *African Descendants Manifesto: Self-Determination and National Independence by 1973* (San Francisco: The Party, ca. 1967), 17, 21, CMSC; Hucks, *Yoruba Traditions*, 155; Karolczyk, "Subjugated Territory," 126–28; and Ogbar, *Black Power*, 132–33.

32. Scholarly literature on reparations contains many examples of African people demanding restitution for slavery and other unjust acts committed against them at the hands of U.S. citizens, often with the blessings of state and federal governments. This scholarship clarifies that New Afrikans were not the first group to call for reparations. For examples, see Berry, *My Face Is Black Is True*; Bittker, *Case of Black Reparations*; Carter, "Radical Critique of the Reparations Movement"; Davidson, "Encountering the Ex-Slave Reparations Movement"; Kelley, *Freedom Dreams*; M. L. King Jr., *Why We Can't Wait*, especially chapter 8; Martin and Yaquinto, *Redress for Historical Injustices*; R. Robinson, *Debt*; Winbush, *Should America Pay*.

33. Reiland Rabaka makes a similar point in passing but does not explore or explain the New Afrikan role. Rabaka, "W.E.B. Du Bois, Reparations," 82.

34. Chokwe Lumumba to unknown, n.d., box 6, folder 14, Alston.

35. Obadele, "Anti-Depression Program," 1.

36. Obadele, "Anti-Depression Program," 2.

37. Obadele, "Anti-Depression Program," 4.

38. Obadele, "Anti-Depression Program," 8. For useful examinations of the criminalization of African Americans since emancipation, see Berger, *Captive Nation*; Cacho, *Social Death*; Gross, *Colored Amazons*; and K. G. Muhammad, *Condemnation of Blackness*.

39. Obadele, "Anti-Depression Program," 10.

40. Obadele, "Anti-Depression Program," 11–12.

41. See Coates, "Case for Reparations." In his "radical" critique of reparations activism, Wilson A. Carter suggests that the movement is plagued by an inability to connect the demand for reparations with modern-day racism. He contends that the overemphasis on compensation for slavery hinders activists from addressing present cultural and political conditions that make such activism ineffective. New Afrikans and others, while they focus some attention on slavery, do connect their arguments for restitution with slavery's "afterlife" and legacy, including poverty, housing conditions, subpar education, and more. See Carter, "Radical Critique of the Reparations Movement."

42. Obadele, "Anti-Depression Program," 20.

43. Obadele, "Anti-Depression Program," 22.

44. Obadele, "Anti-Depression Program," 19.

45. For connections between enslavement and economic development, see Baptist, *Half Has Never Been Told*; Solow, *Slavery and the Rise of the Atlantic System*; and E. Williams, *Capitalism and Slavery*. On the "slavery of emancipation," see Binder, "Slavery of Emancipation."

46. Ibekwe, "Africa and the Capitalist Countries"; Moyo, *Dead Aid*; Offiong, *Imperialism and Dependency*; Okolo, "Dependency in Africa"; and Payer, "World Bank and the Small Farmers."

47. Obadele, *People's Revolt*, 6–9.

48. Dorothy Lewis, "Forty Acres Fifty Dollars and a Mule with Interest: Our Past Due Debt to African Americans Payable upon Demand," n.d., 10–11, GRP. Lewis also replicated a weakness in NAPS by overlooking the struggles of Africans and their descendants in northern states as they faced gradual emancipation and persistent

discrimination. The southern states' postslavery practices resembled those from states like New York and Vermont and the British Caribbean, which had already undergone the process of negotiating the socioeconomic positions and social treatment of their former chattel. For critical attention to these issues, see Lott, "Bearing Witness."

49. Lewis, "Forty Acres," 13–14. In addition to her work on reparations, Lewis also acted as an election commissioner for the 1981 National Black Elections. See "National Black Elections Are Set for October," *New Afrikan Notes*, July 1981, NTP 2; and Dorothy Lewis, Open Letter, September 24, 1981, NTP.

50. *Reparations Now!: ANRO's Bi-Monthly News Organ*, n.d., NTP; and conversation with Taifa.

51. For example, see R. C. Smith, "Imari Obadele"; "N'COBRA Fact Sheet," n.d., GRP. See also Aiyetoro, "National Coalition," 209–25.

52. Recent exceptions with regard to the Black Economic Development Conference include Dye, "Lessons"; and Lechtreck, "'We Are Demanding.'"

53. Imari A. Obadele II, "Reparations Yes . . . ," box 6, folder 16, Alston.

54. In response to the "Reparations Toolkit" issued by the Movement for Black Lives, MXGM released a statement about the importance of land claims as reparations. Malcolm X Grassroots Movement, "Position on Reparations," July 23, 2019. In author's possession courtesy of Malcolm X Grassroots Movement.

Epilogue

1. C-SPAN, "U.S. Anti-terrorism."
2. Spivak, "Can the Subaltern Speak?," 286.

Bibliography

Manuscript Archives

Charles Deering McCormick Library of Special Collections, Northwestern
  University Library
Civil Rights Documentation Project, Moorland Spingarn Research Center,
  Howard University
Freedom Archives (Online), Oakland, California, www.freedomarchives.org
Mississippi State Department of Archives and History, Jackson, Mississippi
  Mississippi Sovereignty Commission Records
  Republic of New Africa Collection
  SF/Republic of New Africa 1970–1971
Sgt. Brown Collection, Tougaloo College, Jackson, Mississippi
Special Collections, Michigan State University
Special Collections Library, University of Michigan
Special Collections Research Center, Temple University Libraries
  Contemporary Culture Collection Periodicals
  Liberation News Service Records
Walter P. Reuther Library, Wayne State University, Detroit, Michigan
  Archives of Labor and Urban Affairs
  Chris and Marti Alston Collection
  City of Detroit Inter-Office Correspondence
  Cockrel, Kenneth V., and Sheila M. Cockrel Papers
  Detroit Commission on Community Relations–Human Rights Department:
    Part 3
  New Detroit, Inc.

Microfilm Collections

Bracey, John, Jr., and Sharon Harley, eds. *The Black Power Movement Part 2:
  The Papers of Robert F. Williams.*
Bracey, John, Jr., and Sharon Harley, eds. *The Black Power Movement Part 3:
  The Papers of the Revolutionary Action Movement, 1962–1996.*

Personal Papers

Rashid, General Kuratibisha X Ali. Personal Papers. Miami, Florida.
Taifa, Nkechi. Personal Papers. Washington, D.C.

Oral Conversations Conducted by the Author.

Abdul-Aziz, Hamid, Khalid Abdur-Rasheed, Nana Kwesi Jumoke Ifetayo Frimpong, and General Kuratibisha X Ali Rashid. October 27, 2017.
Abdur-Rasheed, Khalid. March 14, 2014.
Afrik, Hannibal Tirus. March 29, 2009.
Anderson, Michael Balogun. January 7, 2009.
Ferguson, Herman, and Iyaluua Ferguson. June 19, 2010.
Jackson, Melanie Njeri. October 17, 2009.
Kgositsile, Aneb/Gloria House. July 15, 2014.
Killingham, Marilyn Preston. November 3, 2009.
Lumumba, Chokwe, March 31, 2009; March 28, 2010 (with Paul Karolczyk).
Madhubuti, Haki R. December 14, 2010.
Muhammad, Saladin. September 2, 2018.
Mustafa, Khalil. October 11, 2009.
Mwendo, Ukali. February 4, 2012; April 2, 2017.
Nubyahn, D.B. Aammaa. September 20, 2009; October 10, 2009.
Owusu, Sekou. September 8, 2009; October 11, 2009.
Rashid, Kuratibisha X Ali. March 29, 2009; March 30, 2009; November 1, 2009.
Shakur, Shushanna. July 20, 2014.
Simmons, Gwendolyn Zoharah. February 20, 2010.
Sunni-Ali, Bilal. March 27, 2010 (with Paul Karolczyk).
Taifa, Nkechi. January 11, 2011.
Trice, Richard Bokeba. March 2, 2009; March 4, 2009; February 8, 2012.
Umoja, Akinyele Omowale. March 20, 2010; March 26, 2010 (with Paul Karolczyk).

FBI Records

Group on Advanced Leadership. 100-HQ-442379.
Henry, Milton Robinson. 100-HQ-412654.
HQ of the Republic of New Afrika. 100-HQ-444362.
The Republic of New Afrika, Los Angeles office. 100A-LA-87436.
Shabazz, Betty. 105-71196. https://vault.fbi.gov/betty-shabazz.

Documents in Author's Possession

The Illustrated News. Courtesy of Dr. David Goldberg.
Radical Information Project. Courtesy of Christian Davenport.

Dissertations and Master's Theses

Gaines, Rondee Jeanette. "Race, Power, and Representation: Broadcast News Portrayal of the Republic of New Africa." Master's thesis, University of Alabama, 2003.

———. "I am a Revolutionary Black Female Nationalist: A Womanist Analysis of Fulani Sunni Ali's Role as a New African Citizen and Minister of In-formation in the Provisional Government of the Republic of New Africa." PhD diss., Georgia State University, 2013.

Karolczyk, Paul. "Subjugated Territory: The New Afrikan Independence Movement and the Space of Black Power." PhD diss., Louisiana State University and Agricultural and Mechanical College, 2014.

Lott, Patricia A. "Bearing Witness to a History of Erasures and Traces: The Public Collective Memory of Racial Slavery in the Antebellum North." PhD diss., Northwestern University, 2013.

Ragsdale, Rose. "'They Never Stood a Chance': An Analysis of the Print Media's Coverage of the Republic of New Africa in Mississippi from March 1971 to September 1971." Master's thesis, Stanford University, 1983.

Richards, Assata-Nicole. "A Profile of the Leaders of the Provisional Government of the Republic of New Africa 1968–1980: Employing Intelligence and Counterintelligence Information from State Authorities as Data Sources to Study Social Movement Activists." Master's thesis, Pennsylvania State University, 2005.

Wilkins, Fanon Che. "'Black Power in the Belly of the Beast': Black Power, Anti-Imperialism, and the African Liberation Solidarity Movement, 1968–1975." PhD diss., New York University, 2001.

Articles, Books, Chapters, Pamphlets, and Websites

"About." National Jericho Movement website. Accessed August 29, 2017. http://www.thejerichomovement.com/about.

Achebe, Chinua. "The Politics of Language." In *The Post-Colonial Studies Reader*, edited by Bill Ashcroft, Gareth Griffiths, and Helen Tiffin, 268–71. 2nd ed. London: Routledge, 1995.

Ahmad, Muhammad (Max Stanford). *We Will Return in a Whirlwind: Black Radical Organizations, 1960–1975*. Chicago: Charles H. Kerr, 2007.

Aiyetoro, Adjoa A. "The National Coalition of Blacks for Reparations in America (N'COBRA): Its Creation and Contribution to the Reparations Movement." In *Should America Pay? Slavery and the Raging Debate on Reparations*, edited by Raymond A. Winbush, 209–25. New York: Amistad, 2003.

Akinyela, Makungu M. "Eight Bowls Full of Life." African Names: The Art & Science of African Names. December 11, 2009. http://afrikannames.com/2009/12/11/the-eight-bowl-ceremony/.

Alexander, Leslie M. *African or American? Black Identity and Political Activism in New York City, 1784–1861*. Urbana: University of Illinois Press, 2008.

Alexander, Michelle. *The New Jim Crow: Mass Incarceration in the Age of Colorblindness*. New York: New Press, 2012.

Allen, Ernest, Jr. "Making the Strong Survive: The Contours and Contradictions of Message Rap." In *Droppin' Science: Critical Essays on Rap Music and Hip Hop*

Culture, edited by William Eric Perkins, 159–81. Philadelphia: Temple University Press, 1996.

Allen, James S. *The Negro Question in the United States.* New York: International Publishers, 1936.

Allen, Robert. *Black Awakening in Capitalist America: An Analytic History.* 1969. Reprinted, Garden City, NY: Anchor Books, 1970.

Armah, Ayi Kwei. *Two Thousand Seasons.* Nairobi, Kenya: East African Publishing House, 1973.

Ashcroft, Bill, Gareth Griffiths, and Helen Tiffin, eds. *The Post-Colonial Studies Reader.* 2nd ed. London: Routledge, 1995.

Atanga, Mufor. *The Anglophone Cameroon Predicament.* Mankon, Bamenda: Langaa RPCIG, 2008.

Austin, Curtis J. *Up against the Wall: Violence in the Making and Unmaking of the Black Panther Party.* Fayetteville: University of Arkansas Press, 2006.

Babu, Abdul Rahman Mohamed. *African Socialism or Socialist Africa?* London: Zed, 1981; Dar Es Salaam: Tanzania Publishing House, 1981.

Back, Adina. "Exposing the 'Whole Segregation Myth': The Harlem Nine and New York City's School Desegregation Battles." In *Freedom North: Black Freedom Struggles outside the South, 1940–1980,* edited by Jeanne F. Theoharis and Komozi Woodard, 65–91. New York: Palgrave Macmillan, 2003.

Bambara, Toni Cade, ed. *The Black Woman: An Anthology.* New York: Washington Square Press, 1970.

Baptist, Edward E. *The Half Has Never Been Told: Slavery and the Making of American Capitalism.* New York: Basic Books, 2014.

Barbour, Floyd B. *The Black Power Revolt.* Boston: Extending Horizons Books, 1968.

Barrett, James R. *Work and Community in the Jungle: Chicago's Packinghouse Workers, 1894–1922.* Urbana: University of Illinois Press, 1987.

Bay, Mia, Farah J. Griffin, Martha S. Jones, and Barbara D. Savage, eds. *Toward an Intellectual History of Black Women.* Chapel Hill: University of North Carolina Press, 2015.

Beale, Frances. "Double Jeopardy: To Be Black and Female." In *Words of Fire: An Anthology of African-American Feminist Thought,* edited by Beverly Guy-Sheftall, 146–61. New York: New Press, 1995.

Bennett, W. Lance. "1998 Ithiel De Sola Pool Lecture: The UnCivic Culture; Communication, Identity, and the Rise of Lifestyle Politics." *PS: Political Science and Politics* 31, no. 4 (December 1998): 740–61.

———. "Branded Political Communication: Lifestyle Politics, Logo Campaigns, and the Rise of Global Citizenship." In *The Politics behind Products,* edited by Michele Micheletti, Andreas Follesdal, and Dietlind Stolle, 101–25. New Brunswick, NJ: Transaction Books, 2004.

Berger, Dan. *Captive Nation: Black Prison Organizing in the Civil Rights Era.* Chapel Hill: University of North Carolina Press, 2014.

———, ed. *The Hidden 1970s: Histories of Radicalism.* New Brunswick, NJ: Rutgers University Press, 2010.

———. *Outlaws of America: The Weather Underground and the Politics of Solidarity.* Oakland, CA: AK Press, 2006.

———. "Rescuing Civil Rights from Black Power." *Journal for the Study of Radicalism* 3, no. 2 (2008): 1–27.

Berger, Dan, and Roxanne Dunbar-Ortiz. "'The Struggle Is for the Land!'" In *The Hidden 1970s: Histories of Radicalism*, edited by Dan Berger, 57–76. New Brunswick, NJ: Rutgers University Press, 2010.

Berger, Dan, Mariame Kaba, and David Stein. "What Abolitionists Do." *Jacobin.* Accessed October 10, 2017. https://www.jacobinmag.com/2017/08/prison -abolition-reform-mass-incarceration.

Berlatsky, Noah. "At the United Nations, Chicago Activists Protest Police Brutality." *The Atlantic*, November 17, 2014. http://www.theatlantic.com/national/archive /2014/11/we-charge-genocide-movement-chicago-un/382843/.

Berlin, Ira. *Slaves without Masters: The Free Negro in the Antebellum South.* New York: Pantheon Books, 1974.

Berry, Mary Frances. *Black Resistance/White Law: A Legal History of Constitutional Racism in America.* New York: Penguin Books, 1971. Reprinted, 1994.

———. *My Face Is Black Is True: Callie House and the Struggle for Ex-Slave Reparations.* New York: Alfred A. Knopf, 2005.

Bevill, James. *The Paper Republic: The Struggle for Money, Credit and Independence in the Republic of Texas.* Houston: Bright Sky, 2009.

Binder, Guyora. "The Slavery of Emancipation." *Cordozo Law Review* 17, no. 6 (May 1996): 2063–102.

Bittker, Boris. *The Case of Black Reparations.* Boston: Beacon, 2003.

Black Entertainment Television. "Mutulu Shakur and the Republic of New Afrika." *American Gangster.* Accessed April 2008. www.bet.com/americangangster.

"Black Names." *Newsweek*, July 29, 1968, 88.

Blackstone, N. *Cointelpro: The FBI's Secret War on Political Freedom.* New York: Vintage, 1975.

Blight, David W. *Frederick Douglass' Civil War: Keeping Faith in Jubilee.* Baton Rouge: Louisiana State University Press, 1989.

Boggs, Grace Lee. *Living for Change: An Autobiography.* Minneapolis: University of Minnesota Press, 1998.

Boggs, James. *The American Revolution: Pages from a Negro Worker's Notebook.* New York: Monthly Review Press, 1963.

———. *Racism and Class Struggle: Further Pages from a Black Worker's Notebook.* New York: Monthly Review Press, 1970.

Bond, Jean Carey, and Patricia Peery. "Is the Black Male Castrated?" In *The Black Woman: An Anthology*, edited by Toni Cade Bambara, 141–48. New York: Washington Square, 1970.

Boyle, Kevin. *Arc of Justice: A Saga of Race, Civil Rights, and Murder in the Jazz Age.* New York: H. H. Holt, 2004.

Brent, William Lee. *Long Time Gone: A Black Panther's True-Life Story of His Hijacking and Twenty-Five Years in Cuba.* Bloomington: iUniverse, 2000.

Brickell, Katherine. "'Mapping' and 'Doing' Critical Geographies of Home." *Progress in Human Geography* 32, no. 2 (April 2012): 225–44.

Brisbane, Robert H. *Black Activism: Racial Revolution in the United States, 1954–1970.* Valley Forge, PA: Judson, 1974.

Brooks, Roy L., ed. *When Sorry Isn't Enough: The Controversy over Apologies and Reparations for Human Justice.* New York: New York University Press, 1999.

Brown, Claude. *Manchild in the Promised Land.* New York: Macmillan, 1965.

Brown, H. Rap. *Die Nigger Die!* Chicago: Lawrence Hill Books, 2002.

Brown, Oscar C. "What Chance Freedom!" *The Crisis* 42, no. 5 (May 1935): 134–55.

Brown, Robert A., and Todd C. Shaw. "Separate Nations: Two Attitudinal Dimensions of Black Nationalism." *Journal of Politics* 64, no. 1 (February 2003): 22–44.

Brown, Scot. *Fighting for US: Maulana Karenga, the US Organization, and Black Cultural Nationalism.* New York: New York University Press, 2003.

——. "The Politics of Culture: The US Organization and the Quest for Black 'Unity.'" In *Freedom North: Black Freedom Struggles Outside the South, 1940–1980,* edited by Jeanne F. Theoharis and Komozi Woodard, 223–53. New York: Palgrave Macmillan, 2003.

Browne, Robert S. "A Case for Separation." In *Black Separatism and Social Reality: Rhetoric and Reason,* edited by Raymond L. Hall, 24–28. New York: Pergamon, 1977.

Buffalo, Audreen. "Reclaiming Our Marriage." *Essence,* December 1992, 118.

Bukhari, Safiya. *The War Before: The True Life Story of Becoming a Black Panther, Keeping the Faith in Prison & Fighting for Those Left Behind.* New York: Feminist Press, 2010.

Cabral, Amilcar. *Return to the Source: Selected Speeches of Amilcar Cabral,* edited by the African Information Service. New York: Monthly Review Press, 1973.

Cacho, Lisa Marie. *Social Death: Racialized Rightlessness and the Criminalization of the Unprotected.* New York: New York University Press, 2012.

Cahan, Richard, and Michael Williams. *Revolution in Black and White: Ernest Withers Photographs 1948–1968.* Chicago: CityFiles Press, 2019.

Cameron, Catherine. *The Name Givers.* Englewood Cliffs, NJ: Prentice-Hall, 1983.

Carlisle, Rodney. *The Roots of Black Nationalism.* Port Washington, NY: Kennikat, 1975.

Carmichael, Stokely (Kwame Ture). "Pan-Africanism—Land and Power." *Black Scholar* 1, no. 1 (November 1969): 36–43.

——. *Stokely Speaks: From Black Power to Pan-Africanism.* Chicago: Lawrence Hill, 2007.

Carmichael, Stokely (Kwame Ture), and Charles V. Hamilton. *Black Power: The Politics of Liberation* Vintage ed. New York: Vintage Books, 1992.

Carmichael, Stokely, and Ekwueme Michael Thelwell. *Ready for Revolution: The Life and Struggles of Stokely Carmichael (Kwame Ture).* New York: Scribner, 2003.

Carson, Clayborne. *In Struggle: SNCC and the Black Awakening of the 1960s.* Cambridge, MA: Harvard University Press, 1995. Originally published 1981.

Carson, Clayborne, David J. Garrow, Gerald Gill, Vincent Harding, and Darlene Clark Hine, eds. *The Eyes on the Prize Civil Rights Reader: Documents, Speeches, and Firsthand Accounts from the Black Freedom Struggle*. New York: Penguin Books, 1991.

Carter, Wilson A. "A Radical Critique of the Reparations Movement." In *Beyond the Boundaries: A New Structure of Ambition in African American Politics*, edited by Georgia A. Persons, 205–26. New Brunswick, NJ: Transaction Publishers, 2009.

Castellucci, John. *The Big Dance: The Untold Story of Kathy Boudin and the Terrorist Family that Committed the Brink's Robbery Murders*. New York: Dodd, Mead, 1986.

Cha-Jua, Sundiata Keita. *America's First Black Town: Brooklyn, Illinois, 1830–1915*. Urbana: University of Illinois Press, 2000.

Cha-Jua, Sundiata Keita, and Clarence Lang. "The 'Long Movement' as Vampire: Temporal and Spatial Fallacies in Recent Black Freedom Studies." *Journal of African American History* 91, no. 2 (Spring 2007): 265–88.

Chrisman, Robert. "The Formation of a Revolutionary Black Culture." *The Black Scholar: Journal of Black Studies and Research* 1, no. 8 (June 1970): 2–9.

Churchill, Ward, and Jim Vander Wall. *Agents of Repression: The FBI's Secret Wars against the Black Panther Party and the American Indian Movement*. Boston: South End Press, 1988.

———. *The COINTELPRO Papers: Documents from the FBI's Secret Wars against Domestic Dissent*. Boston: South End Press, 1990.

Civil Rights Congress. *We Charge Genocide: The Historic Petition to the United Nations for Relief from a Crime of the United States Government against the Negro People*. New York: International Publishers, 1951. Reprint 1971.

Clarke, John Henrik. "African Warrior Queens." In *Black Women in Antiquity*. New edition, edited by Ivan Van Sertima. New Brunswick, NJ: Transaction Books, 1998.

———, ed. *Malcolm X: The Man and His Times*. New York: Macmillan, 1969.

Clayton, Lynn. "What's in a Name." *Essence* (June 1978): 48–49.

Cleaver, Eldridge. *Soul on Ice*. New York: Delta, 1991.

Cleaver, Kathleen Neal. "Back to Africa: The Evolution of the International Section of The Black Panther Party." In *The Black Panther Party [Reconsidered]*, edited by Charles E. Jones, 211–54. Baltimore: Black Classic Press, 1998.

Cleaver, Kathleen, and George Katsiaficas, eds. *Liberation, Imagination, and the Black Panther Party*. New York: Routledge, 2001.

Clegg, Claude Andrew, III. *An Original Man: The Life and Times of Elijah Muhammad*. New York: St. Martin's, 1997.

Coates, Ta-Nehisi. "The Case for Reparations." *The Atlantic*, June 2014. http://www.theatlantic.com/features/archive/2014/05/the-case-for-reparations/361631.

Cobb, Charlie. *African Notebook: Views on Returning "Home."* Chicago: Institute of Positive Education, 1972.

Cody, Cheryl Ann. "Naming, Kinship, and Estate Dispersal: Notes on Slave Family on a South Carolina Plantation, 1786 to 1833." *The William and Mary Quarterly,* 3rd ser. 39, no. 1 (January 1982): 192–211.

Coleman, Robin R. Means, and Douglas-Wade Brunton. "'You Might Not Know Her, but You Know Her Brother': Surveillance Technology, Respectability Policing, and the Murder of Janese Talton Jackson." *Souls* 18, no. 2–4 (April–December 2016): 408–20.

A Collection of Biographies. *Can't Jail the Spirit: Political Prisoners in the U.S.* 4th ed. Chicago: Chicago Editorial El Coqui, 1998.

Collier-Thomas, Bettye, and James Turner. "Race, Class, and Color: The African American Discourse on Identity." *Journal of American Ethnic History* 14, no. 1 (Fall 1994): 5–31.

Collins, Lisa Gail, and Margo Natalie Crawford, eds. *New Thoughts on the Black Arts Movement.* New Brunswick, NJ: Rutgers University Press, 2006.

"Communist Party Membership by Districts 1922–1950." *Mapping American Social Movements through the Twentieth Century.* Accessed June 20, 2019. https://depts .washington.edu/moves/CP_map-members.shtml.

Conn, Steven. "Back to the Garden: Communes, the Environment, and Antiurban Pastoralism at the End of the Sixties." *Journal of Urban History* 36, no. 6 (November 2010): 831–48.

"Cops' Version of Gun Battle in Detroit Church Accepted." *Chicago Tribune (1849–1985),* April 9, 1969, A3. *Historical Newspapers: Chicago Tribune.* ProQuest. http://www.proquest.com/.

Countryman, Matthew. *Up South: Civil Rights and Black Power in Philadelphia.* Philadelphia: University of Pennsylvania Press, 2006.

Crawford, Margo Natalie. "Must Revolution Be a Family Affair? Revisiting *The Black Woman.*" In *Want to Start a Revolution? Radical Black Women in the Black Freedom Struggle,* edited by Dayo F. Gore, Jeanne Theoharis, and Komozi Woodard, 185–204. New York: New York University Press, 2009.

Cressler, Matthew J. *Authentically Black and Truly Catholic: The Rise of Black Catholicism in the Great Migration.* New York: New York University Press, 2017.

Cross, William C., Jr. "Toward a Psychology of Black Liberation: The Negro-to-Black Conversion Experience." *Black World* (July 1971): 13–27.

C-SPAN. "U.S. Anti-terrorism Efforts and Muslims." C-SPAN, October 31, 2001. https://www.c-span.org/video/?167057-1/us-anti-terrorism-efforts-muslims& start=1950.

"Cuba Offers U.S. Hijacking Agreement." *Los Angeles Times,* September 27, 1970.

Cunningham, David. *There's Something Happening Here: The New Left, the Klan, and FBI Counterintelligence.* Berkeley: University of California Press, 2004.

Davenport, Christian. *How Social Movements Die: Repression and Demobilization of the Republic of New Africa.* New York: Cambridge University Press, 2015.

———. *Media Bias, Perspective, and State Repression: The Black Panther Party.* New York: Cambridge University Press, 2010.

———. *State Repression and the Domestic Democratic Peace.* New York: Cambridge University Press, 2007.

Davenport, Christian, Hank Johnston, and Carol Mueller, eds. *Repression and Mobilization*. Minneapolis: University of Minnesota Press, 2005.

Davidson, James M. "Encountering the Ex-Slave Reparations Movement from the Grave: The National Industrial Council and National Liberty Party, 1901–1907." *Journal for African American History* 97, nos. 1–2 (Winter–Spring 2012): 13–38.

Davis, Angela. *Angela Y. Davis Reader*. Edited by Joy James. Malden, MA: Blackwell, 1998.

———. *Are Prisons Obsolete?* New York: Seven Stories Press, 2003.

———. "Art on the Frontline." In *Angela Y. Davis Reader*, edited by Joy James, 236–47. Malden, MA: Blackwell, 1998.

———. "Reflections on the Black Woman's Role in the Community of Slaves." *Black Scholar*, 3, no. 1 (December 1971): 3–15.

Dawson, Michael C. *Black Visions: The Roots of Contemporary African-American Political Ideologies*. Chicago: University of Chicago Press, 2001.

DeCuir, Sharlene Sinegal. "'Nothing to Be Feared': Norman C. Francis, Civil Rights Activism, and the Black Catholic Movement." *Journal of African American History* 101, no. 3 (Summer 2016): 312–34.

Dillard, Angela Denise. *Faith in the City: Preaching Radical Social Change in Detroit*. Ann Arbor: University of Michigan Press, 2007.

Dillard, J. L. *Black Names*. The Hague: Mouton & Co., 1976.

Diop, Cheikh Anta. *The African Origin of Civilization: Myth or Reality*, translated by Mercer Cook. Chicago: Lawrence-Hill, 1974.

Draper, Theodore. *The Rediscovery of Black Nationalism*. New York: Viking, 1970.

Du Bois, David Graham. "Afro-American Militants in Africa." *Black World* 21, no. 4 (February 1972): 4–11.

Du Bois, W. E. B. "Criteria of Negro Art." In *Portable Harlem Renaissance Reader*, edited by David Levering Lewis, 100–105. New York: Viking, 1994.

———. *The Souls of Black Folk*. Bantam Classic ed. New York: Bantam Books, 1989.

Dubois, Laurent. *Avengers of the New World: The Story of the Haitian Revolution*. Cambridge, MA: Belknap Press of Harvard University Press, 2004.

Dubois, Laurent, and John D. Garrigus. *Slave Revolution in the Caribbean, 1789–1804: A Brief History with Documents*. Boston: Bedford/St. Martin's, 2006.

Dunbar, Ernest. "The Making of a Militant." *Saturday Night Review of Society* 55, no. 51 (January 1973): 25–32.

Dworkin, Ira. *Congo Love Song: African American Culture and the Crisis of the Colonial State*. Chapel Hill: University of North Carolina Press, 2017.

Dye, Keith A. "Lessons in Hearing Human and Divine Discontent: The Black Manifesto and Episcopal Leaders and Congregations in the Detroit Area." *Journal of African American History* 97, nos. 1–2 (Winter–Spring 2012): 72–91.

Equiano, Olaudah. *The Interesting Life of Olaudah Equiano, Written by Himself with Related Documents*. Edited by Robert J. Allison. New York: Palgrave Macmillan, 2006.

Eskew, Glenn T. "'Bombingham': Black Protest in Postwar Birmingham, Alabama." *The Historian* 59, no. 2 (December 1997): 371–90.

Essien, Kwame. *The Brazilian-African Diaspora in Ghana: The Tabom, Slavery, Dissonance of Memory, Identity, and Locating Home*. East Lansing: Michigan State University Press, 2016.

Essien-Udom, E. U. *Black Nationalism: A Search for an Identity in America*. Chicago: University of Chicago Press, 1962.

Evans, Sara. *Personal Politics: The Roots of Women's Liberation in the Civil Rights Movement and the New Left*. New York: Vintage Books, 1979.

Evanzz, Karl. *The Judas Factor: The Plot to Kill Malcolm X*. New York: Thunder's Mouth, 1992.

Fairchild, Halford H. "Black, Negro, or Afro-American? The Differences Are Crucial." *Journal of Black Studies* 16, no. 1 (September 1985): 47–55.

Falola, Toyin, and Ann Genova, eds. *Orisa: Yoruba Gods and Spiritual Identity in Africa and the Diaspora*. Trenton, NJ: Africa World Press, 2005.

Fanon, Frantz. *Black Skin, White Masks*, translated by Charles Lam Markmann. New York: Grove, 1967.

———. *The Wretched of the Earth*, translated by Constance Farrington. New York: Grove, 1963.

Farmer, Ashley D. *Remaking Black Power: How Black Women Transformed an Era*. Chapel Hill: University of North Carolina Press, 2017.

Ferguson, Iyaluua, and Herman Ferguson. *An Unlikely Warrior, Herman Ferguson: Evolution of a Black Nationalist Revolutionary*. Holly Springs, NC: Ferguson-Swan Publications, 2011.

Ferguson, Kathy E. *Emma Goldman: Political Thinking in the Streets*. Lanham, MD: Rowman & Littlefield, 2016.

Fierce, Milfred C. "Black Struggle for Land during Reconstruction." *Black Scholar* 5, no. 5 (February 1974): 13–18.

Fijnaut, Cyrille, and Gary T. Marx, eds. *Undercover: Police Surveillance in Comparative Perspective*. Boston: Kluwer Law International, 1995.

Fine, Sidney. *"Expanding the Frontiers of Civil Rights": Michigan, 1948–1968*. Detroit: Wayne State University Press, 2000.

———. *Violence in the Model City: The Cavanaugh Administration, Race Relations, and the Detroit Riot of 1967*. Ann Arbor: University of Michigan Press, 1989.

Foner, Eric. *A Short History of Reconstruction, 1863–1877*. New York: Harper Perennial, 1988.

Foner, Phillip S., ed. *The Black Panthers Speak*. 1st Da Capo Press pbk. ed. New York: Da Capo, 1995.

———. *Organized Labor and the Black Worker, 1619–1973*. New York: Praeger, 1974.

Forman, James R. *Self-Determination & the African-American People*. Seattle: Open Hand, 1981.

Franklin, V. P. *Black Self-Determination: A Cultural History of African-American Resistance*. 2nd ed. New York: Lawrence Hill Books, 1992.

Front Line Defenders. "Human Rights Defender Chokwe Lumumba." Frontline defenders.org. Accessed August 30, 2009. http:www.frontlinedefenders.org /node/488.

Fujino, Diane C. *Heartbeat of Struggle: The Revolutionary Life of Yuri Kochiyama*. Minneapolis: University of Minnesota Press, 2005.

Gage, Beverly. *The Day Wall Street Exploded: A Story of America in Its First Age of Terror*. Oxford: Oxford University Press, 2009.

Garcia, Sandra E. "Yasiin Bey Arrest Gives World Passport Visibility." *New York Times*, February 4, 2016. https://www.nytimes.com/2016/02/04/travel/-2016 -02-04-travel-04world-passport-mos-def.html.

Garrow, David J. *The FBI and Martin Luther King, Jr.* New York: Penguin Books, 1981.

Gea, Albert, and Pilar Suarez. "Human Tower Builders in Catalonia Kick Off with Pro-Independence Protest." *Reuters.com*. https://www.reuters.com/article/us -spain-culture-human-towers/human-tower-builders-in-catalonia-kick-off -with-pro-independence-protest-idUSKCN1MH0UA.

Georgakas, Dan, and Marvin Surkins. *Detroit: I Do Mind Dying*. 2nd ed. Cambridge, MA: South End Press, 1998.

Geschwender, James A. *Class, Race, and Worker Insurgency: The League of Revolutionary Black Workers*. Cambridge: Cambridge University Press, 1977.

Geschwender, James A., and Judson L. Jeffries. "The League of Revolutionary Black Workers." In *Black Power: In the Belly of the Beast*, edited by Judson L. Jeffries, 135–62. Urbana: University of Illinois Press, 2006.

Gilbert, Olive. *Narrative of Sojourner Truth*. Champaign: Project Gutenberg, 2000.

Gilmore, Ruth Wilson. *Golden Gulag: Prisons, Surplus, Crisis, and Opposition in Globalizing California*. Chapel Hill: University of North Carolina Press, 2007.

Giugni, Marco G. "Political, Biographical, and Cultural Consequences of Social Movements." *Sociological Compass* 2, no. 5 (2008): 1582–600.

Giugni, Marco, Doug McAdam, and Charles Tilly, eds. *How Movements Matter: Theoretical and Comparative Studies on the Consequences of Social Movements*. Minneapolis: University of Minnesota Press, 1989.

Glanton, Dahleen. "Backers: Al-Amin Victim of Vendetta; Ex-Black Panther No Killer, They Say." *Chicago Tribune*, March 11, 2002. *Historical Newspapers: Chicago Tribune*. ProQuest. http://www.proquest.com.

Glaude, Eddie, Jr., ed. *Is It Nation Time? Contemporary Essays on Black Power and Black Nationalism*. Chicago: University of Chicago Press, 2002.

"Global Acclaim for Black Human Rights." *The Paper*, November 8, 1979, 1. http://digital-archives.ccny.cuny.edu/archival-collections/the_paper/1979 /Vol%2050_No%205_NOVEMBER_8_1979.PDF.

Gomez, Michael A. *Black Crescent: The Experience and Legacy of African Muslims in the Americas*. New York: Cambridge University Press, 2005.

———. *Exchanging Our Country Marks: The Transformation of African Identities in the Colonial and Antebellum South*. Chapel Hill: University of North Carolina Press, 1998.

Gore, Dayo F., Jeanne Theoharis, and Komozi Woodard. *Want to Start a Revolution? Radical Black Women in the Black Freedom Struggle*. New York: New York University Press, 2009.

Grady-Willis, Winston A. *Challenging U.S. Apartheid: Atlanta and Black Struggles for Human Rights, 1960–1977*. Durham, NC: Duke University Press, 2006.

Gregory, James. *The Southern Diaspora: How the Great Migrations of Black and White Southerners Transformed America.* Chapel Hill: University of North Carolina Press, 2005.

Gross, Kali. *Colored Amazons: Crime, Violence, and Black Women in the City of Brotherly Love, 1880–1910.* Durham, NC: Duke University Press, 2006.

Guy, Jasmine. *Afeni Shakur: Evolution of a Revolutionary.* New York: Atria Books, 2004.

Guy-Sheftall, Beverly. *Words of Fire: An Anthology of African-American Feminist Thought.* New York: New Press, 1995.

Hall, Jaqueline Dowd. "The Long Civil Rights Movement and the Political Uses of the Past." *Journal of American History* 91, no. 4 (March 2005): 1233–63.

Hall, Raymond L., ed. *Black Separatism and Social Reality: Rhetoric and Reason.* New York: Pergamon, 1977.

———. *Black Separatism in the United States.* Hanover, NH: University Press of New England, 1978.

Hall, Stuart. "The Problem of Ideology: Marxism without Guarantees." In *Stuart Hall: Critical Dialogues in Cultural Studies,* edited by David Morley and Kuan-Hsing Chen, 25–46. London: Routledge, 1996.

Hamilton, Charles V., ed. "Republic of New Africa." In *The Black Experience in American Politics.* New York: Capricorn Books; G. P. Putman's Sons, 1973.

Hamilton, Tullia Brown. *Up from Canaan: The African American Journey from Mound Bayou to St. Louis.* University City, MO: PenUltimate, 2011.

hampton, dream. *The Black August Hip Hop Project.* Vimeo.com, 2010. mpeg video, 1:17:54. https://vimeo.com/134549172.

Hartman, Saidiya. *Lose Your Mother: A Journey along the Atlantic Slave Route.* New York: Farrar, Straus and Giroux, 2007.

Hayes, Floyd W., III, and Judson L. Jeffries. "Us Does Not Stand for United Slaves!" In *Black Power: In the Belly of the Beast,* edited by Judson L. Jeffries, 67–92. Urbana: University of Illinois Press, 2006.

Henry, Milton R. "An Independent Black Republic in North America." In *Black Separatism and Social Reality: Rhetoric and Reason,* edited by Raymond L. Hall, 33–39. New York: Pergamon, 1977.

Hewitt, Christopher. *Understanding Terrorism in America: From the Klan to Al Qaeda.* London: Routledge, 2003.

Higgins, Chester. "Black Sought Separate State 35 Years Ago." *Jet,* May 30, 1968.

Hill-Collins, Patricia. *Black Feminist Thought: Knowledge, Consciousness and the Politics of Empowerment.* Boston: Unwin Hyman, 1990.

Hilliard, David, and Lewis Cole. *This Side of Glory: The Autobiography of David Hilliard and the Story of the Black Panther Party.* Chicago: Lawrence Hill Books, 1993.

Hogan, Wesley C. *Many Minds, One Heart: SNCC's Dream for a New America.* Chapel Hill: University of North Carolina Press, 2007.

Holland, Catherine A. *The Body Politic: Foundings, Citizenship, and Difference in the American Political Imagination.* New York: Routledge, 2001.

Holland, Dorothy, Gretchen Fox, and Vinci Daro. "Social Movements and Collective Identity: A Decentered, Dialogic View." *Anthropological Quarterly* 81, no. 1 (Winter 2008): 95–126.

Horgan, John, and Kurt Braddock, eds. *Terrorism Studies: A Reader.* London: Routledge, 2012.

Horne, Gerald. *The Counter-Revolution of 1776: Slave Resistance and the Origins of the United States of America.* New York: New York University Press, 2014.

Howard, Reverend Dr. William. *Political Repression and Government Surveillance: An Address by the Rev. Dr. William Howard President, National Council of Churches of Christ White Rock Baptist Church, Philadelphia, Pa. October 30, 1980.* New York: United Methodist Voluntary Service, 1981.

Hucks, Tracey E. *Yoruba Traditions and African American Religious Nationalism.* Albuquerque: University of New Mexico Press, 2012.

Hughes, Langston. "The Negro Artist and the Racial Mountain." In *Portable Harlem Renaissance Reader,* edited by David Levering Lewis, 91–95. New York: Viking, 1994.

Hunt, Alex, and Brian Wheeler. "Brexit: All You Need to Know about the UK Leaving the EU." *BBC News.* https://www.bbc.com/news/uk-politics-32810887.

Ibekwe, Chinweizu. "Africa and the Capitalist Countries." In *General History of Africa: Africa since 1935,* edited by Ali Mazrui and C. Wondji, 769–97. Oxford: Heinemann Educational, 1993.

Intergovernmental Panel on Climate Change (IPCC). "Summary for Policymakers." In *Global Warming of 1.5°C. An IPCC Special Report on the Impacts of Global Warming of 1.5°C above Pre-industrial Levels and Related Global Greenhouse Gas Emission Pathways, in the Context of Strengthening the Global Response to the Threat of Climate Change, Sustainable Development, and Efforts to Eradicate Poverty.* Edited by V. Masson-Delmotte, P. Zhai, H. O. Pörtner, D. Roberts, J. Skea, P. R. Shukla, A. Pirani, W. Moufouma-Okia, C. Péan, R. Pidcock, S. Connors, J. B. R. Matthews, Y. Chen, X. Zhou, M. I. Gomis, E. Lonnoy, T. Maycock, M. Tignor, and T. Waterfield. Geneva, Switzerland: World Meteorological Organization, 2018. http://report.ipcc.ch/sr15/pdf/sr15_spm_final.pdf.

"Interview with Safiya Bukhari." September 27, 1992. https://thejerichomovement.com/profile/safiya-asya-bukhari-1950-2003.

"Jair Bolsonaro: Far-right Candidate Wins." *BBC News,* 8 October 2018. https://www.bbc.com/news/world-latin-america-45780176.

James, Joy, ed. *Warfare in the Homeland: Policing and Prison in a Penal Democracy.* Durham, NC: Duke University Press, 2007.

Jeffries, Hasan Kwame. *Bloody Lowndes: Civil Rights and Black Power in Alabama's Black Belt.* New York: New York University Press, 2009.

Jeffries, Judson L., ed. *Black Power: In the Belly of the Beast.* Urbana: University of Illinois Press, 2006.

——. "Black Radicalism and Political Repression in Baltimore: The Case of the Black Panther Party." *Ethnic and Racial Studies* 25, no. 1 (January 2002): 64–98.

ji Jaga, Geronimo. "Every Nation Struggling to Be Free Has a Right to Struggle, a Duty to Struggle." In *Liberation, Imagination, and the Black Panther Party*, edited by Kathleen Cleaver and George Katsiaficas, 71. New York: Routledge, 2001.

John, Catherine A. "Complicity, Revolution, and Black Female Writing." *Race & Class* 40, no. 4 (1999): 33–43.

Johnson, Cedric. *Revolutionaries to Race Leaders: Black Power and the Making of African American Politics*. Minnesota: University of Minnesota Press, 2007.

Jones, Charles E., ed. *The Black Panther Party [Reconsidered]*. Baltimore: Black Classic Press, 1998.

———. "The Political Repression of the Black Panther Party, 1966–1971: The Case of the Oakland Bay Area." *Journal of Black Studies* 18, no. 4 (June 1988): 415–34.

Joseph, Peniel E. "Black Liberation without Apology: Rethinking the Black Power Movement." *Black Scholar* 31, no. 3–4 (Fall/Winter 2001): 2–17.

———. *The Black Power Movement: Rethinking the Civil Rights–Black Power Era*. New York: Routledge, 2006.

———. "The Black Power Movement: A State of the Field." *Journal of American History* 96, no. 3 (December 2009): 751–76.

———, ed. *Neighborhood Rebels: Black Power at the Local Level*. New York: Palgrave Macmillan, 2010.

———. *Waiting 'til the Midnight Hour: A Narrative History of Black Power in America*. New York: Henry Holt, 2006.

———."Waiting 'til the Midnight Hour: Reconceptualizing the Heroic Period of the Civil Rights Movement, 1954–1965." *Souls* 2, no. 2 (Spring 2000): 6–17.

Kachru, Braj B. "The Alchemy of English." In *The Post-Colonial Studies Reader*, edited by Bill Ashcroft, Gareth Griffiths, and Helen Tiffin, 275. 2nd ed. London: Routledge, 1995.

Kanogo, Tabitha. *African Womanhood in Colonial Kenya, 1900–50*. Athens: Ohio University Press, 2005.

Karenga, Maulana. *Kwanzaa: A Celebration of Family, Community and Culture*. Los Angeles: University of Sankore Press, 2008.

———. *The Quotable Karenga*. Edited by Clyde Halisi and James Mtume. Los Angeles: US Organization, 1967.

Katagiri, Yasuhiro. *The Mississippi State Sovereignty Commission: Civil Rights and States' Rights*. Jackson: University Press of Mississippi, 2001.

Katzman, David M. *Before the Ghetto: Black Detroit in the Nineteenth Century*. Urbana: University of Illinois Press, 1973.

Kelley, Robin D. G. *Freedom Dreams: The Radical Imagination*. Boston: Beacon, 2002.

Kendi, Ibram X. *Stamped from the Beginning: The Definitive History of Racist Ideas in America*. New York: Nation Books, 2016.

Kettner, James H. *The Development of American Citizenship, 1608–1870*. Chapel Hill: University of North Carolina Press, 1978.

Khatib, Syed Malik. "Personal Names and Name Changes." *Journal of Black Studies* 25, no. 3 (January 1995): 349–53.

Kijembe, Adhama Oluwa. "Swahili and Black Americans." *Negro Digest* 18, no. 9 (July 1969): 4–8.

Killingham, Marilyn. "Marilyn Killingham and the Revolutionary Action Movement (RAM)." *Freemix Radio*, January 4, 2010. www.voxunion.com/?p=90.

King, Deborah K. "Multiple Jeopardy, Multiple Consciousness: The Context of a Black Feminist Ideology." *Signs* 14, no. 1 (Autumn 1988): 42–72.

King, Martin Luther, Jr. *Where Do We Go from Here: Chaos or Community?* Boston: Beacon, 1967.

——. *Why We Can't Wait*. New York: Mentor, 1964.

Kornweible, Theodore. *Seeing Red: Federal Campaigns against Black Militancy, 1919–1925*. Bloomington: Indiana University Press, 1998.

Kuykendall, Ronald A. "African Blood Brotherhood, Independent Marxist during the Harlem Renaissance." *Western Journal of Black Studies* 26, no. 1 (March 2002): 17.

La Rue, Linda. "The Black Movement and Women's Liberation." In *Words of Fire: An Anthology of African-American Feminist Thought*, edited by Beverly Guy-Sheftall, 164–73. New York: New Press, 1995.

Ladner, Joyce. "Tanzanian Women and Nation Building." *Black Scholar* 3, no. 4 (December 1972): 22–28.

Ladson-Billings, Gloria. "Toward a Theory of Culturally Relevant Pedagogy." *American Educational Research Journal* 32, no. 3 (Autumn 1995): 465–91.

Lake, Obiagele. *Blue Veins and Kinky Hair: Naming and Color Consciousness in African America*. Westport, CT: Praeger, 2003.

Lang, Clarence. "Between Civil Rights and Black Power in the Gateway City: The Action Committee to Improve Opportunities for Negroes (ACTION), 1964–1975." *Journal of Social History* 37 (Spring 2004): 725–54.

——. *Grassroots at the Gateway: Class Politics and Black Freedom Struggle in St. Louis, 1936–75*. Ann Arbor: University of Michigan Press, 2009.

Lappé, Antony. "Fugitive from Time." *New York Times* (1923–Current File), May 23, 1999, SM54. *Historical Newspapers: New York Times*. ProQuest. http://www.proquest.com/.

Laqueur, Walter. *Terrorism*. Boston: Little, Brown, 1977.

Latner, Teishan A. *Cuban Revolution in America: Havana and the Making of the United States Left, 1968–1992*. Chapel Hill: University of North Carolina Press, 2018.

Lazerow, Jama, and Yohuru Williams, eds. *In Search of the Black Panther Party: New Perspectives on a Revolutionary Movement*. Durham, NC: Duke University Press, 2006.

——. *Liberated Territory: Untold Local Perspectives on the Black Panther Party*. Durham, NC: Duke University Press, 2008.

Lechtreck, Elaine Allen. "'We Are Demanding $500 Million for Reparations': The Black Manifesto, Mainline Religious Denominations, and Black Economic Development." *Journal of African American History* 97, nos. 1–2 (Winter–Spring 2012): 39–71.

Lee, Chana Kai. *For Freedom's Sake: The Life of Fannie Lou Hamer.* Urbana: University of Illinois Press, 1999.

Lee, Helen Shores. *The Gentle Giant of Dynamite Hill: The Untold Story of Arthur Shores and His Family's Fight for Civil Rights.* Grand Rapids: Zondervan, 2012.

Leiden, Carl, and Karl M. Schmitt. *The Politics of Violence: Revolution in the Modern World.* Englewood Cliffs, NJ: Prentice-Hall, 1968.

Lenin, V. I. *Collected Works.* Vol. 20, December 1913–August 1914. Edited by Julius Katzer. Translated by Bernard Isaacs and Joe Fineberg. Moscow: Progress, 1964.

Leonard, R. N. Ashley. "Changing Times and Changing Names: Reasons, Regulations, and Rights." *Names* 19 (1971): 167–87.

Lester, Julius. *Look Out Whitey! Black Power's Gon' Get Your Mama.* New York: Dial, 1968.

Levy, Peter B. *Civil War on Race Street: The Civil Rights Movement in Cambridge, Maryland.* Gainesville: University Press of Florida, 2003.

Lewis-Coleman, David M. *Race against Liberalism: Black Workers and the UAW in Detroit.* Urbana: University of Illinois Press, 2008.

Lincoln, C. Eric. *The Black Muslims in America.* Boston: Beacon, 1960.

Llorens, David. "Black Separatism in Perspective: Movement Reflects Failure of Integration." *Ebony,* September 1968, 89–90, 92–95.

Logan, Rayford W. *The Negro in the United States: A Brief History.* Princeton, NJ: D. Van Nostrand, 1975.

Lowenthal, David. "Past Time, Present Place: Landscape and Memory." *Geographical Review* 65, no. 1 (January 1975): 1–36.

Lumumba, Chokwe. *The Roots of the New Afrikan Independence Movement: A Response to the Inaccurate and Politically Immature Attacks on the New Afrikan Independence Movement by the African People's Socialist Party.* Jackson, MS: New Afrikan Productions, n.d.

———. "Short History of the U.S. War on the R.N.A." *Black Scholar* 12, no. 1 (January–February 1981): 72–81.

Madhubuti, Haki R. "The Latest Purge: The Attack on Black Nationalism and Pan-Afrikanism by the New Left, the Sons and Daughters of the Old Left." *Black Scholar* 6, no. 1 (September 1974): 43–56.

Maglangbayan, Shawna. *Garvey, Lumumba and Malcolm: National-Separatists.* Chicago: Third World Press, 1972.

Makalani, Minkah. *In the Cause of Freedom: Radical Black Internationalism from Harlem to London, 1917–1939.* Chapel Hill: University of North Carolina Press, 2011.

Malcolm X. "The Black Revolution," edited by Imam Benjamin Karim. Accessed April 14, 2008. http://www.malcolmxonline.com/speeches-black-revolution .html.

———. "God's Judgment of White America (The Chickens Come Home to Roost)" edited by Imam Benjamin Karim. Accessed March 15, 2010. http://www .malcolm-x.org/speeches/spc_120463.htm.

———. *Malcolm X Speaks: Selected Speeches and Statements*, edited by George Breitman. New York: Merit Publishers, 1965. Reprint, New York: Grove Weidenfeld, 1990.

———. "Speech to African Summit Conference—Cairo, Egypt." In *Malcolm X: The Man and His Times*, edited by John Henrik Clarke, 288–93. New York: Macmillan, 1969.

Malcolm X, and Alex Haley. *The Autobiography of Malcolm X*. New York: Ballantine Books, 1973.

Malcolm X Grassroots Movement. "Chokwe Lumumba's Election Victory." Accessed August 30, 2009. http://mxgm.org/web/political/chokwe-lumumba -july-campaign-update.html.

Markus, Andrew. "The Far-Right's Creeping Influence on Australian Politics." *The Conversation*, April 12, 2018. http://theconversation.com/the-far-rights -creeping-influence-on-australian-politics-93723.

Marsh, Clifton E. *The Lost-Found Nation of Islam*. Lanham, MD: Scarecrow Press, 2000.

Martin, Michael T., and Marilyn Yaquinto, eds. *Redress for Historical Injustices in the United States: On Reparations for Slavery, Jim Crow, and Their Legacies*. Durham, NC: Duke University Press, 2007.

Marwell, Gerald N. J., III, and Michael Aiken. "1960s Civil Rights Activists Turn Forty: Generational Unit at Mid-Life." *Research in Political Sociology*, Vol. 6 (1993): 175–95.

Marx, Gary T. "Thoughts on a Neglected Category of Social Movement Participant: The Agent Provocateur and the Informant." *American Journal of Sociology* 80, no. 2 (September 1974): 402–42.

Masotti, Louis H., and Jerome R. Corsi. *Shootout in Cleveland: Black Militants and the Police; A Staff Report to the National Commission on the Causes and Prevention of Violence*. Washington, D.C.: U.S. Government Printing Office, May 1969.

Massey, Douglas S. *American Apartheid: Segregation and the Making of the Underclass*. Cambridge, MA: Harvard University Press, 1993.

Matthews, Tracye. "No One Ever Asks What a Man's Place in the Revolution Is." In *Black Panther Party [Reconsidered]*, edited by Charles Jones, 265–304. Baltimore: Black Classic Press.

Mayes, Keith A. *Kwanzaa: Black Power and the Making of the African-American Black Holiday*. New York: Routledge, 2009.

Mazrui, Ali. "Tanzaphilia." *Transition* 31 (June–July 1967): 20–26.

Mazrui, Ali, and C. Wondji, eds. *General History of Africa: Africa since 1935*. Oxford: Heinemann Educational, 1993.

Mbogoni, Lawrence E. Y. *Aspects of Colonial Tanzania History*. Dar es Salaam: Mkuki na Nyota, 2013.

McAdam, Doug. "The Biographical Consequences of Activism." *American Sociological Review* 53, no. 5 (October 1989): 744–60.

———. "The Biographical Impact of Activism." In *How Social Movements Matter*, edited by Marco Giugni, Doug McAdam, and Charles Tilly, 119–46. Vol. 10 of

Social Movements, Protest, and Contention. Minneapolis: University of Minnesota Press, 1999.

——. *Political Process and the Development of Black Insurgency, 1930–1970.* 2nd ed. Chicago: University of Chicago Press, 1999.

McCutcheon, Priscilla. "'Returning Home to Our Rightful Place': The Nation of Islam and Muhammad Farms." *Geoforum* 49 (October 2013): 61–70.

McDuffie, Erik S. "'I Wanted a Communist Philosophy, but I Wanted Us to Have a Chance to Organize Our People': The Diasporic Radicalism of Queen Mother Audley Moore and the Origins of Black Power." *African and Black Diaspora: An International Journal* 3, no. 2 (June 2010): 181–95.

——. *Sojourning for Freedom: Black Women, American Communism, and the Making of Black Left Feminism.* Durham, NC: Duke University Press, 2011.

McNeely, Connie L. "The Determination of Statehood in the United Nations, 1945–1985." *Research in Political Sociology* 6 (1993): 1–38.

McWhorter, Diane. *Carry Me Home: Birmingham, Alabama; The Climactic Battle of the Civil Rights Revolution.* New York: Simon and Schuster, 2001.

Meier, August, and Elliot Rudwick. *Black Detroit and the Rise of the UAW.* New York: Oxford University Press, 1979. Reprint, Ann Arbor: University of Michigan Press, 2007.

Meiners, Erica R. "Ending the School-to-Prison Pipeline/Building Abolition Futures." *Urban Review* 43, no. 4 (November 2011): 547–65.

Meriwether, James H. *Proudly We Can Be Africans: Black Americans and Africa, 1935–1961.* Chapel Hill: University of North Carolina Press, 2002.

Miles, Marvin. "U.S. Skyjackings in '69 Decline Sharply." *Los Angeles Times,* July 14, 1970.

Miles, Tiya. *Ties That Bind: The Story of an Afro-Cherokee Family in Slavery and Freedom.* Berkeley: University of California Press, 2005.

Miller, Edward L. *New Orleans and the Texas Revolution.* College Station: Texas A&M University Press, 2004.

Mills, Brandon. "'The United States of Africa': Liberian Independence and the Contested Meaning of a Black Republic." *Journal of the Early Republic* 34, no. 1 (Spring 2014): 79–107.

Mills, Charles W. *The Racial Contract.* Ithaca, NY: Cornell University Press, 1997.

Minter, William, Gail Hovey, and Charles Cobb, Jr., eds. *No Easy Victories: African Liberation and American Activists over a Half Century, 1950–2000.* Trenton, NJ: Africa World Press, 2007.

Miyakawa, Felicia. *Five Percenter Rap: God Hop's Music, Message, and Black Muslim Mission.* Bloomington: Indiana University Press, 2005.

Mkalimoto, Ernie. "The Cultural Arm of Revolutionary Black Nationalism." *Negro Digest* 29, no. 2 (December 1969): 11–17.

Mlambo, Alois S. *A History of Zimbabwe.* Cambridge: Cambridge University Press, 2014.

Moore, Audley A. *Why Reparations? "Money for Negroes: Reparations If the Battle Cry for the Economic and Social Freedom of More than 25 Million Descendants of American Slaves."* Los Angeles: Reparations Committee, Inc., ca. 1962.

Moore, Richard B. *Richard B. Moore, Caribbean Militant in Harlem: Collected Writings, 1920–1972.* Edited by W. Burghardt Turner and Joyce Moore Turner. Bloomington: Indiana University Press, 1988.

Morgan, Edward P. "Media Culture and the Public Memory of the Black Panther Party." In *In Search of the Black Panther Party: New Perspectives on a Revolutionary Movement,* edited by Jama Lazerow and Yohuru Williams, 324–73. Durham, NC: Duke University Press, 2006.

Morgan, Jennifer. *Laboring Women: Reproduction and Gender in New World Slavery.* Philadelphia: University of Pennsylvania Press, 2004.

Morris, Aldon. *The Origins of the Civil Rights Movement: Black Communities Organizing for Change.* New York: Free Press, 1984.

Mott, Ronni. "Runoffs Provide Decisive Wins." *Jackson Free Press,* May 20, 2009. http://www.jacksonfreepress.com/index.php/site/comments/runoffs_provide _decisive_wins_052009/.

Moye, Todd J. *Let the People Decide: Black Freedom and White Resistance Movements in Sunflower County, Mississippi 1945–1986.* Chapel Hill: University of North Carolina Press, 2004.

Moyo, Dambisa. *Dead Aid: Why Aid Is Not Working and How There Is a Better Way for Africa.* New York: Farrar, Straus and Giroux, 2009.

Muhammad, Askia. "'Black Power' and the Shallow Scholarship at the Smith-sonian." *Black Journalism Review,* March 24, 2009. http://www.black journalism.com/?p=149.

Muhammad, Elijah. *Message to the Blackman in America.* Chicago: Mosque of Islam No. 2, 1965.

———. *Supreme Wisdom: Solution to the So-Called Negroes Problem.* Newport News, VA: National Newport News and Commentator, 1957.

Muhammad, Khalil Gibran. *The Condemnation of Blackness: Race, Crime, and the Making of Modern Urban America.* Cambridge, MA: Harvard University Press, 2010.

Muntaqim, Jalil A. "Jalil A. Muntaqim: The Making of a Movement." *Bay View: National Black Newspaper,* November 6, 2017. https://sfbayview.com/2017/11 /jalil-a-muntaqim-the-making-of-a-movement/.

Mustakeem, Sowande' M. *Slavery at Sea: Terror, Sex, and Sickness in the Middle Passage.* Chicago: University of Illinois Press, 2016.

Muwakkil, Salim. "An Echo from the '60s Rekindles Old Debates [Chicago Sports Final, N Edition]." *Chicago Tribune,* March 27, 2000. *Historical Newspapers: Chicago Tribune.* ProQuest. http://www.proquest.com/.

Neal, Larry. "Any Day Now: Black Art and Liberation." *Ebony Magazine* 1969. Reprinted in *The Black Revolution: An Ebony Special,* 31–53. Chicago: Johnson, 1970.

New Afrikan Notes 1, no. 2 (July 1981): 1.

New Afrikan People's Organization. "Statement on the Transition of Nehanda Isoke Abiodun." 30 January 2019. https://www.mxgm.org/statementonnehanda (accessed January 30, 2019).

———. "Why We Use New Afrikan." Freedom Archives. Accessed January 12, 2018. https://search.freedomarchives.org/search.php?view_collection=12.

Newton, Huey P. "Speech Delivered at Boston College: November 18, 1970." In Huey P. Newton, *To Die for the People: The Writings of Huey P. Newton*, 33. New York: Random House, 1972.

———. *To Die for the People: The Writings of Huey P. Newton*. New York: Random House, 1972.

———. "To the RNA" (letter), September 13, 1969. In *The Black Panthers Speak*, 1st Da Capo Press pbk. ed., edited by Philip Foner, 72. New York: Da Capo, 1995.

Newton, Huey P., and J. Herman Blake. *Revolutionary Suicide*. New York: Harcourt Bruce Jovanovich, 1973.

Ngugi, Wa Thiong'o. *Decolonizing the African Mind: The Politics of Language in African Literature*. Nairobi: East African Educational Publishers, 1986.

Nuessel, Frank. *The Study of Names: A Guide to the Principles and Topics*. Westport, CT: Greenwood, 1992.

Nyerere, Julius K. *Freedom and Socialism: A Selection from Writings and Speeches*. Oxford: Oxford University Press, 1972.

———. "From Uhuru to Ujamaa." *Africa Today* 21, no. 3 (Summer 1974): 3–8.

———. *Ujamaa: Essays on Socialism*. London: Oxford University Press, 1968.

Obadele, Imari Abubakari, ed. *De-Colonization U.S.A.: The Independence Struggle of the Black Nation in the United States Centering on the 1996 United Nations Petition*. Baton Rouge, LA: Malcolm X Generation, 1997.

———. *Foundations of the Black Nation*. Detroit: House of Songhay, 1975.

———. *Free the Land: The True Story of the Trials of the RNA-11 in Mississippi and the Continuing Struggle to Establish an Independent Black Nation in the Five States of the Deep South*. Washington, D.C.: House of Songhay, 1984.

———. "Getting Ready for the United Nations." *Black Scholar* 8, no. 6 (April 1977): 35–45.

———. "National Black Elections Held by Republic of New Africa." *Black Scholar* 7, no. 2 (October 1975): 27–38.

———. *People's Revolt against Poverty A People's Revolt for Power and an Up-Turn in the Black Condition: An Appeal and a Challenge*. Detroit, MI: President Imari Obadele Revolt Against Poverty Campaign Headquarters, 1977.

———. *President to President on the Question of Human Rights: Imari Abubakari, I President, the Republic of New Afrika—Named a Political Amnesty Prisoner by Amnesty International—Challenges U.S. President Jimmy Carter on Oppression of Blacks, Indians, & Others Genocide, Slave Labor in Prisons, Prisoner Exchange and the U.S. Silence on Vicious Anti-Black 'Cointelpro.'* Washington, D.C.: Malcolmite Party, July 16, 1978.

———. "The Republic of New Africa—An Independent Black Nation." *Black World* 20, no. 7 (May 1971): 81–89.

———. *Revolution and Nation Building: Strategy for Building the Black Nation in America*. Detroit: House of Songhay, 1970.

———. "The Struggle Is for Land." *Black Scholar* 3, no. 6 (February 1972): 24–36.

———. "The Struggle of the Republic of New Africa." *Black Scholar* 5, no. 9 (June 1974): 32–41.

——. *Suggested Guidelines for the Land Development Cooperatives*. Washington, D.C.: People's Revolt against Poverty, n.d.

——. *War in America: The Malcolm X Doctrine*. Rev. ed. Detroit: Malcolm X Society, 1968.

Office of Chokwe Lumumba, Esq. "Biographical Sketch of Chokwe Lumumba." Accessed August 30, 2009. http://www.law.howard.edu/dictator/media/220 /BIOGRAPHICAL_OF_CHOKWE_LUMUMBA.doc.

Offiong, Daniel A. *Imperialism and Dependency: Obstacles to African Development*. Washington, D.C.: Howard University Press, 1982.

Ogbar, Jeffrey O. G. *Black Power: Radical Politics and African American Identity*. Baltimore: Johns Hopkins University Press, 2005.

Okolo, Amechi. "Dependency in Africa: Stages of African Political Economy." *Alternatives* 9, no. 2 (Fall 1983): 229–47.

Onaci, Edward. "'I Can Be Your Sun, You Can Be My Earth': Masculinity, Hip Hop, and the Nation of Gods and Earths." In *Message in the Music: Hip Hop, History, and Pedagogy*, edited by Derrick Alridge, V. P. Franklin, and James B. Stewart, 131–51. Washington, D.C.: Association for the Study of African American Life and History Press, 2010.

OpenJurist.org. "288 F. 2d 600—Taylor v. Board of Education of City School District of City of New Rochelle." Accessed November 15, 2009. http://open jurist.org/288/f2d/600/taylor-v-board-of-education-of-city-school-district-of -city-of-new-rochelle.

O'Reilly, Kenneth. *Racial Matters: The FBI's Secret File on Black America, 1960–1972*. New York: Free Press, 1989.

Painter, Nell Irvin. *Standing at Armageddon: The United States, 1877–1919*. New York: W. W. Norton, 1987.

"Pair Termed Envoys." *New York Times (1923–Current file)*, July 14, 1972. *Historical Newspapers: New York Times*. ProQuest. http://www.proquest.com/.

Palatino, Mong. "Is the Philippines' Duterte Really a Leftist?" *The Diplomat*, May 2, 2017. https://thediplomat.com/2017/05/is-the-philippines-duterte-really-a-leftist/.

Patterson, Orlando. *Slavery and Social Death: A Comparative Study*. Cambridge, MA: Harvard University Press, 1982.

Paustian, P. Robert. "The Evolution of Personal Naming Practices among American Blacks." *Names* 26, no. 2 (June 1978): 177–91.

Payer, Cheryl. "The World Bank and the Small Farmers." *Journal for Peace Research* 16, no. 4 (December 1979): 293–312.

Payne, Charles. *I've Got the Light of Freedom*. Berkeley: University of California Press, 1995.

Peery, Nelson. *The Negro National Colonial Question*. 2nd rev. ed. Chicago: Workers Press, 1975.

Perkins, Margo, V. *Autobiography as Activism: Three Black Women of the Sixties*. Jackson: University of Mississippi Press, 2000.

Perreaux, Les. "After 40 Years, Sovereignty off the Table in Quebec Election." *Globe and Mail*, August 19, 2018. https://www.theglobeandmail.com/canada /article-independence-not-a-major-defining-issue-in-quebec-election-campaign/.

Perrusquia, Marc. *A Spy in Canaan: How the FBI Used a Famous Photographer to Infiltrate the Civil Rights Movement.* Brooklyn, NY: Melville House, 2017.

Pharr, Pauline C. "Onomastic Divergence: A Study of Given-Name Trends among African Americans." *American Speech* 68, no. 4 (Winter 1993): 400–409.

Pinkney, Alphonso. *Red, Black, and Green: Black Nationalism in the United States.* Cambridge: Cambridge University Press, 1967.

Pipes, Daniel. "The Curious Case of Jamil Al-Amin." *Daniel Pipes Middle East Forum*, November–December 2001. http://www.danielpipes.org/97/the -curious-case-of-jamil-al-amin.

"Pistol Packers Arrested." *Chicago Daily Defender (Daily Edition) (1960–1973)*, July 17, 1972. *Historical Newspapers.* ProQuest. http://www.proquest.com/.

"Policeman Killed in Detroit Battle: Clash at Church Follows Black Militant Meeting." *New York Times (1851–2004).* March 31, 1969: 1. *Historical Newspapers: New York Times.* ProQuest. http://www.proquest.com/.

Polletta, Francesca. "'It Was Like a Fever . . .': Narrative and Identity in Social Protest." *Social Problems*, 45, no. 2 (May 1998): 137–59.

Polletta, Francesca, and James M. Jasper. "Collective Identity and Social Movements." *Annual Review of Sociology* 27 (August 2001): 283–305.

Popkin, Jeremy D. *A Concise History of the Haitian Revolution.* West Sussex: Wiley-Blackwell, 2012.

Puckett, Newbell Niles. "American Negro Names." *Journal of Negro History* 23, no. 1 (January 1938): 35–48.

———. *Black Names in America: Origins and Usage.* Edited by Murray Heller. Boston: G. K. Hall, 1975.

———. "Names of American Negro Slaves." In *Studies in the Science of Society*, edited by George Peter Murdock. 1937. Reprint, Freeport, New York: Books for Libraries Press, 1969, 471–94.

Purdue, Theda. *Cherokee Women: Gender and Culture Change, 1700–1835.* Lincoln: University of Nebraska Press, 1998.

Rabaka, Reiland. "W.E.B. Du Bois, Reparations, Radical Politics, and Critical Race Theory." In *Racial Structure & Radical Politics in the African Diaspora.* Vol. 2, *Africana Studies*, edited by Georgia A. Persons, 81–112. New York: Routledge, 2017.

Rahman, Ahmad A. "Marching Blind: The Rise and Fall of the Black Panther Party in Detroit." In *Liberated Territory: Untold Local Perspectives on the Black Panther Party*, edited by Jama Lazerow and Yohuru Williams, 181–231. Durham, NC: Duke University Press, 2008.

Ransby, Barbara. *Eslanda: The Large and Unconventional Life of Mrs. Paul Robeson.* New Haven, CT: Yale University Press, 2013.

Rediker, Marcus. *The Slave Ship: A Human History.* New York: Penguin Books, 2007.

Reed, Adolph L., Jr. "Pan-Africanism–Ideology for Liberation?" *Black Scholar* 3, no. 1 (September 1971): 2–13.

Republic of New Africa. *Anti-Depression Program of the Republic of New Africa: To End Poverty, Dependence, Cultural Malnutrition, and Crime among Black People in the United States and Promote Inter-Racial Peace Presented for Enactment to Both Houses of the United States Congress.* Jackson, Miss.: Republic of New Africa, 1972.

———. *New African Ujamaa: The Economics of the Republic of New Africa.* San Francisco: Republic of New Africa, 1970.

Rhodes, Jane. *Framing the Panthers: The Spectacular Rise of the Black Power Icon.* New York: New Press, 2007.

Ricci, David M. *Good Citizenship in America.* New York: Cambridge University Press, 2004.

Richardson, Henry J., III. *The Origins of African-American Interests in International Law.* Durham, NC: Carolina Academic Press, 2008.

Rickford, Russell. *We Are an African People: Independent Education, Black Power, and the Radical Imagination.* Oxford: Oxford University Press, 2016.

———. "'We Can't Grow Food on All This Concrete': The Land Question, Agrarianism, and Black Nationalist Thought in the Late 1960s and 1970s." *Journal of American History* 103, no. 4 (March 2017): 956–80.

Roberson, Erriel D. *The Maafa & Beyond: Remembrance, Ancestral Connections and Nation Building for the African Global Community.* Columbia, MD: Kujichagulia Press, 1995.

Roberts, James. "Sovereignty." *The Internet Encyclopedia of International Relations.* Accessed February 26, 2010. http://www.towson.edu/polsci/irencyc /sovreign.htm.

Robinson, Cedric J. *Black Marxism: The Making of the Black Radical Tradition.* 1983. Reprint, Chapel Hill: University of North Carolina Press, 2000.

Robinson, Dean E. *Black Nationalism in American Politics and Thought.* Cambridge: Cambridge University Press, 2001.

Robinson, Randall. *The Debt: What America Owes to Blacks.* New York: Plume, 2001.

Robnett, Belinda. *How Long? How Long? African-American Women in the Struggle for Civil Rights.* New York: Oxford University Press, 1997.

Rohter, Larry. "25 Years and Exile: An Old Black Panther Sums Up." *New York Times,* April 9, 1996, A4.

Saldaña-Portillo, and María Josefina. *The Revolutionary Imagination in the Americas and the Age of Development.* Durham, NC: Duke University Press, 2003.

Sales, William W., Jr. *From Civil Rights to Black Liberation: Malcolm X and the Organization of Afro-American Unity.* Boston: South End Press, 1994.

Salzberger, Ronald P., and Mary C. Turck. *Reparations for Slavery: A Reader.* Lanham, MD: Rowman & Littlefield, 2004.

"Scottish Independence Referendum." *Gov.uk.* Accessed November 15, 2018, https://www.gov.uk/government/topical-events/scottish-independence -referendum/about.

Seale, Bobby. *Seize the Time: The Story of the Black Panther Party and Huey P. Newton.* Baltimore: Black Classic Press, 1991. Originally published by Random House, 1970.

"Separatists Jailed." *Washington Post, Times Herald (1959–1973)*, October 15, 1972, A22. *Historical Newspapers: Washington Post*. ProQuest. http://www.proquest .com/.

Shakur, Assata. *Assata: An Autobiography*. Chicago: Lawrence Hill Books, 1987.

Shelter, Jan Bender. *Imagining Serengeti: A History of Landscape Memory in Tanzania from Earliest Times to the Present*. Athens: Ohio State University Press, 2007.

Sherkat, Darren E., and T. Jean Blocker. "Explaining the Political and Personal Consequences of Protest." *Social Forces* 75, no. 3 (March 1997): 1049–76.

Sherrill, Robert. "Birth of a (Black) Nation." *Esquire: The Magazine for Men*, January 1969.

Shklar, Judith N. *American Citizenship: The Quest for Inclusion*. Cambridge: Harvard University Press, 1991.

Shockley, Megan Taylor. *"We, Too, Are Americans": African American Women in Detroit and Richmond, 1940–1954*. Urbana: University of Illinois Press, 2004.

Simmons, Aishah Shahida, ed. *Love with Accountability: Digging Up the Roots of Child Sexual Abuse*. Chino, CA: AK Press, 2019.

Singh, Nikhil. *Black Is a Country: Race and the Unfinished Struggle for Democracy*. Cambridge, MA: Harvard University Press, 2003.

Sitkoff, Harvard. "The Detroit Race Riot of 1943." *Michigan History* 53, no. 3 (Fall 1969): 183–206.

Smethurst, James Edward. *The Black Arts Movement: Literary Nationalism in the 1960s and 1970s*. Chapel Hill: University of North Carolina Press, 2005.

Smith, Robert C. "Imari Obadele: The Father of the Modern Reparation Movement." *World History Archives*. June 2000. Accessed November 14, 2019. http://www .hartford-hwp.com/archives/45a/312.html.

Smith, Rogers. *Civic Ideals: Conflicting Visions of Citizenship in U.S. History*. New Haven, CT: Yale University Press, 1997.

Smith, Suzanne E. *Dancing in the Street: Motown and the Cultural Politics of Detroit*. Cambridge, MA: Harvard University Press, 1999.

Smitherman, Geneva. *Talkin and Testifyin: The Language of Black America*. Detroit, MI: Wayne State University Press, 1977.

———. *Talkin that Talk: Language, Culture and Education in African America*. New York: Routledge, 2000.

Solow, Barbara L., ed. *Slavery and the Rise of the Atlantic System*. Cambridge: Cambridge University Press, 1993.

Sonebeyatta, Yusufu (Joseph Brooks). "Ujamaa for Land and Power." *Black Scholar* 3, no. 2 (October 1971): 13–20.

"South Sudan Referendum: 99% Vote for Independence." *BBC News*, January 30, 2011. https://www.bbc.com/news/world-africa-12317927.

Spencer, Robyn C. "Engendering the Black Freedom Struggle: Revolutionary Black Womanhood and the Black Panther Party in the Bay Area, California." *Journal of Women's History* 20, no. 1 (Spring 2008): 90–113.

———. *The Revolution Has Come: Black Power, Gender, and the Black Panther Party in Oakland*. Durham, NC: Duke University Press, 2016.

Spivak, Gayatri Chakravorty. "Can the Subaltern Speak?" In *Marxism and the Interpretation of Culture*, edited by Cary Nelson and Lawrence Grossberg, 271–313. Urbana: University of Illinois Press, 1988.

Springer, Kimberly. *Living for the Revolution: Black Feminist Organizations, 1968–1980*. Durham, NC: Duke University Press, 2005.

"Stewardess Says Her Lies Convinced Africa-bound Hijackers to Go to Cuba." *Baltimore Sun*, November 29, 1971.

Stiner, Larry Watani, and Scot Brown. "The US-Panther Conflict, Exile, and the Black Diaspora: The Plight of Larry Watani Stiner." *Journal of African American History* 92, no. 4 (Fall 2007): 540–52.

Stuckey, Sterling. *Slave Culture: Nationalist Culture: Nationalist Theory and the Foundations of Black America*. New York: Oxford University Press, 1987.

"Study Finds Congress Spends 27% of Its Time Taunting." *Here & Now*. WBUR.org, April 21, 2011. http://hereandnow.wbur.org/2011/04/21/congress-taunting.

Sugrue, Thomas J. *The Origins of the Urban Crisis: Race and Inequality in Postwar Detroit*. Princeton, NJ: Princeton University Press, 1996.

———. *Sweet Land of Liberty: The Forgotten Struggle for Civil Rights in the North*. New York: Random House, 2008.

Taylor, Ula Yvette. "Elijah Muhammad's Nation of Islam: Separatism, Regendering, and a Secular Approach to Black Power after Malcolm X (1965–1975)." In *Freedom North: Black Freedom Struggles outside the South, 1940–1980*, edited by Jeanne F. Theoharis and Komozi Woodard, 190–94. New York: Palgrave Macmillan, 2003.

———. *The Promise of Patriarchy: Women and the Nation of Islam*. Chapel Hill: University of North Carolina Press, 2017.

"Teacher Arraigned in Killing." *New York Times* (1857—Current File), June 22, 1969, 50. *Historical Newspapers: The New York Times*. ProQuest. http://www.proquest.com/.

Theoharis, Jeanne. "'I'd Rather Go to School in the South': How Boston's School Desegregation Complicates the Civil Rights Paradigm." In *Freedom North: Black Freedom Struggles outside the South, 1940–1980*, edited by Jeanne F. Theoharis and Komozi Woodard, 125–51. New York: Palgrave Macmillan, 2003.

Theoharis, Jeanne F., and Komozi Woodard, eds. *Freedom North: Black Freedom Struggles outside the South, 1940–1980*. New York: Palgrave Macmillan, 2003.

———. *Groundwork: Local Black Freedom Movements in America*. New York: New York University Press, 2005.

Thomas, Richard W. *Life for Us Is What We Make It: Building Black Community in Detroit, 1915–1945*. Bloomington: Indiana University Press, 1992.

Thompson, Heather Ann. *Whose Detroit? Politics, Labor, and Race in a Modern American City*. Ithaca, NY: Cornell University Press, 2001.

"Thoughts on the Creed: What It Means to Be 'Deaf, Dumb, & Blind.'" *Re-Build! A New Afrikan Independence Movement Periodical* 1, no. 1 (Fall 2018): 4–6. https://www.rebuildcollective.org/events-1.

"3 Slaying Suspects Hijack Airliner and Crew to Cuba." *New York Times*, November 28, 1971.

"3 Suspects in Slaying Hijack Jetliner to Cuba." *Los Angeles Times*, November 28, 1971.

Trotsky, Leon. "The Permanent Revolution." Marxists.org. Accessed October 20, 2011. http://www.marxists.org/archive/trotsky/1931/tpr/pr-index.htm.

Tutu, Desmond. *No Future without Forgiveness*. New York: Doubleday, 1999.

"2 ARRESTED NEAR HOTEL OF McGOVERN." *Atlanta Daily World (1932–2003)*, July 14, 1972. *Historical Newspapers: Atlanta Daily World*. ProQuest. http://www.proquest.com/.

"2 Held at Hotel of McGovern; Guns Seized." *Washington Post, Times Herald (1959–1973)*, July 13, 1972. *Historical Newspapers: Washington Post*. ProQuest. http://www.proquest.com/.

"2 with Guns Held near M'Govern: Black Separatists Arrested after They Leave Car at Senator's Hotel." *New York Times (1923–Current file)*, July 13, 1972. *Historical Newspapers: New York Times*. ProQuest. http://www.proquest.com/.

Tyson, Timothy B. *"Radio Free Dixie": Robert F. Williams & the Roots of Black Power*. Chapel Hill: University of North Carolina Press, 1999.

Umoja, Akinyele Omowale. "The Black Liberation Army and the Radical Legacy of the Black Panther Party." In *Black Power: in the Belly of the Beast*, edited by Judson L. Jeffries, 224–51. Urbana: University of Illinois Press, 2006.

———. *We Will Shoot Back: Armed Resistance in the Mississippi Freedom Movement*. New York: New York University Press, 2013.

UN General Assembly. Resolution 1514 (XV), Declaration on the Granting of Independence to Colonial Countries and Peoples. December 14, 1960. Accessed September 2, 2009. https://www.ohchr.org/EN/ProfessionalInterest/Pages/Independence.aspx.

———. The Universal Declaration of Human Rights. December 10, 1948. Accessed September 2, 2009. https://www.un.org/en/universal-declaration-human-rights/index.html.

United States Congress. Senate Committee on the Judiciary, Subcommittee to Investigate the Administration of the Internal Security Act and Other Internal Security Laws. March 25, 1970. *Testimony of Stokely Carmichael: Hearing, Ninety-first Congress, second session*. Washington: U.S. Govt. Print. Off.

United States House of Representatives, House Committee on Foreign Affairs. *Hijacking Accord between the United States and Cuba*. Washington, D.C., February 20, 1973.

United States Kerner Commission, U.S. National Advisory Commission on Civil Disorders. *Report of the National Advisory Commission on Civil Disorders*. New York: Bantam Books, 1968.

Uzoigwe, G. N. "Background to the Nigerian Civil War." In *Writing the Nigeria-Biafra War*, edited by Toyin Falola and Ogechwukwu Ezekwem, 17–39. Rochester, NY: Boydell & Brewer, 2016.

Van Deburg, William L. *New Day in Babylon: The Black Power Movement and American Culture, 1965–1975*. Chicago: University of Chicago Press, 1992.

Van Dyke, Nella, Doug McAdam, and Brenda Wilhelm. "Gendered Outcomes: Gender Differences in the Biographical Consequences of Activism." *Mobilization: An International Journal* 5, no. 2 (Fall 2000): 161–77.

Vaughn, Edward. *RED BLACK and GREEN: The History and Meaning of the Black Man's Flag.* Detroit: Edward Vaughn & Associates, 1975.

Vincent, Theodore G., ed. *Voice of a Black Nation: Political Journalism in the Harlem Renaissance.* San Francisco: Ramparts, 1973.

Von Eschen, Penny M. *Race against Empire: Black Americans and Anticolonialism, 1937–1957.* Ithaca, NY: Cornell University Press, 1997.

Walzer, Michael. *What It Means to Be an American.* New York: Marsilo, 1992.

Ward, Stephen M. *In Love and Struggle: The Revolutionary Lives of James and Grace Lee Boggs.* Chapel Hill: University of North Carolina Press, 2016.

Warrant, Mac, ed. *Independent Black Political Action, 1954–78: The Struggle to Break with the Democratic and Republic Parties.* New York: Pathfinder, 1982.

Watkins, Rychetta. *Black Power, Yellow Power, and the Making of Revolutionary Identities.* Jackson: University Press of Mississippi, 2012.

Wechsler, Nancy. "Activists Jailed for Refusing to Cooperate with Grand Jury." *Gay Community News,* December 26, 1981, 3. Accessed January 19, 2012, *Historical Newspapers.* ProQuest. http://www.proquest.com/.

Welch, Susan, Lee Sigelman, Timothy Bledsoe, and Michael Combs. *Race and Place: Race Relations in an American City.* Cambridge: Cambridge University Press, 2001.

Whalen, Jack, and Richard Flacks. *Beyond the Barricades: The Sixties Generation Grows Up.* Philadelphia: Temple University Press, 1989.

Whitaker, Matthew C. *Race Work: The Rise of Civil Rights in the Urban West.* Lincoln: University of Nebraska Press, 2005.

White, E. Francis. "Africa on My Mind: Gender, Counter Discourse and African-American Nationalism." *Journal of Women's History* 2, no. 1 (Spring 1990): 72–97.

Widick, B. J. *Detroit: City of Race and Class Violence.* Chicago: Quadrangle Books, 1972.

Wilhelm, Brenda. "Changes in Cohabitation across Cohorts: The Influence of Political Activism." *Social Forces* 77, no. 1 (September 1998): 289–310.

Williams, Eric. *Capitalism and Slavery.* Chapel Hill: University of North Carolina Press, 1993.

Williams, Raymond. *The Country and the City.* New York: Oxford University Press, 1973.

Williams, Rhonda Y. "Black Women and Black Power." *OAH Magazine of History* 22, no. 3 (July 2008): 22–26.

———. *Concrete Demands: The Search for Black Power in the 20th Century.* New York: Routledge, 2015.

———. "'I'm a Keeper of Information': History-Telling and Voice." *Oral History Review* 28, no. 1 (Winter/Spring 2001): 41–63.

———. *The Politics of Public Housing: Black Women's Struggles against Urban Inequality.* New York: Oxford University Press, 2004.

Williams, Yohuru. *Black Politics/White Power: Civil Rights, Black Power, and the Black Panthers in New Haven*. New York: Brandywine, 2000.

Willis, Gary. *The Second Civil War: Arming for Armageddon*. New York: New American Library, 1968.

Wilson, Stephen. *The Means of Naming: A Social and Cultural History of Personal Naming in Western Europe*. London: UCL, 1998.

Winbush, Raymond A. *Should America Pay? Slavery and the Raging Debate on Reparations*. New York: Amistad, 2003.

Winch, Julie. *Philadelphia's Black Elite: Activism, Accommodation, and the Struggle for Autonomy, 1787–1848*. Philadelphia: Temple University Press, 1988.

Wolf, Brian. "Trump on Offense after Kavanaugh Confirmation." *CNN*, October 8, 2018. https://www.cnn.com/2018/10/08/politics/election-2018-midterm-brett -kavanaugh/index.html.

Wolfe, Alan. *The Seamy Side of Democracy: Repression in the United States*. New York: David McKay, 1973.

Wood, Peter H. *Black Majority: Negroes in Colonial South Carolina from 1670 through the Stono Rebellion*. New York: Alfred A. Knopf, 1974.

Woodard, Komozi. *Nation within a Nation: Amiri Baraka (LeRoi Jones) and Black Power Politics*. Chapel Hill: University of North Carolina Press, 1999.

Woodruff, Nan Elizabeth. *American Congo: The African American Freedom Struggle in the Delta*. Cambridge, MA: Harvard University Press, 2003.

Wright, Richard. "Blueprint for Negro Writing." In *Portable Harlem Renaissance Reader*, edited by David Levering Lewis, 194–205. New York: Viking Press, 1994.

Ya Salaam, Kalamu. "African American Cultural Empowerment: A Struggle to Identify and Institutionalize Ourselves as a People." In *Voices from the Battlefront: Achieving Cultural Equity*, edited by Moreno Vega and Cheryll Y. Greene, 119–34. Trenton, NJ: Africa World Press, 1993.

———. "We Are New Afrika: RNA and the Promise of Pan-Afrikan Nationalism in America." *Black Books Bulletin* 4, no. 4 (Winter 1976): 62–71.

Yakubu, Owusu Yaki. "Who Are New Afrikan Political Prisoners and Prisoners of War?" *Crossroad* 4, no. 3 (Winter 1992). Reprinted in *New Afrikan Political Prisoners & Prisoners of War Profiles*. Chicago: Spear & Shield, 1998, 5.

Young, Cynthia A. *Soul Power: Culture, Radicalism, and the Making of a U.S. Third World Left*. Durham, NC: Duke University Press, 2006.

Index

9/11, 205

Abdur-Rasheed, Khalid, 28, 119, 124, 145, 151–52, 155, 183
Abiodun, Nehanda Isoke, 193
Abubakari, Dara (Virginia Collins), 38, 40–41, 184–85, 187, 192
Abubakari-Lumumba group, 41, 190, 200. *See also* constitutional crises
Acoli, Sundiata (Clark Squire), 52, 176, 177
Adefunmi, Nana Oseijeman, 63, 90, 93, 98. *See also* Yoruba
Adegbalola, Alajo, 38, 39, 68, 138, 152, 158
African Blood Brotherhood, 25, 218n5
African-centered schools: Aisha Shule/ DuBois Preparatory Academy (formerly known as Alexander Crummell Center) (Detroit), 151; Shule ya Watoto (Chicago), 140; Watoto School (Washington, D.C.), 141
African Descendants Nationalist Independence Partition Party (AD NIP), 195. *See also* reparations
African Liberation Support Committee (ALSC), 188
African Methodist Episcopal (AME) Church, 125, 128, 132, 153–54. *See also* Christianity; lifestyle politics
African National Reparations Organization, 203. *See also* reparations
African People's Socialist Party, 201
Afrik, Hannibal Tirus, 94–95, 125, 131, 139–40, 147–48, 154
Afrikan names, 80, 88–102, 227n43. *See also* names

Afrikan People's Party, 40–41, 44, 92, 101, 176, 187–89, 190–93, 240n14. *See also* Black Liberation Party
Afro-American Anti-Bicentennial Committee, 41, 189. *See also* bicentennial; July 4th Coalition
Ahidiana, 194, 207
Ahmad, Akbar Muhammad (Maxwell Stanford, Jr.), 21, 25, 35, 191
Akan, 125, 153–54. *See also* lifestyle politics
Al-Amin, Imam Jamil, 57
Alston, Christopher, 20
alter versions. *See* identity
American Civil Liberties Union (ACLU), 19
American Descendants of Slavery, 203. *See also* reparations
American Indian Movement (AIM), 77, 189, 224n114
Ana, Hekima (Thomas Norman), 38, 74–75
Ana, Tamu (Ann Lockhart), 75
Anderson, Michael Balogun, 97–99, 135–36, 138, 140–41, 143, 155, 170, 177
Anti-Depression Program, 164, 196–99. *See also* reparations
Aptheker, Herbert, 69–70
Association of Black Psychologists, 40

Babu, Abdul Rahman Mohamed, 31, 56
Baraka, Amiri, 1, 26, 57, 92, 184, 201
Barashango, Reverend Ishakamusa, 141, 151. *See also* Temple of the Black Messiah
Bell, Derrick, 200

Bell, Eric, 21
Bellecourt, Clyde, 189
bicentennial, 76, 188–89. *See also*
Afro-American Anti-Bicentennial
Committee; people's bicentennial
biographical consequences, 8–10, 114,
156. *See also* life course analysis
Black August Hip-Hop Festival, 193.
See also Malcolm X Grassroots
Movement
Black Government Conference. *See*
Black Government Convention
Black Government Convention: and
Declaration of Independence, 1, 45,
57; participants in, 1, 11, 16, 24, 184,
186; overview of, 26–27; precursors
to, 25–26; and strategic issues, 68,
156, 159, 194, 196, 210n1, 237n56
Black Identity Extremist, 14
Black Legion (also known as the New
Afrikan Legion and the New Afrikan
Security Forces): and the Black
Panther Party, 21; internal conflict,
36; PG-RNA organizational strategy,
29–31, 58, 67–69; lifestyle politics,
97, 135–36, 140, 143, 146–47; New
Bethel Incident, 15, 33, 65, 75, 170;
repression, 168–72, 236n34; as
security, 34, 171. *See also,* Provisional
Government of the Republic of New
Afrika (PG-RNA)
Black Liberation Army, 52, 66, 158,
175–76, 180–82, 192, 207
Black Liberation Party, 138, 187, 232n57.
See also Afrikan People's Party
Black Panther Party for Self Defense
(BPP): in Detroit, 20–21, 26, 35, 48,
66; ideas within, 48, 143, 187, 218n9;
lifestyle, 9–10; and New Afrikan
activism, 119, 131, 138, 178–79; and
plebiscite, 6, 50–52; repression of,
137, 176; tensions with cultural
nationalists, 91–92
Black Power (concept), 6, 13, 16, 37, 42,
49–53, 78, 106, 212n3, 219n20

Black Solidarity Day, 191–93. *See also*
National Black Human Rights
Coalition
Black United Front, 35, 192
Boggs, Grace Lee, 19, 22–23, 212n14
Boggs, James, 19, 22–23, 212n14
Boston, Cynthia. *See* Sunni-Ali, Fulani
Boston, Leroy. *See* Adegbalola, Alajo
Boudin, Kathy, 181–82
Brexit, 4
Brinks Expropriation, 72, 101, 140, 158,
180–83, 185
Brown, H. Rap, 57. *See also* Al-Amin,
Imam Jamil
Buckley, William, 138
Bukhari, Safiya Asya (formerly known
as Bernice Jones), 52, 66–67, 175–76,
181, 182

Cain, Bernadette. *See* Shakur,
Shushanna
Carmichael, Stokely (aka Kwame Ture),
89, 126, 161, 226n29
Castro, Fidel, 142, 179
Cavanaugh, Jerome, 19
Central State University, 94, 132,
134, 139
Chavis, Reverend Ben, 184
Chesimard, JoAnne. *See* Shakur, Assata
Chicanos, 77. *See also* Third World
Christianity: African Methodist
Episcopal Church (AME), 125, 128;
Baptist Church, 124, 128; black
liberation theology, 124; Catholic
Church, 121–23; Christian national-
ism, 213n14; Church of Jesus Christ of
the Latter Day Saints (Mormon
Church), 120–21; Our Memorial
United Church, 125; Presbyterian
Church, 123. *See also* lifestyle politics
Church of the Advocate (Philadelphia),
188–89
citizenship, 1, 4–6, 10, 12, 26–27, 30, 32,
44–45, 59–67
Citywide Citizens Action Committee, 43

272 Index

civil rights: citizenship, 63–64; Detroit activism, 18–19; Henry brothers' activism, 15, 21; lifestyle politics, 116, 126, 130, 133, 143, 161

Clark, Judy, 181

Clark, Mark, 205

Cleage, Reverend Albert, 19–21, 23, 136, 153, 213n14

Code of Umoja (RNA Constitution), 37, 38, 39–40, 44, 56–59, 76

COINTELPRO (Counter Intelligence Program), 158, 160–62, 177, 235n30. *See also* Federal Bureau of Investigation

collective identity. *See* identity

Collins, Virginia. *See* Abubakari, Dara

Collins, Walter, 191

Combahee River Collective, 47

Committee to Free the RNA-11, 137

Communist Party, 18, 25, 105, 188

Congress of African Peoples (CAP), 52, 92, 187, 218n9

constitutional crises, 31–41, 58, 72, 89, 190

Conyers, John, 142

Crockett, George, 15, 18, 169. *See also* New Bethel Incident

Cuba, 152–53, 178–81, 193, 219n23

Cultural Nationalism, 91–92

Czapski, Michael, 15, 33, 169–70. *See also* New Bethel Incident

Damballah Hwedo Ancestor Temple, 124

Davis, Angela, 92, 162

Deacons for Defense and Justice, 22

Declaration of Independence. *See* New Afrikan Declaration of Independence

Democratic National Convention (Miami), 164–65

Detroit Association of Women's Clubs, 18

Detroit Commission on Community Relations (DCCR), 18

Detroit Free Press (Newspaper), 36

Detroit News (Newspaper), 36, 64–65

Detroit Rebellion of 1967, 24, 41–42, 136, 168, 213n20

Detroit Riot of 1943, 17

Discrimination, 17–19, 131; employment, 17, 132–33; in education, 116–17, 131–32; in housing, 17, 126–27; in public accommodations, 116; in voting, 18

Double Consciousness. *See* New Afrikan

Douglass, Frederick, 62, 188, 218n5

Dred Scott v. Sanford, 62, 197, 199

Du Bois, W. E. B., 60, 69, 92, 103

Ehehose, Masai, 66–67

Eight Bowl Ceremony, 113

Eight Strategic Elements (speech), 29. *See also* lifestyle politics

El Malik, 37, 108, 171

Federal Bureau of Investigation (FBI), 13, 24, 69, 92, 158–60; agents, 34, 38; COINTELPRO, 34–35, 65, 93, 159, 193; goals, 160; infiltration and informants, 32, 35, 101, 159, 161–62, 163, 179, 228n43, 235n11, 236n34, 240n14; shootouts, 38, 173; tactics, 160–66, 170–71

Ferguson, Chui, 182

Ferguson, Constance Iyaluua, 90, 119, 123, 131, 154–55, 228n45

Ferguson, Herman, 90–93, 97, 101, 125, 128–29, 131, 137, 154, 227n43

Finney, Michael "Macheo," 90, 152–53, 178–79

Firing Line (television show), 138

Five Percent Nation of Gods and Earths, 99–101, 126

Forman, James, 13, 202

Fox and Wolf Hunt Club, 22. *See also* rifle and shooting clubs

Franklin, C. L., 15

Frederick Douglas Shooting Club, 30. *See also* rifle and shooting clubs

Freedom Now Party (FNP), 11, 19–20

free love, 145. *See also* polygamy
Fuller, Clarence "Chaka," 33, 140, 168–70

Gaines, Jerry, 158, 185
Gallman, Mississippi (Byrdtown), 158–60, 167
Garvey, Marcus, 25, 95, 103, 127, 161, 192, 218n5. *See also* Universal Negro Improvement Association (UNIA)
Geneva Convention, 26–27, 141
Gilbert, David, 181
Ginzburg, Ralph, 69–70
Goodwin, Ralph "Antar Ra," 178–79
Government Administration Handbook, 36, 57, 69–70
grand jury investigation, 158–59, 185. *See also* Sunni-Ali, Fulani
Gregory, Dick, 176, 201
Group on Advanced Leadership (GOAL), 11, 16, 20–22, 162–63
guerilla warfare, 22, 30, 181
Guyot, Lawrence, 1

Haiti, 47, 51, 62, 92, 218n5, 219n23
Hamer, Fannie Lou, 174, 237n56
Hampton, Fred, 205
Harambee, 79
Henry, Milton. *See* Obadele, Gaidi
Henry, Richard Bullock. *See* Obadele, I, Imari Abubakari
Hibbit, Alfred (Alfred 2x), 169–70
Hill, Charles (Fela Olatunji), 178–80
Hilliard, David, 91
Hoover, J. Edgar, 161–63, 168–69, 253n27, 253n30
House, Gloria. *See* Kgositsile, Aneb
House of Umoja (HOU), 40, 59, 92, 101, 113, 188, 194
House Un-American Activities Committee, 18
human rights, 1, 4, 26–27, 30, 46, 119, 141, 161, 190, 199–200

identity: alter versions, 74, 159, 162, 166–78; collective identity, 4, 6, 12–13, 71, 89; and names, 82–88, 97–98, 102–6; and the New Afrikan Creed, 48–49; and Third World, 12, 47, 54, 75–78, 81, 101–2, 105, 111, 192, 218n9, 225n2
incarceration. *See* PP/POW
independence referendum, 4
infiltration. *See* Federal Bureau of Investigation
informants. *See* Federal Bureau of Investigation
integration, 120, 122, 126–27
International Solidarity Day for African Prison of War, 176–77, 187–88
Islam: and lifestyle politics, 118, 123–25, 146, 151, 153, 154, 155; Nation of Islam, 21, 84–85, 143, 219n14, 226n23. *See also* lifestyle politics

Jackson, George, 176
Jackson, Jonathan, 162
Jackson, Larry. *See* Njabafudi, Karim
Jackson, Melanie Njeri, 90, 119–21, 145, 152–53, 154, 227n35
Jackson, Mississippi: political organizing, 38, 152, 170, 172–73, 178; Lewis Street shootout, 65, 71, 137, 173, 205
Jaga, Geronimo ji (Elmer Pratt), 158, 175
James, C. L. R., 212n14
Jones, Bernice. *See* Bukhari, Safiya Asya
Jones, LeRoi. *See* Baraka, Amiri
July 4th Coalition, 188–89

Kalimara, Kwame-Osagyefo, 77
Karenga, Maulana, 1, 26, 53, 57, 91, 105, 143
Kgositsile, Aneb (Gloria House), 69, 117, 136, 141, 151, 232n62
Killingham, Marilyn Preston, 93–94, 115–16, 125, 127–28, 134–35, 138, 143, 147, 151, 164, 205
King, Martin Luther, Jr., 15, 18, 135–36, 161, 174, 192
Kochiyama, Yuri, 71, 75

Ku Klux Klan (KKK), 30, 171
Kush District, 108–9
Kwanzaa, 148

Labor unions, 18
League of Revolutionary Black Workers, 20–21, 23, 31, 48
Letlaka, Tsepo Tiisetso, 32
Lewis, Dorothy, 201–2, 242n49
life course analysis, 8–10, 12, 114, 143, 230n5. *See also* biographical consequences
lifestyle politics: definition of, 5–6; diet, 121; education, 115–19; employment, 139–43; family, 125–33, 143–53; government repression; incarceration, 117; marriage, 113–14, 143–46; spirituality & religion, 119–29, 153–56; youth activism, 121, 122, 130–31, 135. *See also* Afrikan names; names
Lockhart, Ann. *See* Ana, Tamu
Lumumba, Chokwe (formerly known as Edwin Taliaferro): Black Solidarity Day (1979), 192; forming the New Afrikan People's Organization, 185, 187–93; lifestyle politics, 72, 136, 139–41; Malcolm X Grassroots Movement, 193; name choice, 88, 95–97, 145, 165; in National Coalition of Blacks for Reparations in America, 202; New Afrikan independence history, 25–26; PG-RNA internal conflict, 35, 37–41; political offices, 72; responses to repression, 176, 180
Lumumba-Umoja, Mamadou, 188

Maafa, 45, 81
Madhabuti, Haki R., 220n35
Maglangayan, Shawna, 218n9
Malcolm X, 20. *See also* Shabazz, El Hajj Malik
Malcolm X Grassroots Movement, 11, 72, 141, 186, 193, 242n54. *See also* New Afrikan People's Organization
Malcolm X Party, 40, 217n2

Malcolm X Society, 16, 20, 23–26
March on Washington for Jobs and Freedom, 19
Marriage, 9, 75, 99, 113, 116, 123, 128, 145–48
Mason, Lofton, 108, 171
Matsimela, Muntu, 192
Medgar Evers Rifle Club, 22, 163. *See also* rifle and shooting clubs
Miami Democratic National Convention, 164–65
Mississippi Sovereignty Commission, 170, 172
Moore, Audley. *See* Queen Mother Moore
Movement for Black Lives, 203
Muhammad, Elijah, 25, 48, 84–86, 219n14
Muhammad, Saladin, 188–89
Mwendo, Ukali, 117–18, 132–34
Mweusi, Chui (John Taylor), 68
Mweusi, Jumaani, 99

names, 83; group names, 103–6. *See also* Afrikan names
name studies. *See* onomastics
naming ceremony, 79–80
National Association for the Advancement of Colored People (NAACP), 18–19, 21–23, 26–27, 126, 161
National Black Economic Development Conference, 20, 202
National Black Human Rights Coalition, 41, 191–92
National Black Political Convention (Gary Indiana), 38
National Committee to Combat Fascism, 21. *See also* Black Panther Party for Self Defense (BPP)
National Ex-Slave Mutual Relief, Bounty, and Pension Association, 194–95. *See also* reparations
National Industrial Council and National Liberty Party, 195. *See also* reparations

National Task Force for Cointelpro Litigation and Research, 41
National Territory (the five states), 2, 25, 29, 77, 107, 109, 172, 193, 203
nation building classes, 69–71
Nation of Islam. *See* Islam
Native Americans, 44, 61, 72, 76–77, 88, 103, 189, 197, 224n114
Negro-to-Black Conversion Experience (Nigrescence), 86–87
New African Ujamaa: The Economics of the Republic of New Africa, 53–56
New Afrikan: citizenship, 56, 60, 62–64, 67–75; identity, 70–71, 78, 89, 103, 105–6, 159, 166
New Afrikan Creed, 44, 48–49, 53, 68, 71, 139, 153
New Afrikan Declaration of Independence, 1–2, 45–48
New Afrikan family, 143–53
New Afrikan Flag, 43, 217n2
New Afrikan Independence Movement (NAIM): basic tenets, 2–5, 156; and Black Power, 49–50; forerunners to, 63; goals of, 25–27, 45; ideological challenges to, 51–52, 74; lifestyle politics, 114, 122, 132, 135–36, 147, 152–53; New Afrikan Nation Day, 184–85; PP/POW, 175; reparations, 201–202; repression of, 16, 159, 206; tensions within, 35–41
New Afrikan Legion. *See* Black Legion
New Afrikan Oath, 12, 44, 49–53, 71, 138–39, 148, 152, 223n93
New Afrikan People's Organization (NAPO), 41, 141, 186, 189–94, 201, 229n75
New Afrikan Political Science, 6, 16, 42, 44, 49, 67, 72, 113, 193, 206, 241n48; and lifestyle politics, 10–12, 44–45, 113–14, 130, 134, 139, 143–52; and name choices, 79, 109, 111
New Afrikan Security Forces. *See* Black Legion
New Bethel Baptist Church, 136

New Bethel Incident, 167–68
Newton, Huey P., 48, 51–52, 91–92, 109, 219n23, 230n87
Nixon, Richard, 37, 52, 179
Njabafudi, Karim (Larry Jackson), 171
Nkrumah, Kwame, 23, 89, 126, 212n14
North American Anti-Imperialists, 180
Northern Racism, 116–17, 126–27, 131
Nubyahn, Brother-D. B., 74, 99–101
Nyerere, Julius K., 54–55, 126, 220n36, 220n37

Obadele, I, Imari Abubakari (Richard Bullock Henry), 1, 16, 49, 77, 106, 135; background of, 19–24, 26; constitutional crises, 13, 28, 31–37, 39–41, 164, 189–91; Eight Strategic Elements speech, 29, 178; ideas about marriage, 145; incarceration, 137, 152; in Jackson, Mississippi, 65, 171–73; leadership style, 35, 79, 88, 136, 164, 172, 184, 193; and New Afrikan citizenship, 66–67, 70–72, 166; and religion, 155–56; and reparations, 195–200, 202; RNA-11, 137
Obadele, II, Imari Abubakari, 135, 202–3
Obadele, Gaidi (Milton R. Henry), 1, 15–16, 49; background of, 19–24, 26; and constitutional crisis, 13, 28, 31–37, 43, 105, 186; on *Firing Line*, 138; ideas about marriage, 145; name, 105; and New Afrikan citizenship, 64–65; religion, 125, 136
Obafemi, Ahmed, 164–65
Ocean Hill-Brownsville, 30
Odinga, Sekou, 158
onomastics, 81–82. *See also* names
Organization of African Unity (OAU), 105
Organization of Afro-American Unity (OAAU), 26, 105

Panther Underground, 175. *See also* Black Panther Party for Self Defense (BPP)
paper-citizen, 5, 12, 44, 46, 56, 62–64, 76

Pasha, Anwar (Henry "Papa" Wells), 37, 184
people's bicentennial, 188
People's Center Council (PCC), 39–40, 58, 90, 93, 233n75, 240n14. See also Provisional Government of the Republic of New Afrika (PG-RNA)
People's Revolt Against Poverty, 67, 200. See also reparations
People's Revolutionary Leadership Council, 58. See also Provisional Government of the Republic of New Afrika (PG-RNA)
plebiscite, 1–2, 6, 51–52, 109, 196, 201
political nationalism. See revolutionary nationalism
political prisoner. See PP/POW
polygamy, 145–47. See also lifestyle politics
Pontiac City Commission, 23
PP/POW, 40, 71, 177, 185
Prisoner of War. See PP/POW
Provisional Government of the Republic of New Afrika (PG-RNA), 5, 20–21; creation of, 2, 24–28; objectives of, 11, 14, 30; organizational structure, 10; rationale for, 27
Puerto Ricans, 12, 33, 44, 77, 170, 188

Quebec, 4
Queen Mother Moore (Audley Moore): alleged abuse of, 191; at the Black Government Convention of 1968, 1–2; at Black Solidarity Day, 192; ideas about marriage, 145; influence of, 11, 25–27, 63–64, 104–5, 139, 146, 186; and name, 90, 228n45; with the Provisional Government, 37, 56–57, 90, 156, 184; and reparations, 194–95, 203

racially motivated extremist. See Black Identity Extremist
Racketeering Influenced and Corrupt Organization (RICO), 182

Rashid, Kuratibisha X Ali (Ulysses S. Garth), 1–2, 68, 98–99, 129, 146–47, 216n47
Rebuild Collective, 219n14
reparations: historical background of, 194–95; National Black Economic Development Conference, 20, 202; National Coalition of Blacks for Reparations in America, 14, 186, 201–3. See also Anti-Depression Program
Reparations Committee for United States Slaves' Descendants, Inc., 195. See also reparations
Republic of New Afrika (RNA): as a captive black nation, 5; conflict within, 35–37; five state territory, 2, 25, 107–10; forerunners to, 18–24, 63–64, 194–95; founding of, 1–2, 26–27; provisional government, 27–29, 58–59; strategy, 29–30, 159; ideology, 43–45
Revolutionary Action Movement (RAM), 20–23, 26, 27, 35, 40, 63, 93, 134–35, 163, 186–87
Revolutionary Armed Task Force (RATF), 181–82
revolutionary nationalism, 91–92
Richardson, David, 192
Rich Off Our Backs, 188
rifle and shooting clubs, 22, 30, 163
RNA-11, 38, 66–67, 72, 137, 141–42, 173, 175, 191, 200, 210n1
Robideau, Robert, 77
Romney, George, 18–19
Rusk, Dean, 28, 57

Salim, Ahmed Salim, 192
Sanchez, Sonia, 142, 201
Scotland, 4
Scott, Ron, 21
Second strike capability, 30, 178
segregation, 116–17, 126, 129, 132
self-determination, 2, 210n10
Shabazz, Betty, 1, 26–27, 37, 56–57, 162–63, 192, 217n56

Shabazz, El Hajj Malik (Malcolm X): influence on NAIM activists, 11, 20–26, 49, 70–71, 93, 106, 136, 179, 192–93; and name choices, 84–87, 104–5, 226n17

Shakur, Afeni, 145, 231n25

Shakur, Assata, 52, 93, 96–97, 176, 180–82, 192, 228n54, 231n25

Shakur, Mutulu, 72, 101, 137, 175, 182–83, 231n25

Shakur, Shushanna (Bernadette Cain), 88, 90, 135–36, 138, 141

Shakur, Zayd, 176

Shrine of the Black Madonna, 136, 213n14

Shule ya Watoto (Chicago), 140. See also African-centered schools

Simmons, Gwendolyn Zoharah, 124, 155, 163–64, 171, 235n22

Skyjacking, 179–80

Slave names, 80, 84–86. See also Afrikan names

slavery: and African American citizenship, 27, 62, 69, 75; effects of, 4, 62, 81, 89, 134, 167, 198–99, 203; and the law, 4, 242n48; and names, 81–85, 98; in prisons, 130, 241n32, 241n41; resistance, 47, 83, 94–95, 110, 167; reparations for, 4, 194–99

Smith, Davis, 171

socialism. See New African Ujamaa

Socialist Workers Party, 20, 22, 212n14

solidarity efforts, 76–78. See also identity

Sonebeyatta, Tarik, 164–65

South Sudan, 4

Stanford, Maxwell, Jr. See Ahmad, Akbar Muhammad

Student Nonviolent Coordinating Committee (SNCC), 1, 13, 16, 26, 15–16, 126, 141, 230n5

Sunni-Ali, Bilal, 72, 118, 123–24, 155, 191, 229n75

Sunni-Ali, Fulani (fka Cynthia Boston), 72, 138, 158–59, 182, 185

Swainson, John B., 18

Sweet, Ossian, 17

Taifa, Nkechi (Anita Caldwell), 40, 99, 119, 126, 137, 141, 145, 154, 202

Taliaferro, Edwin. See Lumumba, Chokwe

Tanzania, 30–32, 54–56, 70, 180, 192

Tanzania African National Union (TANU), 54–56

Taylor, John. See Mweusi, Chui

Taylor v. The Board of Education, 116–17. See also segregation

Temple of the Black Messiah (Washington, D.C.), 141. See also Barashango, Reverend Ishakamusa

territorial nationalism, 13, 23, 53, 63, 109

terrorism, 4, 62–63, 205–6

Third World. See identity

Till, Emmett, 117

Trade Union Leadership Council (TULC), 19, 22, 23

Trice, Richard (Bokeba Wantu Enjuenti): lifestyle politics, 119, 121–22, 126–27, 135, 138, 142, 150, 154–55; name choice, 90, 97–98, 107, 150; naming ceremony, 79–80; nation-building classes, 69

Ture, Kwame (Stokely Carmichael), 86, 126, 161, 184, 226n29

Uhuru, 20, 22, 23

Ujamaa, 53–54, 220n37

Umoja, Akinyele Omowale, 101, 113, 227n43

United Kingdom, 4

United Nations (UN): demonstrations at, 191–92, 231n32; plebiscite, 1–2, 6, 51; recognition by, 26, 28, 30, 32, 51, 57–59, 63, 78; self-determination, 14, 64, 67, 111, 200

United States Armed Forces, 68
Universal Declaration of Human Rights.
 See United Nations
Universal Negro Improvement Associa-
 tion (UNIA), 43, 95, 127
Urban renewal, 22. *See also*
 Discrimination
Us Organization, 26, 87, 91, 143, 162,
 225n10

Vaughan, Edward, 43
vegetarianism, 121. *See also* lifestyle
 politics
Viera, Rafael, 33, 170
violence: discrimination, 17–19, 131, 132;
 independent actions, 181; lynching,
 69, 129; rape and sexual abuse,
 127–28, 129, 212n3; torture, 129,
 130–31, 231n11, 237n56
voting, 18

War in America: The Malcolm X
 Doctrine, 57, 70
Watoto School (Washington, D.C.), 141.
 See also African-centered schools
Weather Underground Organization, 181
Wells, Henry "Papa." *See* Pasha,
 Anwar
Williams, G. Mennen, 18
Williams, Robert F., 20, 27–28, 30–35,
 51, 57, 64, 164, 172, 195
Willis, Raymond, 27
Worobec, Richard, 15. *See also* New
 Bethel Incident
Worthy, William, 19

Yakubu, Owusu Yaki (James
 Sayles), 175
Yoruba, 90, 93, 98, 153–55, 227n34,
 231n27. *See also* lifestyle politics
Young, Coleman, 19

www.ingramcontent.com/pod-product-compliance
Lightning Source LLC
Chambersburg PA
CBHW031412270326
41929CB00010BA/1427